Second Edition

ETHICS, CRIME, AND CRIMINAL JUSTICE

Christopher R. Williams
Bradley University

Bruce A. Arrigo
University of North Carolina at Charlotte

PEARSON

Boston   Columbus   Indianapolis   New York   San Francisco   Upper Saddle River
Amsterdam   Cape Town   Dubai   London   Madrid   Milan   Munich   Paris   Montreal   Toronto
Delhi   Mexico City   Sao Paulo   Sydney   Hong Kong   Seoul   Singapore   Taipei   Tokyo

Editorial Director: Vernon R. Anthony
Senior Acquisitions Editor: Eric Krassow
Assistant Editor: Tiffany Bitzel
Editorial Assistant: Lynda Cramer
Director of Marketing: David Gessell
Executive Marketing Manager: Cyndi Eller
Senior Marketing Coordinator: Alicia Wozniak
Senior Marketing Assistant: Les Roberts
Project Manager: Holly Shufeldt
Senior Art Director: Jayne Conte
Cover Designer: Suzanne Behnke
Cover Art: Fotolia
Full-Service Project Management and Composition: Anand Natarajan, Integra Software Services, Pvt. Ltd.
Text and Cover Printer/Binder: R.R. Donnelley & Sons

Credits and acknowledgments borrowed from other sources and reproduced, with permission, in this textbook appear on the appropriate page within the text.

Library of Congress Cataloging-in-Publication Data
Williams, Christopher R.,
    Ethics, crime, and criminal justice / Christopher R. Williams, Bruce A. Arrigo. — 2nd ed.
      p. cm.
    Includes bibliographical references and index.
    ISBN-13: 978-0-13-507154-0
    ISBN-10: 0-13-507154-2
    1. Criminal law—Philosophy.   2. Criminal law—Moral and ethical aspects.   I. Arrigo, Bruce A.   II. Title.
K5018.W548 2012
345—dc23

                                                                                        2011029621

10 9 8 7 6 5 4 3 2 1

PEARSON

ISBN 10:   0-13-507154-2
ISBN 13: 978-0-13-507154-0

For Justus and Blaise, Rebecca and Anthony

CONTENTS

level will also be suitable for analyzing data obtained at all higher measurement levels, but not vice versa. Note this actually means that higher level data can always be "collapsed" or categorized to suit statistical treatments at the lower levels. Such treatments may have some unique features in certain computer software packages that you may want to use.

It is also important to identify the *number of variables* involved in an analysis. Bearing in mind the two different kinds of research and the special requirements for a relational analysis (cf. chapter five), we will further divide our discussion around univariate analysis, bivariate analysis, and multivariate analysis. Univariate analysis examines a single variable and bivariate analysis examines a single correlation or other kind of relationship between two variables in either a controlled or an uncontrolled situation. If the situation is uncontrolled, the behavior of the variable or the relationship between the two variables under examination could be spurious, or caused more or less by some other variables. We will first discuss statistics without control as a preliminary stage of data analysis, where the role of other variables is simply ignored. Then we will focus on the possible ways of applying statistical control in terms of the logic of various analytical models. Statistical control is a means of isolation used to rule out the effect of other variables. When more than two variables are taken into consideration at once, it is called a multivariate analysis. Multivariate analysis examines variables in a relational context most close to the real situation. In this sense, multivariate analysis best addresses our research purpose. Unfortunately, the learning process is often trapped in some elementary tasks. Many people are unable to reach the multivariate stage, and they are left with a very narrow view. Conceptually, multivariate analysis is more comprehensive and enlightening, although the statistical tools used are more complex. You are encouraged to gain a multivariate perspective by paying attention to the logic of causal modeling even if you do not quite understand the mathematical/statistical details.

Descriptive analysis

Univariate analysis

Suppose your data are ready for analysis. Now what are you going to do about them? You can ask the computer to list out all the variables and values, but the data will not provide you with much useful information. You may try to find out

PREFACE

On its most basic level, this book was written as an introduction to the subject and scope of ethics, particularly as its many problems and diverse perspectives intersect with those ongoing controversies found in the everyday world of crime, law, and justice. Ethics involves the study of many different themes and issues, including concepts such as good, right, duty, obligation, virtue, freedom, rationality, and choice, as well as the ways in which each of these notions informs the dilemmas we face, the choices we make, and the actions we undertake. The themes that ethics explores underlie many circumstances we routinely confront as individuals, groups, organizations, communities, and cultures. The immediate aim of ethics is simply to encourage critical reflection on these concepts and concerns, recognizing their significance to and contemplating their value for people in various social contexts. Ultimately, if this aim is realized, ethics enables all citizens to adopt more informed beliefs, to make better decisions, to undertake healthier actions, to be better people and, consequently, to live more rewarding and fulfilling lives.

Ethics, Crime, and Criminal Justice explores, in an accessible, stimulating, and practical way, a range of value-based concepts and perspectives designed to familiarize students with their importance both within the complex world of crime and justice and outside of it. Indeed, as Chapter 1 suggests, the fundamental purpose of morality (in thought and action) is to facilitate living a good life in a just society. Accordingly, this book was conceived, written, and organized with this in mind. It is our hope that this volume's content helps students, practitioners, and other readers achieve the essential objectives of ethical reflection, decision-making, and conduct.

THE SUBJECT OF ETHICS

Contemporary ethics is typically divided into three general categories or subject areas: (1) metaethics, (2) normative ethics, and (3) applied ethics. When most people think of "ethics," they are thinking of its *normative* and *applied* elements—those dedicated to setting, establishing, or recommending norms or guidelines for human behavior, and those that address specific moral issues such as those of police corruption, criminal punishment, judicial integrity, and the like. The normative dimension of ethics proffers moral standards, principles, and guidelines of "right" and "wrong," answering questions such as, "What should I do?" and "How should I live my life?" Applied ethics utilizes normative ethical principles and frameworks to determine what we should do about particular dilemmas or issues of personal or social significance. In this respect, normative and applied ethics are very much intertwined, with applied ethics sometimes recognized as part of normative ethics rather than a separate subfield.

The purpose of studying ethics—and criminal justice ethics—is to help us become "good" people and to make "good" decisions. Ultimately, then, ethics is a practical discipline. Yet the various controversies that constitute applied ethical matters cannot be critically discussed or meaningfully resolved without making use of the concepts or "tools" provided to us by normative ethics. As is the case in nearly every field, we must have a sufficient theoretical foundation and point of reference for our more practical endeavors. Imagine, if you will, a cardiologist treating patients—an applied undertaking—without a firm footing in the "hows" and "whys" of heart structure and function. Becoming good people and making good decisions work in much the same way and are subject to the same sorts of concerns.

some pattern or regularity from the distribution of the values on each variable, yet this will immediately prove to be very difficult. To make it easier, you can group the cases (subjects) with the same value together and then count how many groups you have and how many cases are in each group. Oftentimes, with relatively few group values as well as the counts (frequencies) of the cases in those groups, you may greatly simplify the presentation of data without losing any information. The frequency distribution reveals the pattern or regularity in the data that you are looking for. For example, if you have a sample of 10,000 subjects and you want to know what their marital statuses look like, the original data matrix that runs into 10,000 lines would be simply bewildering and give you no idea about the pattern of distribution. On the other hand, a frequency table can be easily produced by the FREQUENCIES procedure in SPSS, which may contain just a few lines depending on the number of categories (codes) you use for marital status. By examining the frequency table, you can immediately capture the information essential for the kind of study, in which you are not interested in identifying each individual but looking for the condition of aggregation. In this example, you are interested in how many people are married, how many are single (never married), how many are divorced or widowed, how many are just separated, how many are simply living together, and how many belong to none of the above categories. You can also get percentages covering all cases, and/or valid percentages excluding cases missing information on the variable for all the categories you may use.

Frequency and percentage distribution is a basic statistical technique for simplifying the data and summarizing the information. We have discussed the use of this technique in data management for the purpose of double checking. The percentages, or generally the rates or relative proportions, are especially useful for gauging the extent and making comparisons in data analysis. The various charts and curves that may be produced by computer software based on frequency and percentage distributions can further give you a visual aid. The information obtained and patterns discerned from frequency tables may constitute a significant portion of the findings in your research report, especially when you claim yours is merely an exploratory study. Although this technique may appear too simplistic to you in view of the various advanced statistical methods now available, it is widely used in practical research. The kind of information is actually a major concern of many funded research projects. Unless your research has a focus on specific methodological issues, you should not neglect such a basic technique that may serve your research objective by providing needed

Most texts on criminal justice ethics focus primarily, if not exclusively, on applied ethical problems and issues (with, perhaps, some limited attention to normative theory). Yet matters of normative and applied concerns represent only part of the interplay between ethics and crime, law, and justice. Consider the following: Are the moral values and principles we employ to justify our choices socially constructed and relative? Grounded in biology and universal? Are there influences on our choice-making sufficiently powerful to question whether we have free will and moral accountability for those choices? From where does morality come and what is its grounding and purpose? Does a genuine concern for others really exist, or are we necessarily self-interested and motivated to moral action only if there is some good in it for ourselves? What, specifically, do we mean by terms such as "good" or "just" as they appear in our ethical vocabulary?

Entertaining these kinds of questions brings us into the often-interrelated realms of metaethics and moral psychology. In a way, *metaethics* is interested in the very foundations of ethics—the meaning of its language, the validity of its claims to knowledge. More importantly for our purposes, it also subsumes a number of critical concerns that are properly regarded as matters of *moral psychology*, which investigates the psychological foundations of moral decision-making and behavior. Of especial relevance to crime, law, and justice are questions of human nature and social cooperation, the role of emotion and intuition in moral decision-making, our motivation to be moral, the role of self-interest in human behavior, and the development of morality.

ORGANIZING THEMES

The organization of *Ethics, Crime, and Criminal Justice* differs appreciably from those other texts found in the market today. For example, rather than focusing primarily on ethical issues in criminal justice, readers are introduced to a number of concepts that function as critical thinking "tools." These tools enable the student or professional to recognize and assess a host of moral and ethical concerns that arise within the study and practice of crime, law, and justice. Rather than reviewing the facts and figures pertaining to criminal punishment, for example, the problems of human freedom, choice-making, and determinism are examined (see Chapter 3). This commentary leads to a more fully informed discussion and treatment of the moral context in which criminal punishment takes place. Moreover, rather than showcasing the topic of racism in policing or in court processing, thinking and reasoning skills are featured (see Chapter 11). This includes practical advice for the criminal justice professional on how to avoid labels, categories, and stereotypes, as well as other fundamental problems that occur when constructing arguments or taking positions that can lead to misguided perspectives, biased decision-making, and questionable actions.

Not surprisingly, then, the guiding organizational premise for *Ethics, Crime, and Criminal Justice* is the emphasis it places on unpacking the assorted philosophical ideas that inform various crime and justice controversies. Moreover, this emphasis includes a targeted reliance on those conceptual tools essential for evaluating thought, choice, and conduct, especially as they relate to criminal justice dilemmas. "Ethics," as it is presented throughout this volume, is not intended to tell us what to do when faced with a conflict between, for example, loyalty toward a fellow police or correctional officer and honesty in one's work setting. Instead, the purpose of ethics is to explore more generally the relevance of duties, obligations, and principles; to encourage sound reflection on those particular explorations; and, ideally, to be better equipped to resolve any (criminal justice) situation in which conflict might arise.

To effectively identify, assess, and reach conclusions on issues of moral significance (e.g., how to balance loyalty and honestly), one must first have an adequate appreciation for the conceptual grounding that represents ethical thought. To accomplish this, *Ethics, Crime, and Criminal Justice* draws attention to those relevant and prominent ethical theories, principles, and perspectives that have emerged throughout the history of Western civilization. In doing so, it exposes students and practitioners to the foundational thought necessary for any critical reflection about ethical choice-making and moral behavior in criminal justice settings as well as any other sphere of personal or professional life.

APPROACH, KEY FEATURES, AND PEDAGOGY

The organizing themes outlined above give rise to a basic approach, several key features, and a number of unique pedagogical aids that separate *Ethics, Crime, and Criminal Justice* from existing texts of its kind. Nearly all ethics texts in the criminal justice discipline present generous amounts of information on issues that are properly ethical or moral in nature (e.g., police corruption, prosecutorial misconduct, juvenile delinquency); however, few texts present these issues in a way that meaningfully links them to the broader study of ethics and morality. The goal in writing *Ethics, Crime, and Criminal Justice* was to offer a provocative yet accessible overview of the subject and scope of ethics, with specific attention to its relevance and value in the context of crime, law, and justice. The aim was to respond to the need for a comprehensive and illustrative text: one that provides a meaningful examination of both ethics *and* ethical concerns in criminal justice. *Ethics, Crime, and Criminal Justice* not only introduces students to the field of ethics, but also demonstrates how this field can inform our understanding of moral issues in criminal justice, thereby aiding the practitioner in reasoning through situational dilemmas that require thoughtful reflection and reasoned decisions.

There are several key (and unique) features to *Ethics, Crime, and Criminal Justice*. The most noteworthy of these include the following:

Comprehensive overview of ethical concepts, principles, and theories and their relevance to crime, law, and criminal justice. Many existing books on ethics and criminal justice provide limited treatment of the concepts and theories that constitute the foundations of ethical thinking, choosing instead to focus primarily or, in some cases, exclusively on criminal justice issues and dilemmas. While not excluding concerns of crime, law, and justice, *Ethics, Crime, and Criminal Justice* offers an informed and relevant exploration of the theoretical and conceptual foundations of ethics—foundations that, in turn, allow for the problems and concerns of criminal justice to be more thoughtfully and critically deliberated.

Emphasis on reasoning and critical thinking skills. Throughout the text, the importance of reasoning and critical thinking in ethics and criminal justice is emphasized. Particularly in the final two chapters, this book challenges students to overcome common obstacles to good ethical thinking and to approach ethical issues and moral dilemmas critically and intelligently. In addition to these chapters, which are dedicated entirely to exploring the importance of reasoning and critical thinking in ethics and criminal justice, many of the in-text illustrations and boxed inserts throughout each of the chapters are designed to encourage students to thoughtfully entertain issues and dilemmas of significance to ethics and criminal justice.

Unique treatment of metaethical and moral psychological concerns of significance to crime, law, and justice. The concerns of metaethics and moral psychology—free will and determinism, relativism, self-interest, moral motivation, and development—are topics that are not only crucial to ethics, but also to understanding many of the issues and controversies in criminal justice (e.g., lawmaking, criminal punishment, unethical professional behavior). Notwithstanding their significance to the study of crime, law, and justice, many existing texts on ethics and criminal justice offer very little—and oftentimes no—attention to these key issues. *Ethics, Crime, and Criminal Justice* treats them as central concerns that must necessarily be addressed and contemplated for meaningful discussion about moral issues and dilemmas to occur. In Part II of the text ("Metaethics and Moral Psychology"), we dedicate ample space to exploring many of these central issues and to examining their impact on, and importance for, crime, law, and justice.

Integrative approach. A key organizational feature of *Ethics, Crime, and Criminal Justice* is its integrative approach. Most books on criminal justice ethics dedicate one or more chapters near the beginning of the text to exploring ethical and moral concepts, and utilize the remaining chapters to examine ethical issues and dilemmas in criminal justice. As the issues and dilemmas explored later in the text often require utilization of the concepts presented at the beginning of the text, this approach typically has the effect of forcing instructors and students to *refer back* to the conceptual chapters throughout the course. In contrast, we have attempted to integrate criminal justice issues, conflicts, and dilemmas into the substantive conceptual chapters. Rather than including separate chapters that address issues or categories of issues in criminal justice (e.g., ethics and law enforcement, ethics and corrections), presentation and discussion of these issues occur throughout the text. This approach allows for the issues and dilemmas to be better illuminated and more thoughtfully examined in relevant conceptual contexts.

Examination of practical issues and/or controversies relevant to careers in criminal justice, the "helping" professions, and justice studies. Most books on ethics and criminal justice are directed toward current and future criminal justice professionals. As such, they tend to dedicate the majority of their content to exploring issues or dilemmas that might arise within the context of a criminal justice career. Although dedicating ample space to these sorts of concerns, *Ethics, Crime, and Criminal Justice* is written to be of value to anyone concerned with law, crime, and justice. Consequently, the book's content is relevant to those pursuing careers ancillary to criminal justice. Examples of these related professions include social work, counseling, public policy, public administration, and forensic science.

Additionally, *Ethics, Crime, and Criminal Justice* offers numerous pedagogical features. These instructional devices enable students to think critically about the twin subjects of ethics and criminal justice and the many contentious points on which they intersect. These features include:

- Lists of key terms and concepts
- Questions for review and discussion
- Ample illustrations, examples, and counterexamples throughout the text to clarify concepts, ideas, and applications of concepts and ideas
- Boxed inserts that encourage reflection on the *application* of ethical concepts and principles to "real-life" issues and scenarios in criminal justice

- Boxed inserts designed to encourage students to *critically reflect* upon controversial ethical themes, topics, arguments, and scenarios in criminal justice
- Boxed inserts that offer *case studies* of people and/or events from the world of crime, law, and justice

NEW TO THE SECOND EDITION

The second edition of *Ethics, Crime, and Criminal Justice* features numerous updates, revisions, and additions designed to more firmly ground and better illustrate the relationship between morality and crime, law, and justice. In several places, deeply theoretical discussions contained within the first edition have been moderated, and cumbersome terminology restricted to create a free-flowing and more widely accessible text. In addition to substantially reshaping discussions in numerous places throughout the second edition for purposes of clarity and cohesiveness, we have supplemented the text with updated studies, fresh case studies and examples, and new boxed inserts. Highlights of the second edition include:

- Chapter 12, "Applying Ethics: Utilizing Normative Frameworks for Decision-Making" is a *new chapter* with a practical emphasis on the application of normative frameworks to ethical issues and dilemmas.
- Chapter 6, "Morality, Human Nature, and Social Cooperation" is a largely new chapter, introducing *game theory*, *evolutionary psychology*, and concepts such as reciprocal altruism, indirect reciprocity, altruistic punishment, non-zero-sum games, and moral intuition.
- Chapter 6 also contains an expanded discussion of the *social contract* (formerly in Chapter 8), linking it to human nature, social cooperation, and the question of *justice*.
- Illustrations and references to new developments in *cognitive neuroscience* have been added to Chapter 3, "Free Will and Moral Responsibility."
- The treatment of Carol Gilligan's *ethic of care* in Chapter 10, "The Virtuous and the Vicious: Considering Character," has been broadened and amplified.
- Substantive chapters *begin with an engaging case study or example*, designed to generate critical thinking and discussion concerning issues to be emphasized in that chapter's text.

Highlights of case studies, examples, and inserts new to the second edition:

- No-knock warrants
- Statutory rape
- Consent to murder and cannibalism
- The "Tavern Rape" and acts of omission
- Violence and the media
- Sodomy laws
- The cases of Susan Smith and Andrea Yates
- Lie detection
- Child abuse
- Violence and video games
- Substance abuse treatment
- Honor killings
- Blood feuds

- The role of science in ethics
- Incest
- The relativity of prostitution laws
- John Rawls' theory of justice
- Criminal informants
- The "Heinz Dilemma"
- Robert Anthony Williams and the "Christian Burial Speech"
- The "Trolley Problem"
- Ethics, crime, and the Internet

ORGANIZATION OF THE TEXT

Ethics, Crime, and Criminal Justice consists of twelve substantive chapters organized into three primary parts or sections. In each of the three sections, a fundamental domain of inquiry within ethics is explored, and in each chapter a substantive issue within that domain is reviewed. Consistent with the underlying focus on ethics in criminal justice, the text addresses key issues mindful of their importance for the general study of crime, law, and justice. Wherever relevant, practical illustrations and useful examples drawn from the fields of law, criminology, criminal justice, and justice studies are strategically located throughout each chapter.

Part I of the text is entitled "An Invitation to Ethics." It contains two chapters. The commentary here introduces students to the field of ethics by emphasizing its value, subject, and scope, particularly in light of criminal justice concerns. Chapter 1 explains the role and importance of morality and the value of ethical inquiry, both within and outside of the criminal justice context. Additionally, routine questions about why ethics is needed—especially given the existence of laws and professional codes of conduct that outline moral ideals and standards—are both raised and addressed. Highlighting several key problems with laws and codes of conduct, the need for morality and ethical inquiry for criminal justice practitioners and nonpractitioners alike is discussed. Moreover, specific concerns impacting the three main "spheres" of criminal justice (laws and lawmaking, social justice, and criminal justice practice) are described and the special moral requirements placed on professionals within the system of criminal justice are reviewed.

In Chapter 2, a more thorough introduction to the field of ethics is provided. Focusing on the importance of choice-making, readers are encouraged to reflect upon their responsibility for making ethically responsible decisions. With this in mind, the role that values play in the choices that we make is considered. This includes outlining types of moral values and problems that can arise when values are in conflict. Chapter 2 concludes with a brief introduction to the three primary domains of normative ethical inquiry (consequentialism, deontology, and virtue ethics). Given that Parts II and III of this volume explore these domains in significantly more depth, this latter segment of the chapter helps situate and organize the balance of the text.

Part II of the book is entitled "Metaethics and Moral Psychology." Several crucial concerns of metaethics and moral psychology are examined, with specific attention directed toward their relevance for criminal justice. When most people think of ethics, they consider its normative domain. This domain considers what we *should* do or how we *should* live, whether in the context of individual decision-making and behavior occurring in personal or professional settings, or in the context of organizational and institutional policy and practice. Interestingly, however, there are a number of important assumptions and concerns about human nature and social conduct that must be addressed before doing any meaningful thinking about what we should do and how we should live. Included among these concerns are questions about (1) human freedom and the determination of human behavior; (2) the relativity of moral values and the possibility of moral objectivity and universality; (3) the degree to which self-interest necessarily informs our decisions; (4) the age-old question of why we should be moral; and (5) the psychological question of how morality develops.

In some respects, concerns of freedom, relativity, and self-interest can be thought of as potential obstacles or, at least, challenges to moral decision-making and behavior. They are given particular focus in Chapters 3, 4, and 5. Chapters 6 and 7 build upon questions raised in Chapter 5, transitioning into a consideration of the moral psychological concerns of moral motivation ("Why be moral?") and moral development.

Part III is entitled "Normative Ethics: Theory and Application." This section investigates the normative domain of ethical decision-making. As the chapters in this portion of the book make clear, normative ethics attempts to formulate guidelines, standards, and/or principles of right and wrong, good and evil, and to provide answers to questions such as, "What should I do?" and "How should I be?" Of course, these questions do not lend themselves to easy or patented answers. In fact, moral philosophy has collected over two thousand years worth of responses to these and similarly complex concerns. And while a review of all such perspectives is unnecessary in the context of a text such as this, an examination of several of the most influential and widely discussed responses is worthwhile. These responses or, more accurately, "theories" or frameworks, function as "tools" with which to assess various types of policy- and practice-based concerns in criminal justice, ideally yielding both reasoned judgments and informed solutions.

Typically, normative ethics is broken down into three basic frameworks. These frameworks consist of consequentialism, deontology, and virtue-based ethics. Part III of *Ethics, Crime, and Criminal Justice* dedicates a full chapter to each of these perspectives. The objective over the course of these three chapters is to explore the merits of weighing consequences, duties, and character when faced with moral issues and ethical dilemmas. Chapter 8 examines the importance of considering the effects—the likely benefits and costs—of our decisions and actions. Chapter 9 explores those perspectives that place less emphasis on the consequences of our actions and, instead, focuses on whether our actions themselves conform to relevant duties, principles, and obligations. Chapter 10 addresses the importance of developing good moral character and a healthy sense of integrity. Once again, relevant illustrations from law, crime, and justice are utilized to help demonstrate how these philosophical ideas and topics routinely operate within the discipline of criminal justice.

Each of these three general frameworks (consequentialism, deontology, and virtue ethics) has many variations. Several of these variations are discussed in the respective chapters throughout Part III. However, what is perhaps most important is the degree to which the theoretical frameworks offered by normative ethics represent useful templates for critical reflection and decision-making on matters of morality. To this extent, the chapters that comprise Part III offer students and professionals a number of essential "tools" to interpret their everyday experiences and to direct their work-related practices in ways that are consistent with ethically sensible decision-making and conduct.

The final two chapters of *Ethics, Crime, and Criminal Justice* serve as "guides" to thinking about and applying ethics and for living a virtuous life. Chapter 11 showcases a range of fundamental ideas about reasoning, thinking, and judgment that foster careful reflection on moral beliefs and values. Not necessarily intended to be "taught," this guide exposes readers to a number of sensible, though informative, points and directives about *how* to engage in sound reasoning and critical thinking. To this extent, then, Chapter 11 provides direction not only in how to pursue and maintain thought, choice, and conduct that are ethical, but also outlines a workable series of strategies for how to live virtuously and bring about justice in one's own life, those of others, and in society. Chapter 12, new to this edition, is designed to encourage practical application of the ethical ideas outlined in Chapters 8, 9, and 10. It provides a basic framework for moral decision-making and addresses the ways in which theories of normative ethics can be used within that basic framework. The chapter concludes by posing a number of scenarios and dilemmas with which to "practice" the application of ethical frameworks to "real life" issues.

ACKNOWLEDGMENTS

The authors wish to thank the following reviewers for their suggestions and comments on this and the previous edition: Dan Ashment, Ball State University; Dr. Susan Brinkley, University of Tampa; J. Virgil Costley Jr., DeKalb Technical College; Dr. Lois Presser, University of Tennessee, Knoxville; Beverly Quist, Mohawk Valley Community College; Michael Stevenson, University of Toledo; and Beverly Strickland, Fayetteville Technical Community College.

ABOUT THE AUTHORS

Christopher R. Williams, Ph.D., is Professor and Chair of the Department of Criminal Justice Studies at Bradley University. His books include, *Law, Psychology, and Justice: Chaos Theory and the New (Dis)Order; Theory, Justice, and Social Change: Theoretical Integrations and Critical Applications;* and the edited volume, *Philosophy, Crime, and Criminology.* Dr. Williams has also published numerous scholarly articles and book chapters, most confronting issues and controversies in social and criminological theory, the sociology of deviance, the philosophical foundations of crime, law, and justice, and the sociological and legal dimensions of mental health and illness. He did both undergraduate and graduate work in psychology before pursuing doctoral studies in psychology, law, and public policy. Dr. Williams currently resides in Peoria, Illinois, with his wife and two children.

Bruce A. Arrigo, Ph.D., is Professor of Criminology, Law, and Society within the Department of Criminal Justice and Criminology at the University of North Carolina—Charlotte. In the College of Liberal Arts and Sciences, he holds additional faculty appointments in the Psychology Department and the Public Policy Program. In the College of Health and Human Services, he holds an appointment in the Department of Public Health Sciences. Professor Arrigo is also a Faculty Associate in the Center for Professional and Applied Ethics—a teaching, research, and service unit of the Philosophy Department, a senior member of the University Honors College Council, and a Faculty Affiliate of Wake Forest University's Bioethics, Health, and Society Program. His recent books include *Revolution in penology: Rethinking the society of captives* (2009), *Postmodernist and Post-structuralist theories of crime* (2010), and *The ethics of total confinement: A critique of madness, citizenship, and social justice* (2011). Dr. Arrigo also is the author of more than 150 peer-reviewed journal articles, law reviews, chapters in books, and scholarly essays on the normative, theoretical, empirical, clinical, and policy dimensions of various human justice and social change issues. Professor Arrigo is a past recipient of the Criminologist of the Year Award (2000), sponsored by the Division on Critical Criminology of the American Society of Criminology, an elected Fellow of the American Psychological Association (2002), and an elected Fellow of the Academy of Criminal Justice Sciences (2005). In 2007 he received the Bruce Smith Sr. Award (for distinguished research), sponsored by the Academy of Criminal Justice Sciences. In 2008 he was the recipient of the First Citizens Bank Scholars Medal, the most prestigious research honor bestowed upon a single UNC-Charlotte faculty member annually. He currently lives in Concord, North Carolina, with his wife, two children, and their dog, Mowgli.

ETHICS, CRIME, AND CRIMINAL JUSTICE

information.

The application of this technique is sometimes problematic, however. If you use too many categories to code the answers of a question, or the variable is a relatively continuous one at the interval or ratio level, the frequency table will not add much simplification to the data. For instance, if the age variable goes by year, the frequency table could run from 0 to possibly 80 plus, which would take as much space as two full pages and is awkward to use. To further simplify the presentation you need to reduce the data by omitting some details, even though that means you will lose some information while obtaining more concise findings about the data pattern. For this purpose, you can group the values into fewer and larger categories in a frequency table. For the data on age, for instance, you can "collapse" them into 5-year or 10-year age groups and re-run the frequency tables.

The desire for more concise representation of data spurs the search for more general means of data reduction, although it is at the expense of certain detailed information. The idea develops from relying on a distribution table to using a few distribution parameters to represent the data. The latter approach is especially suitable for continuous data. In real terms, there are two kinds of parameters that characterize a distribution, that is, central tendency and dispersion.

A central tendency is measured by an average, which is, in a sense, the most representative of the values of a variable or its data as a whole. There are three kinds of average, or measure of central tendency: the mode (the most frequent value for the cases of a sample), the median (the midpoint or middle value: half of the values given by the cases can be ranked above it, and half below), and the mean (the arithmetic center). Categorical or nominal data can only use the mode as a central tendency measure. Ordinal data may use the mode and the median, but cannot use the mean. Although all the three measures can be applied to interval and ratio data, they have different meanings and should be used scrupulously. For example, if mean income is not a good or meaningful indicator of the economic situation of the sample due to the huge discrepancy between the rich and the poor, you may use the median income instead. Each measure has its use as well as limitation. In some distributions (e.g., symmetric ones), the three measures can be the same even though conceptually they are not.

It is easy to obtain these measures of central tendency. The mode is the largest category in the percentage distribution of a variable. The median can be determined by using the cumulative percentages in a frequency table, where the cases are sorted by their values and the median is the category that carries the

PART ONE

An Invitation to Ethics

Criminal Justice and the Study of Morality

The realities of crime, law, and justice hold—and likely will always hold—appeal in the popular imagination. The daily news is littered with headlines of intrigue: "Murderer and Accused Cannibal to Be Freed in August"; "Calif. Woman Charged with Scamming $285,000 from Nuns"; "Mom Admits Fatally Stabbing Her 3 Kids"; "Cops: Woman Disguised as Dead Mom Arrested in Bank Fraud"; "$5 Million Bond for Mother of Boy Found Dead in Oven."[1] Indeed, the problems and issues as well as people and personalities associated with crime, law, and justice arouse our feelings, inflame our passions, and provoke our thoughts. Consider the following:

- In 2005, Genarlow Wilson was convicted in Atlanta, Georgia, of engaging in oral sex with a fifteen-year-old girl when he was seventeen. Wilson had been an honors student, homecoming king, and football star, soon to be enrolled at Vanderbilt University on an athletic scholarship. At the time, Georgia state law defined Wilson's behavior as felony aggravated child molestation, and he was sentenced to a mandatory ten years in prison and made to register as a sex offender. In 2007, the Georgia Supreme Court ruled Wilson's sentence cruel and unusual. He was released later that day, though his conviction was not overturned.

- In December of 2002, Armin Meiwes was arrested in Germany and later sentenced to 8½; years in prison after being convicted on manslaughter charges. The previous year, Meiwes had placed a personal advertisement on the Internet looking for a "well-built 18 to 30-year-old to be slaughtered and then consumed."[2] Bernd Jürgen Brandes responded to the advertisement. Sometime thereafter, Brandes went to Meiwes' home for purposes of completing the act (though others had responded to the ad, none had followed through). Meiwes proceeded to castrate Brandes, and the two attempted to consume the flesh together. A bit later, Meiwes—having provided Brandes plenty of painkillers and alcohol—proceeded to stab him to death, cut his body into pieces, and freeze it. Meiwes would, for some ten months, consume the remains of Brandes.

- On November 21, 2006, ninety two-year-old Atlanta resident Kathryn Johnston was shot and killed in her home by undercover police officers. The officers broke down her door, entering her home on a **no-knock warrant**—a type of warrant which allows officers to enter homes without first notifying the resident/s of their intent to enter. Presumably not recognizing the plainclothes intruders as police officers, she fired a shot from a gun she kept for self-defense. The officers responded by firing several dozen shots upon Mrs. Johnston, a handful of which struck and ultimately killed her. It was later determined that officers had falsified paperwork to get the warrant, claiming to have purchased cocaine from that residence earlier in the day (in fact, they had not). To cover their tracks following the shooting, one of the officers planted marijuana at the scene. Criminal charges were brought against three officers, each of whom received a prison term.

Chances are, several elements of these stories grabbed your attention. A mandatory ten-year prison sentence for a consensual sexual act between two teenagers? People agreeing to be killed and eaten by other people? An innocent elderly woman gunned down in her own home by police? Part of what makes these stories immediately appealing is that, whether we realize it or not, they are steeped in *morality*. Homicide, suicide, sex, cannibalism, lying, and cheating have been subjects of moral evaluation for thousands of years. So too have more nuanced concepts such as rights, liberties, justice, free will, consent, and intentionality that we regularly use to do the evaluating. Out of concern for these kinds of behaviors and regard for these kinds of concepts, criminal justice—in both theory and practice—is an inherently moral subject.

Not surprisingly, then, the topics and questions of interest to criminal justice are often personally meaningful and extremely provocative. Discussions on the death penalty, abortion, flag burning, war, racial profiling, or terrorism present disparate opinions and clashes of values that arise from conflicting views about right and wrong. Some may oppose abortion, arguing that it is wrong to take a life; similarly, some may oppose the death penalty because, again, it is wrong to take a life. Others may support abortion, reasoning that people should be free to do as they see fit with their own bodies—that is, to enjoy some sense of privacy, control, and self-determination when it comes to that which is most private and most uniquely "ours." Yet which values and whose principles are, in fact, valid and desirable in these and other contexts? Should the value of life take precedence over the right to privacy and self-determination? If so, under what specific conditions should this occur? Should the value of life supersede the value of what some define as "just" punishment? Knowingly or not, when we contemplate issues such as capital punishment, sentencing disparity, or drug legalization in criminal justice courses; reference the desirability of "liberty" in friendly discussions with parents or roommates; or take action to respect or protect the "rights" of ourselves or others, we are immersed in the realm of morality and participants in the realm of *ethics*.

ETHICS AND MORALITY

At its most elemental level, **ethics** can be defined as *the philosophical study of morality*. More specifically, ethics can be described, in part, as:

- The study of what is morally "right," "wrong," "good," "bad," "obligatory," and "permissible."
- An effort to understand and justify moral concepts, principles, and theories.
- An effort to establish (justified) principles of moral behavior that can serve as guides for individuals and groups.[3]
- An investigation into the values and virtues that are important—even necessary—to leading and living a (or the) "good" life, as individuals and as societies.

Morality is typically understood to refer to *people's values, their beliefs about right and wrong, good and bad, and the choices they make and the actions that they take as a result of those values and beliefs*. Resorting to violence in retaliation for verbal insult might be described as "wrong" or "immoral"; ethics is the critical contemplation of whether it is, in fact, immoral and on what basis we can make such a judgment. A law enforcement officer telling the truth in a court of law, even though it results in the dismissal of the case, might be described as "moral" and illustrative of integrity; ethics defines, describes, and evaluates honesty, including when and under what circumstances it is a morally desirable course of action. Ethics is thus an investigation into or critical consideration of morality—of values, beliefs, choices, and actions. In this respect, ethics encourages conscientious reflection on how we should live, the decisions we should make, and the actions we should take as we confront a variety of personal and professional scenarios over the course of our lives.

Yet, ethics is not simply the study of morality. Anthropology, sociology, and other social sciences routinely study morality; ethics is better understood as a certain *way* of studying morality. To illustrate, let us revisit the case of Armin Meiwes, one of the three with which we opened the chapter:

A key consideration in the case of Armin Meiwes is that his "victim" consented to being killed and eaten. In other words, he was a willing participant in his own death. With respect to many kinds of encounters, *consent* changes the moral quality of what transpires. As might also be relevant to the case of Genarlow Wilson, consent marks the difference between sex and rape. It also differentiates masochism from criminal torture, and even assault from a routine trip to the dentist's office.[4] The fact that Miewes' victim consented thus begs several questions of interest to ethics: Should the "victim" in this case be considered a homicide victim? Should Meiwes be held criminally responsible? If so, how should he be punished? Should the reason for the victim's consent matter (e.g., he was terminally ill, he was participating in a spiritual or religious ritual)? Is consenting to one's own death better regarded as suicide? Is cannibalism "wrong," even when those being consumed have previously consented to being consumed? Should it matter if the cannibalistic activities were necessary to prevent the deaths of a larger number of people, as when stranded with no access to an alternative food supply?

Each of these questions has something in common with the others that distinguishes them from the kinds of inquiries common to the natural and social sciences. When scientists and social scientists study morality they are typically interested in offering **descriptive** accounts; that is to say, they offer descriptions, explanations, and sometimes predictions of the moral beliefs and practices within a given society or culture. With respect to the Meiwes case, descriptive approaches might offer interpretations of the existing laws pertaining to consent, homicide, and suicide; they might offer explanations for why someone would want to kill, eat human flesh, or have one's own flesh eaten by others; they might offer statistics on the prevalence of suicide or descriptions of cannibalism in other cultures. Ethics, on the other hand, is largely **prescriptive**. It attempts to evaluate moral beliefs, principles, practices, and so forth, and makes normative statements about what *should* be or *should not* be done in light of its evaluations. Thus, unlike anthropology or other social science disciplines, ethics is not the study of what *is*, but of what *should* or *ought* to be.[5]

To further illustrate the distinction between descriptive and prescriptive forms of inquiry, let us consider the example of laws prohibiting murder. If we approached the issue of homicide through the study of criminal law, we would endeavor to understand what is. We would be interested in ascertaining the existing state of the criminal law with respect to murder—how, precisely, this crime is defined; what exceptions, if any, apply to the general rule; what punishments are ascribed to the act of murder; and other considerations that allow us to better grasp what murder is and how it is understood from a legal perspective. As soon as we begin to entertain questions such as what punishments *should* or *ought* to apply to murder, whether murder *should* be legally prohibited, whether there *should* be exceptions to the general rule, and whether existing exceptions are morally justifiable, we step into the realm of ethics (see Box 1.1). In a way, ethics is interested in "taking a step back" from common beliefs and practices, subjecting them to critical examination, and reaching normative conclusions about what *should be* the case rather than what *is* the case.

BOX 1.1
The Moral Problem of Punishment

While we often entertain *practical* questions of criminal punishment, we less often consider the moral underpinnings of those practices. Why do we punish? When do we punish? What is the appropriate amount of punishment for a given infraction? While each of these questions can be answered in a practical sense, they also have moral foundations that require our critical consideration.

Utilitarian philosopher Jeremy Bentham once argued that "all punishment is evil"—"evil" being anything people do not want inflicted upon them. He was not, of course, suggesting that we not ever practice the punishment of criminal offenders. Rather, he was simply stating an often-overlooked moral reality that punishment involves the infliction of pain, the causing of suffering, and/or the infliction of deprivation—all actions that, morally, we ought to avoid wherever possible. Beyond simply being an evil in this sense, punishment is an evil that we *intentionally* inflict upon other human beings.

If we accept the notion that all punishment is evil and, further, agree that evil generally should not be caused and evil actions not done, we recognize the ethical problem of punishment. "If the infliction of evil ought not be done under most circumstances, how can we justify the infliction of evil on criminal offenders?" Outside the context of criminal justice operations, depriving persons of things that they value and/or inflicting pain and suffering upon persons is often grounds *for punishment*. Yet within the system of justice, these pains and deprivations represent the operative mode by which "justice" is often carried out. The **moral problem of punishment**, then, is this: How can we *justify* intentionally inflicting evil upon other human beings? What justifications can you think of for punishing criminals? What justifications might exist for dealing with criminal offenders in ways *other than* punishment?

Source: Igor Primoratz, *Justifying Legal Punishment* (New Jersey: Humanities Press, 1989), pp. 1–9.

Part of the significance of ethics, especially within criminology and criminal justice curricula, is that it encourages students (and teachers) to reflect critically on matters that are all too frequently taken for granted. Definitions of crimes and corresponding punishments; the rights of citizens, suspects, and incarcerated criminals; and law enforcement techniques and tactics for apprehending persons who have (or are thought to have) violated the law are examples of topics that people encounter over the course of their criminal justice and/or criminology education. Most often, however, students are simply asked to learn these things in their existing everyday forms (e.g., facts, techniques), rather than more deeply contemplate what *should* be. Thus, ethics challenges us to experience a deeper understanding of what crime and justice are or could be, directs our attention to the "rights" and "wrongs" of the criminal justice system, and invites students to consider what their (potential) roles should be as current or future practitioners within the field.

Never Kill an Innocent Human Being

In the examples used near the beginning of this chapter, several values and principles were mentioned as common justifications for opposing or supporting practices such as abortion and capital punishment. In everyday discourse, we usually make judgments as to the "rightness" or "goodness" of behavior by referencing values or principles that we hold to be important. The values and principles that ethics investigates are not that different from those that factor into our own moral decision-making and judgment (e.g., honesty and fairness, duty and obligation). However, ethics removes these notions from everyday discussions and subjects them to careful scrutiny. The goal is to identify values and construct principles that are sound, worthwhile, and applicable in a number of situations or contexts (including those that occur within criminal justice contexts). Consider the following questions that could be raised in response to the idea (i.e., principle) that we should *never kill an innocent human being*:

- Is the idea that we should never kill an innocent human being a worthwhile principle?
- Does it apply to all situations or are there exceptions? If there are exceptions, what are they and why? What makes these exceptions legitimate?
- What if the principle of never killing an innocent human being conflicts with other principles also considered important? Can we rank-order principles such that some "trump" others when there is a conflict? If so, who decides this and by what process?
- What if, for example, killing an innocent human being can save the lives of ten other innocent human beings? Is this killing ethically justified?
- What is a "human being"?
- What constitutes innocence?
- What constitutes life and therefore "killing"?

You probably had an easier time with the first question than those that followed. Despite the fact that most people would probably agree that not killing innocent human beings is a valid moral principle worth following, they would likely run into some difficulties with one or more of the subsequent queries. Exceptions to this principle could be many and varied. For instance, in times of war military forces routinely kill innocent human beings (both citizens of other countries and, on occasion, their own civilians). Could we argue that citizens of other countries, by virtue of supporting their governments, are somehow less "innocent" and therefore exempt from the principle? When terrorists attacked the United States on September 11, 2001, flying hijacked aircraft toward buildings occupied by thousands of people, would it have been morally justifiable for the U.S. military to shoot down the hijacked aircraft—thereby killing dozens of innocent citizens on board—in order to prevent these planes from reaching their targets? In other words, to what extent are innocent lives expendable? Which ones? By what moral principles might we make such determinations? (Russian parliament has since passed a law allowing for "flying bombs" to be shot down, while Germany's Federal Constitution Court did just the opposite, citing concern for human dignity as reason that sacrificing innocent citizens in such cases is unlawful).[6]

Defining the contours of moral values and principles can be more difficult than often imagined. The same is true when describing the specific situations in which these values and principles do or do not apply. Even something as seemingly straightforward as defining "human being" can be a matter of significant moral contention. Is an unborn fetus a "human being" by moral standards? If so, at what point does it *become* a human being? Historically, entire groups of people have been exempt from human status. For instance, Nazi Germany subscribed to something similar to the above principle that we should never kill an innocent human being. However, Jews and certain other citizen groups (e.g., gays, various ethnic constituencies) were not legally regarded as fully human. Therefore, killing persons within these collectives was not a violation of the accepted principle within Nazi Germany.[7]

Ethics examines and encourages us to consider these sorts of questions. It seeks to develop valid principles that can be used by individuals, groups, organizations, communities, and even entire societies as guides along the path of life. Some issues (e.g., What constitutes innocence?) may seem academic and of little relevance to our everyday realities. However, investigating such questions forces us to reflect profoundly upon our own values and beliefs, as well as why we have them and how we can or should apply them in our personal and professional lives.

THE ROLE OF MORALITY AND THE VALUE OF ETHICAL INQUIRY

Given this very provisional understanding of morality and ethics, we can begin to consider not only what both are, but also what they *do*; that is, why we need morality and why the study of morality (i.e., ethics) can be of value to individuals, professionals, institutions, cultures, and societies. What role does morality play in cultural settings and in social contexts? What value does morality bring to us as individuals—both in our personal and professional lives? Why do social institutions such as law or the criminal justice apparatus (as well as their component parts) need to function in a moral fashion?

Overall, we might say that the purpose of morality is to *enable us to live a good life in a just society*. Though morality has many more specific purposes, almost all of them tend either to enable us to live good, fulfilling lives as individuals, or promote the kind of society, social conditions, and human relationships that allow all citizens to experience the same. Among other things, morality plays a significant role in preventing and reducing harm and suffering, enhances human and nonhuman well-being, provides the necessary tools to resolve conflict fairly and orderly, and encourages people to recognize and attend to the needs of others.[8] All of these things, in turn, contribute in some way to the development and sustenance of a just society—to conditions and relationships that allow us to be well and to flourish as individuals, that allow others to be well and to flourish as citizens, and that promote the greater health of the community and of society.

All of this may seem rather vague. This is because ethics—the study of morality—is not as simple as concluding that we need morality to enable us to live good lives in just societies. Ethics forces us to reflect more deeply upon what, exactly, we mean by "goodness," "justice," and how and why they are important in a social context. Even if we begin with the basic idea that morality enables us to live a good life in a just society, ethics then forces us to further address related questions and concerns:

- What is "justice" and a "just" society?
- What is a (or the) "good" life?
- How, exactly, does morality function to promote justice (or fail to do so)?
- How does morality further our interest in living a good life? A happy life? A fulfilled life?

Unfortunately, these questions do not lend themselves to easy or straightforward responses. You may be distraught to learn that despite more than two thousand years of moral philosophy—of critical reflection, argumentation, and analysis—ethical inquiry has not produced definitive, irrefutable answers to these sorts of questions. To be clear, this is not a consequence of limited efforts or misguided attempts. Moreover, a variety of provisional answers to these very questions are discernible and they are worth considering (indeed, several of them will be entertained over the course of this book). However, the point is that ethics is not something to be undertaken with the intent of finding all possible solutions. Unlike scientific and social scientific inquiries that provide factual (descriptive and explanatory) information, ethics primarily encourages us to question, to develop our own answers, and then to question some more.

Fortunately or otherwise, ethics is not an exact science. It is not an exercise in learning and applying rules and principles (such as the law). Additionally, ethics does not tell us exactly how we should lead our lives or what we should do in every situation. While ethics certainly encourages us to think about principles and to think about how they might apply in specific, concrete instances, it is perhaps best thought of as an ongoing process of critical reflection. Part of what ethical inquiry is—and part of what it means to be moral—concerns this *process* of thinking and rethinking, developing provisional answers only to recognize their limitations and reflect a bit more. How will studying ethics help you in your personal and professional life? Not, as you might think by providing solutions but instead, by encouraging you to continually reflect upon the questions themselves.

The Examined Life: What Does It Mean to Be Moral?

The Greek philosopher Socrates (469–399 B.C.E.) is reputed to have once said that "the unexamined life is not worth living."[9] What he meant is that it is important to critically reflect upon our own lives, the principles by which we live them, the values we cherish, and the cognitive and affective (i.e., emotional) forces and processes that inform our decisions and actions—in short, the people we are, have been, and want to be. Socrates also instructed his students to be true to themselves; that is, to "know thyself" (a then-familiar philosophical slogan reputed to have been inscribed on the temple of Apollo in ancient Greece). Thus, ethics not only asks that we reflect upon the issues and/or controversies that we encounter in our personal and professional lives, it also asks us to examine ourselves. Another way of saying this is that ethics asks that we live *mindfully*—to take some care in how we act, what and how we feel, what we think and believe.[10] Morality is not possible without self-knowledge; and "knowing thyself" requires the kind of critical, self-searching introspection that ethics encourages us to undertake.

In a way, then, we can understand morality as "*the self-conscious living of life*."[11] To be moral is to have knowledge about one's self; that is, what you are about and, thus, what you are doing and why you are doing it. Searching ourselves—coming to "know ourselves"—brings us to one of the most important functions of morality in the context of our personal existence as individuals: *Morality gives meaning to and provides purpose in our lives.* Knowing one's self in the way that Socrates advocated is ultimately what enables us to experience a sense of identity, meaning, purpose, direction, and motivation. To illustrate, if we selfishly strive for money and power, lying and exploiting others for our own benefit, we not only live a less-than-moral life from the perspective of others, but also lack something important: a personal sense of virtue and goodness. Meaning and purpose come from being in touch with our values and principles and from being aware of and motivated by things beyond ourselves. In short, having a sense of goodness and justice serves as a way of measuring ourselves—where we have been, where we are, and where we are going—and as a guide for our decisions and actions.

If our lives are directed by a deeper sense of goodness and justice, arguably we live more complete, satisfying, and fulfilling existences. Part of what Socrates meant when he proclaimed that the unexamined life was not worth living was that a relationship could be discerned between ethics, morality, and happiness—between being moral and living a fulfilled life. Socrates, Plato, Aristotle, and other early Greek philosophers each, in their own way, suggested that being moral *was* being happy and well. In other words, when people lead good lives, notwithstanding difficulties or inconveniences they may bring to themselves because of it, they embrace happier, more fulfilling existences. This reasoning may be somewhat difficult for us to accept, especially when being moral seems often to result in unhappiness or, at least, inconvenience. However, the temporary frustrations and nuisances that can follow from setting aside our own pleasures, wants, and interests are not contrary to being well and to leading a good life. Indeed, on a deeper level, the inconveniences directly contribute to our own well-being and to that of others, as well as to the general health of the community and society of which we are a part. In other words, they directly contribute to living a good life in a just society.

WHY ETHICS WHEN WE HAVE LAWS?

Like many students of criminology and criminal justice who come upon ethics for the first time, you may be asking yourself, "don't we already have laws that serve to create and sustain a just society in which we can lead good lives?" Isn't this precisely their purpose? And, if so, why do we need to bother with ethics at all?[12]

Let us consider the example of drugs and society as a basis to examine this matter. Whether as students or teachers, both authors of this volume have discussed the phenomenon of illicit substance use/abuse and crime on a number of occasions. Invariably, when the class discussion focuses on drug decriminalization or legalization, some very strong sentiments in favor of or opposed to this policy are voiced. Eventually, after some considerable classroom debate, a student typically weighs in and says emphatically that "It's against the law, period!" When pursuing this position with students who express such deeply held convictions, often (although not always) they are persuaded that the law is, in and of itself, sufficient justification for their views concerning illicit drug use. In other words, for them the mere fact that something is against the law is itself an indicator that further discussion on the matter is unwarranted. The question becomes whether such a position or argument is sound. Does the fact that something is against the law mean that subjecting it to critical scrutiny is pointless? That is, does the legality or illegality of a certain behavior "end the argument," so to speak?

In our joint experiences within the field of criminology and criminal justice, there are literally thousands of students who question the need for critical discourse around issues such as illicit drugs (other than, perhaps, how to control them and the people who sell and use them). In relation to ethics, the question might be asked, "why do we need to study ethics, particularly in the context of a profession that relies heavily on laws, codes of professional conduct, and the like?" Why, one might ask, do we need ethics when we already have laws and guidelines in place to *tell* us how we can and cannot act and what we should and should not do? Why study the moral dimensions of drugs, abortion, euthanasia, prostitution, gambling, rape, arson, robbery, and even murder when other people have already done so and codified (written into law) their conclusions? Why waste time on these matters when it is quicker and easier to rely on the answers that legislators and judges have already provided and that, ultimately, we must abide by anyway?

Laws Are Not Infallible

There are several important considerations that arise in response to these and similar questions. First, we might ask ourselves how and by whom laws are made. It is always important to remember that *laws are made by people*, generally through a process of ethical reasoning that involves moral considerations. More specifically, statutory laws are created by local, state, and federal legislators; regulatory law is created by administrative agencies; and case law is created by judges and justices. In all instances, it is important to remember that laws, policies, rules, guidelines, codes, and so on are made by *fallible* people who are subject to the same sorts of biases, pressures, conflicts, and errors in reasoning as the rest of us (though to a lesser degree, we would hope). To illustrate, simply because state legislators conclude that gambling is harmless and remove it from the list of prohibited acts, does not mean that gambling *is* harmless or that it *should* be removed from the list of prohibited acts. Further, even if state legislators legalize gambling, they do so for what they believe are valid *reasons*. Of particular interest to us should be *what reasons* and whether they represented *good reasons*.[13] For instance, if economic considerations played a role in the state's legalization of gambling, then increased revenues, jobs, commerce, and so forth were likely identified as more important than those factors weighing against the decision. These types of considerations make the legalization of gambling a decidedly *moral judgment*.

cumulative percentage over 50% (the middle position). The mean needs to be calculated by summing up all the values that the sample has taken, and then dividing the result by the number of cases in the sample. In SPSS, these measures of central tendency can be obtained simply by specifying the corresponding statistics in the FREQUENCIES procedure. It should be noted that for a continuous variable, the data had better not be collapsed before calculating any of the parameters, including dispersion measures to be discussed later. Even the computation of a simple average might become very complicated for grouped data.

Any of the central tendency measures can be used as a general expectation to predict the value of a case on a variable, and the total error for the entire sample (i.e., chances of being wrong, or distance of being away from the average) should be the minimum among all the values that are considered. This is, however, only in a relative sense. The error of prediction using an average may be really small, yet it could also be considerable. This will depend on how different the subjects (cases) in a sample are from one another. We need to measure the differences among the cases. This will indicate how representative those measures of central tendency are and what might be the errors when they are used to predict the values on a variable. In other words, we need a measure of dispersion, which, together with the measure of central tendency, would portray a more complete picture of the data distribution.

For the mode as a measure of central tendency, its representativeness depends on the number of cases that fail to take on that particular (mode) value, or more precisely, the ratio of that number to the sample size. Let f_m stand for the frequency of the mode and N for the sample size, then $v=(N-f_m)/N$. This v, called variation ratio, is a measure of dispersion showing that the more cases fall aside the mode value, the larger the total error when the mode is used for predicting the value of a case. Like the mode, this measure can be used at any measurement level (note in a sample or population constituted by individual cases, all variables will turn out to be discrete and no one will really be continuous).

The median can be used in place of the mode to represent the values of the entire sample more precisely in the sense that it takes into account the rank order of those values. Yet to predict the value of any case on an ordinal variable in this way, there is no accurate measure to indicate what the total error or how exact the prediction would be. You may only get a rough idea from the number of ranks included between the median and a quartile, which by definition includes 25% of the total number of cases in between. The fewer the different ranks included,

Laws Can Be Immoral

Concerns of law and lawmaking will reappear throughout subsequent chapters. For now, what is important is that we understand the value of and need for ethics even when we have law. In short, we need ethics—even if we have laws—because *law is not possible without ethics*.[14] In making laws, legislators, judges, and others with lawmaking power are invariably making decisions that are moral in nature or have moral implications; they are arriving at conclusions about what is right and wrong based on what they believe, at the time, amount to good reasons or sound justifications. These reasons and justifications, in turn, may or may not be suspect. Laws may or may not be moral; they may or may not promote moral behavior.

Consider, for example, the **Nuremberg laws** enacted by the Nazi German government which deprived persons classified as "Jews" of German citizenship and basic rights belonging to citizens, or the keeping of slaves in the pre–Civil War United States—a practice that was legal both under state law and under the U.S. Constitution at the time. Persecuting Jews and the keeping of slaves are today acts that most of us would agree are less than moral by nearly all standards. Yet they were also acts that were legal at one time. What can we learn from these examples? Simply put, *legality does not necessarily equal morality*; and, likewise, *morality does not necessarily equal legality*. Ethics may determine that some laws (e.g., those permitting slavery or those promoting or maintaining discrimination on the basis of class, race, gender, etc.) are *immoral*. There are many acts that are legal, yet immoral by many standards; and, at the same time, there are many practices that were, are, or might be illegal, while being moral by at least some ethical standards (see Boxes 1.2 and 1.3). For instance, some environmentalists drive spikes into trees to prevent them from being harvested by the lumber industry (if the trees are then harvested, the spikes break the expensive saws in the lumber mills).[15] Are such practices ethical? Despite questions of legality, the principles that drive environmentalists are unquestionably moral in nature.

BOX 1.2
Jury Nullification

Jury nullification occurs when jurors return a verdict that is consistent with their own sense of justice, but inconsistent with the law. Often, this occurs when a verdict of "not guilty" is returned despite evidence that the defendant is legally guilty of the crime for which she or he is charged. In effect, the jurors determine that the existing law is immoral or has been wrongfully applied in a particular instance and decide the case on the basis of their own *moral* standards rather than applicable *legal* standards. Jurors may, for instance, refuse to find a defendant guilty of a "mercy killing," despite overwhelming evidence that the killing was in violation of criminal law (e.g., see the cases of Jack Kevorkian who, via *physician-assisted suicide*, claims to have "helped" over a hundred people end their lives).

• Given the problems with law outlined in this chapter (e.g., that laws can be misguided, outdated, immoral, unjust), do you feel that jury nullification

could be morally acceptable in some situations? If so, under what circumstances and for which types of crimes/criminals? Keep in mind that the role of jurors is not to make or change laws, but to judge cases on the basis of legal facts with which they are presented.

• Is jury nullification a desirable part of criminal justice? Does it promote or interfere with justice? Keep in mind that it was not long ago that juries in the South regularly returned "not guilty" verdicts for white offenders who were charged with crimes against blacks, notwithstanding strong evidence of guilt. Similarly, black defendants were regularly found "guilty" on the basis of very little evidence.

Source: Murray Levine and Leah Wallach, *Psychological Problems, Social Issues, and the Law* (Boston, MA: Allyn & Bacon, 2002).

BOX 1.3
Morality in Law: The Case of Sodomy

In 1982, Michael Hardwick was arrested in his own bedroom on charges of *sodomy*—at that time a crime in Georgia carrying a penalty of up to twenty years in prison. Hardwick had missed a court appearance on an unrelated matter, resulting in a warrant being issued for his arrest. Police went to Hardwick's home at 3 A.M. to serve the warrant and, having been let inside by his roommate, found Hardwick engaged in oral sex with a male partner. He and his partner were subsequently arrested under a Georgia law which prohibited certain forms of sexual relations. At the time, Georgia was one of a number of states to have **sodomy laws**—laws that criminalize a variety of "deviant" sexual acts, including oral and anal inter-course (even when done in private and between consenting adults).

Although the sodomy charges were later dropped, Hardwick proceeded to sue Michael Bowers, then attorney general of the state of Georgia, hoping to have the Georgia law declared unconstitutional. The case eventually reached the Supreme Court of the United State of America, and the *Bowers v. Hardwick* decision would become one of the most infamous and widely discussed cases involving morality and law in recent decades. By a 5–4 decision, the Supreme Court held that the Constitution does not "extend a fundamental right to homosexuals to engage in acts of consensual sodomy" and that "to hold that the act of homo-sexual sodomy is somehow protected as a fundamental right would be to cast aside millennia of moral teaching."

The publicity and debate generated by the *Bowers* case ultimately set the stage for the eradication of sodomy laws. The Georgia Supreme Court would, in the 1998 case of *Powell v. State*, declare the 182-year-old Georgia sodomy law unconstitutional. Seventeen years after *Bowers*, the U.S. Supreme Court reconsidered the issue in *Lawrence & Garner v. State of Texas* (2003), this time declaring unconstitutional all state laws that made private sexual acts between consenting adults (except for prostitution) crimes. Before the 2003 decision, Alabama, Florida, Idaho, Kansas, Louisiana, Michigan, Mississippi, Missouri, North Carolina, Oklahoma, South Carolina, Texas, Utah, and Virginia still had some variation of sodomy laws (and corre-sponding criminal punishments) on the books.

The *Bowers* case not only raises interesting questions about the relationship between morality and the law: What is the appropriate relationship between morality and law? Does the state have an interest in maintaining the moral integrity of the community and, thus, legislating morality? *Bowers* also raises some interesting questions about the enforcement of laws. Though a person need not have been homosexual to have violated sodomy laws, the Court repeatedly refer-enced "homosexual sodomy," and the "crime" of sodomy was historically enforced selectively (with arrests and prosecutions for sodomy typically involving homosexual rather than heterosexual offenders). What, if any, moral concerns are raised by **selective enforcement** of the law? For what reasons, if any, might it be acceptable to overlook some violations of law while arresting others for the same offense?

Right Does Not Always Make *Good*

These discrepancies are an important reason for studying ethics and morality even when we have laws to guide us. It is always important to keep in mind that even if we "do the right thing" by legal standards, we are not necessarily acting morally. Similarly, even if we do the wrong thing by legal standards, we are not necessarily acting immorally. Throughout your studies of crime and justice, politics, society, and life more generally, always keep in mind that *right* does not equal *righteous*. That is to say, just because something is a *legal* right does not make it a *moral* right. These are two very different uses of the term "right." While my friend Sara may have the "right" to have an abortion, this certainly does not mean that it is morally "right" for her to do so. Similarly, simply because it may be morally wrong for her to do so, this does not necessarily mean that it is or should be legally wrong. The relationship between morality and law is one that is as complex as it is important. While we will have occasion to return to it, for now we simply should recognize that law and morality—though arguably interrelated—are not one and the same. We cannot and should not abandon our study of ethics simply because we have laws. Laws are not definitions of morality; rather, laws are *subjects* of ethical scrutiny in the same way as everything else.

Law Is Not Inclusive of All Moral Concerns

While morality is closely linked with law, they are not one and the same. Law and morality are similar in that they are both intended to promote well-being, resolve conflicts, and generally enhance social harmony.[16] As the previous section attempted to clarify, however, there are some important differences between law and morality. In addition to laws not always being moral, and morality not always being legal, there is at least one other difference that is worth noting—that *some aspects of morality are not covered by law.*[17] Most all of us would agree that lying is, in most instances, morally wrong. Yet other than those laws prohibiting perjury, various forms of fraud, and a few other situations, there are no specified laws against lying. It would be perfectly legal to live our lives lying whenever we could reap some personal gain from doing so. Yet in so doing, we would certainly not be leading moral (or, at least, morally virtuous) lives. Being a good person and doing the right thing are not equivalent to being a law-abiding citizen and avoiding illegal acts. In short, there is much more to morality than law.

It Is Not Enough to Do the Right Thing

Another important reason to study ethics is that, just as lawmakers have good (and sometimes not-so-good) reasons for passing laws, people need to have good reasons for acting one way or another, thinking one way or another, and believing in one thing or another. It is not enough to simply do the right thing; rather, we must *know why it is right.* This applies not only to laws, policies, and codes of conduct, but also to all standards of conduct—whether they be professional, legal, religious, or merely social. All legal and all religious systems have some form of prohibition against the taking of life. Can we say that we are moral simply because we follow God's commandment not to kill? The short answer is, "no." To be moral people, we must not only follow moral rules, but also *understand why* the conduct in question is moral or immoral. We must reflect upon *why* it is wrong to take life. We must, in a sense, reach the same conclusions that lawmakers, religious authorities, professional organizations, and the like have reached by reasoning through principles, scenarios, arguments, and so forth for ourselves. Some would argue, for instance, that the Christian God prohibits killing *because* it is wrong. In other words, even God has good reasons for asking us not to kill. What is important is not simply that we know *that* we should not kill and lead our lives accordingly; rather, what is important is that we know *why* we should refrain from killing.

MORALITY, ETHICAL INQUIRY, AND CRIMINAL JUSTICE

Morality, then, assumes an important role in our own lives, as well as the lives of the communities and societies of which we are a part. As valuable as morality and ethical inquiry are for human social and personal existence, most of you are probably reading this book (and/or taking this course) not because of a deep interest in ethics, but because of an interest in criminology, criminal justice, or justice studies. Thus, in the remainder of this chapter, it will be helpful to look more closely at the role of morality in this context, as well as the value of ethical inquiry for students and practitioners of criminal justice.

We might begin by laying out the role of ethics and morality in relation to what could be termed the **spheres of criminal justice**. Ethics is applicable to a number of different (but interrelated) levels, or spheres, that collectively make up crime and the behavior of the criminal justice system: criminal justice practice, laws and lawmaking, and social justice.[18] Each of these spheres always exists in relation to the others. Consequently, we should not regard them as mutually exclusive, but as interrelated and interdependent. Changes in law, for example, impact the practice of criminal justice as well as broader concerns of societal well-being, and changes in the practices of the criminal justice system impact the form and content of laws as well as have a more far-reaching effect on larger social concerns such as race, class, and gender relations. In light of these interactions, it is important to approach ethical inquiry in criminology and criminal justice from the perspective of each of these spheres, attending equally to concerns that emerge from within and between all of them. Throughout this volume, many ethical concerns of criminal justice practice, law and lawmaking, and social justice are featured. Here, we offer some preliminary observations on each of these spheres of criminal justice.

Criminal Justice Practice

Ethics is not limited to considerations of prominent moral and political issues such as abortion, capital punishment, and euthanasia. Ethics is equally relevant to other significant realms for criminologists and criminal justicians. Specifically, many students of criminal justice ethics are likely to be current or future *practitioners*. Criminal justice ethics encourages practitioners to confront not only contentious moral and legal issues, but also to assess their personal behavior as members of a profession. These are matters of *professional ethics*. **Professional ethics** is interested in utilizing ethical values, principles, obligations, and so on, in applying them to particular issues and practical scenarios that emerge within the context of a given field or occupation. Thus, medical ethics, business ethics, legal ethics, and police ethics are each efforts to understand the moral dimensions that characterize these professions and to formulate principles that might serve as guides for individual behavior within the context of these professions. For example, what principles do we want police officers to practice with regard to honesty or integrity? Is it ever morally acceptable for officers of the law to be dishonest? Does the context matter? What if being less than virtuous helps to achieve the aims of policing as a profession?

Each of these is a question of fundamental importance to criminal justice. Collectively, they are questions of police practice; that is, *how* police officers should go about achieving the aims of the profession. At the same time, though, they are inescapably moral concerns. *How* we behave, be it in our personal or professional lives, always has a moral dimension. Indeed, whether we realize it, nearly everything we do has some ethical relevance. Moreover, as discussed in the previous section, part of the value of studying ethics is to recognize the various ways in which our lives unmistakably possess ethical dimensions and moral significance. Once we come to this realization, we are in a position to consider how to make good ethical choices, both as everyday citizens and as stalwart professionals.

The practical sphere of criminal justice is composed of the choices and behaviors of each individual working within the system—from police dispatchers to jury members to death row executioners. We can further subdivide the ethics of criminal justice practice into three primary components. These include police, courts, and corrections. Each of these components includes unique moral dimensions that fundamentally characterize it. Similarly, each one of these subsystems encompasses concerns shared with the other two. Again, it is important to recognize that these three components of the criminal justice system are interrelated, and, as such, so are the moral concerns that emerge from within them. To illustrate, whether a police officer fully respects the legal rights of a suspect has ramifications for courts and, potentially, corrections as well.

We cannot, however, engage in any meaningful discussion about moral concerns linked to criminal justice practice without first having had some introduction to and having engaged in some critical reflection on ethical values, principles, and beliefs, more generally. We will examine the various facets of ethics, as well as practical concerns with which they intersect, throughout the remainder of this text. For now, consider the following list of questions as a way to acquaint yourself with the kinds of issues and controversies that characterize the practical aspects of criminal justice:

- Does a defense attorney have a moral obligation to defend her or his client's interests, even if in so doing a guilty person will likely be acquitted?
- Should illegally obtained evidence be excluded from trial—even if it clearly suggests that, without a doubt, the defendant is responsible for the crime(s) in question?
- Under what, if any, circumstances should law enforcement officers be permitted to use deceptive methods or techniques to gain consent for searches, to obtain evidence, to apprehend suspects?

Laws and Lawmaking

The sphere of law and lawmaking encompasses both substantive and procedural criminal law, as well as family, civil, and other types of legal decision-making that have a direct or indirect influence on crime and justice. In the context of substantive criminal law, ethics not only encourages us to confront the moral dimensions of specific statutes and cases, but also invites us to reflect upon some of the foundational questions of criminal law: What should constitute a crime? How should we treat persons who offend existing criminal laws? What are appropriate punishments for culpable offenders? What defines culpability or criminal responsibility? What moral principles should be codified into law, both as crimes and as rules that practitioners of criminal justice must follow? What relationship does morality have in general to criminal law in particular? What relationship *should* morality maintain with criminal law?

Much of what the three main branches of the criminal justice system do revolves around criminal law. In large part, the practice of policing entails upholding or enforcing substantive criminal laws in ways that are consistent with existing procedural guidelines or laws. Courts try persons accused of violating criminal laws according to the principles of criminal procedure. The correctional sphere is responsible for dealing with persons convicted of violating such laws, again doing so in a manner that conforms to the standards and regulations set forth through procedural laws and relevant court decisions. Yet, what moral values and principles are embedded in these laws? What moral values and principles are relied upon in the process of arriving at legal decisions, be they at trial or appellate levels? Perhaps more importantly, what moral values and principles *should* be relied upon and thereby embedded in the various dimensions and types of law?

In the context of criminal justice, the importance of law cannot be overstated. Consequently, it becomes that much more significant to reflect upon the moral foundations of law and lawmaking, as well as the ways in which the law impacts the moral dimensions of criminal justice practice.

Social Justice

"Social justice" is a term that routinely surfaces in sociological, criminological, political, and social philosophical discourse. However, it is a concept that is rarely defined to any satisfactory degree.

In part, this is for good reason. Social justice is not easily definable, and its contours tend to change depending on the perspective from which it is approached. This being said, there are several considerations that may help us better understand what is meant by social justice and how and why it is relevant to morality, crime, law, and justice.

In his book, *Social Justice/Criminal Justice*, Bruce Arrigo defines **social justice** as a, "perspective of justice that evaluates how a society provides for the needs of its members and the extent to which it treats its subgroups equally."[19] Social justice concerns the laws, policies, programs, and practices of various societies as they pertain to the distribution of and access to housing, health care, education, employment, and other social goods. It may, however, be easier to define or at least provide instances of social injustice than to describe social justice itself. To illustrate, most of us regard racism, sexism, and poverty as social problems. As such, social justice might entail promoting minorities, women, and the disenfranchised, thereby eliminating discrimination or significantly reducing it in an effort to improve the life circumstances of everyone. What each of these problems has in common, however, is that they are *social* rather than individual concerns. If criminal justice seeks to achieve justice through its decisions and practices as they pertain to criminal offenders, then social justice is more concerned with the conditions within which both criminal offenders and criminal justice practitioners live and operate. Thus, an ethical focus on social justice does not ask whether a given court decision (i.e., outcome) is just or fair; rather, it examines the various conditions (e.g., legal, political, economic, religious) that exist that shape and give rise to the court outcome, fostering (or failing to foster) a climate of fairness, opportunity, and access to comparable social resources that are necessary for pursuing the "good life" for all.

The concerns of social justice, then, are best understood as macro-level or large-scale interests that impact both lawmaking and the practice of criminal justice. As an example of how and why these issues are of relevance to lawmaking and criminal justice, consider the phenomenon of theft. In the context of law and lawmaking, significant moral concerns arise with regard to what we consider to be theft and how we should go about dealing with persons accused and/or convicted of thievery.[20] However, what if society on the whole was organized such that the ways in which property was distributed was itself unjust? If so, then we might query whether the very laws against theft were similarly unjust. In fact, laws that protect or maintain the existing distribution of property may reproduce, aggravate, or intensify injustices that already exist. Consequently, we need to consider that criminal justice policy and practice can only be as "just" as the social organization and the institutional dynamics that they seek to maintain.[21]

While social justice and the issues that contribute to its daily functioning are not a focal concern of this book, they will arise on occasion—and in some instances only implicitly. However, we should keep in mind that almost everything about crime, law, and criminology is in some sense linked to matters involving social justice.

THE SPECIAL MORAL REQUIREMENTS OF CRIMINAL JUSTICE

By now you should have some indication of the role and importance of morality in personal, professional, and social contexts. In addition to what has already been said, there are several reasons why morality takes on even greater significance within the criminal justice field than in most other professions. Those occupations that compose the profession are in many ways unique when compared with most other fields of endeavor. To illustrate, many of the things that make the occupation of police and prosecution work unique is that those individuals employed in these areas are expected—even required—to exhibit an increased level of moral character and to exercise a heightened degree of moral judgment than we might expect of persons employed in many other professional contexts. While it is unrealistic to expect criminal justice practitioners to be perfect moral agents, it is not unreasonable to expect that they display a commitment to and strong respect for the moral dimensions inherent in their professional work. For a number of reasons, agents of criminal justice should be and commonly are held to *higher moral standards* than the general public. Though there are certainly many examples of and reasons for this, several such considerations include the following.

Authority, Power, and Discretion

Practitioners within the criminal justice profession carry with them *authority* and *power*, as well as considerable *freedom of choice* and *discretion* to impose authority and employ force in various situations.[22] Along with power comes an increased *responsibility* to use it in appropriate ways. This includes methods that are consistent with the aims of the profession, that benefit a given community and society more generally, and that promote the larger concern of justice. Earlier in the chapter, we briefly examined the ethical principle of "never kill an innocent human being." However, principles such as this assume an entirely different form when the persons to whom the notion applies have the authority and (to some extent) the discretion to take lives under specified conditions (see Box 1.4). Additionally, it is one thing to say that we should not steal; however, a different level of moral character is required to refrain from stealing when, given the routine circumstances of a profession, practitioners find themselves surrounded by things that are "there for the taking" and find that their possible apprehension is essentially eliminated. In short, with the presence of increased power, discretion, and thus opportunity, the need for morality increases considerably. Because of the power that prosecutors, defense attorneys, judges, juries, police officers, and members of parole boards have, it is especially important that such persons exhibit a heightened sense of morality, making ethically sound choices and engaging in morally responsible behavior.

Criminal Justice Agents as Public Servants

Criminal justice agents are servants of the public. The authority and discretion they enjoy is entrusted to them by those whom they serve and exercised in the name of that public; that is, in the interest of protecting and serving others.[23] Socrates would have suggested that agents of criminal justice are in many ways like teachers or educators. Thus, legislators, judges, attorneys, police officers, correctional personnel, and nearly all other persons employed in a criminal justice context have a responsibility not only to fulfill the functions of their respective jobs, but must do so in ways consistent with serving as "role models" for others. When considering laws, policies, and practices operating within criminal justice, it is always helpful to ask the following: "What messages are we sending and to whom?" If police officers, politicians, and other public officials routinely engage in dishonesty, what point are we making on behalf of the general public about the importance of honesty?[24] On a more controversial note, some criminologists have argued that the practice of capital punishment sends an irresponsible message to the American public; namely, that violence is acceptable—at least in some circumstances—as a means of dealing with our social and economic problems.[25] When considering laws and policies, as well as individual choices and behaviors, it is always helpful to ask: "Are we setting an example that we would want others to adopt?"

Individual Behavior Reflects Institutional Morality

The behavior of individuals within criminal justice not only reflects the personal character of the acting agent, but also the character of the institution of which the individual is a part. When

BOX 1.4
Police Use of Force

Policing is one of the few professions in which the use of force can be a necessary part of the performance of one's professional duties. As well, it is one of the few professions in which practitioners are granted the legal right and discretion to employ force for those purposes. For these reasons, the use of force in policing is one of the more controversial topics in literature on police behavior. Whereas most would agree that the use of force by police officers is in some circumstances justifiable and not morally problematic, there is far less agreement about what those circumstances are. What constitutes necessary and unnecessary force? What constitutes excessive force?

Police scholar John Kleinig has identified several factors that he feels are important in determining the appropriateness of the use of force. He argues, for instance, that the use of legitimate force is not morally problematic if the officer believes it is necessary for purposes of restraining a suspect and if an appropriate amount of force is employed solely for that purpose. In contrast, the use of force becomes a moral concern where officers employ it as a means of punishment, or where its use is excessive in relation to the purposes for which it is needed. The *intention* of the officer is crucial

to distinguishing ethical from unethical use of force. As well, force used should be *proportionate* to the seriousness of the offense and/or to the threat present in the situation. The type and amount of force legitimately used against a jaywalking suspect will be different from that of a fleeing robbery suspect who is believed to be armed and dangerous. A final implication is that force used should be the *minimal amount necessary* to achieve the aim for which it is employed.

- In what circumstances do you feel law enforcement officers can justifiably use force? In what circumstances do you feel law enforcement officers can justifiably use *deadly* force?
- At what point or in what circumstances does the use of force become morally problematic? Why?
- How might emotions such as anger, hatred, intolerance, frustration, and fear impact an officer's decision to use force or the amount of force used in a given scenario? What might be done to minimize this impact?

_____

Source: John Kleinig, *The Ethics of Policing* (New York: Cambridge University Press, 1996).

police officers are accused of brutality or corruption, most citizens do not recall the particular officers involved; rather, they identify the instance of violence or dishonesty as indicative of a larger set of unethical behaviors attributable to the institution of law enforcement. Thus, the individual officers involved are often faceless and nameless (without any personal characteristics that distinguish them), symbolizing the system itself and calling it into question or disrepute when ethical concerns arise. Similarly, many people speak of "the law" rather than the individual justices, judges, or politicians who make or contribute to the interpretation/formation of the laws. In short, although criminal justice is practiced by people, the institutions to which those individuals are connected are significantly implicated in their actions. In 1995, for instance, President William Jefferson Clinton became involved in an extramarital sexual relationship with twenty two-year-old White House intern Monica Lewinsky. When details of the affair became public, President Clinton was widely criticized for his private, though morally questionable, sexual behavior and his publicly dishonest comments (he had lied about having the affair). Although President Clinton—like the rest of us—is "only human," his mistakes became far more consequential than they would have for most others similarly embroiled in an inappropriate sexual relationship. Because his choices and behaviors were much like a mirror reflecting on the institution of the presidency, most Americans expected that he exhibit higher moral standards—choices and behaviors that positively reflected on government, politics, civility, and so forth.

WHAT ABOUT PROFESSIONAL CODES OF CONDUCT?

Thus far we have considered the crucial role morality plays in our personal, professional, and social well-being; that law itself is not sufficient for ensuring that individuals make good moral choices, acting on them accordingly; and that the professions within the criminal justice system demand an even higher level of morality than most other professions. Yet you may still be wondering whether the agencies and organizations that compose the system have their own ethical standards that obligate employees, specifying how they must conduct themselves professionally. Moreover, if they do, why is it necessary to study ethics in the classroom?

Over the years, the criminal justice professions have developed increasingly sophisticated *codes of conduct*. In fact, most corporations and organizations in nearly every field of endeavor have some code of ethics. These codes are intended to articulate the values and commitments identified as important for members or employees to embody. **Ethical codes** are sets of standards designed to regulate the ways in which participants or workers pursue their activities as professionals. They also educate and guide individuals along their professional path. For example, the American Correctional Association's (ACA) code of ethics includes the following:

- Members shall respect and protect the civil and legal rights of all individuals.
- Members shall treat every professional situation with concern for the welfare of the individuals involved and with no intent to personal gain.
- Members shall refrain from allowing personal interest to impair objectivity in the performance of duty while acting in an official capacity.[26]

Each of these elements of the ACA's code of ethics is offered as a guideline by which members of that organization (many of whom are correctional practitioners) *should* pursue their profession. Similar to questioning the need for ethics in a society that has an intricate system of law, the same can be asked about the necessity of ethics in criminal justice when the system's various agencies already have their own professional codes of conduct or moral guidelines. For now, we note that while codes have their workplace value, they also possess their situational limitations. It is thus important to understand the need for ethics despite the existence of professional value systems and codes of conduct. Moreover, while there are significant differences in ethical codes across agencies, several noteworthy concerns are generally applicable to all of them.

The Problem of Enforcement

Think for a moment about the number of times over the course of your college career that you had knowledge of cheating by a friend or classmate. In how many of those cases did you report the violation(s) to the professor or to someone else in a position to impose appropriate sanctions? If you elected to report it, why did you? The requirement that college students do honest work is not entirely unlike the provisions of many professional codes of conduct. Codes express organizational values and ideals; they reflect what the organization has determined to be the desirable character traits of and/or appropriate behaviors for its members. Yet violations of these values and ideals are almost certain to occur. The question, then, is whether those violations are reported and enforced.

The **problem of enforcement** is that, similar to college guidelines regarding academic honesty, the provisions found in professional codes are not easily *enforced*. This is true for several reasons. Assuming that, for at least some people, no deep motivation exists for being moral; that is, for following specified laws and codes, these individuals will likely adhere to them only if penalties are imposed when failing to follow them.[27] However, two concerns are worth noting here. First, violations of both laws and professional codes routinely go unnoticed. Second, even when violations of professional codes are detected, they are unlikely to be reported and even less likely to be met with (serious) disciplinary sanction. This is because within most professional communities, there exists a general unwillingness to report peer and colleague infractions, and there is an even greater unwillingness to testify against those who have breached workplace standards. This is especially true in occupations such as policing and corrections where informal rules (e.g., the "blue wall of silence") often override formalized codes.[28] Thus, much like the criminal law, we cannot expect that because rules or guidelines exist, people will abide by them. In other words, without a deeper appreciation for ethics, the impact and thus value of codes will be of negligible utility.

Minimalism

When we think of persons of exceptional moral character—perhaps Jesus the Nazarene, Gandhi, or Mother Teresa—we tend to think of people who have gone above and beyond what is asked of them by law, custom, or convention. Consequently, we do not regard the person who pays her taxes as embodying exemplary moral character because of this activity. She may have other admirable moral qualities; however, contributing in tax dollars what is required of her by law is certainly not one of them. On the other hand, persons who pay their taxes *and* devote additional portions of their time and/or income to charitable organizations or the needs and interests of other people *are* often regarded as demonstrating commendable moral character. Why is this?

We tend not to equate morality or moral character with simply meeting duties, obligations, ideals, and responsibilities that are expected of us. Rather, embodying exemplary moral character demands, at least in some instances, that we go beyond mere expectations or requirements. The danger here, however, is that when laws, duties, and ideals are set forth, they may be read not as minimal expectations or requirements, but as portraits of moral character and conduct.

The idea of **ethical minimalism** is that when rules or standards are in place to guide our behavior, people may be inclined to adopt a "minimalistic" or nominal attitude toward morality, doing only what is dictated by the rules and standards in place and nothing more.[29] In other words, we may believe that as long as we follow the laws, rules, or standards set forth, we are doing all that is expected of us and, thus, all that is necessary. However, persons of good moral character often do not simply meet minimum moral standards or requirements. They routinely go above and beyond what is necessary and expected. Laws and codes are intended to be minimum guidelines for conduct; however, the provision of nominal standards is not the same as saying that we should adopt a minimalistic attitude toward them. Thus, we should be careful to understand professional codes not as *replacements* for ethical inquiry, but as supplements and, perhaps, points of departure for engaging in integrity-based reasoning, decision-making, and behavior.

Codes Are External, Ethics Are Internal

One of the most important statements that can be made about morality—and one that will resurface on several occasions throughout this book—is that our reasons for being a certain way or doing a certain thing must be *our own*. In our previous discussion of law, we saw that doing the right thing was not sufficient for expressing genuine morality. This is because our reasons for being moral must come from within us—they must be representations of our moral

The research assistant (RA) experience

Perhaps the best way to gain research experience and prepare for your own project is to be someone else's research assistant (RA) first. A student could be awarded a research assistantship as part of his financial aid package (merit- or need-based). Usually doctoral students have the greatest chance to obtain research assistantships, yet sometimes the master's and even undergraduate students may also win such awards. You should keep in mind that no matter what was offered you when you were admitted into the program, there are always new opportunities opening up that are worth exploring. You need to keep your eyes open and make your interest known to those prospective principal investigators. The possibilities will include the funded research projects of your advisor and/or other faculty members in the department, the research projects housed in other departments, and the research projects located off-campus.

To the students, research assistantship is an important source of personal finances. For this reason, few would turn down this job opportunity when it becomes available. The point is, the experience of being a research assistant should also help expedite the thesis/dissertation process. After all, in monetary terms a real job after graduation is likely to be more rewarding than remaining a working student. On the other hand, you should not let yourself miss valuable learning opportunities by putting too much emphasis on economic earnings.

The experience of working as a research assistant may vary considerably. Generally speaking, you may look to part or all of the following aspects of knowledge and skills by taking it as a learning process:

(1) How to conceive of a research project and put the ideas together. If you are involved in a proposal writing process, you will have the opportunity to learn how to set up a research project carefully and efficiently. You will also learn what to do to get your research project funded. No matter what kind of assignment you have, including clerical and library work, the opportunity of seeing through the process and having a copy of the final product will be a good experience for launching your own project later. The talks you have with your supervisor and the meetings you attend among the co-principal investigators will give you more understanding of the planning of research. You will also learn something about the impact of such things as cooperation and contracting on a specific research project.

(2) How to implement a research design. If you are working in a newly approved and funded research project, your responsibility will be to help

2

the smaller the error the median prediction would involve. When the median is used to predict an interval or ratio variable, nevertheless, a more precise measure can be constructed to indicate its representativeness (see the following discussion).

For data obtained at the interval or the ratio level, the simplest measure of dispersion is the range, i.e., the distance separating the highest value from the lowest value, which can go with both the median and the mean in describing a potential pattern of the data distribution. For the median used for an interval or ratio variable, however, the full range seems less useful than the interquartile range. This is the distance between the upper quartile and the lower quartile relative to the median, which includes 25% of the cases respectively. The larger the distance, the lower the representativeness of the median. In addition to the interquartile range, sometimes more detailed interdecile range and even interpercentile range may be used. Their meanings and calculations are similar to those of the interquartile range. Generally speaking, the use of various ranges ignores the details of distribution between two extreme values and, therefore, cannot be considered as a precise measure of dispersion.

The most frequently used and precise measure of dispersion at the interval and ratio levels is called standard deviation (SD). Standard deviation is the positive square root of a more general measure called variance, which is a fundamental building block of statistical analysis. The meaning of the variance as well as the standard deviation, however, is not straightforward and often appears hard for novice users to understand. To overcome this hurdle, it may be helpful to go back to some original thinking associated with this idea.

As in the logic of variation ratio discussed earlier, we may calculate the "mean deviation" of an interval or ratio variable by taking the sum of the difference between each case and the mean (or median) and then divide the total with the sample size. There is a sign problem, however. Some cases will have values greater than the mean and others will have smaller values. Accordingly, subtracting the values from the mean will lead to both plus and minus results. If we simply sum up the plus and minus differences, the positives and the negatives will offset each other and the result will not be the total amount of deviation of the sample as a whole from its mean. One way to get around this is to take the absolute values of the differences before summing them up. And the "mean deviation" (MD) can be calculated in this simple way: $MD = (\Sigma|X_i - M|)/N$, where M is the median (or the mean), N is sample size, X_i is the value of individual cases, and $i = 1, 2, \ldots N$. The problem with this approach is that taking absolute character rather than efforts to abide by laws, codes, guidelines, and so forth. In other words, morality should be an *authentic* expression of the self—of our own beliefs, values, virtues, and moral sensibilities.

John Kleinig observes that moral worth "attaches to conduct not just by virtue of the good that it does or the evil that it prevents, but because it was done for certain kinds of reasons or was expressive of a certain kind of character."[30] Morality is not simply about *what* we do, but more importantly it is about *why* we do what we do. Unfortunately, laws and codes tend to *externalize* morality. In this way, morality appears to be imposed upon us from above and, consequently, conformity functions as a requirement rather than as a reflection of our virtuous character. While in some sense we are required to conform to laws, codes, and other codified versions of morality, our moral decisions and actions should ultimately come from within us. As we will see in Chapters 6 and 7, our motivation to make good choices and to engage in right action should come from within rather than from without. Our empathy toward others should reflect our compassionate character rather than a law or standard that requires us to be compassionate. Our honesty should reflect an honest character and an underlying integrity—one that stems from recognition of the value, worth, and importance of honesty and integrity. Codes are generally well intended; however, it is important that we internalize moral values and principles, making them part of who we are as people rather than endorsing them as mere followers of rules.

Generality and Moral Dilemmas

Similar to the law, professional codes of conduct do not provide answers to all moral dilemmas or situations we will encounter in our professional lives. In fact, most professional codes tend to suffer from the **problem of generality**. They consist of broad guidelines rather than specific solutions to ethically charged scenarios. Sometimes applying these general principles to concrete instances can be complicated, especially if the guidelines do not appear to perfectly fit the situation at hand or if there are other circumstances that need to be considered but are not specifically addressed by the professional code in use. Consider the following guidelines on discretionary decision-making, drawn from the Law Enforcement Code of Conduct of the International Association of Chiefs of Police (IACP), and adopted by numerous law enforcement agencies throughout the nation:

> *Discretion*—A police officer will use responsibly the discretion vested in his [or her] position and exercise it within the law. The principle of reasonableness will guide the officer's determinations, and the officer will consider all surrounding circumstances in determining whether any legal action shall be taken. Consistent and wise use of discretion, based on professional policing competence, will do much to preserve good relationships and retain the confidence of the public. There can be difficulty in choosing between conflicting courses of action. It is important to remember that a timely word of advice rather than arrest—which may be correct in appropriate circumstances—can be a more effective means of achieving a desired end.[31]

The value and intention of this statement notwithstanding, the limits of its practical utility— particularly in a number of "real-life" situations—are quite apparent. To illustrate, the "principle of reasonableness" and "consider[ation] of all surrounding circumstances" will minimally help officers resolve the manifold and diverse dilemmas they encounter while on patrol. Indeed, while it is certainly important to abide by these (and similar) guidelines, what is being recommended on the issue of discretion is, in effect, that police officers should use professional *judgment* when dealing with practical situations. Honing one's skills regarding judgment—that is, considering all circumstances, values, and principles, and making sound and prudent choices in the face of them—is a good part of what the study of ethics attempts to accomplish.

Consequently, professional codes of conduct often have limited practical utility. In fact, they tend to be of minimal value in those situations where they are most needed.[32] When discretionary judgments are called for, or where conflicts arise between equally important moral values, duties, or responsibilities, reliance on professional codes for precise guidance typically yields limited direction. Most often, codes fail to prioritize values and principles. Thus, workers/employees do not know what is most important when encountering various types of conflict. Moreover, codes frequently fail to identify exceptions to general principles, and they do not account for all situational factors that might deserve consideration in diverse instances.

Summary

Morality and ethical inquiry are relevant to all personal, social, and professional spheres of human existence. More specifically, the concerns of morality—and those of crime, law, and justice—are not only intriguing but also essential for our individual well-being and for our collective, indeed global, sense of social cohesion. Consequently, ethics asks not simply that we entertain questions and dilemmas of a moral nature; rather, it asks that we do so responsibly, attending to and examining the many points, principles, values, and questions that underlie any moral issue or situational ethical dilemma. This requires living mindfully, examining and continually reexamining one's self in the interest of living a good life—and assisting others in doing the same—within a just and civil society. However, as we have tentatively explained, laws, codes, rules, and other guidelines for professional conduct can be problematic and, consequently, insufficient for this purpose. As such, morality should be thought of as something other than or, at least, in addition to these things. While each law, code, and rule has value and assumes an important function in the workplace or elsewhere, there is considerably more to being moral than learning about and abiding by formal norms and conforming to social expectations. As well, there is substantially more to ethics and ethical inquiry than simply learning moral standards and principles. Over the next several chapters, a more specific treatment of what ethics is, of what morality entails, and of the notable problems and pitfalls that arise in these contexts will be entertained. Chapter 2 initiates the examination of these matters, providing a more thorough assessment of the subject and scope of ethics.

Key Terms and Concepts

codes of conduct (ethical codes) *18*
descriptive versus prescriptive
    inquiry *4*
ethics *3*
jury nullification *10*
minimalism (ethical
    minimalism) *19*

moral problem of
    punishment *5*
morality *3*
no-knock warrant *2*
Nuremberg laws *10*
problem of enforcement
    (and ethical codes) *18*

problem of generality
    (and ethical codes) *20*
professional ethics *13*
selective enforcement *11*
social justice *15*
sodomy laws *11*
spheres of criminal justice *13*

Discussion Questions

1. What is the relationship between ethics and morality? How are they related, and how are they distinct? Give an example from your own experience that illustrates the relationship between ethics and morality.

2. What is the purpose of morality? How does ethics increase the likelihood that the purpose of morality is fulfilled?

3. According to Socrates, "an unexamined life is not worth living." What did Socrates mean by this? When ethics asks that we live mindfully, how does this notion advance Socrates' observation about living life?

4. Some people question why we need ethics when we have laws. What is your position on this? Please list and explain the five limitations of law.

5. Generally speaking, how are ethics and moral inquiry relevant to criminal justice? Give an example from the field of criminology/criminal justice to support your position.

6. How are criminal justice practice, law and lawmaking, and social justice linked to ethics? Be specific!

7. According to the chapter, agents of the criminal justice system (police, court, corrections personnel) are held to higher moral standards. In view of the power invested in agents of criminal justice and the discretionary nature of much criminal justice work, explain why such higher standards are necessary.

8. What are professional codes of conduct/ethics and how are they problematic in the criminal justice system? In what ways might they be beneficial to criminal justice practitioners?

Endnotes

1. *AOL News* (March 4, 2011). Available at http://www.aolnews.com/category/crime/ (retrieved March 8, 2011).

2. "German Cannibal Tells of Fantasy," *BBC News* (December 3, 2003). Available at http://news.bbc.co.uk/2/hi/europe/3286721.stm (retrieved March 8, 2011).

3. Louis Pojman, *Life and Death: Grappling with the Moral Dilemmas of Our Time,* 2nd ed. (Belmont, CA: Wadsworth, 2000), p. 2.

4. J. Jeremy Wisnewski, "Murder, Cannibalism, and Indirect Suicide: A Philosophical Study of a Recent Case," *Philosophy in the Contemporary World*, 14(1), 11–21 (Spring, 2007).

5. John Hospers, *Human Conduct: An Introduction to the Problems of Ethics* (New York: Harcourt, Brace & World, 1961), p. 4.

6. Gerd Gigerenzer, *Gut Feelings: The Intelligence of the Unconscious* (New York: Penguin Press, 2007).

7. Gunter Grau and Claudia Shoppman, *The Hidden Holocaust: Gay and Lesbian Persecution in Germany 1933–1945* (Chicago, IL: Fitzroy Dearborn Publishers, 1995); Clarence Lusane, *Hitler's Black Victims: The Historical Experience of Afro-Germans, European Blacks, Africans and African Americans in the Nazi Era* (New York: Routledge, 2002).

8. Pojman, *Life and Death*, p. 2.

9. Plato, *Apology*, 38A. In *Euthyphro, Apology, Crito*, F. J. Church (trans.) (Indianapolis, IN: Bobbs-Merrill, 1956), p. 45.

10. Anthony Weston, *A Practical Companion to Ethics*, 2nd ed. (New York: Oxford University Press, 2002), p. 2.

11. Warner Fite, *Moral Philosophy: The Critical View of Life* (Port Washington, NY: Kennikat Press, 1925), p. 2.

12. Vincent Ruggiero, *Thinking Critically About Ethical Issues*, 5th ed. (Boston, MA: McGraw-Hill, 2001).

13. Ibid., p. 5.

14. Ibid.

15. Ibid.

16. Pojman, *Life and Death*, p. 2.

17. Ibid.

18. Cf. Jeffrey Reiman, "Criminal Justice Ethics." In Paul Leighton and Jeffrey Reiman (Eds.), *Criminal Justice Ethics* (Upper Saddle River, NJ: Prentice Hall, 2001), pp. 16–18.

19. Bruce Arrigo, *Social Justice/Criminal Justice: The Maturation of Critical Theory in Law, Crime, and Deviance* (Belmont, CA: Wadsworth, 1999), p. 282.

20. Alfonso Gomez-Lobo, *Morality and the Human Goods: An Introduction to Natural Law Ethics* (Washington, DC: Georgetown University Press, 2002), p. 78.

21. John Monique, *The Origins of Justice: The Evolution of Morality, Human Rights, and Law* (Philadelphia, PA: The University of Pennsylvania Press, 2002).

22. Reiman, "Criminal Justice Ethics."

23. Ibid.

24. See, e.g., Erich Fromm, "The State as Educator: On the Psychology of Criminal Justice." In Kevin Anderson and Richard Quinney (Eds.), *Erich Fromm and Critical Criminology: Beyond the Punitive Society* (Urbana, IL: University of Illinois Press, 2000).

25. Robert Bohm, *Death Quest II: An Introduction to the Theory and Practice of Capital Punishment in the United States* (Cincinnati, OH: Anderson Publishing, 2003); Christopher Williams, "Toward a Transvaluation of Criminal Justice: On Vengeance, Peacemaking, and Punishment," *Humanity and Society,* 26(2), 100–116 (2002).

26. American Correctional Association, *Code of Ethics* (adopted August 1975 at the 105th Congress of Correction). Available at http://www.intech.mnsu.edu/davisj/aca_ethics.htm (retrieved November 2, 2005).

27. John Kleinig, *The Ethics of Policing* (Cambridge: Cambridge University Press, 1996).

28. Ibid.

29. Ibid.

30. John Kleinig, "Ethics and Codes of Ethics." In P. Leighton and J. Reiman (Eds.), *Criminal Justice Ethics* (Upper Saddle River, NJ: Prentice Hall, 2001), p. 247

31. See, e.g., Windcrest, TX (http://www.ci.windcrest.tx.us/index.aspx?NID=123); Clive, IA (http://www.cityofclive.com/departments/police/about-us/); Canton, OH (http://www.cantonohio.gov/police/?pg=316).

32. Kleinig, *The Ethics of Policing.*

2

Choices, Values,
and Ethics

Imagine that you are awakened one morning by the sound of a ringing telephone. Choosing not to answer the call, you roll out of bed, put on some sweatpants and a T-shirt, make your morning coffee, and begin to go about your daily business. To most people, your morning thus far could be considered uneventful and hardly worth discussing—certainly not in the context of ethics, anyway. Yet ethics asks us to consider the ways in which our everyday, seemingly inconsequential choices become more than just mundane details. In fact, nearly everything you did during your hypothetical morning routine can be seen as having ethical and moral significance. To begin with, each of your actions (and nonactions) involved a choice. Many of our everyday choices are as simple as deciding what time to awaken, where to buy that new red T-shirt we need to demonstrate our support for our favorite sports franchise, or what brand and roast of coffee to buy from the grocer this afternoon. Other choices, however, are much more complex and would seem to be far more consequential. We may have to choose whether to lie to our best friend to protect that person's feelings. We may have to choose whether to spend the remains of our next paycheck on a night out or, instead, to use the money to invest in our children's college fund, send aid to a friend or relative experiencing financial hardship, or even to make a charitable contribution to a cause of social or political significance. As criminal justice professionals, we may have to choose whether to arrest the chief of police from your neighboring county for driving while intoxicated, report the deviant sexual behavior of a prominent local politician, grant an inmate an unauthorized phone call to his dying mother, or "rat on" a fellow police officer whom we have discovered is involved in illegal drug activities or simply remain silent (see Box 2.1).

Indeed, ethics reserves a central role for *choice*—what choices we do and should make, why we make them, and what consequences follow from those choices. Part of the reason that choice is of such importance to ethics and morality is that even the seemingly simple, "everyday" choices we make are consequential—not only for ourselves, but often for others. Sometimes the consequences or effects of our choices are good, direct, or intended; other times, they are bad, indirect, or unintended. Some of our decisions affect—or *appear* to affect—only ourselves. Other times, however, the choices we make directly or indirectly affect others in significant ways. Most of the time, our choices affect countless

BOX 2.1

The Tavern Rape and the Duty to Report Crimes or Render Assistance: The Morality of Doing Nothing

Just as we can choose to act one way or another, we can also choose *not* to act (sometimes called **acts of omission**, as opposed to acts of *commission*). For moral purposes, not doing anything can be just as problematic as engaging in the wrong sorts of actions. Remaining silent, overlooking infractions, or failing to get involved in situations that are "not my business" can be immoral choices in the same way as those leading to acts that we commit. Consider the following:

March 6, 1983. After putting her two daughters to bed, twenty-one-year-old Cheryl Ann Araujo stepped out to purchase cigarettes. Finding more customary locations closed, she happened upon "Big Dan's" bar—a reportedly sordid watering hole in the North End of New Bedford to which she had not before been. While inside, Cheryl entered into conversation with another woman and decided to stay for a drink. Sometimes shortly thereafter, the other woman left the bar. Intending to do the same, Cheryl began to exit Big Dan's, but was grabbed from behind by a male patron, stripped of her clothes, and raped on the floor of the bar. The public location, presence of several bystanders, and her kicking, screaming, and pleading notwithstanding, Cheryl would be repeatedly sexually assaulted for over an hour by multiple male patrons. Not only did none of the onlookers intervene, she reported hearing cheers and applause from those witnessing the incident as men took turns forcing themselves upon her.

Cheryl would eventually escape and survive, and four men would be charged and ultimately convicted as direct participants in the sexual assault. In addition, however, two of the witnesses were charged as accessories to rape, but acquitted because, though they had watched, they had not actually been participants in the assault. The "Tavern Rape" (aka "Big Dan's Rape") became a widely publicized and much discussed incident, years later becoming the basis for the film, *The Accused*, for which actress Jodie Foster would win an Academy Award.

Why is the Tavern Rape case of interest in the context of ethics, crime, and justice? Of particular note might be the acquittal of the two men charged as accessories to the sexual assault of Cheryl Ann Araujo. At that time, at least, the state of Massachusetts had no law mandating witnesses of criminal activity to intervene in any fashion. In other words, despite being morally problematic, persons witnessing burglaries, rapes, and even homicides were under no specified legal obligation to protect or assist victims, or even to pick up a phone to report the incident. One question of ethical interest, then, is whether there *should* be legal obligations and to what extent there *should* be moral duties affixed to precisely these sorts of scenarios. Do we, as everyday citizens, have a moral duty to assist those whose lives are in immediate danger and/or to report criminal activities that we have witnessed? What about criminal activities that have not yet occurred, but the future likelihood of which we have knowledge?

Source: "The Tavern Rape: Cheers and No Help," *Newsweek* (March 21, 1983); Press, Taylor and Clause, "The Duties of a Bystander," *Newsweek* (March 28, 1983); Susan J. Hoffman, "Statutes Establishing a Duty to Report Crimes or Render Assistance to Strangers: Making Apathy Criminal," *Kentucky Law Journal*, 72, 827 (1984); Miriam Gur-Arye, "A Failure to Prevent Crime—Should it be Criminal?" *Criminal Justice Ethics*, Summer/Fall, 3–30 (2001).

others in innumerable ways. This fact alone potentially imbues what seem to be simple choices of personal preference with ethical and moral relevance.

Choices are of relevance to ethics and morality when they are freely made and *impact the well-being of others* (see Box 2.2).[1] Child abuse, drug smuggling, and driving while intoxicated are choices of moral significance because they each impinge on others (in these cases, by harming others). Morality does not require nor suggest that we always place the interests of others over and above our own; rather, living an ethical life requires that, at a minimum, we be aware of the interests of others and the ways in which the choices we make impact those interests.

BOX 2.2
Voluntariness and Criminal Defenses

For our choices to be subjected to moral evaluation or judgment, we must be said to have *had* a choice. When we choose between two or more alternatives and engage in an action which reflects that choice, our conduct is said to be **voluntary**.[2] Given the importance of choice-making in ethics described above, we might imagine that actions (or inactions) that are not a product of choice cannot rightfully said to be moral or immoral. Behavior that can be shown to be involuntary or that stemmed from impaired or limited choice-making capacity (e.g., that which is a direct consequence of severe mental disability or structural damage to the brain) typically is not subjected to the same sort of legal response as behavior presumed to be entirely voluntary. This requirement of voluntariness as a prerequisite for judging conduct is evident in our system of law and justice. Criminal law recognizes a number of justifications and excuses for criminal activity on the basis of involuntariness. Involuntary acts are not subject to criminal punishment. **Duress** (or **coercion**), for example, is a legally recognized criminal defense in which the defendant is excused from criminal conduct because she or he was acting under the threat of immediate, serious bodily harm from another person and had no other possibility of escape. **Necessity** or the "choice of evils" is a criminal defense whereby a defendant argues that she or he engaged in criminal conduct to prevent some greater evil. In such cases, the conduct may be considered voluntary in some sense, yet in another sense the only alternative courses of action would have brought about greater harm.

- You take part in a bank robbery because someone has kidnapped and threatened to kill your child (or mother, sister, etc.) if you fail to do so. Have you made a fully voluntary choice? Remember that choice requires the presence of alternative courses of action. In this instance, could we rightfully say that you *had* such options? If so, what were they? How might the consequences of those alternatives been different from the consequences of the actions you took? Should you be exempt from criminal responsibility and your actions exempt from criminal punishment?

- You have recently received your amateur pilot's license and are making the three-hour flight to your sister's to attend her birthday party. Halfway through the flight, you experience engine failure and are forced to make an emergency landing in the mountains. Eight hours later, there is still no sign of rescue and you are very cold, very hungry, and fear that you will not be able to survive much longer. As you begin to search the area around you, you come across a small cabin. The cabin is locked and the owners have clearly not been there in some time. Would you be justified in breaking into the cabin, sleeping in the bed, and eating the stored food? If you did, would your actions be entirely voluntary? Are there any alternative courses of action you could have taken that wouldn't have involved violating the law?

Returning to your hypothetical morning for a moment, consider the potential consequences and moral implications of the following scenarios:[3]

- The phone call that you chose not to answer was from a distressed friend in need of advice. That same friend shortly thereafter made a very poor decision that you may have been able to prevent with a few timely words of guidance.
- The sweatpants and T-shirt that you put on were made in a sweatshop in a developing nation by persons—some of them children—working long hours in poor conditions for very little pay.
- The brand of coffee that you chose to consume is owned largely by an investment bank with known ties to terrorist groups that are hostile to the United States and other countries.

In each instance, your choice has affected or potentially affected far more people in far more serious ways than you might ever have imagined. Though the consequences of our choices are not the only—or necessarily most important—ethical consideration, it is the fact that our choices *have* consequences that make them relevant for ethical analysis. Part of what makes awareness of the unseen consequences of our actions critical for morality is that *people are more likely to engage in immoral activities if there is no apparent victim*. Simply recognizing the often unobserved ways in which our choices affect others thus increases the likelihood that we more fully consider the moral implications of how we choose and what we do. Through increasing our understanding of the consequential nature of our choices, ethics encourages us to think more carefully, indeed critically, about what we do, when we do it, and, most importantly, why we do it.

CHOICES AND OTHERS

Morality, then, concerns the choices that we make that affect other people.[4] This includes the kinds of values we choose to hold and principles by which we live; our chosen beliefs; for whom and what we vote; where we shop; and choices we make about whether to lie, cheat, or steal. In this regard, morality is much broader and covers far more ground than is often thought. We sometimes assume, for instance, that many choices and subsequent behaviors are simply matters of personal preference and affect only ourselves. Such thinking is often used as a basis for arguments of personal liberty—that is, "I should be able to do this or do that because it only affects me" (see Box 2.3). However, closer examination might encourage us to reassess our assumption.

Consider the case of pornography. We may believe that purchasing and watching pornography are choices that affect only ourselves. We may therefore claim that it is not a "moral" decision at all, but merely a matter of how we elect to spend our time and money. We might

---

BOX 2.3

Personal Freedom and Consequences to Others

Ethics challenges us to confront common situations in which our personal liberties seem to conflict with the interests or well-being of others. It is commonly argued by supporters of personal freedom that such behaviors "only affect me." Yet ethics encourages us to realize that nearly *none* of our choices and actions affects only ourselves. Consider the following:

- Most states require drivers and passengers in automobiles to wear seat belts. Yet many people still refuse to wear seat belts, claiming that seat belts are uncomfortable and they should have the freedom to do what they wish with their bodies when the consequences only affect themselves. Yet every one of us feels the burden when others are injured or killed in automobile accidents. Wrightsman, Nietzel, and Fortune point to such consequences as lost wages and taxes, higher medical insurance premiums, and

welfare payments to the dependent family members of the deceased. They cite current estimates that suggest that motor vehicle accidents cost society as much as $90 *billion* per year. How does considering these consequences affect your position on seat belt laws?

- What are the potential consequences and costs of other choices involving the personal freedom to: have an abortion, consume illegal substances, own a handgun, and commit suicide?
- Can you think of other "personal freedoms" that have significant consequences for other people and society as a whole? Should these freedoms be limited by law?

Source: Lawrence S. Wrightsman, Michael T. Nietzel, and William H. Fortune, *Psychology and the Legal System,* 3rd ed. (Belmont, CA: Wadsworth, 1994).

BOX 2.4

Media, Violence, and Morality

Numerous studies over the past several decades have reported findings that violence on television and in motion pictures can have significant effects on viewers—especially younger viewers. Television programs and movies portraying crime can directly "teach" viewers how to be criminals or commit crimes, lower sensitivity to violence, and shape values in ways favorable to criminal and deviant behavior. Critics, however, point out that not everyone is affected in these ways and that, even if they were, the public has an interest in viewing the kinds of media programming that it enjoys—not what others think is best for them.

- If it were to be conclusively that violent television programs and motion pictures correlate with increased levels of violence in viewers, how might this influence your perspective on the morality of violence on television and in movies?
- What is and should be more important: the value we place on freedom of speech/expression

or the best interests of the public? In this case, what are the best interests of the public?

- If we were to take action, how far should we go in restricted public access to violent media? Who should make the call as to what constitutes violence and at what levels it should be subjected to restrictions?
- Many of these same arguments have been made about music—especially that of the rock and rap varieties. If we can demonstrate conclusively that music inspires listeners to rape, homicide, or suicide, could we morally justify placing restrictions on the content of music that is created by artistes? Can we hold those artistes morally responsible for the behavior of listeners?

Source: Steven J. Kirsh, *Children, Adolescents, and Media Violence: A Critical Look at the Research* (Thousand Oaks, CA: Sage, 2006).

---

recognize that pornography itself is a moral and political issue, yet even in recognizing this we may feel that our *personal* choice to purchase and watch sexually explicit material (so long as it continues to be legal) is not so much of a moral concern. However, with some critical reflection, we would soon find that our personal choice may have significant social and, therefore, moral implications. Some feminist critics of the adult film industry, for instance, have pointed out that pornography is an expression of patriarchy and male dominance over women, causing social harm by contributing to the continued exploitation of women and perpetuating gender inequality.[5] As well, watching pornography may have an impact on men's personal relationships in that exposure to the exploitation of women in adult films may "carry over" into the viewer's relationships with women in his personal life.[6] To be fair, however, we might also find feminist scholars who have pointed out the positive consequences of pornography, noting that it is (or can be) liberating and empowering for women, licensing women to exercise a kind of expressive freedom and control over their own sexuality that, historically, they have not enjoyed.[7] We might also find evidence that significant numbers of couples view pornography together and, thus, pornography may have the effect of enhancing intimacy for some people.[8]

Whatever positions we adopt and choices we make on the matter of pornography and other such things, we should recognize that ethics inspires us to think of those positions and decisions as more than matters of personal preference or unreflective choice. This is *not* to say that ethics cannot confirm individual liberties or support them in given situations. Perhaps we value freedom of expression as something which is good and just, even where such expressions potentially have deleterious effects on others; contrarily, perhaps the value we place on the well-being of others and society more broadly is sufficient to warrant curtailing freedom of expression in certain situations (see Box 2.4). Decisions such as these are difficult, and ethics will not provide a single, conclusive answer. What is important is that we recognize the moral nature of issues and decisions, think through alternatives, and that we have good reasons for valuing the things we do and making the choices we make. Too often, we fail to appreciate the moral implications and available alternatives inherent in our choices, and too often we make those choices without sufficient attention to the reasons underlying them.

The Involuntary Nature of Evil?

As we have seen, being "ethical" requires a certain kind of ethical *awareness*; namely, it requires that our choices be informed by an awareness of and active consideration for relevant moral concerns (e.g., the positive and negative consequences for ourselves and others, relevant moral and legal rights, liberties, and concerns for justice). When we are ignorant of the moral elements and implications of our choices, we can potentially cause harm, contribute to injustice, or create problems for ourselves and/or others without even recognizing that we are doing so.[9]

In some ways, the potentially harmful consequences of assuming an uncritical and unreflective posture toward the choices we make are what Socrates had in mind when he said that *no one ever voluntarily chooses evil*.[10] According to Socrates, we can never *choose* evil—*if*, that is, we know good.[11] This last part is obviously significant, as the first seems to fly in the face of everything we believe we know about people. Surely, we think, there are many instances of people choosing evil over good? Socrates would not argue that people make choices, and that those choices sometimes lead to evil actions and/or evil consequences. His point, however, is that those choices are made in *ignorance*.[12] Anytime we act from choice, we are pursuing some chosen end. All of our actions are intended to bring about certain consequences. If we are acting in order to bring about those consequences, Socrates would say, we must at least *believe* the consequences to be good or desirable. How could we ever want anything if it appeared to be bad or painful? Even in those situations where we intentionally bring ourselves pain (e.g., going to the dentist), we do so in pursuit of some end that we perceive as desirable (e.g., taking care of our teeth). In other words, our actions are always aimed at something that we *perceive* to be "good."

For Socrates, leading a "good" life required knowledge of goodness. If we have knowledge of what is good, our actions will automatically follow from that knowledge. If we *know* what is good, our choices and subsequent actions will also be good. We might think of this argument as follows:

> *All of our actions are aimed at something we perceive to be good.*
>
> *If we know what is truly good, our actions will be aimed at what is truly good.*
>
> *Similarly, if we are ignorant of what is truly good, our actions may well be aimed at what we believe to be good, but is truly evil.*

This, then, is what Socrates had in mind when he said that no one can ever voluntarily choose evil. While people sometimes pursue evil ends, it is because they see some good in it—yet they are wrong in believing that whatever good they see is *actually* good. Had their knowledge been more complete, they would have chosen otherwise. No one who *fully* knows the negative consequences of his or her actions can possibly choose those actions.[13] A conspiring bank robber who knows he will be caught and sentenced to twenty years in prison, for example, values gets into the complication of making step-by-step comparisons and judgments which might be inconvenient in mathematical operation and derivation. This leads to the consideration of another frequently used approach in mathematics, that is, having the differences squared before summing them up. The result is called variance of the variable: $S^2 = (\Sigma(X_i - M)^2)/N$ (using the same denotations as above). You might agree that the variance is indeed a measure of dispersion: The larger the variance, the less reliable the mean in representing and predicting the values of different cases on a given variable. However, since the individual differences or deviations are squared, the result can no longer be interpreted as a "mean deviation." It is hard indeed to get an intuitive sense of what this quantity S^2 means. To relate it a little closer to the original idea, statisticians take the square root of the variance and call this (i.e., S) a "standard deviation" (SD) from the mean. However, this treatment makes the formula even harder to remember.

In statistical application and mathematical theory, the variance has found wide use, and made perfect sense as the "second central moment" when compared to mechanical application of the mathematical operations (especially in differential and integral calculus that also underlies much of the statistical analysis). As a result, you will frequently come across this creature. Even if you do not quite understand the reason why it is, the best you can do is to get along with it by memorizing its calculation. You should also notice that measures like variance and standard deviation as well as range and interquartile range cannot be applied to data obtained below the interval level. Computer procedures such as FREQUENCIES and DESCRIPTIVES in SPSS will render you all such measures if you ask for them. It is your responsibility to understand the meaning of each measure and properly use it.

It is also helpful if you are aware that there are other measures that can be used to further describe the shape of the value-frequency (probability) distribution of the sample data on a specific variable. The most important concept in this respect has to do with a special yet most frequently seen pattern called normal distribution. In such cases, the histogram showing the frequency distribution of the cases on different values of a variable approximates a bell-shaped curve, and can be specified by an exponential function. The normal distribution is the basis for much of the statistical analysis work in terms of various parametric procedures. General measures of shape include Skewness, which measures deviation from a symmetrical position, and Kurtosis, which measures peakedness (leptokurtic) or flatness (platykurtic) of the distribution. You can instruct the cannot possibly choose to rob that bank (unless, of course, he had no choice to begin with). If he did, Socrates would say, he would be intentionally choosing something bad. Such a choice would not, of course, make any sense. He robs the bank only because he perceives there to be some good in it (probably for himself).

What Socrates suggested more than two thousand years ago has dramatic implications for how we understand morality in relation to both ourselves and others. It is quite common for us to believe that evil is the result of "evil people" who have voluntarily chosen a life of wickedness. The evil of the world, we may feel, results from the conscious choices of a seemingly increasing number of "bad people." Certainly you and I are excluded from this category. Yet what the study of ethics encourages us to realize (or at least reflect upon) is that we—you, I, and the "bad people"—sometimes make evil choices and contribute to the evil of the world without even being aware that we are doing so. In the words of Socrates, most of us are ignorant of the evil we regularly do. Ethically, then, we cannot regard evil as an outcome of the conscious choices of "evil people." *The majority of evil in the world results from the ill-considered choices of everyday people going about their everyday lives.* The consequences of our actions are often so far-reaching that we cannot even begin to attain a full appreciation for them. We can, however, begin to reflect more thoughtfully on the likely implications of much of what we choose—both personally and professionally.

Recognizing that our decisions and actions have consequences or effects does not necessarily imply that they directly and by themselves *caused* those consequences. The emergence of any given effect or consequence requires the "coming together" of a number of factors—each of which contributes to the eventual manifestation of that consequence. Any given action which I undertake cannot directly—and by itself—cause something else to occur. Instead, a given consequence requires my action *plus* any number of additional actions, events, or circumstances.

Nevertheless, it is important to consider for moral purposes that my actions are *contributing factors* (even if I am unaware or "ignorant" of these effects or of the link between them and my own decisions and actions). A certain effect might not have occurred (at least in the way that it did) had it not been for the contribution of my decision or action. Others, in turn, may well have happened anyway. How morally responsible am I for contributing to events or states of affairs that would persist even if I cease to contribute? While, for example, my failure to recycle aluminum may not cause environmental destruction, I certainly do contribute to it in some minor way. If I do begin to recycle, I will probably not make a significant remedial contribution to environmental improvement. What, then, is my responsibility to the environment and to future generations of people who will live within it?

The Universal Element of Choice

Because every choice we make and every action we take has an impact on the well-being of ourselves and others, our entire lives (both personal and professional) are endowed with moral significance. Not only does every action have consequences, but every consequence has further effects as well, and these effects have their own consequences, and so forth. While the immediate consequences of a given action (e.g., a teenager using a nonprescribed sleeping pill on school grounds, passing out during class, and being suspended from school) may most directly affect the individual, the fallout of those consequences often extends far beyond the person (e.g., the child's parents have to rearrange their work schedule to provide transportation to an alternative school, causing them lost income). For this reason, it might be helpful to think of every choice we make as having a universal aspect. In other words, every choice we make and every action we undertake has consequences—however small—that are felt by many other people. These other people may be family members, friends, colleagues, individuals in our community, or even the people of cultures thousands of miles away from us. Think of actions as a "link" in an endless chain. In many ways, our choices and actions are influenced by what immediately preceded them. In other ways, our choices and actions influence what comes immediately after them. What comes immediately after them, in turn, influences what comes after that, and so on. The "link" we have secured in the chain by choosing a certain action becomes a small, but meaningful, part of a continuing chain of events. Changing our actions—and thus the consequences of our actions—can potentially change the ways in which that entire chain of events unfolds.

Consider the following somewhat unlikely (though not necessarily improbable) scenario. Suppose you are driving to school or work this morning and, as you are peacefully making your way through traffic, a seemingly inconsiderate motorist cuts you off. You have done nothing, of course, to bring this on. Nevertheless, you *do* have an impact on what has yet to occur. Consider the choices you have available to you at this point: You may, for example, simply curse the disrespectful motorist in your head while continuing about your drive; you may lay on your horn while verbally cursing at the motorist out your window; you may speed up, pass the motorist, and then cut him off in retaliation; or, perhaps, you might wave at him in a friendly, understanding manner. Let us suppose that you allow your emotions to get the better of you and, consequently, you choose to lay on your horn and curse the man. Now, let us further suppose that the man (inconsiderate, perhaps, but initially merely in a hurry) becomes angry at you for your retaliatory actions. Though nothing seems to come of it immediately (you both drive off on your separate paths), the now-angry man is so disturbed that upon arriving at work, he curses his boss. In return, he is fired. Now, let us suppose even further that, having been fired, the man becomes even more emotionally unstable (imagine how you might feel!). He peels out of the parking lot at his place of employment and, not being very attentive, hits an unsuspecting pedestrian. The pedestrian is killed immediately.

Most of us—including lawmakers—would be in agreement that the man is responsible for the death of the pedestrian and will most likely face charges of vehicular manslaughter, reckless manslaughter, or in whatever way the offense is applicable in that particular state. Perhaps you see the story on the local news that night, thinking to yourself, "that's the jerk who cut me off today—someone like that deserves whatever he's got coming." Indeed, most of us would feel sympathy for the victim and the victim's family and a corresponding anger toward the inconsiderate (and "dangerous") motorist. Yet most of us would probably *not* stop to reflect upon our own contribution to the unfortunate events.

None of us would argue that, in the above scenario, we should be legally or even morally responsible for the actions of the motorist or the death of the pedestrian. But the issue here is about ethics, choices, and the ways in which we (sometimes unknowingly) contribute to the unfolding of future events through those choices. We might imagine that, had you not responded to the man as you did when he cut you off, he would not have become so angry, cursed his boss, been fired, peeled out of the parking lot, and killed the pedestrian. Of course, we can imagine other scenarios in which your same response might have led to very different consequences. In any case, by choosing one course of action over another, you set in motion or at least made a contribution to a chain of events; where that and other chains of events lead is often beyond our awareness. This is precisely why we typically fail to fully consider the implications of our choices. If we do not *see* the *immediate* consequences, we go on about our lives assuming that nothing bad or troubling has come from our choice. Again, it is important to point out that our choices do not necessarily directly *cause* later events. It is also worth noting that, in any given situation, the choices we make may be morally justifiable or defensible, despite whatever consequences they may bring. What is crucial for ethical purposes is, again, simply that we be aware of the ways in which our choices *are* consequential and, perhaps more importantly, that we strive to always make choices *informed by this awareness* and that reflect good moral reasons (e.g., moral virtue, consequences for ourselves and others, relevant moral principles, duties, and values).

MAKING CHOICES

We have thus far discussed the centrality of the role played by our choices in ethical inquiry. Yet, ethics and morality are not only, and not most importantly, about choices and actions themselves; rather, we could say that they are primarily concerned with how we come to select the courses of action that we pursue—in other words, *how (and why) we make choices*. More than our choices and conduct alone, it is the reasons underlying our choices and conduct that are of particular moral relevance. Studying ethics and, ultimately, living a moral life requires that we have good reasons for our decisions, beliefs, and judgments, and that we be able to articulate those reasons. So what are "good" reasons?

One way of beginning to think about good or right reasons for choices, actions, and beliefs is to explore the values that are important for a "good life in a just society." Consider the following and what they have in common:

happiness, pleasure, justice, equality, fairness, courage, loyalty, human dignity

Recognizing the similarities between the terms above allows us to begin to comprehend the importance of *values* for our choices and actions. Our **values** reflect those things, qualities, or ideals to which we assign importance. When we "value" something, we regard it as desirable, having worth or importance. Similarly, when we *evaluate* something, we judge it to be right or wrong, good or bad, according to our values or some system of values to which we are referring.[14] To "value" something, then, is to advance it as a consideration with regard to our choices and actions.[15] One of the most important commonalities between the values listed above is that each of them, for at least some people some of the time, is used as a basis for making a certain choice, pursuing a certain course of -action, or judging the choices or actions of others. Valuing courage, for example, might lead us to courageous action or, at least, to hold in high regard others who act courageously. Valuing equality might lead us to vote a certain way or participate in social activism, while valuing justice might lead us to support a certain social policy or even pursue certain kinds of career paths.

Values, then, "point out" the things we should pursue in life. They give our lives a sense of meaning and purpose. Part of what the study of ethics is intended to accomplish is the illumination of our values and their role in our choice-making (i.e., "getting in touch" with our own values and understanding from where they came, why we hold them, and how they influence our decisions and actions). More importantly, however, ethics encourages us to critically assess those values and to adopt a set of consistent values that are morally justifiable. Schools of ethical thought (i.e., normative theories of ethics, such as utilitarianism, deontological ethics, and virtue ethics) offer us frameworks for prioritizing values and guidelines for utilizing them in our decision-making. Honesty is almost universally valued, yet what if honesty causes harm? What if being honest involves violating someone's rights? What if, though a violation of rights, being honest brings about better long-term consequences than dishonesty? Are we then justified in violating rights? Honesty, respect for rights, and bringing about good consequences are all examples of values used to make sense of moral dilemmas. How we prioritize these values is a topic to which we will return in later chapters.

It is crucial to note that not all values are *moral* values. While we may value physical strength, for example, it cannot be regarded as a moral value. We may appreciate or admire physical strength and seek to embody it in our lives, though it is wholly unnecessary for moral behavior. Other nonmoral values might include such things as popularity, status, wealth, and even health. While nonmoral values are of consequence in that they commonly influence the decisions we make and the actions we undertake, they are distinct from moral values. **Moral values** are those characteristics or states of affairs that we regard as *necessary to morality*—when pursued or used as a basis for choice-making, they can contribute to leading a good life and creating a just society in which others can do the same. Ethically, *moral values should always take priority over nonmoral values when they come into conflict*. Thus, moral values such as respect, responsibility, humility, and the reduction of pain and suffering should always factor more heavily in our decisions than, for instance, status or popularity.

Of importance to criminal justice are not only values that describe the kinds of people we should be and the ways in which we should approach our professions (e.g., honesty, integrity), but also *social values* such as equality and justice. Evaluating laws, policies, and even court decisions is a matter of determining the degree to which they promote or fail to promote social values that we consider to be important. To say that we value equality, for instance, is to say that we have determined it to be important, worthwhile, desirable, and "good" for society. As such, the decisions that are made at the level of law and public policy should further the goal of equality. Examples of other social values include such concepts as "freedom or liberty," "democracy," "rights," "justice," and "public good." Each of these values, as we will see, is crucial to many ethical concerns within criminal justice.[16] Issues such as gun control and the death penalty lay squarely at the crossroads of ethics, public policy, and law. In fact, many issues that affect the everyday practice of criminal justice are issues of law and public policy with ethical foundations.

Types of Moral Values

Have you ever found yourself wondering what happiness is *for*? Not what it *is* or how to achieve it, but what happiness is used for or what its purpose is? Chances are you haven't. The reason you probably haven't thought about happiness in this way is that happiness is not *for* anything. Rather than being a means to some other desired end, happiness is what philosophers refer to as an *end-in-itself*.[17] Some values, like happiness, are ends-in-themselves. Others, in turn, are "good" because they serve as a *means to an end*. Moral values are commonly characterized in one of these two ways; those that are ends-in-themselves are categorized as *intrinsic* values, while those that are *means to an end* are referred to as *instrumental* values (see below). Depending on how we characterize a value, we will place a different degree of importance on it. Further, the more importance we place upon a value, the more that value factors into our choices and actions. Consequently, understanding the difference between these two types of values is essential to good ethical reasoning and decision-making.[18]

Intrinsic values (also described as intrinsic "goods") are pursued for their own sake. The "goodness" of intrinsic values comes *from the value itself*—not from any desirable consequences that the value might bring about. In this respect, intrinsic values are described as ends-in-themselves rather than as means to an end. Intrinsic values are desirable *as is*, without any consideration for what they help us accomplish, achieve, or for their use. Ancient Greek philosophers, for example, regarded happiness as intrinsically valuable. In fact, not only did the ancient Greeks regard happiness as intrinsically valuable, but they also believed that happiness was the *only* intrinsic value.[19] All other values were good or valuable only so far as they helped bring about happiness. So, for example, while the ancient Greeks valued health, humility, and courage, these values were good only because they served as a means for bringing about happiness.

In contrast to intrinsic values, **instrumental values** are valuable or good for what they can get us. Instrumental values allow us to achieve other things that we regard as valuable or good. Things like wealth, status, and respect are valuable, but only because they help us attain things that are intrinsically valuable. Failure to appreciate this distinction can have profound implications for how we live our lives—for what we pursue, the kinds of people we try to be, the choices that we make, and the ways in which we spend our time.

To illustrate, in the contemporary United States many people mistakenly regard wealth (a nonmoral value) as intrinsically valuable. Many of us know people for whom wealth seems to be the most important thing in life. What many of these people fail to consider, however, is that wealth is only valuable to the degree that it allows us to get other things such as health, knowledge, and, ultimately, happiness. This is not to suggest that wealth is not or cannot be valuable to some degree. However, if the value or good of wealth is to allow us to achieve or attain other things, then these other things must be more valuable than wealth. Imagine, for example, being the wealthiest person on earth, yet having to live alone on a deserted island. For most of us, wealth would suddenly lose all of its value. Wealth and money more generally are thus valuable only in an instrumental sense; that is, they are valuable only to the extent that they allow us to pursue or attain those things like health and knowledge that are intrinsically valuable. This example illustrates the importance of distinguishing different types of values and the role they play and should play in our decision-making (see Box 2.5). As a general rule,

- *Moral values always take precedence over nonmoral values, and intrinsic values always take precedence over instrumental ones.*

BOX 2.5
Intrinsic and Instrumental Values

Generate a short list of values that you consider to be: (a) intrinsic and (b) instrumental. Briefly discuss why they are intrinsic or instrumental.

- Do you agree with the ancient Greeks that happiness is the only intrinsic value? Do you agree that all other values and goods in life are merely means of bringing about happiness? If so, why? If not, why not?
- Take a moment to reflect upon the things that you value in life. Do these things have intrinsic or instrumental value? If, for example, you value family and friends, is it because family and friends bring about happiness or pleasure?
- Using the list you generated for the preceding exercise, attempt to generate a rank-ordered

list of things that you value in life, from most valuable to least valuable. Briefly describe *why* certain things are more valuable to you than others.

- Remember that our sense of morality and the choices we make are often a reflection of the things we value most. Try to think of at least three examples of choices that you have made in the recent past. How have these choices been influenced by values? Based on your rank-ordering of values, were your decisions ultimately informed by your most important values? In reflecting upon your list and those decisions, do you still feel that you made the right choice?

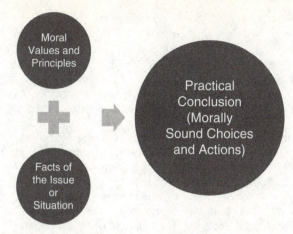

FIGURE 2.1   A Basic Framework for Moral Decision-Making

Normative Ethics and Moral Decision-Making

As we have seen, ethics requires that our choices be grounded in good reasons. Making decisions about matters that carry moral weight without first having the necessary tools with which to make those choices can be challenging, if not ultimately damaging. It is thus important that we have some theoretical grounding which identifies and prioritizes reasonable moral values and principles, and provides guidelines for how we might use them to generate good choices and actions. Conclusions concerning choices and actions of moral significance are derived from the application of relevant moral values and principles to the facts of the issue or situation (see Figure 2.1).

The area of ethics which attempts to identify and prioritize relevant moral values and principles and provide frameworks from within which to embark on moral decision-making is called **normative ethics**. Whether we realize it or not, whenever we make decisions and judgments concerning matters of moral significance we are at least implicitly referencing one or more types of ethical theory. While theories do not tell us exactly what to do in every situation, they guide our reasoning by highlighting values and criteria for decision-making that are of relevance and that are worthy of our consideration (see Box 2.6). While we will explore several normative theories in greater detail in Chapters 8, 9, and 10, we can briefly note their main varieties here (see Table 2.1):

- **Deontological theories** focus on the "rightness" of our actions themselves and whether those actions conform to relevant moral *duties and obligations*. The consequences of our actions are largely irrelevant. If one has a moral duty to keep a promise, one must keep that promise even if doing so brings undesirable consequences for oneself and/or others.
- **Consequentialist theories** focus on the "goodness" of the actual or expected *consequences* of our actions. The effects that our choices produce are more important than whether they conform to duties, respect relevant moral rights, or adequately consider issues of justice. If one can potentially do tremendous good by committing some minor bad, it may be that the "ends justify the means."

BOX 2.6
Values in Practice

Officer Patrick, a married father of three, is having an affair with the daughter of a local real estate agent. As she is also married, their illicit sexual encounters occur during the only times and in the only places they can be together without eliciting suspicion from their spouses or coworkers. The two have recently begun meeting during the afternoons at a vacant home, the key to which she would "borrow" from her mother—the listing agent on the property. Though Officer Patrick is officially on duty during their encounters at the home outside of his department's jurisdiction, his sense of professional ethics easily succumbs to his romantic inclinations. One afternoon, their rendezvous is interrupted by what appears through the window to be a home invasion robbery. Neither sees the suspects clearly, but the car in which the suspects arrived is clearly visible on the side of the road. Officer Patrick's weapon is within reach, as is his radio. Though neither says a thing, they both realize that if he takes action, they will both be exposed. Despite his eight-year tenure on the force, Officer Patrick will almost certainly lose his job. They will both have to face their families, including the very real possibilities of losing their spouses and perhaps their children. If Officer Patrick fails to take action, however, it could result in serious harm to the occupants of the house, and the suspects' remaining at large would certainly represent a continued threat to the community. Should Officer Patrick intervene? Call for assistance? Take a description of the car and/or suspects on their way out and report it later? Find a phone and call in an anonymous report? Do nothing?

In the above scenario, there are a number of values, both moral and nonmoral, that might factor into Officer Patrick's decision (and to our evaluation of his behavior). How might the following be important considerations: honesty, prevention of harm to self and others, professional duty, justice, courage, self-interest, reputation, integrity? Of course, any or all of these values (as well as some not mentioned) might be relevant to this particular scenario. Yet some of these values contradict others. How might we and Officer Patrick prioritize these values? Is his duty to his profession more important than his reputation? Is preventing harm to others more important than his own safety? Is honesty the "best policy," even given the consequences that would likely follow?

Normative ethical frameworks do some of this work for us. Different frameworks ask different questions, prioritize different values, and may lead us to different decisions and judgments:

- *Consequences*: What are the probable consequences of each alternative course of action for Officer Patrick? For his friends and family? For his department? For the victims? For the community? Which course of action would bring about the best consequences for everyone involved?
- *Duties and obligations*: What moral duties and obligations does Officer Patrick have? To whom? Duties and obligations typically must be fulfilled, regardless of the consequences for self and others. Which course of action in this case best respects Officer Patrick's duties to others? His department? His profession? The community?
- *Moral character*: What kind of character traits do we expect law enforcement officers to have? Honesty? Courage? Integrity? What kinds of character traits do we expect law enforcement officers to avoid? Selfishness? Greed? What would a morally admirable person do if faced with the same situation as Officer Patrick?

- **Virtue ethics** focuses on the development and embodiment of moral character. Specifically, it entails identifying the virtues that are important for leading a good life in a just society and striving to exemplify them in our actions. At the same time, we should endeavor to avoid allowing vices such as greed, envy, and jealousy to influence the decisions we make and the actions we undertake.

TABLE 2.1	Types of Normative Theories	
Type of Theory	**Focus**	**What Is Right?**
Deontology (duty-based)	Actions (right/wrong)	Determining one's relevant moral duties and fulfilling those duties irrespective of what consequences might follow
Consequentialism	Consequences of Actions (good/bad)	Determining what course of action will produce the best consequences for all affected by the decision
Virtue Ethics	Character (virtuous/vicious)	Striving to embody virtue and develop one's own moral character; right actions and good consequences will often follow

ETHICS, VALUES, AND CRIMINAL JUSTICE

Like those of academia, the corporate world, or any other professional environment, the institutions and organizations of the criminal justice system are characterized by select values that are deemed crucial to their functioning and that are intended to serve as official guidelines for professionals. As we saw in Chapter 1, codes of ethics typically outline these official or formal values, identify desirable traits of character, and promote moral decision-making on the basis of these core values. Law enforcement organizations, for instance, typically promote values such as justice, fairness, equal treatment and avoidance of discrimination, commitment to serving the community, respect for law, avoidance of decisions based on self-interest, and character traits such as courage, honesty, and self-discipline. The United Nations Code of Conduct for Law Enforcement Officials, for example, specifically describes key values such as commitment to duty, respecting human rights and protecting the dignity of all people, intolerance of torture, cruelty, and degrading treatment of others, and respect for ethical principles.[20] Ideally, individual practitioners will commit themselves to these values and look to them as a basis for making morally sound decisions.

Of course, practitioners in policing and other criminal justice organizations do not always make choices on the basis of values that have been formally identified as desirable. On one hand, individual practitioners bring their own personal system of values with them into their professional careers. As we have seen, personal values can and do influence the decisions we make and the actions we take in both our personal and professional lives. We wouldn't need to look far in any profession to find someone whose decisions were motivated by greed or a desire for popularity rather than by relevant moral values and intrinsic goods. At times, then, personal values and desires may contrast with organizational values and ethical principles, creating a scenario in which an individual practitioner may be inclined to make choices and take actions that are consistent with her or his personal system of values but inconsistent with those promoted by the profession. In some circumstances, we might be able to argue that this is morally defensible (e.g., where laws or policies are themselves immoral); in the vast majority of cases, however, placing one's personal values and interests above those of the law, policy, or organizational directives can produce unethical, harmful—even illegal—results (see Box 2.7).

In addition to personal value systems, one of the most widely discussed ethical challenges facing law enforcement and other criminal justice professions is the existence of organizational or institutional *subcultures*. Virtually all occupations have subcultural elements—*informal values* and norms that, at times, conflict with the formal values to which employees are expected

BOX 2.7
Police Subculture

For new recruits within law enforcement, learning how to "be a cop" sometimes entails exposure to a variety of existing informal norms operating within those organizations—norms that can directly contradict formal values, legal and ethical principles, and the officer's own sense of justice. Numerous researchers in the area of law enforcement have noted the existence of a distinct **police value system** which, troublingly, has been linked with a variety of forms of **police deviance**, including the abuse of discretion and authority, use of dishonesty as a tool, accepting bribes and payoffs, brutality and the use of excessive (or unnecessary) force, and perjury.

Though these norms and themes are not evident in or consistent across all police departments throughout the country, they serve as useful illustrations of the ethical challenges that potentially await future law enforcement officers. Lawrence Sherman, for instance, suggests that through training, interactions with other officers, and on-the-job experience police officers come to understand the "impossibility of doing things 'by the book' and the frequent necessity of 'bending the rules.'" The realities of police work can conflict with the ideals of police work, jeopardizing the "kinds of moral principles [police officers] can afford to have and still 'survive' . . ." New recruits, Sherman suggests, go through a "metamorphosis" whereby, with time, they come to accept a new set of (informal) values and norms:

1. Decisions about whether to enforce the law "should be guided by both what the law says and who the suspect is." Demographic variables such as the race, class, and age of the suspect, as well as the suspect's demeanor, attitude, and level of cooperativeness, should all be taken into consideration.

2. Disrespect for the police should always be met with arrest or the use of force. Even when no law violation has occurred, the officer should find a way to impose punishment—even if this means making an arrest on fake charges.

3. Officers should not hesitate to use force—including deadly force—against those who "deserve it" or where it might otherwise be an effective means of solving a crime. When she or he can get away with it, the officer should employ "as much force as society should use on people like that—force and punishment which bleeding-heart judges are too soft to impose."

4. Due process exists only for the sake of protecting criminals and should be ignored wherever the officer can get away with it. Ignoring Miranda rights, illegal searches and interrogations, and the use of physical force to coerce confessions are all acceptable ways to achieve the goal of fighting crime.

5. Dishonesty—lying and deceptive methods—is "an essential part of the police job." Even perjury should be used if necessary to protect oneself or to get a conviction. Lying in court, to drug dealers, to prostitutes, to muggers, and to burglars are legitimate means of investigating crimes and catching criminals.

6. "You cannot go fast enough to chase a car thief or traffic violator nor slow enough to get to a 'garbage' call; and when there are no calls for service, your time is your own." Hot pursuits are necessary to catch those who challenge police authority; social-work problems such as domestic disputes are not important, and when there are no calls, one can sleep, visit friends, or do anything else one can get away with.

7. It is acceptable to take any extra rewards the public wants to offer an officer. Policing is dangerous work done for low pay, so free meals, gifts, regular payments for special treatment, taking money for not giving a traffic ticket, etc., are legitimate forms of additional compensation.

8. Protecting fellow officers is the "paramount duty"—even if it means risking your own job or life. An officer should do everything she or he can to protect fellow officers, including never cooperating in an investigation against another officer and never "blowing the whistle" by informing on an officer who has taken a bribe, used excessive force, etc.

- In what ways might exposure to the norms described by Sherman lead to unethical and undesirable police behavior?

- Can you think of specific cases from the media where police deviance might be linked to organizational culture?
- What circumstances, conditions, or experiences might make a police officer more or less likely to be influenced by informal norms and values?

Again, it is important to note that the informal norms and values that Sherman describes are not characteristic of every police department. It is more important to recognize that simply because they are operative they are not ideals toward which aspiring law enforcement officers should strive. If anything, they point to the need for courage and commitment to independent moral reasoning about matters of professional significance.

_____

Source: Lawrence Sherman, "Learning Police Ethics." In Michael Braswell, Belinda McCarthy, and Bernard McCarty (Eds.), *Justice, Crime and Ethics* (Cincinnati, OH: Anderson 1998), quotes taken from pages 52 and 55–58.

to embrace and uphold. New employees are exposed to these informal values as they are socialized into the profession, learning how to "be" a member of that profession, as well as how to navigate the day-to-day tasks and responsibilities of the profession in the face of demands that its particular reality presents. This process of socialization and informal learning applies not only to members of criminal justice professions, but equally to professors in colleges and universities, medical doctors, lawyers, newly elected political figures, and even professional athletes. Sociologist Steven Ortiz, for example, describes a "culture of adultery" that permeates professional sports. Over the course of a long season with much time away from home and family, many professional athletes find not only that opportunities for adulterous behavior are common, but also find themselves within a culture of acceptability—even pressure—for that form of behavior.[21] While not all, or even most, professional athletes engage in adulterous behavior, the degree to which institutional, organizational, or professional subcultures promote certain kinds of values and tolerate, accept, or encourage certain forms of unethical behavior is a key consideration when exploring the ethical challenges facing employees within a variety of professional settings.

It is important to point out that the content of informal values and norms will vary from profession to profession and even from organization to organization within those professions, and that not all generate deviance or unethical conduct; some, however, encourage attitudes, beliefs, and commitment to values that make it difficult to maintain a posture of ethical integrity. This is particularly the case in professions such as policing where "fitting in" and maintaining loyalty to one's peers may be essential to one's professional (not to mention, biological) survival. The prevalence and strength of informal organizational values reinforces the suggestion in Chapter 1 that the existence of formal values in criminal justice and other professional organizations is often not enough to ensure good moral decision-making. Equally—if not more—important is the development of our own *internal* moral sensibilities. It is crucial that we come to "know thyself," as Socrates urged, understanding the ways in which our own values shape our choices, contemplating the kinds of values that we consider important, and developing a sense of courage which allows us to adhere to those values in the face of pressures to do otherwise. Just as values point out things we should pursue in life and provide our lives with a sense of meaning and purpose, they also point out the things we should pursue and provide meaning and purpose to our professional lives. The study of ethics helps us understand the importance of making good decisions, and as decisions are often made on the basis of things we value, ethics emphasizes the importance of critical reflection on moral values and how they do and should impact the choices we make.

computer to give you these statistics by putting "Skewness" and "Kurtosis" after the SPSS keyword "/STATISTICS". In addition, it is also good for you to know that at the interval and ratio levels, there are other average measures such as the geometric mean and the harmonic mean in addition to the most frequently used arithmetic mean.

Bivariate analysis

Bivariate analysis is not simply two univariate analyses being put together. In chapter five we talked about two kinds of research. Bivariate analysis is a rudimentary form of relational research. Its focus is on the relationship between two variables rather than the behavior of single variables. It should be noted that the behavior of individual variables can be better understood by putting them in a relational context. This can be further discussed in terms of the idea of applying various controls. The point here is that although we are dealing with the same things (variables), the emphases and angles may appear quite different. Generally speaking, if controlling for one variable makes a difference in another variable or other variables, then we say the control variable is related in some way to the other variable or variables. Of course, controlling for examining the relationship between two variables is different from controlling for examining the behavior of individual variables. The former belongs to multivariate analysis, while the latter mainly refers to bivariate analysis.

How do you conduct a bivariate analysis? Let us further approach the task by illuminating how research control could be realized. In an experimental design, you can achieve the effect of control by randomly assigning the subjects to an experiment group and a control group. This is done before data collection is started. This method of control is usually considered superior to other methods of examining the role of the key variables in a research. The use of this method, however, is very limited because it can only be used to control for one or very few of the variables involved. Researchers, therefore, need to resort to other methods of control that are more flexible and can take into account more variables at a time. This kind of need becomes more apparent at the stage of data analysis and is often satisfied through what is called statistical control. To understand the essence of statistical control, the transition from a univariate analysis to a bivariate analysis can be demonstrated with the following example.

Suppose you have already looked at a variable (e.g., self-rated health) in an individual fashion by examining its frequency and percentage distribution.

Summary

The reach of ethics is perhaps much broader than we might initially imagine. Nearly everything we do has moral significance. More specifically, it is the choices that we make, the reasons underlying those choices, and the actions we take (or not) as a function of those choices that is the "stuff" of ethics. Part of the value of ethical inquiry is that it encourages us to recognize the ways in which just about every choice that we make affects or can potentially affect others. On what basis do we make choices? How can we determine what a "good" choice is? These are questions that implicate moral values and principles—the "tools" that we use,

knowingly or otherwise, to make decisions in our personal and professional lives. The subcategory of ethics that studies these tools and provides frameworks for their use is referred to as *normative ethics*. We will look more closely at several normative frameworks in later chapters. Over the next several chapters, however, we turn our attention to several matters of ethical importance that are commonly described as issues of *metaethics* and *moral psychology*. We begin with an examination of an issue that plays a crucial role in both ethics and in crime, law, and justice: that of *determinism*, or the problem of freedom.

Key Terms and Concepts

acts of omission *25*
duress (or coercion) *26*
instrumental
    values *34*
intrinsic values *33*

involuntary nature
    of evil *29*
moral values *33*
necessity defense *26*
normative ethics *35*

police deviance *38*
police value system *38*
values *32*
voluntariness (voluntary
    conduct) *26*

Discussion Questions

1. How do the choices we make affect other people? Are the consequences emerging from our actions always good? Always intended? Always obvious? Please explain your response.

2. What does it mean to say that our conduct is or can be voluntary? How does the field of ethics help us understand the moral implications of voluntary and involuntary conduct? Use an example from policing, law, or corrections to substantiate your answer.

3. According to the text, no one voluntarily chooses evil. Where choices seem motivated by evil, they are better regarded as stemming from ignorance. Please explain this. How would you reconcile this position with persons who engage in extreme forms of repeated criminal conduct (e.g., a serial rapist, child molester, or murderer)?

4. Because our choices have a universal element, it could be argued that morality requires *universal responsibility*—a responsibility not only to our immediate circle of influence but also to the entire global community (even future generations). Can you think of ways in which the idea of universal responsibility might be applicable to criminal justice? What, if any, responsibilities do we have to rectify injustice or promote justice on a global scale?

5. What is the relationship between values and ethics? What does it mean to say that a value can be instrumental or intrinsic? Police officers and prosecutors value discretion. Is this value a means to an end or an end-in-itself within the criminal justice system? Explain your response.

Endnotes

1. Charles Baylis, *Ethics: The Principles of Wise Choice* (New York: Henry Holt and Company, 1958); See also, Joseph Heath, *Communicative Action and Rational Choice* (Cambridge, MA: MIT Press, 2001).

2. Stephen Pepper, *Ethics* (New York: Appleton-Century-Crofts, 1960), pp. 3, 12–35.

3. Adapted from David Ingram and Jennifer Parks, *Understanding Ethics* (Indianapolis, IN: Alpha Books, 2002), p. 4.

4. Bernard Williams, *Morality: An Introduction to Ethics* (Cambridge, MA: Cambridge University Press, 1993); Bernard Williams, *Ethics and the Limits of Philosophy* (Boston, MA: Harvard University Press, 2004).

5. Diana Russell, *Dangerous Relationships: Pornography, Misogyny, and Rape* (Thousand Oaks, CA: Sage, 1998).

6. Ibid.

7. See generally, Drucilla Cornell, *Feminism and Pornography* (Oxford: Oxford University Press, 2000).

8. See generally, Ferrel M. Christensen, *Pornography: The Other Side* (New York: Praeger, 2008).

9. Paul Ginsborg, *The Politics of Everyday Life: Making Choices, Changing Lives* (New Haven, CT: Yale University Press, 2005), p. 181.

10. Plato raises this issue in his dialogues *Gorgias* and *Protagoras*. See John Cooper (Ed.), *Plato: Complete Works* (Indianapolis, IN: Hackett, 1997).

11. Richard Taylor, *Good and Evil* (Amherst, NY: Prometheus), p. 62. See also, Russ Shaffer-Landau, *Whatever Happened to Good and Evil?* (New York: Oxford University Press, 2003).

12. C. C. W. Taylor, R. M. Hare, and Johnathan Barnes, *Greek Philosophers: Socrates, Plato, and Aristotle* (New York: Oxford University Press, 2001).

13. Taylor, *Good and Evil.*

14. Ingram and Parks, *Understanding Ethics*, p. 19.

15. Ingram and Parks, *Understanding Ethics*; Daniel Kahneman and Amos Tversky (Eds.), *Choice, Values, and Frames* (Cambridge, MA: Cambridge University Press, 2000).

16. Bruce A. Arrigo and Christopher R. Williams (Eds.), *Philosophy, Crime, and Criminology* (Urbana-Champaign, IL: University of Illinois Press, 2006).

17. Robert Spitzer, *Healing the Culture: A Commonsense Philosophy of Happiness, Freedom and the Life Issues* (Fort Collins, CO: Ignatius Press, 2000); Anton Vetroff, *Practical Philosophy of Happiness: The Ultimate Philosophy* (North Hatfield, MA: Troubador Press, 2005).

18. Ingram and Parks, *Understanding Ethics*, pp. 21–22.

19. Holowchak M. Andrew, *Happiness and Greek Ethical Thought* (London: Continuum International Press, 2004).

20. Available at http://www2.ohchr.org/english/law/codeofconduct.htm (retrieved July 28, 2001)

21. Steven Ortiz, "When Sport Heroes Stumble: Stress and Coping Responses to Extramarital Relationships among Wives of Professional Athletes." Paper presented at the annual meeting of the American Sociological Association, Anaheim, CA, 2001.

PART TWO

Metaethics and Moral Psychology

3

Free Will and Moral Responsibility

On October 25, 1994, Susan Smith contacted law enforcement authorities in South Carolina to report that an African American man had hijacked her car and drove away with her two sons—one three years of age, the other fourteen months—still in the car. Nine days after, after initial investigative efforts turned up no supporting evidence or leads, Smith confessed to having strapped her two children in their car seats and rolling her car into a lake. The children both drowned. How could someone do such a thing? The later trial revealed that Smith (who was divorced) had fallen in love with a man who did not want a "ready-made family" and that he had intentions of ending the relationship for that reason. Was Susan Smith simply a callous and depraved human being who valued her own selfish desires more than the lives of her children? At trial, Smith's defense team attempted to portray her in a different light. She was described as deeply depressed, with a history of significant mental health issues—including at least two previous suicide attempts. Her father had committed suicide when Susan was six years old, and she had been repeatedly sexually molested by her later stepfather (who admitted as much). Though jurors were quick to find her guilty on two counts of murder, the information about her troubled (and troubling) past likely had much to do with her being sentenced to life in prison rather than death.[1]

In a similar and also widely publicized case in 2001, Andrea Yates drowned her five children in a bathtub in her home. Again, the question on the collective mind of the public was, "why?" As would become known, Andrea had a history of serious psychiatric impairment, including major depression with psychotic features (e.g., hearing voices, thinking people were out to get her). Experts would argue that her thinking was characterized by an inability to differentiate what was real from what was not. She had had severe postpartum depression after the birth of her fourth child, and again after the birth of her fifth. Psychiatric examinations revealed that Andrea was under the delusion that Satan was inside of her and that drowning her children would destroy Satan; otherwise, her children faced eternity in hell. In Andrea's mind, protecting her children's souls was more important than their lives. Her pronounced history of major mental health concerns was not enough to convince the jury that she was legally insane. Andrea was convicted of murder but, like Susan Smith, the jury elected to spare her the death penalty and sentenced her to life in prison. After a successful appeal, however, a 2006 retrial resulted in a verdict of "not guilty by reason of insanity," and Andrea was indefinitely committed to a maximum-security psychiatric hospital in Texas.

Both of these cases—and many unfortunate others like them—require difficult moral and legal judgments about criminal conduct and human behavior more generally. In particular, they raise crucial questions about *free will* and *moral responsibility*. Though different in important respects (e.g., motive), each illustrates the way in which morality and our evaluations of moral responsibility rest upon our ideas about the extent to which people are *free* to make the choices they make. Were the actions of Susan Smith and/or Andrea Yates freely chosen? Were they influenced or even caused by forces beyond their control? If so, to what extent should the influence of those forces factor into our consideration of their moral responsibility? Even if responsible, are there circumstances surrounding their actions that might warrant leniency in legal sentencing? Psychiatric treatment as opposed to incarceration in prison or capital punishment?

Though historically relegated to the depths of philosophical inquiry, the questions raised about free will and moral responsibility are increasingly not just philosophical; they are *practical* as well. As Jerry Samet writes, "We can't just leave it to philosophers to ponder these problems. We—as citizens, as physicians and therapists, as law enforcers, as parents and children, as jurors, as jurists ... need somehow to draw the line about matters of personal and moral responsibility."[2]

FREE WILL

Though the cases of Susan Smith and Andrea Yates are relatively recent, questions about human freedom as it relates to intentionality, voluntariness, responsibility, and culpability for human conduct date back hundreds—if not thousands—of years. Throughout much of the Middle Ages, for example, dominant explanations of criminal behavior centered upon the notion of supernatural intervention in human affairs.[3] Notably, criminals were often regarded either as having made a "pact" with the devil or having been involuntarily "possessed" by demons that subsequently assumed control of their thoughts, feelings, and behaviors. In cases involving the former, witches and other heretics were subjected to various modes of torture and often punished by death. In cases thought to involve involuntary possession by demons, however, persons were often "treated" through exorcism and other religiously inspired methods of intervention. In such cases, "possessed" persons were not presumed to be *responsible* for their deviant conduct; rather, their actions were *caused* by the demonic forces that inhabited their bodies. Those who had made a "pact" with the devil, in turn, were presumed to have made a voluntary *choice* to join forces with evil. Consequently, they were held to be fully responsible for their conduct and were punished accordingly.[4] While explanations of human behavior derived from **demonology** no longer hold much appeal within philosophy and the social sciences, the notions of choice and freedom continue to factor critically into discussions of morality, human behavior, and moral responsibility.

Importantly, whenever we speak of "shoulds" and "oughts" (e.g., "the officer should not have fired upon the unarmed suspect") in ethics, criminal justice, or other facets of social life, it is important to remember that *should implies can*. In ethics, we assume that we *can* choose between alternative courses of action and proceed to ask what courses of action are desirable. In criminal justice, we assume that (most) persons who have violated the criminal law chose criminality over alternative lifestyles or courses of action and we proceed to ask what form and degree of punishment is called for with reference to the crime. We assume, in other words, that such persons *had* a choice with which to begin. When we judge and place responsibility upon alcoholics for their addiction to alcohol, upon law enforcement officers for using excessive force, or upon mothers for their *filicidal* actions, we are presupposing that each had alternatives but freely chose not to pursue them.

In ethics as in law, the term **culpability** is sometimes used to describe the moral responsibility or moral blameworthiness that accrues when one knows that an action is wrong, but makes a free choice to engage in that action anyway. In contrast, if we are unaware that an action is wrong, lack the mental capacity to understand that something is wrong, or are forced by circumstances beyond our control to engage in wrongful conduct, we would typically be judged not culpable for our actions (though, depending upon the situation, we might still be held *legally* accountable). A four-year-old child who shoots and kills another child would not be regarded as culpable; likewise, the presence of severe developmental disability or mental illness can lessen (or eliminate) culpability, as can instances of duress or necessity such as those described in the previous chapter.[5] In short, morality and moral judgment require that we have the necessary *freedom* to be moral.

The freedom in question is often referred to as **free will**, or the *power to make choices and engage in actions that originate with ourselves*.[6] As ongoing research in the natural and social sciences continues to catalogue the various biological, psychological, and sociological influences on our choices and actions, we are left to critically examine the degree to which our thoughts, feelings, and actions are, in fact, free or voluntary.[7] At every moment of our lives we are subject to a variety of influences acting upon us—from our genetic makeup, to the balance of chemicals in our brains, to our intelligence, personality structure, and social environment. By way of these influences, it is sometimes argued, our capacity for free will is limited.

The threat inherent in this idea is that the kind of freedom necessary for each of us to make moral choices and to engage in moral behavior is either nonexistent or significantly weaker than what we often believe. *If* our choices and actions are not completely voluntary and *if* we lack the freedom to choose and act, both ethical inquiry and our efforts to make moral decisions in our everyday lives (and to act in a moral fashion accordingly) will be largely futile. What we *should* do is more a matter of what we *will* do.[8] While most of us certainly *feel* and *believe* that we are free to choose and act as we desire, the problem of *determinism* is not as simple as what we feel or what we believe.

DETERMINISM AND CHOICE

The idea of free will is opposed by that of **determinism** which, in simplest form, holds that *every event has a cause*.[9] When applied to the natural world, we typically take determinism for granted: clouds form because water vapor condenses in air that is cooled below its saturation point; the law of gravity determines that objects with weight and mass fall to the ground when we drop them. Yet do the same principles of cause-and-effect apply to the world of human behavior? Are we willing to accept that our thoughts, feelings, and behaviors have causes in the same way that events in the natural world do? If determinism is correct, then nothing happens that is not caused to happen by some other event, condition, or set of events and/or conditions—and this includes every thought and feeling we have, every choice we make, and every action we take.[10]

The logic of this idea is, for many people, less of a problem than its moral and legal implications. Not only does free will become limited (if not eliminated) under determinism, so too does moral responsibility or culpability. Supporting the existence of free will amounts to arguing that there are *at least some* (or, at least *one*) events that occur for which no previous event is necessary.[11] The most important of such events for our purposes is the event of human choice. This does not deny that events in the *natural* world are caused or determined, only that cause-and-effect do not operate the same way on human thought, feeling, and behavior. There is a difference, as existentialist philosopher Jean-Paul Sartre (1905–1980) argued, between human beings and other "things" in the universe.[12] While nonconscious objects may be subject to the laws of causation, conscious human subjects are knowing, willing, choosing subjects or beings. We create ourselves through the choices that we make and, while those choices may be *influenced* by factors beyond our control, our choices and actions themselves ultimately are always of our own volition. Consequently, any human action *could have been otherwise* if the acting agent *chose to do otherwise*.

What evidence do we have to support the idea that we choose and act of our own volition? Deterministic accounts of human choice and action have an increasingly robust library of scientific research to back their claims. Yet there exists no solid empirical evidence in support of free will. In fact, free will is only perceivable by way of its effects, leaving us little alternative than to retrospectively attach it to our behavior. We can *believe* that we have free will and continue to live our lives as if we do, but we will find very little in the way of grounds to support our claim. A commonly cited reason in support of free will is simply the **feeling of freedom**, which suggests something as follows: When we make choices, we *feel* that we have freely chosen—we *feel* that we could have chosen or done otherwise if we had wanted to—and, consequently, if we feel that we have made a choice, then we must have freely made that choice.[13] The problem with the "feeling of freedom" is that we may be mistaken or simply ignorant with regard to the forces acting upon us.

CAUSALITY

It is important to recognize that part of the reason that we do not have a causal explanation for everything in the universe is that the process of causation can be prohibitively complex. When we argue that something is *caused*, we are not necessarily arguing that it has *a* cause. Rather, causation is best understood in other, more complex terms. For example, we cannot accurately say that smoking cigarettes causes lung cancer. If this were true, then everyone who smoked cigarettes would develop lung cancer. Because, in turn, we know that not everyone who smokes cigarettes develops lung cancer (at least not after the same length of time or number of cigarettes), we can conclude that there must be other factors that need to be considered. Perhaps smoking cigarettes *in conjunction with* a genetic predisposition to develop cancer leads to lung cancer? Perhaps continual inhalation of cigarette smoke *interacts* with the continual inhalation of polluted air that, through this interaction, encourages cancerous cells to develop? Or, perhaps, there are additional factors that should be considered, such as the effects of stress and anxiety, vitamin and mineral consumption/deficiency, exercise, diet, and others. In any case, the link between smoking and lung cancer—though very much supported by medical research—is not as simple as we might assume.

As an example from within criminology, consider the phenomenon of gang involvement. What, we might ask, *causes* youths to become involved in gangs? Chances are, if you were to research this question you would be led to entertain a number of important factors, including low self-esteem, family conflict, weak attachment to parents, underachievement in school, the need for identity, the need for security, socializing influences of the neighborhood within which one is raised, and early socializing influence of relatives and peers.[14] None of these factors can accurately be said to cause, by itself, gang involvement. Instead, it is likely that involvement in youth gangs depends on the influence of various factors working in conjunction with one another and/or influencing one another that collectively contribute to a protracted process that leads youths toward gang behavior.

For our purposes, the point of both of the above examples is that the process of causation is not always as simple as "A causes B." We should recognize that most often causality is a complex process that includes multiple factors and forces that interact with one another, mutually affect one another, and should be understood only as small pieces of an ongoing dynamic by which the effect or phenomenon in question is produced. This, of course, is not necessarily to be regarded as evidence that all things—including choice—are caused. It is, however, to suggest that while some things seem not to have identifiable causes, it may simply be that the contributing influences and causal dynamics are sufficiently complex that we do not yet understand them. This is the argument posed by determinists—what we believe to be a product of free will may be attributable to a collection of biological, psychological, and social and cultural forces that are too complex to be fully comprehended (at least for now).

FREE WILL AS A BASIS OF BEHAVIOR

Contrary to the notion that human choice and behavior are determined (i.e., caused by some force or combination of factors) is the idea that the choices we make and the behaviors in which we engage are, ultimately, deliberate, voluntary products of human will. If we subscribe to the idea that human choice and behavior are a product of free will, we are suggesting that the choices we make and the actions we undertake are willful, voluntary products of human reasoning. They are not caused in the true sense of the term, but emerge as rational responses to a variety of wants, needs, and desires. And while some of these needs and desires may not be purely voluntary, the ways in which we choose to respond to them are.

The reasons we might have for choosing to be moral or immoral are innumerable. Social philosopher Jeremy Bentham, with whom we will be reacquainted in Chapter 8, argued that human beings are by nature **hedonistic**; that is, we are naturally motivated to pursue pleasure and avoid pain. Everything we do, he noted, is in some way tied to these primary human motivations. Yet pleasures and pains come in a variety of forms and can give rise to an equally wide variety of reasons for our choices and actions. One may, for instance, begin use of illicit substances to more easily "fit in" with peers, thus bringing about the pleasure of friendship and avoiding the pain of social isolation. In this case, we might say that seeking friendship is a *reason* for illicit drug use, but not necessarily a *cause* of that behavior. Consider the following list of additional motives that have been constructed to account for instances of immoral or deviant behavior:

- To satisfy our curiosity
- Because it is fun, exciting
- To relieve feelings of boredom
- To relieve stress, tension, pain, or anxieties
- To establish or further our identity
- To avoid responsibility
- To obtain financial rewards
- To obtain nonfinancial goods or services
- To achieve status or earn prestige
- To "fit in" or, alternately, to "stand out"
- To fulfill expectations (e.g., from culture, religion, parents, friends)
- To live up to ethical or religious beliefs and values
- To experience power over ourselves or others[15]

Though there are certainly many other possible motives, what each of these has in common is that they represent reasons why one might freely choose immoral alternatives. We may want things that we feel we cannot acquire through moral means; we may fear losing something and turn to immoral means to avoid the loss. In the case of Susan Smith described at the beginning of the chapter, it may be that she freely chose to drown her children to avoid losing something that she valued; namely, a relationship with a man with whom she was emotionally attached. Many of these reasons, of course, could apply equally as motivations for *moral* behavior. What is important is the suggestion that these motivations give rise to choices and actions that cannot be said to be caused.

To further illustrate, consider that adults and children lie on a daily basis. We lie to avoid harm, to make ourselves look better, or sometimes for altruistic reasons such as protecting others from harm (see Box 3.1).[16] Each of these is a reason or motivation which might lead someone to freely choose to deceive others, but not a "cause" of the behavior. To suggest that a person lies from free will to obtain financial rewards is to suggest that that person could have done otherwise, but chose dishonesty as a means of achieving what was desired. To apply a reason to his or her behavior is not the same as saying that it was "caused" in the sense that causation is being used here. Consider, however, if we were to learn that this same person endured frontal lobe damage during a workplace accident and has, ever since, lied compulsively. Or, perhaps, that his or her ill child is in desperate need of unreasonably expensive medication without which the child would soon die. Given either of these circumstances, would we be just as willing to describe the individual's behavior as a product of choice? Or, on the other hand, would we be inclined to argue that freedom of choice and action might, at least on occasion, be substantially limited if not altogether eliminated?

BOX 3.1
Probing Dishonesty

Dishonesty has been situated amongst the vices and moral shortcomings of the human species for millennia. The benefits of timely lies for individuals are a matter of common sense. Dishonesty allows us to gain distinct advantages in business, love, sports, academic, and professional pursuits. As well, dishonesty has historically been one of the key methods of avoiding arrest and prosecution for those with something to hide. Over the past century, however, research on the biology of dishonesty (how our brains and bodies react when we lie), has made possible increasingly sophisticated lie-detection devices. The *polygraph*—an early and unreliable attempt at a lie-detection device—measured changes in heart rate, blood pressure, respiration, and other physiological accompaniments of deception. Though still used to some extent in law enforcement, the polygraph is inadmissible in courts of law. Even more recently, however, new knowledge and new technology have made possible the creation of new lie detectors that are more reliable and more effective at determining when people are being dishonest. *Thermal Imaging*, *infrared brain scans*, and, the even more advanced, *brain fingerprinting* each "read" the brain, looking for changes that, in theory, occur even in people who are able to "get around" the old polygraph examinations. Brain fingerprinting consists of electrodes that are attached to a subject and, at the other end, to an EEG (electroencephalograph) machine which records brain waves. When a subject is being dishonest, s/he produces a particular pattern of brain wave (known as P300). While not universally admissible, brain fingerprinting may in the near future be the standard for detecting lies in police departments and courtrooms around the country. Morally, however, perhaps this is an instance where products of science and technology are potentially undesirable. Consider the following:

- Suppose brain fingerprinting, *fMRI* technology, or similar technologies result in accuracy rates of 99 percent or better (the standard of proof in criminal cases). Would you favor the use of lie detectors to determine the guilt of suspected criminals? How much evidence would we need of a person's guilt to subject her or him to such a test? What about probing victims, witnesses, friends, and family members of suspects?
- Even if we support the use of lie-detecting technology in the context of criminal justice, would you also support the same technology being used to interrogate college students about cheating on papers or exams? Grade school students about stealing lunch money? Employment candidates?
- What ethical values and/or principles can you think of that might justify utilizing new lie-detecting technologies? What ethical values and/or principles may present a case against using them?

Source: Lawrence Tancredi, *Hardwired Behavior: What Neuroscience Reveals about Morality* (New York: Cambridge University Press, 2005)

Instead of making predictions about everybody's health based on the general distribution (i.e., mode or median), you may want to introduce another variable, say sex, to reexamine the distribution of self-rated health under a controlled situation. You can select women first and men next and make a frequency table for each group. If you find that men and women are quite different in rating their own health, then using the single general distribution table to predict self-rated health will be undesirable. Using the two subtables of frequency and percentage distribution to predict self-rated health of men and women separately will be more accurate. If you present the two frequency and percentage distributions in a consolidated table with "women" and "men" on the top line to label each distribution column, then you are considered to have come up with a "contingency table." Depending on the specific way you make up the table, it may look like some parallel frequency distributions of a variable put together for subgroup comparison, or it may appear to be a "real" cross-tabulation of two variables.

Generally speaking, the technique of frequency and percentage distribution discussed earlier may be used here for simplifying the material and summarizing the information. And the reduction of data by collapsing response categories is even more desirable, also often necessary, for tabulating a bivariate distribution. The essence of a general frequency table can be kept in bivariate cross-tabulation in the form of a marginal distribution. The emphasis of a bivariate analysis, however, is on the relationship between the two variables under investigation. Each variable can be considered as a control factor for the other variable, though the relationship may actually be asymmetric. The values of the "control variable" set different conditions for examining and comparing different subgroups of the sample in light of their variations on the other variable. The table is thus also called a conditional frequencies/percentages table. The variable treated as a control factor functions as an "independent variable," and the other variable can be considered a "dependent variable." Conventionally, the independent variable is positioned as a column variable in the bivariate cross-tabulation whose name and values are placed in the two top rows of the table. The dependent variable is positioned as a row variable whose name and values are placed in the first two columns on the left-hand side of the table. The size of the table is determined by the data matrix, which contains the counts of cases (frequencies) and their percentages in $r \times c$ cells. Here r is the number of rows and c the number of columns of the data matrix (the rows and columns taken by the variable names and value labels are not counted).

BIOLOGICAL, PSYCHOLOGICAL, AND SOCIOLOGICAL BASES OF BEHAVIOR

We have seen that determinism argues that nothing happens that is not caused to happen. In the context of human choice and behavior, what exactly are these causal forces supposed to be? Influences on human behavior can be roughly placed into three categories: (1) biological, (2) psychological, and (3) sociocultural or environmental. Though there is substantial overlap between the three—not to mention that different kinds of influences work in concert—it is often helpful to discuss them separately.

Internal Factors

Biological and psychological influences on choice-making and behavior each claim that our choices and behaviors are largely a product of events and conditions that occur or exist *within* us. Each, however, differs in terms of how it understands the nature and dynamics of those events and conditions. While biological and psychological models are not mutually exclusive, they differ with respect to what it is within us that shapes our ways of thinking, feeling, and behaving. It should also be noted that not all biological and psychological models are purely deterministic, and those that are come in a variety of forms. While it is not necessary for our purposes to look in detail at the variety of theoretical models employed in biology and psychology, it may be helpful to briefly examine what we mean by biological and psychological determinism.

BIOLOGICAL DETERMINISM   As a general example of biological causation to which most people can relate, consider the feeling of sexual desire. Imagine, for example, a moral prohibition against *experiencing* sexual desire. As much as we may wish to control such desires, they will inevitably arise periodically. Sexual desire is a universal biological element of human life. We are biologically "programmed" to have sexual desires and, in fact, the experience of such desires is necessary on a broader biological level for the continuation of the human (and other) species. Sexual desire is not a "choice" at all. Rather, it is an event that is internally determined to happen by virtue of our being alive and by way of the biological makeup of our species.

Yet biological determinism goes beyond looking simply at the biological makeup that is common to a given species. In some ways, we are all biologically similar because we are all human beings. In important other ways, however, each individual has a unique biological constitution that makes her or him distinct as a member of the human species. Because of this, each individual's thoughts, feelings, choices, and behaviors will be somewhat different from those of other people. Contemporary biological research, for instance, has tended to place a great deal of emphasis on genetics.[17] One implication of this research is that we all think, feel, and behave as we are genetically predisposed or "programmed" to behave. In extreme form, genetic determinism argues that our genes essentially map out a course for us, and we follow that course accordingly. The choices that we make have, in a sense, already been made by the genetic "instructions" that define and dictate who we are and what we do. More commonly, however, our genes are understood to interact with environmental influences, with the environments to which we are exposed "turning on" certain of our genetic predispositions. If there were a gene for violence (a question not yet conclusively answered), those who were genetically predisposed to violence would likely only become violent if they were exposed to certain kinds of experiences that encouraged the predisposition to materialize.[18]

Other hypothesized causal forces or biologically deterministic influences include intellectual deficits, brain disorders or defects, biochemical imbalances, hormonal imbalances, blood chemistry disorders, allergens, as well as vitamin and mineral deficiencies and dietary concerns.[19] In recent years, researchers in the natural and social sciences have looked at each of these in an effort to understand various forms of deviant (and presumably immoral) behavior, including crime, homosexuality, and mental disorder.[20] If these behaviors and conditions are a product of biological forces, then they are not or are not exclusively a product of free will (i.e., they are not freely chosen). Consequently, as we will discuss shortly, we are forced to rethink traditional understandings of personal and social responsibility, as well as reward and blame for one's conduct (see Box 3.2).

PSYCHOLOGICAL DETERMINISM   The logic of psychological determinism is similar to that of its biological counterpart. The idea is that our choices and subsequent actions are largely determined to occur as a function of our particular psychological makeup and tendencies, and/or mental events and processes that occur beyond the level of conscious awareness and over which we have no (or very little) control.[21] Our psychological makeup and tendencies are typically discussed as **personality**, or the collection of traits, characteristics, and patterned ways of thinking, feeling, and behaving that define us as individuals. Our personalities, in turn, are thought to be determined by a variety of interrelated events and conditions, some of them biological (e.g., the balance of chemicals in our brains), and some of them social and environmental (e.g., parenting practices, the influence of significant people in our lives, our education). For some personality theorists, our characters (or identities) are more or less set very early in the life course.[22] They are shaped or structured by the interaction of biological characteristics and early childhood experiences. Moreover, they consist of essentially *permanent* traits and tendencies that dictate how we think,

---

BOX 3.2
Transmitting Child Abuse

Researchers studying rhesus monkeys who were abused and neglected by their mothers during their first month of life found that, as adults, their brains had 10–20 percent less of the neurotransmitter serotonin than those who were not subject to maternal mistreatment. Significantly, they were more likely to be abusive themselves. About half of the monkeys who were exposed to abuse became abusers as adults. Although not yet studied in human populations, this research could have important implications for how we understand the effects of abuse victimization and the causes of later abusive behavior. While not all people (or monkeys) who are abused as children become abusers as adults, they do so at a much higher rate than those who are not abused. It would seem that abuse can be transmitted from one generation to the next, not by example, but by producing permanent changes in the brain. These changes, in turn, also increase the likelihood of aggressive behavior, depression, learning difficulties, and hypersensitivity to perceived threats, to name but a few.

- While biology may not be an excuse for criminal and deviant behavior, are the presumed effects of victimization sufficient to warrant special considerations for lawbreakers with confirmed histories of repeated abuse?
- Would we be willing to consider leniency even for child sex offenders with documented histories of sexual abuse?
- Keeping in mind that not all abused children become abusers themselves, if chemical imbalances (e.g., serotonin level) can be restored with the use of antidepressant drugs, would it be justifiable to treat child abusers or even abused children involuntarily in an effort to stop the cycle of abuse?

Source: Dario Maestripieri, J. Dee Higley, Stephen Lindell, and Timothy Newman, "Low Levels of Neurotransmitter Serotonin May Perpetuate Child Abuse Across Generations," *Science Daily* (November 2, 2006). Available at http://www. sciencedaily.com (retrieved March 14, 2011).

feel, choose, and act. We of course choose neither the characteristics nor the experiences. In the extreme, we might argue that we are predetermined to think, feel, and react in certain ways about and to particular things, and we are predetermined to make specific choices in certain situations. The thoughts and feelings we have and the choices we make are not products of free will or rational decision-making, but are *caused* by our existing psychological makeup.

Many current ideas concerning psychological influences on choices and behaviors stem, in some fashion, from the seminal work of Sigmund Freud (1856–1939). For Freud, many of the mental events and processes that influence our thinking, feeling, and acting happen on an *unconscious* level. That is to say, at any given moment there is much happening within our minds of which we are unaware and over which we have no control. These events and processes, in turn, have a profound, deterministic influence on what happens consciously. For Freud and many others working within the psychoanalytic tradition of psychology, free will is nothing more than an illusion—our personalities are formed *for us* very early in our lives, and the mental events and processes that influence us happen unconsciously, beyond our control. Even infants display personality characteristics, leading many to believe that traits such as shyness and aggressiveness are largely inherited and thus determined for us—particularly when environmental factors encourage the expression of those characteristics. What makes psychological determinism on the whole similar to biological determinism is that ideas such as personality structure and unconscious mental processes are references to influences that affect us in ways that significantly limit our capacity for free will. Much like we cannot choose our genetic makeup or the balance of hormones in our bodies, we also cannot choose our parents, the economic environment in which we were raised, the quality of teachers we had over the course of childhood, the workings of our unconscious minds, and so forth. Arguably, each of these things has a profound impact on our unique way of thinking, feeling, choosing, and acting, yet none of them is a result or function of conscious choices that we deliberately have made.

External Factors

In contrast to internal variations of determinism, external determinism looks to influences *outside* of us that shape and influence our thoughts, feelings, choices, and behaviors. These external influences are many and varied. They can be socializing influences such as parenting, education, religion, and peer influence; they can stem from cultural dynamics such as stereotypes, discrimination, prejudices, social role expectations, and the various demands made by norms, beliefs, and values of cultures and subcultures. Additionally, we can be influenced by structural or institutional forces and behaviors, including the media, the system of education, or the economy (see Box 3.3). Finally, ecological forces such as the neighborhood in which one lives, population density, and even the weather are external variables that serve to influence our everyday thoughts, feelings, and behaviors. If, as researchers have suggested, there is an important correlation between population density and aggressive/violent behavior (see Box 3.4), does living in overcrowded conditions limit expectations of self-control? If instances of urban violence were shown to be a product of overcrowded living conditions, would we be willing to agree that such offenders were less morally and, thus, criminally responsible for their actions?

Generally speaking, the idea of external determinism encourages us to recognize that there are numerous external factors that work to structure or shape our personal lives, thereby limiting our behavioral alternatives (and, consequently, freedom). Additionally, it is important to keep in mind that these various factors can work simultaneously, in combination with one another, or in conjunction with biological and/or psychological factors. Mental illness, for instance, is a commonly cited psychologically deterministic influence that can significantly limit free will. We know, however, that poverty, unemployment, and other social factors are strongly correlated

BOX 3.3
"Mirroring" Violence

In 2003, seventeen-year-old Devin Thompson was suspected of driving a stolen car and subsequently brought to the Fayette police station in Alabama, at which time he grabbed a gun from an officer and proceeded to shoot and kill two police officers and a police dispatcher. In reference to the incident, attorney Jack Thompson noted, "What has happened in Alabama is that four companies participated in the training of Devin … to kill three men." As it turned out, Devin Thompson was obsessed with the video game *Grand Theft Auto: Vice City*, which depicts police killings. Reportedly, when later apprehended for the shootings, Thompson told the arresting officers, "Life is a video game. You've got to die sometime."

Grand Theft Auto is a video game which not only features theft and homicide, but also incorporates various opportunities to kill police officers and a variety of means of doing so, including decapitation, sniping, and burning to death. Is it possible that repeated exposure to a video game such as this can cause or increase the probability that someone will "snap" and act on violent impulses? Two interesting findings from the neurosciences are worth considering. First, the *prefrontal cortex*—the part of the brain associated with judgment, consideration of future consequences, and impulse control—is not fully developed in teenagers such as Devin (in fact, this part of our brain is not fully developed until we are in our mid-20s to early-30s).

A second, though less conclusive, piece of research suggests a potentially important role for what have been termed "*mirror neurons*." These neurons are hypothesized to play a key role in imitative behavior. Areas of the brain respond in similar ways when watching others engage in behavior as when engaging in the behavior oneself. This may help explain why we become so emotionally affected by sports, pornography, etc. In some ways, our brains may be responding as if it were we who were engaging in those behaviors. While the system of mirror neurons may be especially important for human development (e.g., infants brains being primed simply by watching others talk and act) and human morality (e.g., capacities for empathy and human relatedness more generally), it may also help to explain why viewing violence is a reinforcing (and perhaps desensitizing) experience. With this in mind,

- Was Devin being "trained" by video game play?
- Was he simply mirroring in reality what the game encouraged him to do in fantasy?
- Would the shootings still have occurred if Devin had not been repeatedly exposed to that type of violence on *Grand Theft Auto*?
- Does repeated exposure to video game violence by minors in any way diminish culpability for violent crimes? What if the offender were ten years old rather than seventeen?
- Even if we believe Devin to be morally and legally culpable for his actions, is there some sense in which the video game maker, retailer, and/or others should be held accountable?

Source: "Lawsuit: 'Grand Theft Auto' Led Teen to Kill," *FoxNews.com* (February 16, 2005); David Walsh, "Violent and Explicit Video Games: Informing Parents and Protecting Children." Testimony submitted to the U.S. House of Representatives Subcommittee on Commerce, Trade, and Consumer Protection. Available at http://archives.energy-commerce.house.gov/reparchives/108/Hearings/06142006 hearing1921/Walsh.pdf (retrieved July 28, 2011).

with the development of mental illness, such that persons living under these conditions are significantly more likely to develop a mental disorder (and more serious mental disorder) than persons whose living circumstances are more conducive to good mental health and well-being.[23]

Moreover, consider how state underfunding of education may result in the recruitment, hiring, and retention of teachers with minimal qualifications. This practice, in turn, can lead to poor school performance, the absence of quality mentoring, pessimistic future outlook and, ultimately, students dropping out of school and turning to street crime. This is not to suggest, of course, that street crime is directly *caused* by the state's underfunding of education; instead, it simply suggests that crime might be better understood as a complex interplay of forces, variables, pressures, and so forth than a simple expression of free will. Whether this limits free will to the extent that we are willing to concede that behavior is determined and less subject to moral

BOX 3.4
Territoriality, Critical Mass, and Prison Violence

As an example of the ways in which human behavior might be influenced by biological, psychological, and sociological forces, consider the hypothesized importance of *interpersonal space*. In the mid-twentieth century, research on "territoriality" raised some important questions about the relationship between space and animal behavior. Some animals characteristically establish a "territory"—an area of personal space which they will instinctively and aggressively defend if violated by unwelcome others. Researchers found that rats, having been enclosed in a cage with other rats, would instinctively seize areas of the cage (i.e., personal territories). As more and more rats were introduced into the cage, the rats already in the cage became less willing to give up portions of their space. Importantly, when a certain level of crowding was reached, the rats reacted *aggressively*. What was suggested by this area of research is that there exists a *critical mass*—a sort of maximum occupancy for a given space. Once critical mass is reached, any additional rats (or, theoretically, people) will tend to respond with aggression and violence.

Although the implications of territoriality and critical mass for human behavior are less clearly established, this research is commonly referenced in studies examining the effects of *urban overcrowding*. Hypothetically, the absence of sufficient personal space and lost sense of personal control and freedom that accompanies living in overcrowded conditions contributes to physical and psychological deterioration, and perhaps to increased levels of aggression and violence

(almost universally, for instance, rates of physical violence are highest in geographical areas that are most heavily crowded).

With the hypothesized link between critical mass and aggressive behavior in mind, consider the setting of prisons. When prisons are filled beyond their capacity—both in terms of the numbers in the general population and within individual cells—correctional administrators worry about increases in aggression and violence. In fact, both overcrowding and violence are among the most significant problems facing many correctional institutions today. Connecting the research described above with the noted correctional problems, think about the following:

- If human beings are, like many other animals, biologically inclined to react defensively and aggressively to invasions of personal space, how might territoriality and critical mass help account for the problem of *prison violence*?
- What implications might this research have for establishing and maintaining *control* within prisons and jails?
- What implications might this research have for establishing and maintaining *humane conditions* within correctional settings?
- If violence and other correctional problems are at least partly a function of overcrowded conditions, what—if any—moral responsibilities do policy-makers and prison administrators have for reducing overcrowding?

condemnation remains a matter of debate. Even though the influence of such circumstances and conditions may not suggest that free will is eliminated, it perhaps does suggest that we should pay more than passing attention to the ways in which choices and actions can be shaped and constrained, as well as the implications of such constraints for moral and legal responsibility.

Soft Determinism

Is it possible that our choices and behavior are partly determined and, simultaneously, partly a product of free will? Many philosophers and social scientists have come to prefer the ground that lies in between—the gray area between free will and determinism. Very few people are prepared to give up the idea of free will altogether, and very few people would claim that biological, psychological, and social forces do not, to at least some extent, influence the choices we make and the actions in which we engage.

In between the idea that natural and human worlds are entirely subject to the laws of causation (referred to as *hard determinism*) and the notion that we have absolute free will (referred to as *libertarianism*) lies a third possibility.[24] Often referred to as **soft determinism**, this middle ground position argues that while many elements of our world are determined, we are nevertheless free in other respects. Soft determinists do not deny that the laws of causation are operative in the natural world, or even to some degree in the human world, but that the reality of causation does not eliminate the existence of free will. This position recognizes the importance of causal influences, but maintains a perspective on human nature and behavior that allows for the existence of free will and moral responsibility.[25]

Many philosophers and social scientists who subscribe to soft determinism assume that we have some freedom of choice and action, but that choices and courses of action can be *limited* in some important ways. To illustrate, a person with an I.Q. of 60 cannot become a world-renowned physicist.[26] However, *within limits of what is physically, psychologically, and socially possible*, human beings enjoy the freedom to choose and act among several alternatives. Thus, in any given instance, we have whatever *breadth* of choice is granted by our biology, psychology, culture, social background and position, environmental circumstances, and the intricacies of the situation at hand. This breadth can be greater or lesser, depending upon any or all of these factors. However, what becomes important for determining moral responsibility is the *degree of influence* specific causal forces had and the extent to which free will was constrained in a given situation as a consequence of these influences. Importantly, though, proponents of soft determinism maintain that the phenomenon of *choice* is always subject to *some* freedom and thus never completely preordained. While our biological and psychological constitutions, as well as our social background and environment, have a significant impact on our patterns of thinking, feeling, choosing, and acting, we maintain at least some capacity to shape our moral character and to make morally responsible and desirable choices. This capacity to shape our moral character, to be good and engage in right action, is central to morality. As well, the presumption of at least some degree of free will is what provides justification for the study of ethics.

FREE WILL, DETERMINISM, AND THE CRIMINAL JUSTICE SYSTEM

The moral significance of determinism derives from the *lack of freedom* it implies. Morality clearly involves concepts such as choice, voluntariness, intention, and responsibility. However, if hard determinism is true, our thoughts, feelings, and behaviors are not freely chosen; rather, they are determined by prior conditions and events either within us, outside of us, or some combination of the two. Hard determinism eliminates the possibility that we could have selected an alternative course of action than what we did. The choices we make and the actions we take are the *only* ones we *could* have made or followed in light of the influences acting upon us. Even if we *feel* that our choices are voluntary and our actions are intentionally chosen, harder versions of determinism hold that the intentions that lead to our choices are themselves determined and, thus, the choice itself is determined. Simply put, under more extreme variations of determinism, our behavior is largely *beyond our control*.

Being able to choose, however, is an essential component of moral responsibility. If determinism were true in its more extreme form, none of us could act or can act other than the way we did or will. In this regard, none of us can be held morally responsible for our choices or actions because we could not have done otherwise—our choices and actions happened *to us* rather than being a product of intention and choice. How, we would have to ask, can any person be held responsible—morally, legally, or both—for actions the individual undertook based on choices the individual was predetermined to make? What about choices and actions that may not have been necessitated, but were significantly influenced by biological, psychological, and/or social forces acting upon the person who made or engaged in them (see Box 3.5)? These questions are not only central to ethics and morality, but are also a focal point of criminal law.

Criminal Responsibility

Since antiquity, responsibility, blame, and punishment have been reserved for voluntary actions.[27] Criminal law determines guilt and innocence on the basis of a person's intentions, rather than solely on the basis of his or her actions (although the latter are necessary for a crime to have occurred). **Mens rea** ("guilty mind") is a necessary element of criminal responsibility. It requires that a person knowingly and intentionally commit a legal offense. In the U.S. system of jurisprudence, we do not blame or punish people for accidents, for (most) self-defensive actions, for crimes committed under duress, or for crimes committed by persons incapable of making rational choices—of knowingly and willingly choosing and acting (e.g., the legally insane, children).

The assumption underlying the idea of criminal responsibility is that any "guilty" offender *could have done otherwise.* We assume that persons freely chose to commit the offenses that were performed and that such persons did have alternative courses of action that they could have

---

BOX 3.5
The Case of Aileen Wuornos

Aileen Wuornos was raised by her grandparents, Britta and Lori Wuornos. She believed that they were her biological parents until, at the age of twelve, she was told otherwise. During her early childhood, she was often ridiculed by her grandfather. He claimed that "she was no good"; that "she didn't deserve to live in the Wuornos household"; and that "she was stupid." Aileen's grandmother was very cold and distant, displaying little warmth and affection toward her granddaughter. Several reports of sexual abuse at the hands of Aileen's grandfather and her brother, Keith, were also noted. By all accounts, Aileen experienced no positive attachments, no secure bonding, with either of her parental figures.

At the age of nine, Aileen began prostituting herself to a number of neighborhood boys for loose change and cigarettes. This continued for several years into early adolescence. During this time, Aileen was frequently truant or tardy at school, got into fights with other children, and was generally disruptive. Early alcohol and marijuana use occurred during this period as well. Eventually, Aileen left school for good. She found herself increasingly involved in criminal activity including stealing, auto theft, forging bad checks, and, ultimately, murder. In fact, she was convicted of murdering seven men. Aileen alleged that she was the victim of sexual abuse in each of these instances. Aileen Wuornos was executed in Florida in 2002.

- Given her life circumstances, would you argue that Aileen's behaviors were ultimately a product of free will? If so, to what extent could we claim that her freedom was at least limited by factors beyond her control? To what extent might her "choices"—to be promiscuous, to engage in underage drinking, to act criminally—have been determined for her, given the sexual and verbal abuse to which she was subjected as a child?
- If Aileen's behaviors were, at least in part, a product of her early life experiences and formative development, should she still be regarded as morally blameworthy and legally accountable for her actions? If so, should she be sentenced and punished in the same manner as all other murderers? How would you respond to the ethical question posed by the possibility of *executing* her?

Source: Stacey L. Shipley and Bruce A. Arrigo, *The Female Homicide Offender: Serial Murder and the Case of Aileen Wuornos* (Upper Saddle River, NJ: Prentice Hall, 2004).

chosen to follow. Crimes, then, are thought to reflect situations in which offenders "could reasonably have been expected to have conformed [their] behavior to the demands of law."[28]

Criminal law allows for a variety of circumstances under which mens rea is thought not to be present; that is, conditions or circumstances under which persons could not reasonably have been expected to conform to the law. In other words, criminal law recognizes that for some people acting within some circumstances, free will is largely absent or, at least, sufficiently diminished so as to reduce legal responsibility. In a sense, criminal law has always subscribed to a version of soft determinism whereby it presumes and is founded upon the existence of free will and the presumption of freely chosen actions, but nonetheless recognizes the ways in which causal influences can at times constrain free will. The most recognized (and widely accepted) of these influences include circumstances that require a person to choose or to act a certain way in a given situation, and biological/psychological factors that substantially limit or entirely eliminate the possibility of free choice and/or self-control.

Most often, these circumstances or conditions are raised as part of a criminal *defense* that seeks to absolve the defendant of moral and legal responsibility for the individual's actions. Defenses are sometimes grouped into two distinct types: (1) the criminal law recognizes a number of **justifications** for violating legal prohibitions—circumstances that *justify* otherwise wrongful and morally blameworthy actions; and (2) a number of **excuses**, or circumstances under which we *excuse* an offender from her or his criminal conduct.

Justifications include self-defense, defense of others and property, and the notion of necessity that we were exposed to in the previous chapter. Embedded within each of these justifications is the assumption that there exist some situations that may require or compel a person to violate the criminal law, often in order to avoid some greater evil that may result from not doing so. For example, can a person engaged in self-defense from imminent harm truly be said to have a "choice" as to how to react to the situation? If free will is not eliminated under these types of circumstances, most of us would agree that it is at least constrained to the degree that the person is considerably less blameworthy on moral and, thus, legal grounds than if the constraint were not present.

However, excuses are of a different nature. The assumption underlying excuses for criminal conduct is that, although the person violated the law, there is some condition or circumstance in light of which we should not hold the person morally and legally responsible, including circumstances or conditions such as age and soundness of mind. We do not, for instance, hold children morally and legally responsible for criminal acts because they do not have sufficiently developed cognitive capacities for moral decision-making. Other recognized excuses include mistake of fact (e.g., genuinely mistaking someone else's coat for your own and, consequently, "stealing" it), involuntary intoxication (e.g., acting under the influence of alcohol or drugs that were not voluntarily consumed), and what is perhaps the most notable excuse—insanity.

In other cases, the criminal law allows for biological, psychological, and/or social influences to be considered when making determinations as to the appropriate type or amount of punishment to assign to a given offender. Sometimes referred to as **mitigating circumstances**, the criminal law recognizes the possibility that certain circumstances surrounding the commission of a crime can reduce moral responsibility and, consequently, can reduce the severity of punishment. In such cases, defendants may have acted under duress, may have been influenced by other persons, may suffer from a disabling mental illness, or may experience other emotional limitations. Significantly, the presence of mitigating circumstances, though important for reducing moral responsibility, does not eliminate guilt. What is presumed is that while these determining influences were present, the criminal act itself was ultimately a freely *chosen* action. The notion of mitigating circumstances is also very much consistent with the assumptions of *soft determinism*.

In sum, the criminal law requires that to be subject to punishment, an act must have been carried out under the guidance of free will; and in practice, the legal system tends to presume that criminal behavior *is* the product of "a free agent confronted with a choice between doing right and doing wrong and choosing freely to do wrong."[29] To the degree that determinism is true, this reasoning becomes problematic and this presumption should be questioned. Although the criminal law currently recognizes a number of limitations on free will, there are perhaps many other biological, psychological, and/or social conditions and circumstances that arguably restrict free will and for which the law permits no diminished responsibility. As former appellate judge David Bazelon suggested, we would have to consider "whether a free choice to do wrong can be found in the acts of a poverty-stricken and otherwise deprived black youth from the central city who kills a marine who taunted him with a racial epithet," one who steals food to feed his family, or the drug addict who buys drugs only to fulfill the demands of his addiction.[30]

Treatment, Punishment, and Implications for Criminal Justice Policy

The free will versus determinism debate has implications not only for criminal responsibility, but also for how we respond to persons who violate the criminal law and for the approaches or strategies we take to reduce crime. The former entails a consideration of treatment and punishment and their respective effects on offender recidivism. The latter involves an assessment of the type of criminal justice policy that should guide decision-making.

Addressing the questions regarding (1) what measures to take to reduce crime (i.e., criminal justice policy) and (2) how best to respond to criminal offenders (recidivism), in part is a function of whether we generally subscribe to the notion that those who violate the law freely choose to do so, or whether we generally understand human behavior to be determined by personal and/or social characteristics. One noted implication of free will is that reducing or preventing crime might best be achieved by making criminal behavior a *less attractive alternative* than its law-abiding counterpart. If we presume that people freely choose their actions from among a number of alternatives, then making crime less attractive would function to encourage law-abiding choices.

Traditionally, questions of how best to make crime less attractive have received considerably more attention than how to make legality more appealing. Early social and legal philosophers such as Cesare Beccaria (1736–1794) and Jeremy Bentham (1748–1832) were among the first to offer recommendations along these lines. For instance, Beccaria suggested that criminal punishments be made more certain, swift, and, to a minimally necessary extent, severe in an effort to ensure that the costs of criminal activity outweigh its benefits.[31] More recent criminologists working from within rational choice and economic models of crime have made similar arguments, presuming that criminal behavior is a product of free, rational choice and, consequently, that it can be *deterred* by instilling in potential lawbreakers a fear of consequences.[32] **Deterrence** refers to an attempt to instill in citizens (either individual lawbreakers or the public at large) a fear of the consequences for violating the law. The fear of consequences (i.e., legal punishment), in turn, is thought to reinforce compliance with the legal order.[33] What is important is the policy assumption—founded on the notion of free will—that we are more likely to *choose* the moral and/or legal alternative if we are sufficiently afraid of what might happen to us if we do not.

Interestingly, some argue that all of this ignores or neglects to consider the possibility that crime is not simply a function of rationally calculated choice. Indeed, many other philosophers and criminologists have contended that there are a variety of both internal and external influences that can significantly limit either our rationality or the choices we have available.[34] Consequently, following this line of analysis, efforts to prevent crime through deterrence will be largely ineffective for a significant portion of the population. Even among those for whom deterrence is generally effective, it will likely not be so in all situations. In other words, even those who avoid criminal behavior because, for example, of a fear of going to prison, getting a ticket, or attending drug court may at some point be faced with circumstances or situations in which stronger influences will prevail.

Social scientists who subscribe to a deterministic conception of human behavior acknowledge various limitations on free will and generally argue for the futility of attempting to alter behavior through rewards and punishments (i.e., efforts to make certain choices more attractive). In the context of crime and justice, these arguments translate into suggestions that crime control policies aimed at reducing transgressions through reforming the criminal justice system (e.g., tougher penalties, more police, or growing prisons) are equally futile. Instead, determinism implies policies that seek to resolve the underlying causes of crime. Specific policy implications will of course vary depending on whether those causes are presumed to be biological, psychological, sociological, or some combination of them. Proponents of biological determinism, for instance, have advocated everything from extreme measures such as selective breeding, surgical procedures, and **selective incapacitation** (i.e., identifying and incapacitating future criminals before they have an opportunity to break the law) to less invasive techniques such as dietary therapy or drug therapy (see Box 3.6). Advocates of psychological determinism, in turn, have been more supportive of treatment and rehabilitative efforts such as educational training, vocational training, therapy, substance abuse counseling, and other methods that address the underlying psychological causes of criminal behavior. Finally, social determinism implies the necessity of larger and more widespread social and institutional reforms that seek to promote equal opportunity, the end to prejudice and discrimination, the revitalization of neighborhoods and communities, and other efforts intended to rectify underlying social and economic causes of crime.[35]

BOX 3.6
Vaccinating for Substance Use

The abuse of legal and illegal substances is often described as one of the most significant social problems facing the United States. Though legal and policy initiatives to control substance use have taken many forms, none has proven very effective. Some have suggested that many such initiatives fail because they do not account or control for the fact that drug use is demand driven. In other words, people *want* to use drugs. To effectively remedy the social problem of illegal drug use, we need to find ways to reduce the appeal of and demand for drug-induced "highs." Perhaps some help is on the way.

Researchers have recently discovered a "vaccine" which, at least in mice, has the effect of limiting the action of cocaine on the brain. The vaccine allows some cocaine molecules to be "captured" before they reach the brain. In the study, about 40 percent of administered cocaine was prevented from reaching the brain in animals that had been vaccinated, resulting is cocaine having less of an impact and ultimately being less rewarding. Although the cocaine vaccine has not yet been tested on human beings, it is likely only a couple of years away. This potentially raises several interesting questions with moral implications.

- Researchers have suggested that the vaccine is perhaps best suited for persons dependent upon cocaine who want and are ready to quit. However, would it be morally permissible to forcibly administer the vaccine to persons with cocaine dependencies?
- In cases in which convicted criminals have cocaine dependencies, could the vaccine be an effective component of rehabilitation? A morally appropriate component of a person's sentence?
- What, if any, moral concerns might be raised if one day in the not-too-distant future we began vaccinating infants for a variety of illegal drugs (assuming it became possible), thereby substantially reducing the likelihood that they would one day become addicted to or dependent upon harmful substances?

Source: Nathan Seppa, "Cocaine Vaccine Looks Promising," *Science News* (February 12, 2011).

For each of the data columns conditioned by a specific value of the independent or control variable, you can check the frequency (i.e., the count in each cell) and percentage distribution of the subgroup of cases that have this value on the independent variable. Then you can compare the distributions of different columns in a hope to find out whether different values of the independent variable make a difference that can be discerned with any regularity, or pattern. For this purpose, various indicators of the degree of association are important in addition to the parameters of univariate distributions. We will further discuss this later.

Notice that the difference between "independent" and "dependent" variables is only theoretical or hypothetical. Empirical data used this way cannot tell you which variable is really independent (the cause) and which is dependent (the consequence). And the cross-tabulation table does not require you, although it is the usual practice, to consider the column variable on the top as independent and the row variable on the left-hand side as dependent. As a matter of fact, oftentimes you may not know which variable influences which, and in such cases you are studying a symmetrical relationship. All the statistics rendered by the computer will be in a two-way manner; for the measures based on asymmetrical relationship, the computer will give you alternative results by assuming the two variables as independent variables respectively. The thing you need to bear in mind is that you need to instruct your computer to put row percentages instead of column percentages in the cells if you need to consider the row variable as a control but not necessarily independent variable. There are cases in which you may have to control for the dependent variable instead of the independent variable. This is especially needed when the sample is drawn using disproportionate stratified sampling on the independent variable. People who are prone to draw causal inference from the contingency table may feel that is counterintuitive. Yet it really does not make much difference since such analysis cannot support the differentiation between the dependent and the independent variables anyway. The SPSS command for producing the bivariate analysis results in the form of a simplified two-way distribution table with statistics is "CROSSTABS TABLES = row variable names BY column variable names /CELLS COUNT COLUMN (and/or ROW)/STATISTICS LAMBDA GAMMA ETA." The statistical measures in this example will be explained later.

A contingency table is suited for the study of the relationship between two categorical variables. These are usually data obtained at the nominal level. Yet cardinal, interval, and ratio data may also be cross-tabulated if they are properly

Summary

This chapter reviewed the way in which determinism and freedom inform ethical behavior. These matters are central not only to understanding the metaphysical underpinnings of ethics but also to policy, practice, and decision-making in criminal justice. However, more than identifying several important philosophical principles as a basis to understand these doctrines (e.g., choice, causality, free will, incompatibilism), this chapter explained the sort of tensions that are inherent in ethical issues impacting the police, court, and correctional systems, including the problem of responsibility within the criminal law. In the next chapter, we turn our attention to the problem of relativism—a critical ethical issue with important consequences for numerous thorny debates and controversies in criminal justice, as well as for the choices and behaviors of individuals and groups operating within police, court, and correctional systems.

Key Terms and Concepts

culpability *46*

demonology *45*

determinism *46*

deterrence *58*

excuses *57*

feeling of freedom *47*

free will *46*

hedonism (hedonistic) *48*

justifications *57*

mens rea *56*

mitigating circumstances *57*

personality *51*

selective incapacitation *59*

soft determinism *55*

Discussion Questions

1. Police officers typically are called upon to exercise discretion when on patrol. Given the chapter's observations on choice and free will, in what ways or in what situations might the choices of officers be constrained?

2. Please explain the difference between determinism and indeterminism. How is the notion of causality related to these concepts? Do you believe that the choices you make as a student, employee, boyfriend/girlfriend, etc., are determined? Mindful of the determinism versus indeterminism distinction, are the choices of those who break the law different from your own? If so, how?

3. Please list four examples of internal determinism and four examples of external determinism. Do you believe that "biology" or "psychology" determines the choices that people make? If so, to what extent? Using the example of gang membership, how might biological or psychological determinism help account for this choice?

4. Medical professionals and researchers have suggested that, in at least some cases of substance use, people are in effect "self-medicating" through their use of drugs. An argument might be as follows: in some people, brain receptors for the neurotransmitter dopamine are less sensitive than normal. As some drugs act to increase the release of dopamine, users of these drugs might be, in effect, self-medicating to feel "normal" (i.e., restoring a neurochemical balance through the use of drugs). Would an underlying neurochemical imbalance more closely resemble a "cause" of illicit drug use than a freely chosen reason? Would it lessen culpability for drug use? Explore this argument.

5. How does the concept of "soft determinism" help us understand mens rea and criminal responsibility?

Endnotes

1. Andrea Peyser, *Mother Love, Deadly Love: The Susan Smith Murders* (New York: HarperCollins, 1995).

2. Jerry Samet, "Foreward." In Eliezer Sternberg (Ed.), *My Brain Made Me Do It: The Rise of Neuroscience and the Threat to Moral Responsibility* (New York: Prometheus, 2010).

3. Christopher R. Williams and Bruce A. Arrigo, "Philosophy, Crime, and Criminology: An Introduction." In B. A. Arrigo and C. R. Williams (Eds.), *Philosophy, Crime, and Criminology* (Urbana–Champaign, IL: University of Illinois Press, 2006).

4. Stephen Pfohl, *Images of Deviance and Social Control: A Sociological History* (New York: McGraw-Hill, 1985).

5. Vincent Ruggiero, *Thinking Critically About Ethical Issues*, 5th ed. (Boston, MA: McGraw-Hill, 2001), pp. 124–125.

6. Ted Honderich, *How Free Are You? The Determinism Problem* (New York: Oxford University Press, 2002), p. 2; see also, Gary Watson (Ed.), *Free Will,* 2nd ed. (New York: Oxford University Press, 2003).

7. Bruce A. Arrigo, *Criminal Behavior: A Systems Approach* (Upper Saddle River, NJ: Prentice Hall, 2006).

8. Donald Borchert and David Stewart, *Exploring Ethics* (New York: Macmillan, 1986), p. 30.

9. John Hospers, *Human Conduct: An Introduction to the Problems of Ethics* (New York: Harcourt, Brace & World, 1961), p. 502; see also, Borchert and Stewart, *Exploring Ethics*, p. 34.

10. Ibid.

11. Borchert and Stewart, *Exploring Ethics*, p. 35; Timothy O'Connor, *Agents, Causes, and Events: Essays on Indeterminism* (New York: Oxford University Press, 1995); Karl Raimund Popper, *The Open Universe: An Argument for Indeterminism* (London, UK: Routledge, 1992).

12. Jean-Paul Sartre, *Being and Nothingness*, Hazel E. Barnes (trans.) (New York: Routledge, 2003).

13. Borchert and Stewart, *Exploring Ethics*, pp. 35–36.

14. Arrigo, *Criminal Behavior,* pp. 168–189.

15. Stuart Henry, *Degrees of Deviance: Student Accounts of Their Deviant Behavior* (Salem, WI: Sheffield, 1990), pp. 145–146.

16. Laurence Tancredi, *Hardwired Behavior: What Neuroscience Reveals about Morality* (New York: Cambridge University Press, 2005); Bella M. DePaulo, Matthew E. Ansfield, Susan E. Kirkendol, and Joseph M. Boden, "Serious Lies," *Basic and Applied Social Psychology*, 26 (2–3), 147–167 (2004).

17. Ted Peters, *Playing God?: Genetic Determinism and Human Freedom,* 2nd ed. (New York: Routledge, 2002).

18. For an overview, see Matt Ridley, *The Agile Gene: How Nature Turns on Nurture* (New York: Perennial, 2004).

19. Werner Einstadter and Stuart Henry, *Criminological Theory: An Analysis of its Underlying Assumptions* (Forth Worth, TX: Harcourt Brace, 1995), p. 84.

20. Richard J. Hernstein and James Q. Wilson, *Crime and Human Nature: The Definitive Study on the Causes of Crime* (New York: The Free Press, 1998).

21. Adrian Raine, *The Psychopathology of Crime: Criminal Behavior as a Clinical Disorder* (San Diego, CA: Academic Press, 1993).

22. See, e.g., Susan C. Cloninger, *Theories of Personality: Understanding Persons,* 4th ed. (Upper Saddle River, NJ: Prentice Hall, 2003).

23. Jennifer L. Bullock and Bruce A. Arrigo, "The Myth That Mental Illness Causes Crime." In Robert M. Bohm and Jeffrey T. Walker (Eds.), *Demystifying Crime and Criminal Justice* (Los Angeles, CA: Roxbury Press, 2006), pp. 12–19.

24. Robert Young, "The Implications of Determinism." In P. Singer (Ed.), *A Companion to Ethics* (Malden, MA: Blackwell, 1993).

25. Ibid.; Honderich, *How Free Are You?*

26. Charles A. Baylis, *Ethics: The Principles of Wise Choice* (New York: Henry Holt & Co., 1958), pp. 28–33.

27. Williams and Arrigo, "Philosophy, Crime, and Criminology," pp. 3–15.

28. David Bazelon, "The Morality of Criminal Law." In Paul Leighton and Jeffrey Reiman (Eds.), *Criminal Justice Ethics* (Upper Saddle River, NJ: Prentice Hall, 2000), p. 31.

29. Ibid.

30. Ibid.

31. Cesare Beccaria, *On Crimes and Punishments*, Henry Paolucci (trans.) (Indianapolis, IN: Bobbs-Merrill, 1963).

32. See, e.g., Liliana Pezzin, "Earning Prospects, Matching Effects, and the Decision to Terminate a Criminal Career," *Journal of Quantitative Criminology*, 11, 29–50 (1995); Robert A. Rosenthal, "Economics and Crime." In S. Guarino-Ghezzi and A. Javier Trevino (Eds.), *Understanding Crime: A Multidisciplinary*

Perspective (Cincinnati, OH: Anderson Publishing, 2006), pp. 61–90; James Q. Wilson, *Thinking About Crime* (New York: Vintage Books, 1983), p. 260.

33. Daniel Nagin and Greg Pogarsky, "Integrating Celerity, Impulsivity, and Extralegal Sanction Threats into a Model of General Deterrence: Theory and Evidence," *Criminology,* 39(4), 865–892 (2001).

34. See, e.g., Teresa J. Neyhouse, *Positivism in Criminological Thought: A Study in the History and Use of Ideas* (New York: LFB Scholarly Publishing, 2002).

35. Bruce A. Arrrigo, Social Justice/Criminal Justice: The Maturation of Critical Theory in Crime, Law, and Deviance (Belmont, CA: Wadsworth, 1999); Michael J. Lynch, Raymond J. Michalowski, and Byron Groves, The New Primer in Radical Criminology: Critical Perspectives on Crime, Power, and Identity, 3rd ed. (New York: Willow Tree Press, 2000); Martin D. Schwartz and Suzanne E. Hatty, Controversies in Critical Criminology (Cincinnati, OH: Anderson Publishing, 2003).

4

Is Morality Relative? The Variability of Norms and Values

Thirty-two-year-old Nura Asasah, single and pregnant by five months, watched and waited in frightened anticipation as her father welcomed around thirty guests to their home. Once greeted, the guests proceeded to form a circle around Nura, while her father asked her to choose between a rope he was holding in one hand, and an ax which was in the other. Nura selected the rope. Her father then proceeded to pin her to the floor by placing his foot on her head, and tied the rope around her throat. As the audience reportedly cheered him on, he strangled Nura to death. Nura, all the while, did little to resist or protest the attack. Shortly thereafter, Nura's mother and sister served coffee to and visited with the guests. Once the guests had left around midnight, Nura's father and brother sought the village chief and indicated that the "family's honor had been restored."[1]

Tina Isa, a sixteen-year-old Palestinian immigrant and St. Louis resident, was murdered by her father in 1989 for being employed without the permission of her parents and being involved in a romantic relationship with an African American male.

While other family members watched, Samaira Nazir, a twenty-five-year-old Pakistani woman living in Great Britain was stabbed to death by her brother and cousin as her mother held her down. Samaira had "brought shame" upon her family by refusing to marry according to her family's arrangement, desiring to marry instead a man with whom she had fallen in love.[2]

Stories like Nura, Tina, and Samaira's number in the many thousands per year. In fact, the United Nations Commission on Human Rights estimates that there are over five thousand such **honor killings** each year. Most of these are planned, premeditated killings of family members (most often women and girls) whose behavior is judged to have brought shame or dishonor to the family. The killings are often executed by male relatives and, though not always defined as legal, in many cases they are deemed *permissible* acts of violence by cultural tradition. Even where condemned by law, the majority of honor killings go unreported or, at least, unpunished. Why?

Honor killings (also called "karo-kari") occur within cultures characterized by a deep tradition of male dominance, wherein women are considered the property of male relatives—whether husbands, fathers, brothers, cousins, etc. Because the women embody the honor of the family, "deviant" behavior such as having sex outside of marriage, seeking divorce, refusing an arranged marriage, and even being the victim of rape are considered insults to family honor. In many cases, the cultural tradition is so entrenched and widely shared as to be part of the basic cultural worldview and normative order.

Consequently, the law may allow for violence or call for reduced sentences (where prosecutions occur), and law enforcement may view such acts of violence as strictly "private matters"—those with which the police should have no involvement.

By the standards of the majority of the civilized world, the honor killings described above would be regarded as immoral and almost certainly criminal. Yet simply because "most people" share certain standards, beliefs, or behavioral norms does not necessarily mean that they should be shared by all people or that they are more "right" than alternative beliefs or practices. Other than the fact that "most people" believe honor killings to be morally wrong, on what grounds (if any) can we judge them to be so? Since values, beliefs, and practices are often created and shared by people of particular social groups at particular points in history, perhaps they have merit and can be evaluated or judged only within the historical and cultural contexts within which they exist.

Whether "permissible" killings, torture, or less inflammatory practices, judging human behavior requires us to make reference to values and principles that "we" believe to be morally desirable. The values and principles that we feel to be morally desirable, however, may differ significantly from those that other people (e.g., those of other cultures, subcultures, geographical regions, historical eras) believe are acceptable or desirable. For this reason, some moral philosophers have argued that morality is something of a local phenomenon that emerges within particular and unique contexts and that can only be judged from within those contexts. We cannot make a sweeping claim about the immorality of racism for instance. Although harboring racist beliefs and attitudes may result in being ostracized and verbally abused within some cultures or social groups, in others it may be deemed acceptable and even desirable. Further, it might be argued that because there is no basis for determining racist beliefs to be objectively "wrong," we are prohibited from imposing judgment upon those cultures, subcultures, or social groups wherein they are held.

If you agree that in principle human belief and behavior cannot be judged wrong in any absolute sense, you might share in the perspective known as *relativism*, including one or more of its several forms. If this logic seems troublesome to you, however, then you are not alone. Others argue that moral convention does not equal moral truth. Simply because certain values, principles, and standards of behavior are normal within a given culture or time period does not necessarily make these values, principles, and standards "right" or even defensible in the moral sense. Difference—especially differences in values, beliefs, and practices—is a characteristic feature of the human social world. Ethics asks us to critically consider those morally relevant differences and the degree to which they are desirable or undesirable, beneficial or harmful, acceptable and tolerable, or reprehensible and worthy of intervention.

OBJECTIVISM AND UNIVERSALISM IN ETHICS

The key ethical question derived from the idea of relativism is whether there are absolute moral values and universal moral principles, or whether moral values and principles are relative to time, place, and, perhaps, person (referred to as *subjectivism*—each person has her or his own truth, none being more or less right than any other).[3] **Relativism** as an ethical position argues that morality is relative to particular cultures, time periods, and even subcultures within cultures and time periods. To suggest that morality is relative is to acknowledge that morality *varies* from culture to culture, time period to time period, and that the morality of one culture at one time is or should be applicable only to members of that culture at that time. What culture "A" believes to be moral *is* moral; and what culture "B" believes to be moral *also is* moral—even if the two beliefs contradict one another. Because different social groups have different normative beliefs, "moral" actions are simply those that are in agreement with the norms of a given social group.[4]

Before looking at the claims of relativism in more detail, it might be helpful to first consider several other concepts against which it is often contrasted. Relativism can be contrasted with *ethical objectivism* (or *ethical absolutism*) and *ethical universalism*.[5] The first two terms are often used interchangeably, and the third follows from the others. The claims made by ethical objectivism and universalism may shed some light on why relativism has been so attractive to a good number of people—both in philosophical and social scientific circles, as well as within the general public.

Ethical Objectivism

The claim of **objectivity** is a *knowledge* claim. To say that something is "objective" is to say that its quality or character lies within itself and, consequently, can be "uncovered" by any observer who knows where and how to look. Typically, when we say that something is "objectively true," we are making a claim that "true" knowledge of that thing is possible and, further, that everyone should be able to agree on that truth. Objectivity is contrasted with the idea that different observers may have different perceptions, thoughts, feelings, or experiences with something. For example, if I were to say that it is "objectively true" that the desk I am sitting at is brown, I am making a claim that it actually *is* brown and that everyone else who perceives the desk *should* also agree that it is brown. If a different observer perceives the desk to be red, she or he is simply wrong. This is because the "true" color of the desk lies *within the desk itself*, rather than in the perception of the people who are looking at it. It is possible, of course, that everyone who looks at the desk perceives it to be red when it is actually brown. In that case, we would all be wrong. All objectivism suggests is that the desk has a "true" or actual color and that it is an unchanging property of the desk itself.

Ethical objectivism takes the argument just used to describe the color of the desk and applies it to morality. To suggest that certain acts are *objectively wrong* (i.e., immoral) is to suggest that the quality of evil or the immorality of that act lies *within the act itself*. That is to say, the *act* is wrong regardless of who is doing it and when, where, and how it is being done. Another way to say that something is objectively wrong or evil would be to say that it is *inherently* wrong or evil. Much like the color of the desk might be regarded as inherently brown, according to ethical objectivism certain acts are, by nature, right or wrong; that is, they "carry" this quality with them wherever and whenever they go. In this sense, certain behaviors *always have been and always will be* wrong, evil, or immoral. Regardless of how different people *perceive* these behaviors, they are *either* right or wrong—they cannot be both!

Ethical Universalism

Universalism makes a claim very much related to, and following from, the argument of objectivism. While objectivism holds that "true" knowledge of something is possible, **ethical universalism** holds that knowledge can and should be *applied* to everyone in every similar situation. To say that something is "universal," is to say that it is—or at least should be—true of all cultures and all time periods. Something that is not universal, in contrast, would be bound in one or more ways (e.g., applicable only to a given culture, time period, situation, person). The notion of universality follows from the idea that things have true, knowable properties or characters. Because the character of something is inherent in its nature, it has the same character regardless of the individual instance in which it is applied. Every individual instance of something, though seemingly different in many respects, can still appeal to the same general rule that governs or should govern each of those instances. For example, if incest has the property of being morally wrong, then the prohibition against incest is a general rule that is applicable to every situation. Incest practiced two thousand years ago is no different from incest practiced today; incest practiced within a very small Asian culture is no different from incest practiced within the much larger and very different U.S. culture. Incest has the inherent property of being morally wrong and, as a general rule, we can *apply* that property of "wrongness" to all people in all situations.

If morality or certain moral principles are universal, we are obligated to treat alike all cases in which that moral principle is relevant. If something has a universal character, that character supersedes all other situational factors. A potential problem with universal notions of right and wrong is that they depend on the extent to which cases are, indeed, alike. To illustrate, we may make a universal claim that "killing is morally wrong." In doing so, however, we are making a claim that applies equally to all of the following situations: killing animals for sport, killing animals for food, capital punishment, killing in a time of war, killing in self-defense, abortion, and euthanasia. It might seem, then, that the view, "killing is wrong," cannot or should not be a universal moral principle. In this case, we must either allow for situational differences (which defeats universalism) or refine our moral principle so that it is applicable in all situations (e.g., "killing people without a morally good reason is wrong" or "killing people for pleasure is wrong").[6]

Importantly, ethical universalism holds that there are objective moral principles and that such principles can and should be applied equally to everyone. The biggest difficulty, perhaps, lies in identifying those objective moral principles. A second difficulty or, perhaps, criticism involves the source of those principles. In other words, whose principles are they? Where do they come from? What makes a particular source of principles an "authority"? If, for example, 99.9 percent of the population believes that abortion is morally wrong, is the fact that 99.9 percent of the population agrees enough to argue that abortion is objectively wrong? Is that population itself to be regarded as an authority or collective "expert" on matters of morality? Elsewhere in this chapter (see the section on pragmatic relativism), we will demonstrate that the majority opinion can be, and oftentimes is, mistaken or ill-informed, especially on matters of ethics and morality. If we cannot rely on majority opinion, where do we turn to find the "objective truth" about the morality, for instance, of abortion, capital punishment, flag burning, rape, and incest?

At this point, it may be tempting to turn to theological or religious interpretations of right and wrong to settle the dispute. However, we should keep in mind that we would then have to justify what makes one religion "more right" than another or, even further, what makes any religion "more right" than a belief that is not founded upon religious authority. You should begin to see, then, that both ethical objectivism and ethical universalism run into some formidable difficulties. It is precisely these difficulties that make relativism such a provocative and attractive alternative when addressing ethical decision-making throughout much of Western civilization (see Box 4.1).

BOX 4.1
Crimes *Mala in se* and *Mala Prohibita*

In discussions of criminal law, wrongful acts are sometimes classified as **mala in se** ("wrong in themselves") or **mala prohibita** ("wrong because they are prohibited"). Crimes that are wrong-in-themselves are objectively and universally wrong—they have always, everywhere been wrong and will continue to be that way. Behaviors such as murder, rape, cannibalism, and incest are common examples of crimes *mala in se*. In contrast, other behaviors are considered wrong only because a given society has defined them that way. Crimes *mala prohibita* are those that are not objectively or universally recognized as wrong; rather, their wrongfulness varies by time and place. Common examples of behaviors that are wrong only because we have defined them that way include gambling, prostitution, and underage drinking, and other so-called *victimless crimes*. The idea that there is nothing inherently or objectively wrong about these types of behaviors implies that they may be acceptable for some people in some places.

- Do you agree that there are some behaviors that are objectively and universally wrong or evil? Other than those suggested above, can you think of other examples of crimes *mala in se*? Can you think of situations or circumstances in which murder, rape, or cannibalism would be *acceptable*? Are there any ways in which culture, time period, or even specific situations might make them less objectively wrong?

- Consider the practice of homosexuality. Twenty-five years ago, intercourse between two same-sex and consenting adults was considered criminal. It was also recognized as a diagnosable mental disorder. Today, it is not considered criminal, nor is it a diagnosable mental disorder. How does the notion of moral relativism assist us in understanding how the wrongfulness of behaviors can be defined differently at different points in the history of a culture? Why might cultural conceptions of homosexual practices have changed? Do you believe that homosexuality represents behavior that *should* be defined as *mala in se*? Why or why not?

CONTEMPORARY ETHICAL RELATIVISM

Relativism asks us to consider the possibility that there *are no* "true," "absolute," "objective," or "universal" moral principles, right or wrong actions, good or evil characters, and so fourth.[7] No moral sensibilities exist or can exist in unchanging, cross-cultural form. Similarly, we must abandon any search for an ideal ethical system, made up of ideal ethical principles. Rather than appreciating the morality of characters, intentions, actions, and consequences in their own right, it is necessary for us to understand the historical, cultural, subcultural, and, perhaps, personal context within which these all occur. What we find is that while one set of moral values may be "right" in a given time period or within a given culture, these same moral values may not be "right" in a different time period or within a different culture. Yet relativism does not simply acknowledge historical and cultural differences; it suggests that such differences are *ordinal*. In other words, they are merely different without being "better" or "worse" than one another. It may be the case, then, that all morality is nothing more than *convention*. Consequently, if we are to say that morality is purely conventional, we are saying that there is no "right" or "wrong," only what *is* and what *is not*. The distinctions made between right and wrong actions, good and evil intentions, are nothing more than an agreed-upon set of values and norms that were created by human beings in a particular cultural and historical context. If this is indeed the case, then we cannot *judge* other moral frameworks. Instead, we must merely seek to understand morality as a framework of artificially created conventions that are true to a particular group of people at a given time or moment.[8]

If morality can be understood as a set of rules by which human conduct is guided, we must acknowledge that such rules are not the same across time periods, cultures, subcultures, and so on.[9] Previous cultures, for example, have engaged in many practices that, by our present standards, would be judged immoral: the ancient Egyptians practiced incest; the ancient Romans practiced infanticide; and Americans practiced slavery. In each case, the people of those cultures were not performing acts that would have been considered immoral by their own standards. Such practices were perfectly in keeping with the beliefs of the practicing people and, in that sense, were perfectly "moral." In the contemporary United States, racism and sexism were (and, to some degree, still are) common attitudes based on shared beliefs, giving rise to consensual practices.[10] As immoral as such attitudes and practices appear for many of us today, chances are that we, too, would have shared popular sentiments concerning these matters had we been exposed to and

---

BOX 4.2
Defensible Violence?

In some cultures—particularly those lacking centralized law enforcement and formalized criminal law—the family of a murder victim can, by custom, kill a male relative of the offender in retaliation. In northern Albania, for instance, thousands of families are involved in ongoing **blood feuds,** with tens of thousands of males living what amounts to lives of hiding—"prisoners of their own homes." Cultural traditions of *vendetta* can lead to vicious cycles of killing upon killing, all in the name of vengeance and honor. Traditions such as these not only expose us to the existence of cultural differences but also raise important ethical questions about when, if ever, homicide and violence might be defensible.

- Is there any sense in which we can say, objectively and universally, that traditions of vendetta are morally wrong?
- On what grounds, if any, could we argue that retaliatory killings by family members of victims are *defensible* killings?
- If claiming that cultural traditions of vendetta are morally wrong, on what grounds, if any, could we argue that the more "civilized" system to resolve conflicts as practiced in the contemporary United States is superior?
- In what ways, if at all, do vendetta killings resemble gang wars and organized crime practices in the contemporary United States? Does the moral defensibility of one or the other differ? Why?

---

raised within the cultural climate that existed fifty or more years ago. What these examples suggest, then, is the possibility that not only do different "rules" exist, but that we might not be able to impose moral judgments on any of these rules (see Box 4.2).

For purposes of clarity, we need to distinguish several of the claims made above. In particular, we noted: (1) the factual claim that morality differs from culture to culture, time period to time period; (2) that, consequently, there is no objective sense of moral right and wrong; and (3) that because of (1) and (2), we should not judge the beliefs and practices of other cultures and time periods. Ethical relativism generally holds to each of these three beliefs. Importantly, however, these beliefs do not necessarily follow from one another. To distinguish these claims and their implications for ethics, we need to address the key difference between descriptive relativism and its prescriptive or normative counterpart.[11]

Descriptive and Prescriptive Relativism

Moral values and practices can and do vary—sometimes significantly—between cultures. Relativism is founded upon the simple notion that there are fundamental differences between the moral values of different people and cultures.[12] This simple claim is not entirely disagreeable. In fact, there exists ample *descriptive* anthropological and sociological evidence that the moral value attached to different forms of behavior can vary considerably from one culture to the next.[13] This recognition that differences exist between cultures, time periods, and even subcultures within the same culture is commonly referred to as **descriptive relativism**. Descriptive relativism can be thought of as that aspect of or argument within the broader philosophy of relativism that merely acknowledges and describes the presence of moral differences between groups of people. In doing so, descriptive relativism points to the **cultural variability** of norms, beliefs, and moral values.[14] This variability is evident not only historically and cross-culturally, but also between social groups within our own contemporary culture. Race, gender, social class, age, subcultural and religious affiliation, as well as the region of the country in which we live can all impact the norms to which we adhere, the customs in which we participate, the values to which we subscribe, as well as our general moral framework and worldview.

Simply acknowledging this variability is very different from making evaluative or normative claims that some values or customs are better or worse than others. Sometimes, however, descriptive claims concerning cultural variability are used as reasons in support of the idea that there are no objective or universally applicable moral truths (called *metaethical relativism*). Though it may be factually correct to acknowledge that one culture condones infanticide while another condemns it (a description claim), it does not necessarily follow that the differing practices of the two cultures are equally justifiable in the context of morality. Consequently, we can accept the facts of cultural and historical variability without necessarily accepting the idea that there is no "right" answer to conflicts over moral values and practices. *How* we determine which practices are morally "right" or "wrong" is a different species of question (see Box 4.3)

BOX 4.3
Relativism Contra Science

While some things can be *empirically* shown to have certain objective properties, *moral* beliefs, values, and practices are typically regarded differently. The *fact–value distinction* asserts that the empirical techniques of science cannot be employed to resolved disputes about human values. How, for example, is one to show scientifically—through observation and measurement—that polygamy is wrong in the same sense that we can show that the earth is round rather than flat? Is it possible to observe or measure the "rightness" or "wrongness" of moral beliefs or cultural practices?

Some philosophers and scientists have argued that we *can* make such objective distinctions. *Ethical naturalism*, a metaethical position, rejects the fact–value distinction arguing that objective knowledge of moral concerns can be obtained in much the same way that we obtain knowledge of natural or social concerns. Some contemporary naturalists argue for something like a "science" of morality, wherein what is "good," for instance, can be determined by scientific inquiry. If a "good" life involves good health (something which is, in fact, universally valued), the methods of science can determine the kinds of diets, exercise regimes, and even health care policies that promote or lead to good health and the avoidance of physical suffering. On this basis, we may be able to say that certain diets or health care initiatives are objectively better or worse than others. On that basis, we might even make a normative claim that people *should* (or, perhaps, have a moral obligation to) follow certain diets, exercise, or care for themselves in certain ways.

We might also use scientific ("natural") facts to resolve particular ethical issues. Consider the practice of incest. Is the taboo against incest merely a matter of cultural construction? Or, perhaps, is there good scientific reason for the existence of the moral prohibition against it? We know, for instance, that when two closely related human beings procreate, it substantially increases the likelihood of two deleterious ("toxic") recessive genes coming together and producing any of a large variety of conditions that *interfere with health and happiness*. Two unrelated people, because of their differing genetic ancestries, are extremely unlikely to carry the same deleterious genes. Based on scientific knowledge of human genetics, then, we might make a strong case that the practice of incest should be regarded as objectively wrong—not merely a matter of one's relative standpoint.

- With respect to incest, would your opinion change at all if the persons involved (e.g., a brother and sister) used multiple forms of birth control, thus eliminating all chance of a pregnancy and later birth defects? Why? (Be careful of appealing to the notion that the act is offensive for, if they keep it a secret, there is no one to be offended.)
- What role, if any, should science play in describing, defining, or evaluating human morality?
- In what ways, if at all, might scientific research help to resolve the controversy surrounding euthanasia? Appropriate punishments for criminal offenders? Gun control? Justifiable conditions for war?

Sources: Sam Harris, *The Moral Landscape* (New York: Free Press, 2010); Christopher Peterson, *A Primer in Positive Psychology* (Oxford: Oxford University Press, 2006); Daniel Gilbert, *Stumbling on Happiness* (New York: Vintage, 2007). For more on the incest taboo, see Jonathan Haidt, "The Emotional Dog and Its Rational Tail: A Social Intuitionist Approach to Moral Judgment," *Psychological Review*, 108, 814–134(2001).

categorized. Here data reduction through categorization or "collapsing" the responses is even more important than in the univariate situation since a contingency table is more complicated, and the space is more limited. Proper grouping of the responses will also help to meet the statistical requirement for the optimal condition of at least 5 cases in each cell. Like a frequency table in univariate analysis, cross-tabulation is a unique way for showing a bivariate distribution. The contingency table lets you have two marginal frequency and percentage distributions, which is like the combination of two frequency tables. Yet it goes into greater detail, i.e., the cells with the column and/or row percentages listed along with the counts of cases. These form the subdistributions along the columns and/or rows. All the subdistributions provide you with a more detailed view based on which the potential relationship between the two variables may be discerned.

The two variables linked this way are ready to be analyzed for their relationship. For each value of the control variable, you examine the distribution of the other variable and compare it with the distributions under other conditions. The work may turn out to be difficult and elusive, however, especially when you have a large r × c table. Is there a quantitative way to exactly and effectively measure the relationship between the two variables? The answer is yes. You can obtain such parameters of a bivariate distribution by certain statistical calculations. Generally speaking, you can calculate the degree of the association, which usually ranges from 0, indicating that there is no relation or the two variables are independent from each other, to 1 or -1 (the minus sign does not apply to nominal data), meaning that the change of one variable completely determines the change of the other (in the same or the opposite direction). A computer software package like SPSS can produce the cross-tabulation table by laying out the frequency and percentage distributions for you. It can also yield various coefficients as measures of association between the two variables according to your instructions.

There are different kinds of measures of association. Although all of them indicate the relative strength of the relationship between two variables, some are more meaningful than the others since their values can tell us how much risk you will take, or reduce, when using one variable to predict the other based on their correlation. This is called proportionate reduction of error (PRE) model in statistics.

Suppose we want to predict the value of a variable (var_1) and the total error is E_1 for the entire sample. If we know the value of another variable (var_2) which is related to var_1, we can base our prediction of var_1 on the value of var_2, and the

Normative or **prescriptive relativism** (i.e., *prescribing* a certain morality that *should* be accepted) moves beyond the descriptive version in arguing that the presence of cultural variability, combined with the absence of any way of determining objectively "right" answers to moral conflicts, *prohibits us from judging* the beliefs and practices of others. Because differences do exist and, further, because we have no means of showing or proving that any one set of beliefs or practices is more "right" than any other, we *should* modify our own beliefs and practices to account for the recognition that no other belief or practice is necessarily more "right" or "wrong" than our own (see Box 4.4).

What are the consequences of such a position? Perhaps most importantly, relativism is often interpreted as a strategy in support of *tolerance* with regard to the beliefs and practices of others. In other words, we should "live and let live." The problem, however, is that pure relativism implies that *intolerance* should be tolerated as well. That is to say, intolerance is no more "wrong" than tolerance and, therefore, we should simply acknowledge that some people are intolerant of others and place neither moral approval nor condemnation on such attitudes.

Several examples may come to mind. Consider the conflicting beliefs concerning slavery that played an important role in the American Civil War; the conflict over apartheid as practiced for many years in South Africa; and, more recently, the efforts of the United States to "free" the

---

BOX 4.4
Sex Crimes and Normative Relativism

In the sociological literature and in popular opinion, "deviant" sexual acts typically include everything from bisexuality, nudism, topless dancing, and fetish behavior to more extreme acts such as *pedophilia* (sex with children), *zoophilia* (sex with animals), and *necrophilia* (sex with dead persons). However unconventional, most sexually deviant acts are not defined as crimes (in all places and circumstances, at least). On the other hand, more extreme forms of sexual deviance such as sex with children, animals, and dead persons are more universally regarded as unlawful. However, a strict interpretation of relativism would suggest that even these actions, no matter how despicable, could not be defined as categorically immoral—or, for that matter, "criminal." Depending on the persons involved, the culture, time period, circumstances, etc., they may be morally acceptable.

- Using the insights of relativism and objectivism discussed in this chapter, on what basis could you argue that these deviant sexual practices should always, everywhere be "criminal"? On what basis could you argue that they should *not* be? Can you think of specific situations in which sex with children, animals, or dead persons might be acceptable or excusable practices?

- When comparing illegal sexual behaviors with those that are not, what is it about the behaviors in each group that makes them more or less morally reprehensible? In what ways, for instance, do Internet sex, the use of legal pornography, and legal public nudity differ from pedophilia, zoophilia, and necrophilia?

- One of the commonalities shared by the three sex crimes discussed above is that, unlike nude dancing or sadomasochistic behaviors that are consensual acts with no identifiable "victim," children, animals, and dead persons are unable to offer voluntary and knowing *consent*. When it comes to sexual practices, is consent a desirable basis on which to judge something legal or illegal? Can you think of any consensual sexual acts that should be considered immoral and/or illegal? Can you think of any nonconsensual sexual acts that should not be considered immoral and/or illegal?

- How might the observations regarding the distinction between *mala in se* and *mala prohibita* (see Box 4.1) assist you in differentiating between different forms of sexual deviance and in identifying sex *crimes*? What, if any, types of sexual behaviors would you consider wrong-in-themselves? Why?

"oppressed" Iraqi people from tyrannical rule. In its extreme version, relativism cannot regard slavery, apartheid, or oppression in any form as objectively "wrong" in the moral sense. Rather, each concerns the beliefs and practices of a different group of people that may be morally disagreeable to many, but not morally "wrong." Furthermore, our efforts to end slavery, apartheid, and various oppressive practices *are themselves immoral*. In 2003 when the United States invaded Iraq, several differing justifications were given for instigating the war. One such claim was that the Iraqi people were victims of rampant human rights abuse and that the mission of the United States involved freeing the oppressed peoples of Iraq. In the context of relativism, such actions display a demonstrable lack of tolerance for the beliefs and practices of other cultures. Rather than intervening and attempting to change the beliefs and practices of other cultures to bring them into line with what "we" believe to be "right," the appropriate course of action (following normative or prescriptive relativism) would have been no intrusive action at all.

The normative implications of relativism are, of course, difficult for many people to accept. For this reason, as well as others, relativism has been a hotly contested subject in moral philosophy. Nevertheless, the belief that we *should*, for example, intervene to end practices of slavery *requires* an appeal to some objective standard of right and wrong. We must be able to offer some acceptable justification for identifying slavery as morally "wrong"—something more, of course, than merely our feelings, unsupported opinions, or conventional practices. The challenge that relativism presents is that of finding an adequate source of moral authority by which to justify our beliefs and subsequent practices.[15] Various moral philosophies have responded to this dilemma in manifold ways: by appealing to theological sources; by appealing to science; by appealing to the best interests of the people involved; by appealing to universal rules derived from logical argument. We will explore several of these potential sources in some detail in later chapters. However, before we conclude our discussion of relativism, it is worth considering one further variation: pragmatic ethical relativism and, relatedly, sociological functionalism.

PRAGMATIC MORALITY

Protagoras (c. 490–c. 420 B.C.E.) is often recognized as one of the earliest proponents of—and by some accounts the "father" of—what we now refer to as relativism. His famous epigram, "Man is the measure of all things . . .," succinctly summarizes his position. For Protagoras, there is no "natural" morality, truth, justice, and so on.[16] Rather, the laws and moral rules governing human behavior vary from time to time and from place to place. Further, none of these variations is "more true" or "more right" than any other because none is objectively true or false. When faced with conflicting sets of moral standards, we often want to ask, "Which is right?" Yet to judge a set of practices, laws, and customs as more moral than another requires an objective set of moral standards with which to compare them. The difficulty is that such standards do not seem to exist. Though we often mistake convention and majority opinion for truth, these things are not truth. This certainly does not mean that we do not *believe* that one set of standards (typically those of our own time period, culture, religion, etc.) is more right than another. Yet Protagoras and later relativists suggest that none actually *is* more right.[17]

Protagoras did, however, say that some beliefs and practices were "better" in light of their *consequences*.[18] To be clear, the implication is not that what is "better" is "right" or even "more right" than any other belief or practice. What Protagoras was acknowledging was simply that, for example, if everyone else agrees that today is Friday, it would be in my best interest to also agree with (or "go along with") the popular and conventional belief that today is Friday.[19] My life will certainly be easier and not subject to any of the potential negative consequences that might result from my dissension. In the context of an orderly social world, perhaps that dissenting "truth" is not as important as simply finding points of agreement to which we can refer in order to make life more predictable and, in that way, more smooth.

To illustrate, it may not be the case that 65 miles per hour is the "right" speed limit on the interstate near my home. Given individual differences in driving ability, differences in the quality and safety of automobiles, and the relative traction effects with various highway road surfaces, it certainly may not be the "right" speed limit for all cars and all individual persons on all interstates. However, it does create a point of agreement and a point of reference to which we can all refer in determining how fast to drive on that particular highway. In other words, imposing a speed limit of 65 miles per hour on the interstate, while not necessarily the "correct" velocity by any objective standard, makes driving predictable and orderly. In this regard, setting a speed limit is beneficial or "good" in its *consequences* or in the *practical value* that it has for social life.

In referring to "practical value," we come across a potentially important idea in ethics or any other field of study; namely, *pragmatism*. **Pragmatism** comes in a variety of forms, though the basic idea of each is that the purpose of anything—values, beliefs, laws, research—is not to uncover or represent the truth, but to allow us to more effectively and/or comfortably live our lives. The function of lawmakers, for example, is not to find the "right" law for a particular purpose, but to develop an *effective* law for that purpose. In other words, a good law becomes a law that *works*.[20] If, for instance, our goal is to achieve and maintain social order, then law and practices of law enforcement that serve that purpose—those that *work*—are good laws and practices. We cannot rightfully judge behaviors, customs, beliefs, and laws, except by reference to their context and effectiveness (or **functionality**) within that context.

So what are the implications of Protagorean philosophy for ethics? In short, it means that our search for objective and universal standards of truth, justice, goodness, beauty, and so forth is futile and pointless. We should discard accounts of absolute truth and, further, abandon any related pursuits we might subsequently undertake. Moral laws do not exist, at least in any objective or "natural" sense. Social reality consists merely of human constructions that are not "right" nor "wrong," but *functional* for a given culture at a given time. "Justice" is what is believed to be "just" by a certain group of people, and what therefore works for that group of people within that historical period. "Killing" cannot be objectively wrong, yet prohibitions against killing can be functional. A culture which did not have prohibitions against killing—at least many forms of killing—would be a culture that was not primed for survival. A culture in which it was customary for men to have five wives might eventually run into practical problems if there were considerably more men than women living within that culture. By contrast, *polygyny* might function positively in a culture where there were considerably more women than men.

Thus, while it is quite natural for us to think about killing and polygamy as moral issues, if Protagoras is correct, we should cease judging the morality of practices and beliefs and begin seeking to understand the practicality and functionality of those practices and beliefs. This, in turn, requires abandonment of philosophical thinking about ethics and a turn toward investigating the beliefs and practices of social groups or collectives *sociologically*. What is functional for a group of people is a purely sociological question, void of any deeper moral philosophical content.

Consider the following two examples—the first pertains to cultural variability and its relation to a pragmatic conception of relativism; the second is a functionalist sociological perspective on an often-debated social and legal issue:

- European explorers discovered that Inuit (Eskimo) tribes regularly engaged in practices very different from their own. In particular, the Eskimos seemed to practice *infanticide* and a crude form of *euthanasia*. Female babies were sometimes killed off, and elderly members of the tribe were sometimes left out in the cold to die. What may have initially seemed to Europeans to reflect a remarkable lack of moral sensibilities, however, were discovered to be sensible practices. Later explorers would recognize that the Eskimo people were a nomadic tribe, traveling constantly in search of new food sources. As hunters and food gatherers, males were far more likely to die prematurely. If all female babies were to survive, the number of female adults would quickly far outweigh the number of healthy males, thereby jeopardizing the well-being of the tribe. Further, some of the elderly members of the tribe were simply too frail to keep up. Leaving them behind to die was less a moral matter, and more a matter of doing what was necessary to ensure the survival of the group. As James Rachels suggests, "[t]he Eskimos' values are not all that different from our values. It is only that life forces upon them choices that we do not have to make."[21]

- In a much-discussed article, sociologist Kingsley Davis argued that *prostitution* is "good" for society in that it serves the overall function of maintaining the social system by performing several smaller functions.[22] Prostitution (1) satisfies sexual desires without the associated expenses of dating or marriage and without the often-required emotional investment; (2) maintains the institution of the family by relieving wives of the necessity of satisfying the "perverse" sexual desires of their husbands, thus enabling husbands to continue to respect their wives; (3) allows a small number of women to satisfy the needs of a large number of men, including those who have difficulty finding conventional outlets for those needs; and (4) allows prostitutes themselves to earn considerably more money than they would in most other occupations.

In both of these examples, we are faced with a controversial moral issue: the first concerning life and death; the second concerning human sexuality. In the first instance, many would be quick to point out the assumed immoral nature of infanticide or allowing elderly persons to die. However, what would seem to most of us today as a profound disrespect for life and a cruelty of character might be better regarded as a practice conducted within the context of a certain cultural reality. Approached in this way, it may seem less morally reprehensible and, perhaps, even acceptable as a practice necessary (functional) for group survival. We could say the same for the second case as well: Prostitution may be morally reprehensible, yet it could also be understood as a practice that meets the needs of a large group of people within a given society. In neither case do we necessarily commit ourselves to accepting the practice as *moral*. Rather, what seems initially to be a moral question becomes a pragmatic question when viewed in a different light.

THE VALUE OF RELATIVISM

Relativism has brought mixed blessings to ethics and morality. In one sense, it represents a serious threat to the very idea of morality, as well as ethical inquiries into morality. In another sense, it alerts us to some common faults in our own thinking about moral issues. Some would argue that it is only a short step from relativism to an "anything goes" attitude in which morality can no longer serve as a foundation or point of reference for social health, happiness, and relations more generally. At the same time, others contend that a failure to recognize the diversity of moral values that exists within and between cultures (and the corresponding benefits of that diversity) can lead us to potentially more dangerous ways of thinking and potentially harmful laws, policies, and practices emerging from those ways of thinking. What are the dangers of relativism? What are the dangers of *not* taking relativism into consideration?

A significant consequence of accepting a purely relativistic ethics is that it requires us to abandon our common practice of judging other people and cultures and the often accompanying practice of attempting to change those same people and cultures by imposing our own values onto them. For relativists, this consequence is not entirely detrimental to human relations. Different laws, rules, customs, practices, and beliefs may be entirely at odds with one another and yet work equally well for different groups of people. We should keep in mind that historical development, economic and social conditions, educational standards, and so forth of different groups of people can vary tremendously. Thus, while a given common practice may work quite well for one culture, region, or subculture, it may be devastating for another. Recognizing these differences does not require us to abandon our own sense of morality. Rather, it asks that we not be so quick to judge and impose ourselves in every situation in which there exists a conflict. It might be possible to differentiate between moral principles that are legitimately universal and moral practices that are legitimately variable.

If we subscribe to some variation of relativism, we would have to concede that practices such as capital punishment cannot be judged moral or immoral. From a pragmatic standpoint, we might better ask whether the death penalty "works" or serves some greater purpose for which it is intended.[23] Assuming that capital punishment has practical or pragmatic value as a deterrent, then executing convicted criminals would be morally acceptably and desirable so long as it fulfilled this purpose. On the other hand, if it failed to fulfill its intended function, we would have to judge the practice of capital punishment to be morally undesirable and unacceptable. Most of us, however, are probably a bit uncomfortable with the idea that practices such as capital punishment are not moral or immoral, but could be either depending on where and when the act is undertaken and who is engaged in undertaking it. Must there not be some standard or principles by which we could say conclusively that certain laws, policies, or practices are *either* moral *or* immoral?

As unsettling as it may be for some, most people do tend to think of morality as relative— at least to situational circumstances. Thus the act of killing is generally regarded as immoral, but could be moral if done in a time of war or as part of a heroic effort to prevent some greater evil. Some philosophers and social scientists (including criminologists) suggest that even if we cannot say conclusively that certain laws, policies, or practices are right or wrong on a moral level, we *can* make judgments concerning the underlying *reasons* for them. For instance, while we may not be able to make a determination one way or the other about the morality of war, we may be able to make moral judgments about the underlying reasons for going to war. Starting or entering a war in an effort to satisfy an underlying desire for vengeance against another country or our hatred for that country may be objectively less moral than if motivated by a desire to improve the well-being of the general public (consider, for example, the recent U.S. war in Iraq). Additionally, while we may not be able to conclusively say that stealing is immoral, we can say conclusively that stealing for personal material gain is immoral—leaving open the possibility that some reasons for stealing (e.g., feeding a starving family) may be socially undesirable, but not necessarily immoral.

One of the benefits that the notion of relativism provides is that it encourages us to be more open-minded and considerate of perspectives other than our own when faced with moral issues and scenarios.[24] Most people, for instance, tend to be ethnocentric. **Ethnocentrism** refers to a way of perceiving the world and all aspects of the world from the perspective of one's own culture or social group.[25] From an early age, a respect for our own culture is instilled in us. This respect is not based on any experience or objective knowledge we have acquired concerning the values and practices of our culture or those of any other; rather, we are simply socialized such that we come to have this respect. The danger of ethnocentrism lies in the sequencing of thought and action that is commonly made: perceiving the world from the perspective of one's own social group (a more or less inevitable phenomenon), to believing that that perspective is the "right" one. In other words, when respect for one's own culture turns into a belief in the *superiority* of one's own culture, we endanger our capacity for open-minded reasoning.

In relation to morality, ethnocentric persons believe not only that there are objective moral values, but also that their own moral values *are* the objectively right ones. Ethnocentric morality, then, entails a belief in the moral superiority of one's own culture or social group. Ethnocentrism often affects people such that they reject the possibility that their own values are wrong and that those of another culture or social group *might* be right or in some ways "better." It is only another small step from believing that the moral sensibilities of one's own group are correct to judging the moral values of other groups and attempting to change those other groups so that they are consistent with one's own culturally bound views.

What makes ethnocentrism problematic is that it often can lead to *dogmatism* and *intolerance*.[26] **Dogma** refers to a belief or belief system that is held unquestioningly and with absolute certainty. **Dogmatism** refers to the refusal to entertain criticisms of or challenges to those beliefs.[27] Often, such beliefs are not justified or backed by sound reasons—they are merely held as unquestionable truths. Dogmatism leads to narrow-mindedness (rather than open-mindedness) and an unwillingness to reconsider one's own values and beliefs even in light of contrary evidence. As well, a dogmatic stance can lead us to reject beliefs that are inconsistent with our own without ever considering them for what they are or might be worth. The problem, of course, is that our own beliefs may well be false or, at the very least, may be capable of improvement or refinement.

Moreover, dogmatism prevents one from assuming an objective perspective on one's own moral beliefs and values, as well as those of other people. If we are certain that our own beliefs are true—even without evidence to support them—we can easily become intolerant of the beliefs and practices of others who do not share in our value-based perspective. Because tremendous diversity exists both within and between cultures with regard to moral values, beliefs, and practices, conflict becomes inevitable. Dogmatism prevents agreeable resolution to such conflicts because both parties believe themselves to be absolutely right and the other to be absolutely wrong. Thus, each party or faction will try to force the other to adopt its perspective. Of course, this does not necessarily mean that either party is, in fact, right or wrong; rather, it simply means that neither is willing to consider the perspective of the other.

While much has been said both in support of and opposed to the virtue of tolerance, we should keep in mind that the kind of openness implied by relativism is not necessarily one that advocates tolerance of *all* values, beliefs, and practices. Instead, we should think of tolerance as a willingness to *understand* the perspectives of others and to not make judgments until we have done so. Tolerance or acceptance of this sort suggests that we should make some effort to keep an open mind and reserve judgment until we are able to do so in light of all relevant information. Thus, the value of tolerance is perhaps best understood as a means of *avoiding intolerance*.

On the whole, relativism reminds us that we are *fallible*—as much as we may cling to certain values and beliefs, our own moral sensibilities are not necessarily absolute truths that should be applied to everyone and in all situations. As well, becoming familiar with difference and diversity can help us recognize and understand the moral perspectives of other persons, groups, and cultures in various situations and utilize this understanding before passing judgment or imposing solutions in those involving conflict. Although recognizing the relativity of moral values and norms does not mean that we should abandon our own values or adopt an "anything goes" attitude, it does encourage us to refrain from thinking in "black-and-white" terms and to maintain a willingness to understand and even learn from other perspectives.

Recognizing the variability of moral values and norms and maintaining a certain degree of open-mindedness not only seems necessary for anyone living in a complex and diverse society such as the United States, but is especially important for current and future criminal justice practitioners. Agents of criminal justice are exposed to difference and diversity of cultural and subcultural values routinely, whether through the policing of different communities, the guarding of a diverse population of prison inmates, or through representing the interests of diverse clients in a courtroom environment. In fact, most formal codes of ethics in law enforcement, correctional, and court-related professions emphasize and promote equal treatment and the avoidance of prejudice and discriminatory treatment—values that would seem to demand a certain level of understanding and respect for group and individual differences.

RELATIVISM AND THE CRIMINAL JUSTICE SYSTEM: THE MORALITY OF CRIMINAL LAW

Over the course of this chapter, we have seen that moral values and norms can and often do vary—even within the same society or culture; from region to region; from religion to religion; along group, class, racial, and ethnic lines; and between subcultures. We have also been exposed to the argument that, because of this variability, there is no "true" morality or, at the very least, that "true" morality is not immediately evident and therefore we should not be so quick to pass judgment on those whose values and practices differ from our own. These ideas have important but often overlooked implications for crime, law, and justice. Within the criminal justice context, the relativity of moral values—as well as the idea that morality should not be imposed on others—perhaps poses the greatest difficulties and dilemmas within the sphere of lawmaking (see Box 4.5). In this final section, we look briefly at some of the dilemmas that relativity of moral values poses for the practice of lawmaking.

When lawmakers create laws, they often cannot escape the influence of moral interests. Even when moral interests are not specifically stated, laws almost always have a moral dimension. Yet many advanced industrial societies such as the United States are characterized by moral diversity and conflict over key moral (and legal) issues. Almost universally, citizens cannot murder, rape, or rob other citizens—behaviors that directly harm the person or property of others. There tends to be a strong *consensus* among the public concerning the wrongfulness of these behaviors and the desirability of prohibiting them. Other forms of behavior, however, are less a matter of public consensus. Gambling, the sale and distribution of sexually explicit materials and alcoholic beverages, and the possession and use of various substances are, for example, behaviors over which there has always been and continues to be moral disagreement. Where conflict over moral values and appropriate behavior exists, it is law that ultimately must supply "working answers." Importantly, laws are not written to apply only to those people who happen to agree with them or share in their underlying moral values; rather, laws are created to apply to all people, everywhere within a given jurisdiction. In other words, the nature of lawmaking is such that certain values *must* be imposed upon citizens.

Within criminal law, the existence of moral diversity and conflict is perhaps most evident in discussions about *what should be a crime*. In the United States, as in other civilized countries, citizens are not free to do whatever they wish. Federal, state, and local governments place various

BOX 4.5
The Relativity of Things Lawful and Unlawful

Part of the difficulty of relying solely on the law to define what is right and wrong is that *laws vary and change*. Consequently, the behaviors that are defined as lawful or unlawful vary and change with them. Laws prohibiting or allowing certain forms of behavior vary from one place to the next (e.g., by country, state, and even by county and city). What is legal at one location, may be illegal at another. In addition to varying from place to place, laws also change over time. What is legal at one point in history, may be illegal at another (previous or future) historical point. Consider the following:

- Nevada is well known for being the only state in the United States to have legalized prostitution. More accurately, prostitution is legal in some counties in Nevada and illegal in others. In Clark County, for instance, which houses the city of Las Vegas, prostitution is explicitly prohibited and punishable as a misdemeanor offense. Nevada Revised Statute 244.345 maintains that houses of "ill fame or repute" or other businesses employing persons for purposes of prostitution are not lawful in Nevada counties with a population greater than 400,000. Counties with a population of under 400,000 can, under state law, prohibit or regulate prostitution as they see fit. While prostitution and the solicitation of prostitution are illegal in the major cities of Las Vegas, Reno, and Carson City, these practices are perfectly legal (though regulated) at other locations. One will find houses of prostitution about 50 miles from Las Vegas, and less than 10 miles from Reno and Carson City.
- Well into the 1960s, the distribution, sale and/or use of contraceptives was illegal in many U.S. states. In the 1860s and 1870s, Anthony Comstock launched an anti–birth control crusade, claiming that the contraceptives encouraged lustful and immoral sexual behavior. In 1873,

U.S. Congress passed a federal law (the **Comstock Act**) which defined contraceptives as obscene material and placed regulations on their distribution. Shortly thereafter, a number of individual states passed similar laws. In the state of Connecticut, for instance, the *use* of birth control was outlawed. Even married couples could be arrested and sentenced to as much as a year in jail for the use of contraceptives. In *Griswold v. Connecticut* (1965), the U.S. Supreme Court ruled that laws prohibiting the use of contraceptives violated privacy rights and, thus, were unconstitutional.

Each of these examples illustrates a basic reality of crime: what is a crime at one place may not be at another, and what is a crime at one time may not be at another. Whereas one could be arrested and sentenced on misdemeanor charges for prostitution in the city of Reno, one could lawfully engage in the same behavior only a short drive down the road. Whereas one could, today, purchase and use various forms of contraceptives available at the local drug store, one could legally have been arrested and sentenced on misdemeanor charges for the use of birth control only several decades ago.

Because laws change from time to time, the same people who are lawbreakers today may not be tomorrow; the same people who are law-abiding citizens today, may be tomorrow's criminals. Because laws change from place to place, the same people who are lawbreakers at one location, may not be at another. Clearly, this creates problems for our efforts to define crime and criminals, as well as for studying crime and criminals. In our efforts to understand the "crime" of prostitution, should we study the prostitute in Las Vegas who is a criminal and not the prostitute 50 miles down the road who is not? Should we define as "criminal" the prostitute who works the streets in Reno but define as a law-abiding citizen the prostitute who works at a legal prostitution business a few minutes from town?

restrictions on individual liberties by passing laws that prohibit some forms of behavior and require others. Debate arises, however, when we begin to ask *which* behaviors should be subject to restrictions. Further, we might ask, on what grounds can we justify restricting or criminalizing some behaviors but not others? How and why is it that certain behaviors are determined to be "crimes" while others—irrespective of how harmful, immoral, or offensive they may be to some—are not? On what basis can we justify governments defining appropriate behavior and forcing citizens to comply with moral standards that they might find objectionable or disagreeable?

In his widely discussed four-volume work, *The Moral Limits of Criminal Law*, Joel Feinberg explores four principles that might be used to determine whether the government can legitimately prohibit or criminalize certain forms of behavior: the harm principle, paternalism, legal moralism, and offensive conduct. In the remainder of this section, we briefly explore each of these principles and conclude with an exercise in applying them to contemporary controversies in law and society (see Box 4.6).

The Harm Principle

One of the most commonly discussed justifications for the prohibition of certain types of behavior is the **harm principle**, derived from John Stuart Mill. The harm principle is also commonly used as justification for *not* criminalizing certain forms of behavior. In short, the question to which Mill responds is, "When is it morally acceptable for governments to coerce people through law?" To this question, he suggests a simple principle: Governments can

---

BOX 4.6
Justifying Legal Prohibitions

Moral values and norms tend to vary across and within cultures and over time. There are many behaviors about which there is a lack of moral consensus. Conflict and disagreement over which behaviors should be criminalized is reflected in the fact that laws concerning these behaviors often vary over time and from place to place at a given time. In other words, criminal law is, to some extent, *relative*. How, then, do governments determine which behaviors should be subject to legal coercion?

As we have seen in this section, over the course of his four-volume work, *The Moral Limits of Criminal Law*, Joel Feinberg suggests that there are four principles that might be used to determine whether the government can legitimately prohibit certain forms of behavior:

1. *The Harm Principle*. Behavior can be legitimately prohibited if it causes or has a high risk of causing serious harm to other people.
2. *Paternalism*. Governments can legitimately prohibit behavior that might cause serious harm to the acting agent, even if no one else might be harmed.
3. *Legal Moralism*. Governments are justified in prohibiting behavior that is immoral, even when it does not harm or offend anyone.

4. *The Offense Principle*. Behavior can be legitimately prohibited if it seriously offends others.

As a concluding exercise, consider how the above principles might *justify* or *fail to justify* legal prohibition of the following behaviors. For those behaviors that are currently illegal, consider whether and how any of Feinberg's four principles might justify their legalization.

- Physician-assisted suicide
- Abortion
- Burning the American flag in public
- Possession and use of marijuana
- Buying and selling sex
- Buying and selling sexually explicit material
- Owning weapons, including automatic weapons and grenades
- Polluting the environment
- Gay marriage
- Sunbathing nude in public
- An employer refusing to hire women or African Americans
- A therapist having sexual relations with his or her clients
- Treating mentally ill persons by medicating them against their will

legitimately prohibit or require certain behavior when it is necessary to *prevent people from harming others*—and *only* when it is necessary for this purpose. In Mill's own terms,

> . . . the only purpose for which power can be rightfully exercised over any member of a civilized community, against his will, is to prevent harm to others. His own good, either physical or moral, is not a sufficient warrant. . . . Over himself, over his own body and mind, the individual is sovereign.[28]

Clearly, the harm principle would justify the government passing and enforcing laws against murder, rape, robbery, theft, driving under the influence, and other forms of behavior that either cause objective harm to others or have a strong likelihood of doing so. Where laws prohibit non-harmful behaviors, Mill would suggest, the government is crossing boundaries that it has no moral right to cross.

For Mill, *liberty* is a key feature of human existence and wherever possible should not be limited by government. Harm or the possibility of harm to others is the only morally legitimate reason for placing limitations on liberty through the passing and enforcing of laws. Importantly, the harm principle suggests that people should be free to do anything else they may choose—even if their actions harm themselves, offend others, or are regarded as immoral. Advocates of *decriminalization* of so-called victimless crimes often appeal to the harm principle in support of their position. Arguably, behaviors such as personal recreational drug use, paying for sex, and gambling may be regarded as immoral by some but do not create any objective harm for anyone other than those who are voluntarily involved in the behavior. So long as the participants are competent adults, *consent* negates any wrongfulness. As such, citizens should enjoy the freedom to legally engage in such behaviors.

Appealing to the harmfulness or harmlessness of certain behaviors as justification for criminalization or legalization begs an important question: namely, "What counts as harm?" Aside from obvious instances of harm that result from violent behavior, there are numerous ways in which citizens harm one another physically, emotionally, and financially. As we saw in Chapter 2, most everything we do has some effect, however small it may be, on others. In many cases, the harms we do to others are not obvious, direct, or immediately experienced. One could argue, however, that they are harms nevertheless. Thus one of the biggest difficulties in applying the harm principle—as well as in the making of laws—is determining what types of "harms" warrant legal coercion.

To this question, Feinberg suggests that the Harm Principle justifies coercive government action where behaviors harm people's *basic welfare interests*, including "continued life, health, economic sufficiency, and political liberty."[29] Wearing a T-shirt with a radical political message may cause anger and disgust, but is not likely to jeopardize the basic interests listed above. In addition, driving while intoxicated carries a significant risk of harming others' interests in continued life and physical health and the government may therefore be justified in prohibiting it.

Paternalism

In his description of the harm principle, John Stuart Mill suggested that laws are designed to protect people from *one another*, not from themselves. Of course, laws sometimes *are* intended to protect people from themselves, and governments *do* use coercion for this purpose (e.g., seat belt laws, laws prohibiting the possession of dangerous drugs). When governments seek to protect citizens from themselves, this is called **paternalism**. In its most general sense, total error is E_2. The possible reduction of error $E_1 - E_2$ compared to the original error E_1 is called proportionate reduction of error (PRE). Here is how to express the idea in a mathematical form: PRE = $(E_1 - E_2)/E_1$. What this formula tells us is that the stronger the association between var_1 and var_2, the larger the difference between E_1 and E_2 ($E_1 - E_2$) and thus also the PRE. Apparently, a measure of association with such an excellent sense of proportionate reduction of error is preferred in statistical analysis.

In addition to the PRE meaning, there are other criteria for the selection of a measure of association. The most important consideration is measurement level. A measure used at a higher level (e.g., interval or ratio) may not be applicable to the lower (e.g., ordinal and nominal) levels. A measure used at a lower level can be applied to a higher level, though the data may need be categorized or regrouped to facilitate the calculations. Symmetry is another factor in the selection which may have an impact on measurement precision. Some measures are based on symmetrical assumptions while others are designed for asymmetrical relations. Sometimes linearity of the relationship should also be taken into account.

<u>Measuring associations at the nominal level.</u> The measurement of association between two nominal variables reflects an idea of "frequency correspondence." The most frequently used measure is called Lambda (λ), sometimes also called Guttman's coefficient of predictability, which is based on the distribution of the modes of one variable under different conditions defined by different values of the other variable. The PRE logic for calculating the asymmetrical version of λ (i.e., λ_{yx}) goes like this. To predict the value of Y by its own mode (i.e., using the mode to represent all the possible values of Y) would have a total error of $E_1 = N - M_y$ (N is the sample size and M_y is the frequency of the mode or the count of cases that actually take the mode value on Y). Now, suppose we know the values of another variable X and that X is related to Y. To predict the value of Y by its mode under each condition corresponding to each value of X would have a total error of $E_2 = N - \Sigma m_y$ (m_y is the frequency of the mode of Y under each value of X). The reduction of error of predicting Y by basing on X should be: $E_1 - E_2 = (N - M_y) - (N - \Sigma m_y) = \Sigma m_y - M_y$. Thus, λ_{yx} = PRE = $(E_1 - E_2)/E_1 = (\Sigma m_y - M_y)/(N - M_y)$. If the relationship is symmetrical, λ = PRE = $(E_1 - E_2)/E_1 = [(\Sigma m_x + \Sigma m_y) - (M_x + M_y)]/[2N - (M_x + M_y)]$.

The Lambda has a perfect PRE meaning as well as two different versions for accommodating both symmetrical and asymmetrical patterns of relations. It is also relatively easy to calculate. Therefore, it is frequently used at the nominal paternalism refers to a relationship of giving or aiding others in which an authority (e.g., government, organization) relates to those in need as a father would to his dependent children (*paternal* = "fatherly"). In the context of social policy, paternalism is evident where governmental power brokers assume responsibility for the (presumed) needs of its citizens, taking action through law or policy (e.g., penal, psychiatric) to meet those needs.

As a principle, paternalism holds that it is justifiable and morally permissible for the government to use law and policy to coercively protect people from themselves. Many would agree that persons who are *incompetent* (e.g., children, those with developmental disabilities) should be subject to paternalistic treatment. Feinberg, in fact, suggests that the government has a moral *duty* to intervene in such situations. However, protecting competent, rational adults from themselves is another matter. As Feinberg writes, doing so is "arrogant and demeaning." When involving competent adults, paternalism implies that "there are sharp limits to my right to govern myself . . . that others may intervene . . . to 'correct' my choices and then (worst of all) justify interference on the ground (how patronizing) that they know my own good better than I know it myself."[30] As most of us value *self-determination* or our capacity to find our own way through life and to make our own choices in everyday encounters, paternalistic laws can seem offensive and degrading—especially since these actions suggest that people are incapable of caring for themselves and need to be looked after by those who presumably "know best" or, at least, know better than they do.

A contemporary controversy involving paternalistic government policy is the practice of **civil commitment** or involuntary hospitalization for persons deemed mentally ill (though not necessarily legally incompetent) and presumed to be in need of psychiatric treatment. In such cases, the state confines a person to a hospital against that individual's will because it has judged the person to be: (1) mentally ill *and* (2) a "clear and present" danger to others, a danger to self, or "grossly disabled" and unable to adequately care for oneself. Where civil commitment is intended to protect the public from presumably dangerous persons, it might be justified by the harm principle. However, where it is used to protect people from themselves and impose psychiatric care on those who are judged unable to care for themselves, it is paternalistic in nature. Problematically, to some persons with mental health issues, the deprivation of liberty and the infringement on self-determination that accompanies such hospitalization is greatly resented. With this in mind, we might ask, "Is it morally permissible for governments to deprive persons of basic interests in liberty and self-determination for purposes of treating them when they are not a danger to others and do not want psychiatric treatment?"[31]

Legal Moralism

Legal moralism is a position which holds that governments can and should pass laws to prohibit behaviors *if those behaviors are considered to be immoral*—even if they do not cause harm to self or others. When grounded in the perceived immorality of the behavior, laws that prohibit forms of private, consensual sexual behavior are examples of legal moralism. For example, sexual behaviors collectively referred to as "sodomy" were illegal in some states until relatively recently in U.S. history. Sodomy laws were not created to protect individuals from themselves or one another, but in the interest of preserving the moral integrity and tradition of communities.

It is this perceived need to preserve certain ways of life that is often used as a justification for legal moralism. The question, however, is whether the majority—or those with the power to create laws or influence the lawmaking process—have a moral right to force others to conform to their moral standards. In what, if any, cases does a group of people have a moral right to impose laws (and thus moral values) on other people who do not agree with them and have not consented to living by those rules and values?[32]

Legal scholar Joel Feinberg argues that every community needs certain core moral values by which all of its members should live. These core values are necessary for the well-being of the community and the survival of its members (e.g., those that prevent people from harming one another). Outside of these few, basic values, however, Feinberg suggests that communities are made *stronger* by leaving room for *diversity*. On this note, Emmett Barcalow offers the following observations:[33]

- History has demonstrated that forcing people to comply with rules with which they do not agree often produces resistance—sometimes of the violent, revolutionary type.
- Recognizing and accepting a certain degree of moral relativism within communities may be necessary for social cohesion.
- Communities change and, "it is futile and probably dangerous to try to block all changes to a community's way of life."
- Some ways of life are oppressive and immoral. Consider the keeping of slaves of the American South and the subordination of women and racial/ethnic minorities. Preserving certain ways of life is not desirable if those ways of life are morally questionable.
- Behavior which might be regarded as immoral or offensive is not usually "contagious." If homosexuality is tolerated or even accepted, for instance, most people will still be heterosexual; if prostitution were legalized, most people are still not going to seek out and solicit the services of prostitutes. Tolerating moral diversity will not likely produce significant changes to a community's way of life, as most members will remain committed to conventional values and behaviors.

Offensive Conduct

All of us are occasionally negatively affected—perhaps "harmed" in some sense—by others' rudeness, insensitivity, loud music, offensive body odor, distasteful clothing, and so on. According to Feinberg, however, these behaviors cannot rightfully be classified as "harmful":

> Not everything that we dislike or resent, and wish to avoid, is harmful to us . . . [E]xperiences can distress, offend, or irritate us without harming any of our [physical, psychological, or financial] interests. They come to us, are suffered for a time, and then go, leaving us as whole and undamaged as we were before.[34]

In other words, Feinberg argues that while experiences such as those listed above might cause temporary "unhappy mental states," they should not count as harms for legal purposes. While your body odor may cause me a brief unpleasant sensation, your insult may for a short time wound my pride, hurt my feelings, or cause me anger, and your T-shirt may momentarily shock my sensibilities, I have not been "harmed" in such a way that your behavior should be criminalized or otherwise prohibited or restricted by law. While I may experience temporary physical and psychological discomfort as a result of your behavior, you have not had any substantial negative effect on my basic interests. While many would agree that the effects of these behaviors are not "harmful" enough to justify legal intervention, they are nonetheless *offensive*. The question becomes, "Is the government morally justified in prohibiting behavior that *offends* others even if it produces no substantial harm?"

While Feinberg describes "harms" as those behaviors that impose upon others basic interests, "offensive" behavior "produces unpleasant or uncomfortable experiences—affronts to sense or sensibility, disgust, shock, shame, embarrassment, annoyance, boredom, anger, fear, or humiliation."[35] As examples, he suggests behaviors such as playing loud music in public; vomiting in public; using the American flag as a handkerchief; copulating in public; and wearing an ethnically, racially, or religiously derogatory T-shirt. While most people would agree that some offensive conduct should be prohibited, the question remains, which such behaviors are sufficiently offensive to warrant legal prohibition?

In response to the above question, Feinberg suggests that some offensive behavior may be considered a violation of people's *right to privacy* when it invades private space. If people have a moral right to be protected from certain experiences, the offensive behavior could be considered wrongful where it "deprive[s] . . . unwilling spectators of the power to determine for themselves whether or not to undergo a certain experience."[36] As well, the *seriousness* of the offense must be considered. Seriousness depends on the intensity and duration of the unpleasantness or discomfort, the number of people offended, as well as how much inconvenience would be caused in order to avoid or escape the experience.

Feinberg also notes that we should consider the social utility of the offensive behavior. Loud trains rumbling through our neighborhood at 2:00 A.M. or the smell of manure from a nearby farm may be offensive, yet both serve important social purposes. Their social utility may outweigh any unpleasant experience that we may be forced to endure. As well, we need to consider the importance of offensive behavior to those who engage in it. Some behaviors are important parts of people's lives and prohibiting them may stand to cause significant harm to their interests. The sight of an interracial or gay couple may offend some people, but the importance of love and friendship to those couples may outweigh the offense it (temporarily) causes others.

Finally, Feinberg tells us that the *intentions* of the actor must be considered. There is clearly a difference between conduct that is intended to be offensive and that of which offending others is not the primary purpose. For instance, wearing an offensive T-shirt for the mere purpose of offending others may be less permissible than wearing the same T-shirt because one is making a political statement. As well, it is easy enough for spectators to avoid looking at an offensive T-shirt.[37]

Summary

We have now spent some time exploring two significant issues in metaethics: determinism (in Chapter 3) and moral relativism (in this chapter). Clearly, both determinism and relativism present ethical challenges that warrant careful attention before doing any meaningful thinking about other moral concerns. This includes issues within the criminal justice system or those that otherwise involve criminal behavior.

Specifically within this chapter, the notion of moral relativism was contrasted with ethical objectivism and ethical universalism, and contemporary ethical relativism was examined mindful of its descriptive and normative variants. Finally, pragmatic relativism was considered. In part, this included commentary on the ways in which sociological functionalism helps account for ethical decision-making and whether these choices should be guided by the extent to which actions, laws, or policies fulfill (or fail to fulfill) their stated and useful purposes.

Regardless of our personal resolution to the issue of moral relativism, it encourages us to remember that each of us navigates our day-to-day responsibilities within a *pluralistic* society. As of this writing—and likely for the foreseeable future—there is not a single, overarching ethical code or series of principles to which we all subscribe. Even the U.S. Supreme Court has insisted that the moral permissibility of certain behaviors (e.g., sodomy, prostitution, pornography) be decided by "community standards" which, of course, vary from one community to another.[38] At the very least, we must seek to understand and be mindful of these differences. Ethnocentrism, dogmatism, and intolerance often produce more problems than they do good.

In the next chapter, we move on to a third problem of metaethics; namely, that of whether we *can* be moral. This question and the follow-up question of why we *should* be moral are matters of *moral psychology*. Having explored concerns of determinism and relativism, it is to the metaethical problem of *egoism* that we now turn.

Key Terms and Concepts

blood feuds *68*

civil commitment *80*

Comstock Act *77*

cultural variability *68*

descriptive relativism *68*

dogma *75*

dogmatism *75*

ethical objectivism *65*

ethical universalism *65*

ethnocentrism *74*

functionality (of moral beliefs and practices) *74*

harm principle *78*

honor killings *63*

legal moralism *80*

mala in se 66

mala prohibita 66

normative relativism *70*

objectivity *65*

paternalism *79*

pragmatism *72*

prescriptive relativism *70*

relativism *64*

Discussion Questions

1. Relativism argues that morality is linked to culture, historical time periods, and even subgroups. Explain what this means. How do the doctrines of ethical objectivism and ethical universalism contrast with the notion of relativism?

2. Using the example of "victimless" crimes (e.g., gambling, prostitution, drug use), explain how descriptive relativism provides an ethical basis for their decriminalization or their legalization. Do you believe that descriptive relativism is a sensible basis to propose the decriminalization or legalization of these offenses? To what extent does the notion of cultural variability assist you in your analysis? Justify your response.

3. Do you believe there is an objective sense in which "right" and "wrong" can be identified? What does the notion of metaethical relativism say about this? If there is no objective ethical basis by which behavior can be deemed "right" or "wrong," what are the implications for criminal justice practice (consider law enforcement, court administration, and correctional work, specifically)?

4. Explain the doctrine of pragmatic relativism. In what way is sociological functionalism related to it? How

does the doctrine of pragmatic relativism (and sociological functionalism) operate in everyday criminal courtroom deliberations? In decisions linked to probation or parole? In decisions to waive (or not) juveniles to the adult system?

5. How might ethnocentrism and dogmatism impact police decisions to stop and arrest suspects? Consider the phenomena of racial and criminal profiling. Ethically speaking, how would you reconcile the presence of ethnocentrism and dogmatism in criminal justice with decisions to arrest, convict, and sentence the undocumented, foreign nationals, or those who live in the United States but whose values, beliefs, customs, and practices differ from those found within mainstream culture?

6. Identify a recent criminal case in which cultural variability was an important component of determining how the criminal justice system functioned. Do you believe that the criminal justice system is obligated to demonstrate tolerance and open-mindedness when confronted with behavior deemed unlawful? Why or why not? Justify your response.

Endnotes

1. Neve Gordon, "Honor Killings," *Iris: A Journal about Women* (April 1, 2001). Available at http://www.israelsoccupation.info (retrieved July 28 2011).

2. "Missouri Couple Sentenced to Die in Murder of their Daughter," 16, *New York Times* (December 20, 1991); Steve Bird, "Sister is Stabbed to Death for Loving the Wrong Man," *The Times* (June 17, 2006).

3. Gilbert Harman and Judith Jarvis Thomson, *Moral Relativism and Moral Objectivity* (London: Blackwell, 1996).

4. Donald Borchert and David Stewart, *Exploring Ethics* (New York: Macmillan, 1986), pp. 68–69.

5. Ibid.; Harman and Thomson, *Moral Relativism and Moral Objectivity*.

6. Emmett Barcalow, *Moral Philosophy: Theories and Issues* (Belmont, CA: Wadsworth, 1998), quotes from page 44.

7. Paul K. Moser and Thomas L. Carson (Eds.), *Moral Relativism: A Reader* (New York: Oxford University Press, 2000).

8. Harman and Thomson, *Moral Relativism and Moral Objectivity*.

9. Brett L. Billet, *Cultural Relativism in the Face of the West: The Plight of Women and Children* (New York: Palgrave MacMillan, 2005); Samuel Fleischacker, *Integrity and Moral Relativism* (Boston, MA: Brill Academic Publisher, 1997).

10. See, e.g., Lisa Heldke and Peg O'Connor, *Oppression, Privilege and Resistance: Theoretical Readings on Racism, Sexism, and Heterosexism* (New York: McGraw-Hill, 2003).

11. David Wong, "Relativism." In P. Singer (Ed.), *A Companion to Ethics* (Malden, MA: Blackwell, 1993).

12. Robert Streiffer, *Moral Relativism and Reasons for Action* (New York: Routledge, 2003)

13. Jane K. Cowan and Marie-Benedicte Dembour (Eds.), *Culture and Rights: Anthropological Perspectives* (Cambridge: Cambridge University Press, 2001).

14. Wong, "Relativism."

15. Lawrence E. Hazelrigg, *Social Science and the Challenge of Relativism: Claims of Knowledge* (Tallahassee, FL: Florida State University, 1989).

16. Richard Taylor, *Good and Evil* (Amherst, NY: Prometheus, 1999), p. 56.

17. Mi-Kyoung Lee, *Epistemology After Protagoras: Responses to Relativism in Plato, Aristotle, and Democritus* (New York: Oxford University Press, 2005).

18. Taylor, *Good and Evil*, p. 59.

19. Ibid.

20. Ibid.

21. James Rachels, *The Elements of Moral Philosophy* (New York: McGraw-Hill, 1986), pp. 13, 20–21.

22. Kingsley Davis, "The Sociology of Prostitution," *American Sociological Review*, 2(5), 746–755 (1937).

23. Hugo Bedau and Paul G. Cassell, *Debating the Death Penalty: Should America Have Capital Punishment? The Experts on Both Sides Make Their Best Case* (New York: Oxford University Press, 2006).

24. Rachels, *The Elements of Moral Philosophy*, pp. 23–24.

25. See, e.g., Kwame Anthony Appiah, *Ethics and Identity* (Princeton, NJ: Princeton University Press, 2005).

26. James Davidson Hunter, *Culture Wars: The Struggle to Define America* (New York: Basic Books, 1992).

27. Anthony Weston, *A 21st Century Ethical Toolbox* (New York: Oxford University Press, 2001), pp. 11–14.

28. John Stuart Mill, *On Liberty* (Indianapolis, IN: Hackett, 1978), p. 5.

29. Joel Feinberg, *Harm to Others* (vol. 1 of *The Moral Limits of Criminal Law*) (New York: Oxford University Press, 1984), p. 45; quoted in Barcalow, *Moral Philosophy*, p. 236.

30. Joel Feinberg, *Harm to Self* (vol. 3 of *The Moral Limits of Criminal Law*) (New York: Oxford University Press, 1986), p. 23.

31. See, e.g., Bruce A. Arrigo, *Punishing the Mentally Ill: A Critical Analysis of Law and Psychiatry* (Albany, NY: State University of New York Press, 2002); Judith Lynn Failer, *Who Qualifies for Rights: Homelessness, Mental Illness and Civil Commitment* (Ithaca, NY: Cornell University Press, 2002); Elyn R. Saks, *Refusing Care: Forced Treatment and the Rights of the Mentally Ill* (Chicago, IL: University of Chicago Press, 2002).

32. Barcalow, *Moral Philosophy*.

33. Ibid., pp. 244–245.

34. Joel Feinberg, *Harm to Others,* p. 188; quoted in Barcalow, *Moral Philosophy,* p. 239.

35. Joel Feinberg, *Offense to Others* (vol. 2 of *The Moral Limits of Criminal Law*) (New York: Oxford University Press, 1984), p. 5; quoted in Barcalow, *Moral Philosophy*, p. 239.

36. Feinberg, *Offense to Others*, p. 23.

37. Barcalow, *Moral Philosophy,* p. 241.

38. Robert Solomon, *Ethics: A Brief Introduction* (New York: McGraw-Hill, 1984), quote from page 4.

5

Why Should We Be Good?

In 2008, Jonathan Lutman—a two-year veteran of the Slidell (Louisiana) Police Department—was arrested and charged with nine counts of theft and four counts of malfeasance. On each of the nine occasions, Lutman's thefts occurred while he was on duty, during legal traffic stops of Hispanic males. Allegedly, he would ask for their wallets, remove the cash, and then return the wallets (often without the victims knowing anything was missing). In all likelihood, Lutman singled out Hispanics as victims assuming that they would not report the thefts to police—assuming that, through careful selection of victims, he could get away with wrongdoing. Slidell Chief of Police Freddie Drennan commented, "He used his position to steal from these people. He used his position for personal gain."[1]

In an incident similar in an important respect, in 2009 two Pennsylvania judges were charged with accepting $2.6 million in kickbacks for putting teenagers in private detention centers run by PA Child Care LLC and Western PA Child Care LLC from 2003 to 2006. Teenagers were brought before the judges without attorneys, given trials lasting only minutes, and routinely sentenced to incarceration in privately run juvenile facilities for minor offenses. Many of the teenagers had no prior records, and some were incarcerated for offenses as petty as writing prank notes and stealing loose change from cars.[2]

Each of the cases above features criminal justice professionals who exploited opportunities to reap personal benefit from moral wrongdoing. *Opportunistic theft* by police officers and judges accepting *kickbacks* for sentencing delinquents to incarceration are but two examples of ethically and morally impermissible behaviors that occur with some frequency in criminal justice and other professional contexts. Of course, moral wrongdoing is not limited to criminal justice, nor is it limited to the professional environment. Avoiding acts that are morally forbidden and engaging in acts that are morally obligatory present challenges around every corner of our personal and professional lives—particularly when we stand to benefit from doing the wrong thing, or bring some harm or inconvenience to ourselves by doing the right thing.

Morality demands maintaining integrity in both personal and professional realms. Yet morality is not simply about having the capacity for integrity; it is about exercising that capacity. An important question thus becomes, "*What motivates us to exercise (or fail to exercise) that capacity?*" What reason do we have to avoid moral wrongdoing? To do the "right" thing? To act with justice, and to be honest, giving, tolerant, or caring? In short, what motivates us to be moral, especially when we stand to benefit from immorality?

THE RING OF GYGES

The case of Jonathan Lutman described above is in some ways similar to the tale of Gyges, as told by Plato (427 B.C.E.–347 B.C.E.) in his *Republic*.[3] Gyges was a poor shepherd who lived in the service of the King of Lydia. One day, a violent rainstorm and earthquake opened a hole in the ground. Coming upon this chasm, he proceeded to explore it, finding a corpse wearing nothing but a gold ring. Gyges put on the ring, ascended from the hole in the ground, and continued about his normal business. Shortly thereafter, as he was sitting among several others at a monthly meeting, he began playing with the ring. As he twisted the hoop of the ring toward himself, he became invisible. The others went on talking as if he had left. As he turned the hoop outward, he became visible again. The ring, it seemed, had the power to make the wearer disappear. Recognizing the opportunities for personal gain the ring presented, Gyges began to make use of his newfound power. He immediately became one of the king's messengers and, from within his new position, proceeded to seduce the queen, plot with her to murder the king, and to take over the kingdom. By way of his power of invisibility, Gyges went from poor shepherd to powerful and wealthy ruler of Lydia.[4]

The ethical question that arises from Plato's tale is as follows: "Why should we be moral when we know (or, at least, think) that we can reap tremendous benefit from acting immorally?" Moreover, why should we do the "right" thing if we can (or, again, think we can) do the "wrong" thing *and get away with it*? None of us will likely have the opportunity to become invisible, but we all certainly have had and will be faced with situations in which we stand to benefit personally and/or professionally from immoral actions that can easily go overlooked or for which there are no negative consequences. What, then, motivates or should motivate us to avoid moral wrong-doing and to undertake that which is morally good?

THE FORMS AND EFFECTIVENESS OF REWARD AND PUNISHMENT

One possible response to the question, "why be moral?" draws upon reward and punishment as incentives for behavior. In the story of Gyges, Plato implies a human nature that is **egoistic**, or *motivated by self-interest*. We do the right thing, Plato assumes, only because we fear that if we do the wrong thing we will be caught and punished. If, like Gyges, we could do whatever we wanted—knowing we would never be caught—we would all act with little or no concern for the welfare of others, quite possibly even causing harm to others along the way. That people will act immorally if not somehow prevented from doing so is a common theme informing many depictions of human nature, and is a key assumption informing systems of government, codes of law, religion, and professional conduct, and other sets of rules and regulations. Each of these either explicitly or implicitly relates to the threat of sanctions to encourage compliance with identified standards of right and wrong conduct. In other words, they are efforts to motivate people to do the right thing by, in part, instilling a fear of doing the wrong thing. Various forms and degrees of sanction are presumed necessary to keep our egoistic tendencies "in check" and to motivate us to balance our own interests against the welfare of others.[5] But is the motivation derived from fear of sanctions enough to ensure that we do the right thing? Even if so, does doing the "right" thing because we fear being caught and punished make us "moral" people?

External Sanctions: From the Law and God

Modern legal systems were constructed as a source of formal social control—to ensure behavioral conformity and social order by threatening citizens with various forms of sanction for violating criminal codes, breaching contracts, disobeying authority, and so forth. Yet how effective is the threat of sanctions posed by law? As a matter of fact, violations of the law *usually* go unpunished. Most of us have committed at least minor infractions of the law at one time or another (e.g., speeding, underage alcohol consumption, illegally copying or downloading music). It is likely that, when contemplating these behaviors, we concluded that there was little *chance* of being caught, and/or that the *consequences* of being caught were not significant enough to be of much concern. In other words, we feel fairly certain that, most of the time, we can get away with it or that we can live with whatever consequences may come. The threat of sanction thus proves often to be ineffective in preventing moral wrongdoing.

Even if deterrence by threat of sanction were an effective motivator, however, it is still insufficient for morality. Our reason for not speeding, not stealing, and not lying must be something other than or at least in addition to simply attempting to avoid negative consequences. Even where laws, codes, and regulations are effective in reducing wrongdoing, they do little in the way of influencing our underlying desires. In other words, just because we are afraid to commit wrongdoings does not mean that we do not still want to. Increasing *fear* by, for example, increasing the severity of punishment may increase conformity, but it does not serve to develop our moral sensibilities.

In fact, people do not always engage in moral wrongdoing even in situations where they know they can get away with it. Think of opportunities you may have had to take something that does not belong to you, "cheat" on a spouse or lover, break a promise to a friend, or lie for personal gain but elected to do otherwise. Why? Most likely, you were motivated by something other than the simple fear of being caught. Moreover, most of us would probably agree that we would not *want* to live in such a world. Would we feel comfortable with a spouse or lover who was faithful only because she or he was afraid of being caught? Would we want our friends to keep promises only because they feared the consequences of not doing so?

Some will argue that, even where moral wrongdoing goes undetected by human authorities, it is nonetheless always detected by divine authority. In these cases, it is argued that God provides a *source of motivation* or *reason* for avoiding wrongdoing and honoring our moral obligations.[6] More specifically, the belief that gives rise to that motivation is that God rewards the good and punishes the evil—in this world or some other. The answer to the question, "Why be moral?" becomes the promise of divine reward and the avoidance of divine punishment. Although religion may have an important role to play in morality, in this case we must confront the same problem raised above; namely, that behaving morally simply because we fear the consequences of not doing so is insufficient for genuine morality. Even if religion has a role in our motivation, the promise of divine reward and the fear of divine punishment should not be our sole source of inspiration for moral behavior (more on this below).

Internal Sanctions: Conscience and Guilt

Punishment for immoral behavior need not come from only external sources such as the legal system or divine authorities. An equally important type of sanction emerges from our own conscience when our choices and behaviors contradict moral values and principles.[7] **Conscience** typically refers to our awareness that certain actions are morally right or wrong. To "have a conscience" implies that we are aware that the actions we undertake or those that we intend to undertake have a *moral quality*.[8] Such an awareness typically includes a set of internally felt standards by which we judge ourselves, and a corresponding experience of "bad conscience" when our actions contradict those internal standards.[9] Importantly, conscience is not something we have to "use"; rather, it is part of who we are. We need not consciously reflect upon whether our actions are congruent with our inner standards for our conscience to have influence. Our self-evaluations operate largely beneath our conscious awareness.

The experience of "bad conscience" noted above is typically described as **guilt**—the anxiety or emotional discomfort felt when we deviate from those internalized values and standards of conduct.[10] Unlike legal guilt, the "guilt" derived from our conscience is something personal that results from a psychological process. In this way, guilt differs from religious or legal punishment in that it is a *self-imposed punishment* or sanction; moreover, it is *emotional self-punishment.*[11] Because it is self-imposed and emotional in nature, guilt differs from other forms of sanction in its tendency to continue *even after* other forms of sanction disappear. In this sense, it may be the strongest of all sanctions. In another sense, however, it may be the weakest and *least reliable* of sanctions.

On one hand, guilt's effectiveness as a motivation for moral behavior is limited in that it is contingent upon our *belief* that we have harmed someone or violated some moral standard. Absent this belief (or if we *rationalize* our conduct), guilt fails to function as an effective sanction (see Box 5.1). We must, of course, already have developed moral sensibilities or inner standards for the process of self-judgment to unfold. If we haven't such sensibilities, we will not experience guilt; if we do not *feel* or *experience* guilt or remorse how is it to serve as a motivating factor in our choices and actions?

BOX 5.1
Rationalizing Police Deviance

In their theory of delinquent behavior, Sykes and Matza proposed that lawbreakers are able to protect themselves from feelings of guilt and negative self-image by rationalizing or justifying their conduct. What they referred to as "techniques of neutralization" are of five basic types: denial of responsibility, denial of injury, denial of victim, condemnation of condemners, and appeal to higher loyalties. As Kappeler et al. suggest, these methods of rationalization or justification may also be useful in helping us understand forms of police deviance:

- *Denial of responsibility* ("they made me do it"). The injury caused (or that could have been caused) by an officer's actions was due to forces beyond her or his control. In the context of police work, *violence* may be regarded as an appropriate and necessary reaction to defiant citizens/suspects. Where force or excessive force is used, the officer's belief that she or he was provoked by the citizen may allow the officer to rationalize her or his behavior. Doing so shifts responsibility for the use of force away from the officer and onto the citizen.
- *Denial of injury* ("no innocent got hurt"). Wrongfulness depends upon whether anyone— or anyone innocent—was hurt by the action. Stealing from suspects (e.g., drugs, money) for personal gain, violating constitutional rights of suspects to make an arrest or secure a conviction,

and abusing authority to maintain order are each excusable as no real injury was caused.
- *Denial of victim* ("they deserved it"). The injury or harm caused was not wrong given the circumstances under which they occurred. In many cases, this involves rationalizing the harm as a form of punishment or as justice. The use of force, for instance, can be rationalized as justifiable punishment in certain situations or with respect to certain types of people. Those who run from police, use illegal drugs, or defy authority are "threats"—predetermined as dangerous by virtue of who they are and in need of "punishment."
- *Condemnation of condemners* ("they don't know anything"). Attention is shifted away from the wrongdoing and the wrongdoer and toward those who disapprove of the action(s): the exclusionary rule is simply a "loophole" for criminals which makes police work more difficult; judges are "soft on crime"; citizens who bring lawsuits or complaints against officers are "hostile" or resentful toward the police; those who would pass judgment on the behavior of officers do not understand the realities of the job. In each case, the problem lies not with the officer's motives or behaviors, but with the rules, motives, perception of those who would control and judge them.

- *Appeal to higher loyalties* ("protect your own"). The most powerful of techniques of neutralization, appeal to higher loyalties involves perceiving certain (informal) norms as more important or as involving a higher loyalty than abidance by formal laws, rules, or norms. Larger societal norms or the formal norms of the organization can and should be sacrificed in the interest of abiding by norms of the smaller group to which the officer belongs (i.e., those of police subculture). The informal norm of secrecy and loyalty to other officers overrides the formal norm of not lying, giving rise to perjury or false testimony. Protecting another officer—even when this involves unethical and/or illegal conduct—is expected and regarded as noble as it demonstrates loyalty and solidarity.

Sources: Victor Kappeler, Richard Sluder, and Geoffrey Alpert, *Forces of Deviance: Understanding the Dark Side of Policing*, 2nd ed. (Prospect Heights, IL: Waveland Press, 1998), pp. 113–125; Gresham Sykes and David Matza, "Techniques of Neutralization: A Theory of Delinquency," *American Sociological Review*, 22(6), 664–670 (1957).

A second problem with conscience and guilt as motivations for moral behavior is that their strength is, for many people, limited. Most of us have at some point in our lives done something or some things for which we harbor no pride. Perhaps we hurt a close friend, either intentionally or through neglect. Perhaps we even "felt bad" or guilty about our actions. Nevertheless, we *learned to live with it*. The simple fact about guilt is that, even when we experience it, we typically "get over it."[12] For several reasons, then, guilt and conscience seem to have limited power in our everyday moral lives. Some people seem incapable of guilt, perhaps "having no conscience"; others rationalize individual instances of immoral behavior to avoid feeling guilt in that situation; and still others feel some sense of *temporary* guilt, but soon get over it. Because guilt and conscience are *internal*, we can confront and deal with them internally as well (see Boxes 5.1 and 5.2). Consequently, while conscience may play a role—and perhaps an important one—in morality, it is not sufficient in itself as a motivation for ethical conduct.

BOX 5.2

Rationalization and Cheating among College Students

As we saw in Box 5.1, oftentimes we can avoid the feeling of guilt if we *rationalize* or in some way justify our behaviors to ourselves. Another example might be the various justifications that college students sometimes use to excuse cheating or plagiarism. Research indicates that as many as two-thirds of college students have cheated on a major exam/assignment at some point in their college career. While rationalizing our immoral conduct may not allow us to escape punishment from authorities (e.g., professors, university officials), it often protects us from self-punishment. Consider how the following types of thinking allow students to avoid the feeling of guilt that would otherwise be attached to academic dishonesty:

- "Here at the University of _____, you must cheat to stay alive. There's so much work and the quality of materials from which to learn, books, professors, is so bad that there's no other choice."

- "Everyone has test files in fraternities . . . If you don't [cheat], you're at a great disadvantage."
- "If our leaders can commit heinous acts and then lie before Senate committees about their total ignorance and innocence, *then why can't I cheat at least a little?*"

In each of these cases, students are justifying their behavior. In other words, they are identifying what they believe to be reasons that defensibly excuse their immoral conduct. Rationalization prevents the psychological mechanism of guilt from working as it should. If we can convince ourselves that we were justified in behaving immorally, we will not "feel bad" about acting immorally.

Source: Donald McCabe, "The Influence of Situational Ethics on Cheating Among College Students," *Sociological Inquiry*, 62(3), 365–374 (1992).

level. Relying solely on the mode while ignoring other values, however, presents a problem of various degrees of insensitivity. Especially when the modes of one variable remain the same across the values of the other variable, Lambda would become zero even if there is an actual relationship between the two variables.

In view of this problem, researchers may need to use more precise measures of association based on the cross-tabulation of data. One such measure is Goodman and Kruskal's tau-y, which applies to asymmetrical relations. The advantage of tau-y is that it takes into account all conditional as well as marginal frequency distributions, and therefore is usually more accurate and sensitive than λ_{yx}. The calculation of tau-y follows the PRE logic. We will leave this out as it is more complicated than Lambda. Computer statistical software sometimes produces other measures of association as well. In SPSS/PC+, for example, a measure called uncertainty coefficient is also calculated and the specific logic can be found in its statistical manual. Another measure is the famous Chi-square (X^2), which does not have exact PRE meaning but is very important in statistical testing. We will discuss some of the measures of association based on X^2 in the next section.

<u>Measuring associations at the ordinal level.</u> The measurement of association between two ordinal variables reflects an idea of "rank-order correlation." The correlation has a positive or negative sign to indicate its direction (note the notions of correlation and direction make little sense, if any, at the nominal level). The most frequently used measure is Goodman and Kruskal's Gamma (G). Instead of focusing on the mode or the median, Gamma captures the relationships between all pairs of values on the two variables. This is similar to the logic of tau-y in improving the measurement precision from λ_{yx}. The PRE logic for calculating Gamma addresses the question of how much error could be reduced when predicting the relative rank-order of any two cases on one variable according to their known rank-order on another variable. The calculation of Gamma requires figuring out two quantities: (1) the number of same-ordered pairs (called concordant pairs) of cases, which have the same ranking on both variables; and (2) the number of different-ordered pairs (called discordant pairs) of cases, which have the opposite ranking on the two variables involved. The first quantity is denoted by N_s, and the second, N_d. The sum of N_s and N_d is always $N(N-1)/2$ (N is the sample size), if these are the only values of the variables. Here it is the difference of N_s and N_d that interests us. The larger the difference, the stronger the relationship between the two variables. If N_s is bigger than N_d, then the relationship will be positive; if N_s is smaller than N_d, then the relationship will

THE MORAL SUFFICIENCY OF REWARD AND PUNISHMENT

What each of the above discussions—guilt, God, and the law—have in common is the idea that we are or at least can be motivated to be moral by either expectation of reward or, more commonly, fear of punishment or other negative consequences. Consequences—both positive and negative—can, in some cases, be *useful*. Yet the utility of consequences is limited to instances where there is a *need to compensate* for a lack of morality. To illustrate, consider the situation of young children. Most parenting practices rely on the imposition of punishment or the granting of rewards for right and wrong actions. However, parents rely on reward and punishment only because children have yet to acquire a sufficient understanding of right and wrong (see Chapter 7 on moral development for more details). However, in adults with presumably more developed moral capacities, being a good person or doing the right thing requires motivation other than or in addition to reward and punishment. Several reasons for this are worth considering.

Reward, Punishment, and Self-Interest

For most moral philosophers and the general public alike, morality does not consist solely of doing what is in one's own best interest.[13] Concern for one's self is inevitable and perhaps desirable. As well, there are many ways and situations in which morality and self-interest coincide. Being honest, for example, can be both moral *and* in one's personal best interests (more on this in the next chapter). Yet when our response to the question, "Why be moral?" principally focuses on the possibility of suffering negative consequences or securing some reward for ourselves, then we are indirectly citing self-interest as the most salient reason for our actions. As we will see in Chapter 7, developed moral decision-making is typically thought to involve more than a concern for consequences to oneself.

The Need for Reward/Punishment Reflects an Absence of Morality

Prussian philosopher Immanuel Kant (1724–1804) argued that neither reward nor punishment should be regarded as incentives to action. We should not do good deeds because of the expectation of some reward; and we should not avoid evil deeds because of the expectation of punishment. Kant makes a provocative argument that motivations involving reward and punishment in fact demonstrate a *lack of morality*.[14] If, for instance, correctional officers refrain from accepting bribes for fear of being disciplined, they have failed to recognize either the wrongfulness inherent in the act of bribery, or the harm potentially caused to others (e.g., family, fellow officers, the image of the department) as a result of those actions. If we are truthful or honor our obligations only because we fear the consequences of not being or doing so, we cannot say that we embody honesty or that we recognize the moral value of honoring obligations in the first place. One who embodies the virtue of honesty, for example, will be so inclined even in the absence of rewards, punishments, and other nonmoral incentives.

As has been emphasized several times throughout the beginning chapters of this text, morality is not merely a matter of doing the right thing, but also of having the right reasons for doing those things. While many of us may believe that we are moral because we refrain from acting immorally, Kant reminds us that the *absence of immorality does not equal morality*.[15] It may be unsettling to consider that simply because we have abided by the law, been faithful to our lovers, and displayed honesty, trustworthiness, responsibility, and so on throughout the majority of our lives, we are not necessarily "moral" people by this logic. In short, being good is as much about character, intention, values, virtues, and principles—in short, *why* we do the right thing— as it is about *whether* we do the right thing.

Reward and Punishment Are Impediments to Morality

Might it be that rewards and punishments are not only insufficient for morality, but also serve to *prevent* the development and sustenance of morality? As Kant suggests, "a man [sic] who is rewarded for good conduct will repeat that conduct *because it is rewarded*."[16] Similarly, "one who is punished for evil conduct *will hate not the conduct, but the punishment*."[17] Rewards and punishments do tend to shape our decisions and actions, but their ultimate purpose is simply to encourage us to repeat the good and refrain from the bad. In other words, reward and punishment are not intended to encourage us to reflect on the morality of those decisions and actions. Indeed, we can encourage people to refrain from undesirable behavior by putting rewards and sanctions in place to mold behavior; yet doing so will do nothing to alter the underlying motivations that gave rise to the behavior in the first place.[18]

If our goal is simply to encourage certain forms of conduct and to discourage other forms of conduct, sanctions of various sorts can be effective. On the other hand, if our goal is to encourage the development of thoughts and feelings conducive to morality, reward and punishment will be of little value. Again, we should keep in mind that morality consists not only of "doing" the right thing, but also of understanding *why* it is right or, alternatively, why it is wrong. Instilling fear of consequences through the imposition of punishment is, as Kant noted, *teaching a person to hate the consequences rather than the act itself*. Rather than being or becoming moral people, we simply live in fear of being immoral.

For this reason, Kant argued that "it is wrong for religion to preach that men [sic] should avoid doing evil in order to escape eternal punishment," because people will fear the punishment rather than recognize and accept the wrongfulness of the deed itself.[19] We could say the same about law, parenting, the system of education, health, professional codes of conduct within criminal justice, and so forth. Morality requires us to develop an appreciation for the wrongfulness of our actions and be motivated to avoid them because of that wrongfulness rather than (or at least in addition to) negative consequences (see Box 5.3).

BOX 5.3

Desistance from Crime and Offender Rehabilitation

In Chapter 9, we will look more closely at the moral problem of criminal punishment and the purported goals of punishing offenders. For now, let's consider how the logic of reward and punishment might be applied in the context of desistance from crime and offender rehabilitation. It is often claimed that deterrence is an effective crime-reduction strategy. Yet a person who is successfully deterred from committing criminal offenses is not likely to refrain from such behavior because she or he genuinely understands that these actions are wrong. Instead, the individual simply fears the consequences attached to the ongoing commission of these criminal acts. These consequences or penalties are likely to include additional if not increasing amounts of prison time, resulting in devastating outcomes for the individual's personal and professional life.

Offender recovery and reform, on the other hand, depend on meaningful forms of rehabilitation that teach ex-offenders to reconstruct various facets of their lives. This includes such things as their relationships, their outlook toward work, their commitment to change, their response to authority figures, etc. In short, the key is to identify the barriers that stand in the way of recovery (whether self-imposed or imposed by society), to work through them, and then to learn from these impediments. In contrast with deterred offenders, reformed or rehabilitated offenders come to appreciate the wrongfulness of their past criminal actions when experiencing a change in character and, thus, motivation. In other words, "making good" entails a form of "moral development," if you will (more on this in Chapter 7). In this context, rewards and/or punishments are simply inadequate when it comes to rebuilding one's life and doing things for the right reason. In fact, the problem with a system of rewards and punishments is that, in some ways, it can function to prevent or inhibit precisely the sort of moral character necessary to desist from crime, and to experience personal insight.

_____

Source: David Garland, *Punishment and Modern Society* (Chicago, IL: University of Chicago Press, 1990); Elliott Currie, *Confronting Crime: An American Challenge* (New York: Pantheon, 1985); for an interesting study of crime desistance, see Shadd Maruna, *Making Good: How Ex-Convicts Reform and Rebuild Their Lives* (Washington, DC: American Psychological Association, 2002).

RELIGION AS SOURCE AND MOTIVATION FOR MORALITY

Ethics and religion have become nearly synonymous for many people, with religion serving as both a source of morality and a as a point of moral reference (see Box 5.4).[20] Indeed, nearly all cultures in all time periods evidence religious belief, and in many those beliefs are regarded as a source of and motivation for morality.[21] Yet to what extent can and should religion serve as a foundation for morality? Within ethics, answers to questions of morality and moral psychology that appeal to religion are typically categorized as variations of **Divine Command Theory**, which argues that certain actions are good or bad, moral or immoral, because they are approved or disapproved of by God (i.e., because God, the Bible, Koran, etc., say so). While religion plays an important role in the lives of many people, reliance on any religion as a source of moral values and a reason for moral belief should proceed with several reservations in mind.

Necessary Belief?

One of the biggest limitations of relying on religion to answer questions of moral significance is the implication that *there is no morality unless one believes in God*. Having certain kinds of religious belief is thus a *necessary condition* for morality. As such, people who do not believe in a higher power or some otherworldly source that accounts for our very existences cannot hope to be moral unless they first convert to the particular faith in question. Most of us, however, would agree that it is at least possible for a person to be moral without sharing in a particular set of religious or spiritual beliefs. In fact, many moral philosophers would argue that *belief in God is not necessary for morality*.[22] It is not only possible but common for people to embody integrity, to make morally sound choices, and to act in virtuous ways out of concern for humanity, respect for other people, compassion, and other motives that are not necessarily linked with a belief in a higher power. While religion may help some people to clarify their moral values and principles, it is not *necessary* as motivation for morality.

Common Ground

A second important limitation of relying on religion as a source of morality is what is termed the **problem of common ground**. It is notable that religious reasoning often extends only to people who share in that reasoning. It is generally understood within ethics, however, that for something to

BOX 5.4
Civil Religion and Flag Desecration

There are many controversies in criminology/criminal justice that have a religious or near-religious dimension to them. One such act that has brought decades of public concern, intense legal battles, and various forms of social control is that of desecrating the American flag. Throughout American history, repeated efforts have been made—sometimes successfully, other times less so—to criminalize what are thought to be improper and offensive uses of the Stars and Stripes. From politically charged acts such as flag burnings to controversial (and arguably distasteful) creative and artistic representations of Old Glory, destruction and desecration of the American flag has always elicited powerful emotional reactions from many among the American public. Yet why and how is it that a piece of cloth generates so much controversy?

In virtually all cultures, certain symbols are held to be "sacred" and expected to be cherished, honored, and revered. Because, as Michael Welch writes, it is "imbued with patriotic qualities of sacred proportion" and is characterized by "deep emotional—virtually religious—attachment," desecration of the flag often provokes particularly strong sentiments. The American flag is "emblematic of patriotism," and represents freedom, opportunity, and all that is good and right about the United States—it is the foremost icon of America's history, power, and way of life. Should we be surprised that, in a 1992 Gallop poll, 77 percent of Americans indicated that the burning of the flag should *not* be protected by the First Amendment?

Michael Welch argues that the American flag embodies *civil religion*—a "nonsectarian faith in which secular objects are transformed into sacred icons." In part because it embodies civil religion, social movements intent on protecting the flag have arisen and persisted throughout much of recent American history. Welch describes "rallying around the flag" as "a ritual infused with patriotic fervor ... resemble[ing] nondescript religion." Movements seeking to criminalize flag burning are one example of the interweaving of religion and the state. Though in principle they are to remain separate, church and state "frequently operate in concert to promote religion and patriotism, together becoming a potent unifying force in American culture." The influence of religious forces is evident even within the language of law, where the flag is a "venerated" object, its destruction a form of "desecration."

- What does the American flag symbolize to you and others around you (e.g., family, friends)?
- Do you consider the American flag to be a "sacred" object in the same way that religious symbols might be?
- How important is the American flag compared with other objects and symbols that you or others may hold to be "sacred"?
- Should desecration of the flag be protected under the First Amendment of the Constitution (freedom of speech)?
- If not, should burning of the flag be illegal? What about wearing a skirt made from the American flag? Wearing a T-shirt with a political message superimposed upon the flag? Flying the flag upside down? In what, if any, ways are these forms of flag "desecration" different?
- If illegal, what punishment should be proscribed for various forms of flag desecration?

Source: Michael Welch, *Flag Burning: Moral Panic and the Criminalization of Protest* (New York: Aldine de Gruyter, 2001), quotes taken from pages 4, 5, 31, and 32.

---

be a sufficient foundation for morality and/or a sufficient motivation for moral behavior, it should be reasonable to all people—regardless of religious beliefs, personal values, degree of education, and so forth. It should at least be possible for people of all faiths (as well as atheists and agnostics) to find *common ground* on important moral issues. Where this is not possible, principles and arguments drawn from religious sources lack the *universalizability* (or *generality*) toward which ethics strives.[23]

Ethical discussions should occur on some ground that is common for *all* interested parties.[24] Imagine, for example, that you must spend the rest of your life on an island with ten other people, each with a different religious or spiritual background. Obviously, there will be a need for some common moral foundation to ensure that you all could lead safe, secure, and satisfying lives together. While threats of divine punishment might be effective for those who share in that fear, you would be better off appealing to other kinds of values and principles that all could agree are necessary for the mutual benefit of everyone. In fact, resorting to religion in such a circumstance may well generate conflict and interfere with your building a mutually beneficial social climate (see Box 5.5).

BOX 5.5
Religion and the Practice of Capital Punishment

Notwithstanding the supposed need for separation of Church and state, some have argued that religious considerations *should* play an important role in the development and implementation of public policy. Exactly *what* religious teachings say about these issues is often a matter of interpretative conflict. One such issue over which much controversy exists and about which many Americans turn to religion for guidance and/or support for their position is that of the death penalty, or capital punishment for criminal offenders. As Christianity is by far the largest religious group in the United States, it is on Christian teachings that we focus.

Religious Support for Capital Punishment

Within the Christian faith groups, passages from the Old Testament (a.k.a. Hebrew Scriptures or Judaic Bible) are common reference points for the justification of capital punishment on retributive grounds (e.g., an "eye for an eye"). Problematically, a literal interpretation of the Old Testament would also have us support slavery and prescribe the death penalty for theft, blasphemy, laboring on the Sabbath, cursing one's parents, adultery, and a good number of other "crimes" that are no longer capital offenses and for which few—if any—people would continue to support death as a punishment. The wide range of offenses (no less than thirty-six) punishable by death in biblical times notwithstanding, in practice the penalty was rarely used. Procedural rules made it difficult, if not impossible, to impose a sentence of death. Accused offenders enjoyed a variety of safeguards designed to protect against wrongful execution. The lack of such safeguards in today's criminal justice system (or, at least, the seeming ineffectiveness of those that do exist) is sometimes cited by contemporary religious authorities as grounds for supporting capital punishment in principle, yet opposing it in practice.

Religious Opposition to Capital Punishment

Most Christian denominations and groups—both Eastern and Western—oppose capital punishment and support its abolition. In fact, since the 1950s and 1960s, the Catholic Church as well as all major denominations of Protestantism—save the Southern Baptists—have officially aligned themselves against the death penalty. Religious leaders who advocate the abolition of the death penalty have pointed generally to teachings advocating love (even for one's enemies), mercy, and forgiveness in the New Testament and to capital punishment's inconsistency with the effort "to promote respect for human life, to stem the tide of violence in our society and to embody the message of God's redemptive love." As well, some have argued that by executing a murderer, we are taking away her or his opportunity to repent. Finally, capital punishment is believed to "institutionalize retribution and revenge and to exacerbate violence by giving it official sanction."

The ambiguous and sometimes contradictory nature of scriptural references has given rise to a storied history of disparate interpretations and a general lack of consensus within the Christian tradition concerning the morality of capital punishment. Interestingly, not all—or even most—members of Christian denominations share in the official position of their group. Notwithstanding the opposition to capital punishment by virtually all major Christian denominations, as many as 80 percent of Christians continue to support capital punishment—slightly higher than support within the American population at large. As Robert Bohm suggests following Protestant scholar and journalist Reverend G. Aiken Taylor, much of the confusion may be a function of unanswered questions concerning the difference between the Christian personal ethic and Christian ethics as they apply to the maintenance of social order. Most Christians "tend to apply what the

Bible teaches us about how we—personally—should behave toward our neighbors . . . " However, it may be that this personal ethic should be understood differently from what the Bible teaches about ethics and the preservation of order within society. Perhaps the Bible encourages individual Christians to love, show mercy, and forgive, yet allows for governing bodies to impose capital punishment where it is in the interests of the common good. Indeed, as Bohm asks, does God have two different sets of rules—one ethic for individual Christians and a different ethic for governments and rulers?

We would seem to be without an authoritative answer to this and similar questions. Given the ambiguous nature of the Christian scriptures on the issue of capital punishment, the controversy over whether death is a morally acceptable sanction within the Christian paradigm will surely continue. In the meantime, as Bohm implies, the fact that such a lack of consensus is evident even within the Christian tradition should encourage us to question the value and desirability of religious influence on lawmaking and conceptions of justice—whether in the context of capital punishment or elsewhere.

Sources: Robert Bohm, *Deathquest II: An Introduction to the Theory and Practice of Capital Punishment* (Cincinnati, OH: Anderson, 2003), pp. 242–243; Avery Dulles, "Catholicism and Capital Punishment," *First Things*, 112, 30–35 (April 2001); Gail B. Szumski, Lynn Hall, and Susan Bursell (Eds.), *The Death Penalty: Opposing Viewpoints* (St. Paul, MN: Greenhaven, 1986), pp. 86–91.

Independent Good

In his *Euthyphro*, Plato narrates a conversation between Socrates and Euthyphro during which he posed the now-famous question, "Why does God command something?" Certainly, what God directs is good and right, but what Socrates was asking is why are *these things* commanded? Socrates proceeded to argue that God commands *that which is good*. There is a subtle but important logic to this: conduct is not right or good because God commands it; rather, God commands it because *it is* good. Murder, for instance, is not wrong because God commands that it is; rather, the wrongness of murder itself is what makes God command that it is so. In other words, murder is wrong because it *is* wrong.[25]

By the logic of Divine Command Theory, if God had commanded that we always lie, then lying would be good. If God had ordered that we murder our neighbors, be unfaithful to our spouses, and steal from our friends, then murder, infidelity, and stealing would be right. We could respond, however, that God would never command such things. If so, the question is *why?* If God would never direct us to lie, cheat, and steal, then God must understand that these things are not good, right, and just. If this is the case, then what is good, right, and just must exist *independent* of God's command.[26]

Arguably, God thus has some conception of goodness and justice and, through commanding it, shares and imparts this conception. If this is true, one implication is that determining what is good and right does not depend on a higher power—anyone could reach the same conclusions about what is right and good without relying on God to tell them. Consequently, religion may be beneficial, but is not *necessary* for morality. Even if we reserve an essential role for religion in our own lives, we should always be thinking critically about the underlying reasons for religious imperatives, not simply accepting them as presented.

EGOISM AND THE CRIMINAL JUSTICE SYSTEM: CORRUPTION IN POLICING AND CORRECTIONS

The motivation to consider our own interests when making choices may be an inevitable aspect of human nature. In fact, in and of itself the rational pursuit of self-interest is not necessarily morally problematic. However, excessive egoism can lead us to pursue personal gain at great expense to others—at times, directly and intentionally causing harm to others along the way. In the same respect, we can say that egoism is evident in criminal justice wherever practitioners place personal gain above morality and legality, acting so as to further self-interest at the expense of ethical considerations and the welfare of others and the greater community. In this way, self-interest and the desire for personal gain pose formidable challenges to everyday personal and professional decision-making.[27] For this reason, virtually every professional code of ethics either explicitly or implicitly cautions against allowing personal gain or self-interest to influence the performance of professional duties. For instance,

- A lawyer should not accept proffered employment if his personal interests or desires will . . . affect adversely the advice to be given or services to be rendered . . . (American Bar Association Model Code of Professional Responsibility)
- Members shall refrain from allowing personal interest to impair objectivity in the performance of duty . . . (American Correctional Association Code of Ethics)
- Psychologists refrain from taking on a professional role when personal [or other] interests [could] . . . impair their objectivity, competence, or effectiveness . . . (American Psychological Association Ethical Principles of Psychologists and Code of Conduct)

These formal prohibitions notwithstanding, instances of egoistic behavior in all fields of criminal justice are not uncommon. In fact, many forms of unethical conduct in criminal justice ultimately stem from egoistic motivations. Although there are other forms of professional deviance that are egoistically motivated, in this section we highlight several examples of *corruption* in both police and correctional contexts that illustrate the ways in which egoism can and sometimes does interfere with ethical responsibilities of criminal justice practitioners.

Police Corruption

Michael Johnston defines **police corruption** as actions that "exploit the powers of law enforcement in return for considerations of private-regarding benefit and that violate formal standards governing his or her conduct."[28] Corrupt acts, John Kleinig writes elsewhere, occur wherever officers "act with the primary intention of furthering private or departmental/divisional advantage."[29] What makes corrupt acts egoistic is that their underlying motivation is personal gain. By virtue of their authority, discretion, and the nature of their everyday work, police officers are routinely placed in situations where personal advantage can easily be furthered through unethical and even illegal means. As one might imagine, examples of acts motivated by personal gain are numerous. In his *Police Ethics: Crisis in Law Enforcement*, for instance, Tom Barker offers the following typology of police corruption:[30]

- *Corruption of Authority.* Accepting unearned rewards for doing one's regular duties, including free meals, liquor, sex, discounts of various sorts from businesses, and payments from businesses to more closely monitor premises.
- *Kickbacks.* Receiving goods or services for referring business to attorneys or bondmen.
- *Opportunistic Theft.* Stealing money or property from suspects or victims, goods not taken by a burglar, evidence that has been confiscated (e.g., drugs or money from drug busts).
- *Shakedowns.* Accepting money or other forms of payment for not making an arrest.
- *Protection of Illegal Activities.* Accepting money from vice operators or companies operating illegally.
- *Fixes.* Accepting money or other rewards/favors for overlooking traffic violations, quashing prosecution proceedings by, for instance, tampering with evidence or committing perjury.

- *Direct Criminal Activities.* Engaging directly in various forms of criminal activity, such as selling drugs, robbing stores, or burglarizing homes or businesses.
- *Internal Payoffs.* Buying or selling employment-related benefits, such as off days, holidays, work assignment, evidence, or promotions.

Each of the above-listed activities is an unethical, and in many cases illegal, means of furthering one's own advantage. They illustrate some of the ways in which police authority and discretion can be used improperly and egoistically to advance personal gain.

Various attempts have been made to *explain* the persistence of police corruption. One popular set of explanations focuses on *predispositions* or characteristics of individual officers. The so-called **rotten-apple explanation** was widely accepted prior to the 1960s. It implies that the cause of corruption is to be found in the questionable moral character of a few individuals who, by virtue of their psychological makeup, were predisposed to engage in corrupt practices even before they joined the police force. More recent research on the "police personality" suggests that persons with certain personality traits such as *authoritarianism* that are linked to unethical conduct are more likely to be drawn to law enforcement. Corruption is thus the result of traits and values that a significant percentage of officers bring with them to the job or, in some cases, develop over the course of socialization and on-the-job experience.[31]

In effect, suggesting that corrupt practices are limited to a small number of "bad apples" or are otherwise the result of predispositions of individual officers diverts attention from departmental, institutional, and systemic factors. Explanations that involve the latter focus less on individual (psychological) characteristics of officers, and more on sociological variables. Implicated in departmental, institutional, and systemic explanations are factors such as ineffective anticorruption protocols, the wide discretion enjoyed by police officers, the difficulties of supervising officers, the lack of public visibility keeping officers "in check," and norms of secrecy and loyalty that pervade law enforcement.

Whatever its causes, corruption potentially brings a number of negative consequences for individual officers, departments, and the greater community. For instance, area residents may experience increased crime/victimization, offenders who cannot or do not pay may receive relatively harsher treatment, inner-city and other high-vice neighborhoods may experience stronger organized crime presence and increased deterioration, and the general public may lose trust and confidence in the police.[32] In light of these and other troubling effects of police corruption, a number of suggestions have been proposed as to how best to *combat* police corruption. Some have suggested that departments do more to detect corruption and increase accountability.[33] Others have suggested that reducing corruption begins with the recruitment, hiring, and training of ethical officers. Hiring officers with higher levels of moral character and placing greater emphasis on ethics in education and training will, in principle, reduce the likelihood that new officers will become involved in corrupt activities. Police training, as Alpert and Dunham suggest, "must help officers to *think* as well as to react and respond."[34] Officers "must not only be trained, they must be educated. . . . training must teach critical thinking and problem-solving techniques."[35] It is in part because of this need that more and more colleges and universities are requiring students to take ethics courses as one dimension of their criminal justice curriculum.

Prison Corruption

Prison corruption has been, in Bernard McCarthy's words, "a persistent and pervasive feature of corrections."[36] While patterns of corruption in prisons are in many respects similar to those in policing, there is at least one notable difference. Prisons are secluded, protected environments—existing and operating largely outside of the public's view. Because of this, corruption in prisons is often unpublicized, and small-scale unethical practices are often not even reported. Other than the relatively few instances where prison corruption erupts into a publicized scandal, very little is known about it. Although corruption exists at higher levels of prison operations (e.g., administration), in this subsection we focus on forms of and motivations for *staff corruption*.

Corruption in prisons exists in a variety of forms, from relatively minor instances of theft, to large-scale, organized drug-trafficking and counterfeit rings. What each has in common, however, is underlying egoistic motivation—whatever its form, corruption is fueled by the desire for personal gain and the willingness and opportunity to neglect moral and legal obligations in its favor. Through his examination of official records of an internal affairs unit, Bernard McCarthy identified several general categories of corrupt conduct in prisons:[37]

- *Theft.* Stealing valuables and other personal items from inmates during frisks and cell searches; stealing items from visitors during processing; and stealing items from other staff members.
- *Trafficking.* Conspiring with inmates and civilians to smuggle contraband into prisons in exchange for money, drugs, or other services. Common forms of contraband include much demanded and highly marketable items such as drugs, alcohol, and weapons. In some cases, guards act on their own, while others are of a much larger scale, involving street gangs and organized crime officials.
- *Embezzlement.* Appropriating goods belonging to the state for one's own use. Unlike petty acts of theft, embezzlement involves "employees, sometimes with the help of inmates, systematically stealing money or materials from state accounts (inmate canteens or employee credit unions) and from warehouses."
- *Misuse of authority.* Intentionally misusing one's discretion for personal gain. Misuse of authority involves three basic offenses: (1) "the acceptance of gratuities from inmates for special consideration in obtaining legitimate prison privileges (e.g., payoffs to receive choice cells or job assignments)," (2) "the acceptance of gratuities for special consideration in obtaining or protecting illicit prison activities (e.g., allowing illegal drugs sales or gambling)," and (3) "the mistreatment or extortion of inmates by staff for personal material gain (e.g., threatening to punish or otherwise harm an inmate if a payment is not forthcoming)."[38]

Corrupt acts in prisons can be further classified according to the traditional typology of misfeasance, malfeasance, and nonfeasance (a typology that is also sometimes used to categorize forms of police misconduct). Each involves the misuse of discretionary powers:

- **Misfeasance** is the "improper performance of some act that an official may lawfully do." Included herein are practices such as the accepting of gratuities in exchange for special privileges, selectively offering formal rewards and punishments for a fee, and the misuse of state resources for personal gain. The handing out of privileges (e.g., assignment to desirable cell block), rewards and punishment, and use of state resources are lawful acts falling within the authority of prison employees. Misfeasance occurs where this lawful authority is used in an unethical fashion for furtherance of self-interest.
- Whereas misfeasance involves the "improper use of legitimate power or authority," **malfeasance** is "direct misconduct or wrongful conduct by a public official or employee." Malfeasance includes such corrupt acts as theft, embezzlement, trafficking

in contraband, extortion, assisting escapes, and conspiring with inmates in forgery, drug, or counterfeiting rings.

- In contrast to both misfeasance and malfeasance, nonfeasance does not involve the commission of unethical or unlawful acts. Instead, **nonfeasance** is the "failure to act according to one's responsibilities, or the omission of an act that an official ought to perform." Nonfeasance may include not reporting inmate violations (e.g., allowing inmates to have sex with visitors, looking the other way when drugs are smuggled into the prison), and may also include not reporting violations of other employees.

Efforts to explain correctional corruption have focused on both individual and institutional factors. Similar to individualistic explanations of police corruption, attention is sometimes drawn to characteristics and quality of prison personnel. Because correctional institutions typically offer low pay and provide poor working conditions, they often have difficulties hiring and retaining qualified, well-trained, and educated personnel. Less than half of the states in the United States, for instance, require even a high school diploma for correctional officer work. Coupled with authority, discretion, and a low-visibility environment, opportunities for and chances of corrupt behavior arguably increase. In this light, some have suggested that strategies such as increasing pay, improving working conditions, utilizing psychological testing or screening techniques at the hiring stage, and better emphasizing moral duties and ethical responsibilities may help to reduce corruption.[39]

On the other hand, structural and organizational characteristics of prisons must also be taken into consideration. The prison environment and the day-to-day realities of the prison experience, for instance, may provide incentives for corrupt behavior. As Cloward and others have noted, maintaining order and control in prisons may be perceived as *requiring* some level of corruption. In order to successfully maintain order and control—their primary objective—line staff may recognize that "coercive power must be supplemented with informal exchange relations with inmates."[40] In other words, correctional officers come to adopt a "you scratch my back and I'll scratch yours" attitude, tolerating violations of minor rules when doing so can assist in the performance of their job. We will have much more to say about this kind of reciprocity in the next chapter.

Summary

The basic purpose of this chapter was to introduce psychological questions about the foundations and sources of morality, our personal motivation for moral behavior, and to explore several ways in which the pursuit of personal gain can interfere with our efforts to be good people and do the right thing. Several limitations of reward and punishments— including the threat of sanctions from the law, God, and our own conscience—as incentives for moral behavior were reviewed. Not only is the threat of sanction oftentimes ineffective, it is also undesirable (at least, in and of itself) as a source of moral motivation. Our reasons for moral behavior should be something more or other than the promise of reward for good behavior or the fear of punishment for immoral behavior. As well, while religion and spirituality may have valuable roles to play in our personal lives, we should remain cognizant of the problems associated with relying primarily on religion as a source or morality and as a motivation for moral behavior. We are still left with the crucial question, "Why be moral?" With this question in mind, the next chapter addresses several additional sources of and motivations for moral behavior.

be negative. If N_s and N_d are the same, then the two variables have nothing to do with each other or are not related. The formula for computing Gamma (G) is simple: $G = (N_s - N_d)/(N_s + N_d)$. The calculation of N_s and N_d however, could be very strenuous. Fortunately, the computer will do all the calculations and computations. All you have to do is to put GAMMA along with other measures (e.g., LAMBDA) after the keyword /STATISTICS in the CROSSTABS command of SPSS.

Gamma is a frequently seen measure that tells you about the magnitude and direction of the correlation between two ordinal variables, which may range from -1 to +1. For a 2×2 table, Gamma is the same as Yule's Q coefficient, which applies only to dichotomous variables. There are two problems with Gamma, nevertheless. First, it is only (or mainly) for measuring symmetrical relations. Second, its computational logic does not take into account case pairs with the same values on a variable. This involves a problem of over-sensitivity of the measure, in contrast to the insensitivity problem with Lambda, when the number of such case pairs is considerable.

In view of that issue, Somers' D appears to be a better choice. This is also a PRE measure, which may range from -1 to +1. Using the same denotations as those for calculating the Gamma, the formula for measuring the asymmetrical type of relations is: $d_{yx} = (N_s - N_d)/(N_s + N_d + T_y)$. The strength of Somers' D is that it takes into consideration case pairs with the same values on either of the variables. Here T_y is the number of case pairs with the same values on the dependent variable. Due to the inclusion of T_y (as well as T_x when the formula takes its symmetrical form), the value of Somers' D will be smaller than Gamma. That means it will be more accurate than Gamma when there are case pairs with the same values on either of the variables. When there are no such case pairs (i.e. $T_y = 0$), of course, the formulas as well as the results will become the same as Gamma's.

There are still more rank-order correlation measures available. For example, computer software packages can provide you with such statistics as Kendall's tau coefficients (tau-a, tau-b, and tau-c), which are also based on the numbers of concordant pairs, discordant pairs, and same-value pairs. Spearman's rho coefficient is another measure, which is not only based on rank-order but also takes into account the specific rank difference (i.e., not only a general rank order but how many ranks are there differentiating between any two cases). These measures all apply to symmetrical relations. However refined, they do not have the PRE meaning, and thus are not so widely used as Gamma and d_{yx}.

Key Terms and Concepts

common ground
  (problem of) *92*
conscience *87*
Divine Command Theory *92*

egoistic *86*
guilt *88*
malfeasance *98*
misfeasance *98*

nonfeasance *99*
police corruption *96*
rotten-apple (explanation
  of police deviance) *97*

Discussion Questions

1. Is self-interest at all necessary or desirable for practitioners within the criminal justice field? Discuss several ways in which egoistic motivations might produce positive and negative effects in the following: (1) police officers, (2) district attorneys and prosecutors, (3) defense attorneys.

2. To what extent does the fear of punishment motivate you to act morally? To what extent are you motivated to obey the law because of the existence of punishments for violating the law? To what extent does divine sanction or the expectation of divine reward motivate your behavior?

3. How do conscience and/or guilt serve as motivators resulting in moral action? What are their limitations and in what ways can conscience/guilt "go wrong" as motivations? Do you believe that most people behave morally because they fear being guilt-ridden? Use an example from your own personal or professional life to illustrate the power—or lack of power—that conscience and guilt have over our behavior.

4. Psychopathic offenders are said to lack conscience. Examples of psychopathic offenders are individuals who demonstrate a callous disregard for the feelings or welfare of others; who are impulsive, manipulative, and deceitful; and who have a larger-than-life sense about themselves. One case of a (sexual) psychopathic offender was Jeffrey Dahmer. Dahmer tortured, mutilated, and killed a number of young men before having sexual intercourse with them. Eventually, he was caught by the police and sentenced to multiple life prison terms in Wisconsin. He was murdered by a fellow prisoner. Are persons like Dahmer capable of forming a conscience? If not, then how can we expect moral/ethical behavior from them?

Endnotes

1. Erik Sanzenbach, "Slidell Police Officer Charged with Theft, Malfeasance; Resigns," *St. Tammany News* (July 15, 2008).

2. Michael Rubinkam and Maryclaire Dale, "U.S. Judges Accused of Jailing Kids for Cash," *FoxNews.com* (February 12, 2009).

3. Plato, *The Republic,* G. M. A. Grube (trans.) (Indianapolis, IN: Hackett, 1974), pp. 31–33.

4. See also, Christopher Falzon, *Philosophy Goes to the Movies: An Introduction to Philosophy* (New York, Routledge, 2002), p. 88.

5. Jeremy Bentham, *The Principles of Morals and Legislation* (New York: Prometheus Books, 1988); see also, William Sahakian, *Ethics: An Introduction to Theories and Problems* (New York: Barnes and Noble, 1974), p. 30.

6. For a biologically informed account of this notion, see Donald M. Broom, *The Evolution of Morality and Religion* (Cambridge: Cambridge University Press, 2004).

7. Vincent Ruggiero, *Thinking Critically About Ethical Issues,* 5th ed. (New York: McGraw-Hill, 2001), pp. 32–40.

8. Nicholas Dent, "Conscience." In Edward Craig (Ed.), *The Concise Routledge Encyclopedia of Philosophy* (New York: Routledge, 2000), p. 167.

9. Ibid.; see also, Tom Kitwood, *Concern for Others: A New Psychology of Conscience and Morality* (New York: Routledge, 1990).

10. Patricia S. Greenspan, *Practical Guilt: Moral Dilemmas, Emotions, and Social Norms* (Oxford: Oxford University Press, 1995).

11. Ibid.
12. Falzon, *Philosophy Goes to the Movies.*
13. See generally, Alison Hills, *The Beloved Self: Morality and the Challenge from Egoism* (Oxford: Oxford University Press, 2010).
14. Immanuel Kant, *Lectures on Ethics,* Louis Infield (trans.) (Indianapolis, IN: Hackett, 1963), pp. 52–57.
15. Ibid.
16. Ibid., p. 56 (authors' emphasis).
17. Ibid.
18. William M. Baum, *Understanding Behaviorism: Behavior, Culture, and Evolution,* 2nd ed. (New York: Blackwell Publishers, 2004).
19. Kant, *Lectures on Ethics,* p. 57.
20. See Jonarthan Berg, "How Could Ethics Depend on Religion?" In Peter Singer (Ed.), *A Companion to Ethics* (Oxford: Blackwell, 1993).
21. Regina Wentzel Wolfe and Christine E. Gudorf, *Ethics and World Religions: Cross-Cultural Case Studies* (Maryknoll, NY: Orbis Books, 1999); see also, Judith Boss, *Ethics for Life* (Mountain View, CA: Mayfield, 2001), pp. 151–189.
22. Ibid.
23. Richard Brandt, *Ethical Theory* (Englewood Cliffs, NJ: Prentice Hall, 1959), p. 19.
24. Ruggiero, *Thinking Critically About Ethical Issues,* p. 7.
25. James Rachels, *The Elements of Moral Philosophy* (New York: McGraw-Hill, 1986), p. 42.
26. Ibid.
27. For an accessible analysis which attempts to bridge the divide between self-interest and morality, see Craig Biddle, *Loving Life: The Morality of Self-Interest and the Facts That Support It* (Glen Allen, VA: Glen Allen Press LLC, 2002).
28. Michael Johnston, *Political Corruption and Public Policy in America* (Monterey, CA: Brooks/Cole, 1982), p. 287.
29. John Kleinig, *The Ethics of Policing* (New York: Cambridge University Press, 1996), p. 166.
30. Tom Barker, *Police Ethics: Crisis in Law Enforcement,* 2nd ed. (Springfield, IL: Charles C. Thomas, 2006).
31. Johnston, *Political Corruption and Public Policy in America.*
32. Ibid., p. 305.
33. See, generally, Victor Kappeler, Richard Sluder, and Geoffrey Alpert, *Forces of Deviance: Understanding the Dark Side of Policing,* 2nd ed. (Prospect Heights, IL: Waveland Press, 1998), pp. 216–243.
34. Geoffrey P. Alpert and Roger G. Dunham, *Policing Multi-ethnic Neighborhoods* (Westport, CT: Greenwood, 1988). Quoted in Kappeler, Sluder, and Alpert, *Forces of Deviance,* p. 221.
35. Kappeler, Sluder, and Alpert, *Forces of Deviance.*
36. Bernard McCarthy, "Keeping an Eye on the Keeper: Prison Corruption and its Control." In Michael Braswell, Belinda McCarthy, and Bernard McCarthy (Eds.), *Justice, Crime, and Ethics,* 3rd ed. (Cincinnati, OH: Anderson, 1998), p. 251.
37. Bernard McCarthy, "Keeping an Eye on the Keeper: Prison Corruption and its Control," *The Prison Journal,* 64 (2), 113–125 (1984). Reprinted in Michael Braswell, Belinda McCarthy, and Bernard McCarthy, *Justice, Crime, and Ethics,* 3rd ed. (Cincinnati, OH: Anderson, 1998), pp. 251–262.
38. McCarthy, "Keeping an Eye on the Keeper," p. 254.
39. Ibid.
40. Ibid., p. 258. See also, Richard A. Cloward, *Theoretical Studies in the Social Organization of the Prison* (New York: Social Science Research Council, 1960); Gresham M. Sykes, *The Society of Captives: A Study of a Maximum Security Prison* (Princeton, NJ: Princeton University Press, 1958), pp. 63–108; and John Irwin, *Prisons in Turmoil* (Boston, MA: Little, Brown & Co., 1980).

Morality, Human Nature, and Social Cooperation

Ralph and Renaldo are arrested for the crime of robbery, which carries a maximum sentence of seven years in prison in their jurisdiction. Each suspect is transported to the police station in a separate car, and placed in a separate cell, unable to communicate with the other. The local prosecutor realizes that the police have collected only enough evidence to ensure convictions for possession of stolen property, which carries a sentence of eighteen months. Realizing this, the prosecutor approaches Ralph and indicates that she will offer him a reduced sentence of twelve months in exchange for his statement and future testimony against Renaldo, who would then almost certainly be convicted of burglary and sentenced to the maximum seven-year sentence. "However, you should know," the prosecutor tells Ralph, "that I have made the same offer to Renaldo." If Renaldo accepts the prosecutor's offer and Ralph does not, then Ralph is facing the seven-year maximum prison sentence while Renaldo will face only twelve months. As additional incentive, the prosecutor indicates that "in the event that each of you implicates the other, I will have sufficient evidence to convict each of you of robbery, but I will see to it that neither of you is sentenced to more than four years." What should Ralph do?

SELF-INTEREST

The above story is a modified version of the **prisoner's dilemma**. Scenarios such as that involving Ralph and Renaldo are commonly employed within *game theory*, which explores the strategies we use and those that are best used in our interactions with others.[1] In part, game theory contributes to our understanding of morality in revealing the extent to which people are, and should be, motivated by *self-interest*. Most of us would agree that it is often expected and even acceptable that we pursue our own interests to some extent. Yet is it possible to do otherwise? To what extent is the pursuit of self-interest desirable and beneficial, for both self and others?

In response to the first question posed above, many philosophers and nonphilosophers alike have noted that self-interest seems to be a fundamental part of human nature. Within ethics, this view is known as psychological egoism. **Psychological egoism** is a *descriptive* argument holding that human beings are, by nature, always motivated by self-interest; that all people, all of the time, act so as to promote (what they think are) their own interests.[2] We may not do so knowingly or intentionally, but we nevertheless are always influenced by self-interest. By this logic, it is not possible to set aside concern for ourselves and act wholly out of concern for the welfare of others (see Box 6.1).

BOX 6.1
Can We Be Moral?

Psychological egoism suggests that what seem to be altruistic acts are merely self-interested actions in disguise. What are we to make, you might ask, of cases that seem clearly to be motivated by concern for the welfare or interests of others—that involve the willing risk their life, liberty, happiness, health, status, or wealth to benefit others? Proponents of psychological egoism argue that altruistic or other-regarding behavior can be *reinterpreted* in egoistic terms. In other words, we can always find self-serving interests underlying what seem to be altruistic behaviors. To illustrate, consider the examples of *charity* and *pity* as described by philosopher Thomas Hobbes (1588–1679):

Charity

Charity seems to be a case of human benevolence—of kindness toward and concern for one's fellow human beings. However, Hobbes argued that if we look more closely we find that acts of charity are better understood as individuals *taking delight in demonstrating their own power*. The charitable person revels in her own superiority by showing both herself and the world that she is more capable than others. The pleasant sensation that most of us feel when giving to others comes from knowing that "I not only have enough to take care of myself, but I have 'enough left over for others who are not so able.'" Most likely, we *believe* ourselves to be acting in a manner that is selfless; yet, as Hobbes further suggests, we typically interpret our own behavior in a way that is most flattering to ourselves.

Pity

We often understand "pity" to entail some degree of sympathy or even empathy for some other person or persons experiencing misfortune. Yet perhaps our concern for others—the "feeling" we have for the misfortunate others—is nothing more than a *reminder* that we, too, could experience the same misfortune. As Hobbes noted, "[p]ity is imagination or fiction of future calamity to ourselves, proceeding from the sense of another man's calamity." In other words, what we are genuinely concerned for is our *own* well-being. Pity, then, is simply the experience of our own potential suffering through witnessing the present misfortune of others.

Unfortunately, psychological egoism is an assumption which cannot be tested scientifically and cannot be shown to be empirically true or false. However, there is good reason to believe that human beings are at least capable of altruistic or other-regarding behavior. It is likely true that when we act unselfishly, we feel good about ourselves. Yet we cannot assume that simply because doing good things for others makes us "feel good" that this feeling is the *reason* why we undertake these actions. An important counterargument is that in order to feel satisfaction in something, we must want that something in the first place. The pleasant sensations associated with moral behavior perhaps require that we already attach *value* to that behavior. In that case, our primary motivation is to help others, with the pleasant sensation simply being a consequence of achieving something that we find valuable or worthwhile. If we derive satisfaction from enhancing the well-being of others, it seems likely that we must have first desired the happiness and/or well-being of other people in the first place; likewise, if we attach value to human dignity or justice, for instance, then we will derive satisfaction from protecting dignity or acting with justice.

Source: James Rachels and Stuart Rachels, *Elements of Moral Philosophy*, 6th ed. (New York: McGraw-Hill, 2010); Thomas Hobbes, *Human Nature and DeCorpore Politico* (New York: Oxford University Press, 1999).

A related *prescriptive* argument concerning self-interest comes by way of **ethical egoism**, which holds that we *should* act from self-interest—that our motivation for moral behavior should be our own rationally derived interests. As was discussed in the last chapter, however, conventional moral sensibilities seem to entail a requirement that, at least on some occasions, we restrain our pursuit of self-interest in light of the wants or needs of others. At the very least, we should avoid harming others and, where appropriate, even try to be helpful. Moreover, we often have obligations to others (e.g., parents, spouses, friends, work associates, the community) that, most would agree, should be honored even when doing so is not in our own immediate best interest. Taking this logic a step further, perhaps admirable moral character even requires that, at least on occasion, we engage in **altruistic** acts—those that are selfless and undertaken solely for the benefit of others. If human beings are egoistic by nature, however, then altruistic acts are merely disguised effects of the pull of self-interest.[3] Yet even if these egoistic depictions of human nature are accurate, does that necessarily mean that we are incapable of moral behavior? That cooperation and concern for the welfare of others have and should have no role on our decisions and actions? That self-interest is necessarily *opposed* to morality?

As we will see, our own interests are not necessarily opposed to those of others. It may be that, in at least some situations, the most effective way to bring some advantage to ourselves is to assist others or behave so as to further their welfare. Neither psychological nor ethical egoism should be confused with the idea that we should never act out of regard for others; rather, both perspectives simply maintain that our motivation for doing so is to gain some advantage for ourselves.

THE PRISONER'S DILEMMA

Let us return for a moment to the dilemma involving Ralph and Renaldo outlined at the beginning of the chapter. We can break down the possible outcomes of the scenario as follows:

- If one of the suspects accepts the deal and agrees to testify against the other, he will get twelve months while the other receives a seven-year sentence.
- If *both* suspects accept the deal, they will each receive a sentence of four years.
- If *neither* suspect accepts the deal, each will be convicted only on charges of possession of stolen property and receive a sentence of two years.

From the perspective of either one of the suspects, the rational (self-interested) approach to this dilemma is to testify against the other (see Table 6.1). Ralph knows that if Renaldo testifies against him, then his own interests are served by also testifying against Renaldo, in which case he would be sentenced to four years rather than seven. However, Ralph also knows that if Renaldo does not testify against him, his interests are still best served by testifying against Renaldo, in which case he would only serve only twelve months. *No matter what* Renaldo does, Ralph's best move seems to be to accept the deal, and no matter what Ralph does, Renaldo's best move seems to be to accept the deal. If each is motivated by rational self-interest, both will accept the deal, confess to their own participation and that of the other, and ultimately serve four years of a sentence for robbery.

From the perspective of either individual alone, mutual confession results in only the third most desirable scenario out of four possible scenarios. When considered together rather than

TABLE 6.1	The Prisoner's Dilemma	
	Ralph Accepts the Deal	**Ralph Remains Silent**
Renaldo Accepts the Deal	4 years for *both* Ralph *and* Renaldo	12 months for Renaldo, 7 years for Ralph
	Third best scenario for both suspects	***Best scenario for Renaldo, worst for Ralph***
Renaldo Remains Silent	12 months for Ralph, 7 years for Renaldo	2 years for *both* Ralph *and* Renaldo
	Best scenario for Ralph, worst for Renaldo	***Second best scenario for both suspects***

individually, the best scenario is for both to remain silent (i.e., cooperate with one another, rather than the prosecution). The problem, however, is that by not confessing, either individual opens himself up to the possibility of being taken advantage of by his partner and, ultimately, facing the worst case scenario of seven years in prison. Even if each suspect were allowed to communicate with the other and made a pact not to cooperate with the prosecution, would both suspects then choose to remain silent? If motivated purely by personal gain, the answer must be, "no." If Ralph knows that Renaldo will remain silent, Ralph can exploit his trust by testifying against him and thus securing the greatest possible reward (or least possible punishment) for himself.

As a further consideration, suppose that Ralph was not a participant in the robbery—he is, in fact, innocent of all charges. If Ralph maintains his innocence, nothing prevents Renaldo from cooperating with the prosecutor to save himself. If this series of events were to unfold, the guilty party (Renaldo) would face a twelve-month sentence while Ralph, innocent of any involvement in the crime, would serve seven years behind bars. Even if truly innocent, Ralph's best option is to falsely confess to his own involvement and serve no more than four years to protect himself from the greater punishment of seven years. It is because of this kind of dilemma that the practice of *plea bargaining* is illegal in many countries. In at least some instances, the rational course of action for a criminal defendant is to confess to something of which she or he is innocent in order to prevent or protect against the possibility of suffering some greater harm.

In sum, then: (1) the most rational, self-interested choice for either suspect is to cooperate with the prosecution and testify against the other; (2) however, they would both be better off had they each kept quiet; thus, (3) by pursuing their own interests exclusively, they each come off worse than had they acted for the benefit of the other or in the interest of some cooperative (though necessarily implicit) arrangement between them. In part, the prisoner's dilemma suggests that the only way for *both* suspects to benefit from the situation is through *cooperation*, *trust*, and/or *concern for the welfare of the other person* (see Box 6.2).

BOX 6.2

Criminal Informants and the Prisoner's Dilemma

As another example of a social dilemma in which mutual cooperation provides greater payoff than cheating for personal gain, consider the practice of law enforcement agencies utilizing *criminal informants* to secure information about illegal activities. Most often, informants provide information to law enforcement only in exchange for some consideration for themselves (e.g., having their own criminal activities overlooked or even protected, cash incentives). Law enforcement agencies are sometimes willing to offer such compensation to criminals because of what they get in return; namely, assistance in solving crimes, tracking down suspects, or for general information about criminal enterprises that they may not otherwise have. With both this and our discussion of the prisoner's dilemma in mind, consider the following scenario:

Officer Pate has agreed to supply Informant John with $100 in exchange for information about a robbery which occurred three nights ago. They arrange to meet in an alley, at which point Officer Pate will hand Informant John a bag containing the cash, and Informant John will hand Officer Pate a notebook containing the information. Both have an opportunity to get something without giving anything in return by handing over either an empty bag (Officer Pate), or a blank notebook (Informant John).

- Using the logic of the prisoner's dilemma, discuss whether the interests of either or both would be better served by "defecting" or cheating if this were a one-time encounter.

(continued)

- Now, suppose that each has agreed to meet once a week, every week, for the same exchange. Officer Pate will hand Informant John a bag containing $100, and Informant John will hand Officer Pate a notebook with useful information on criminal activities. Under this condition of meeting again, are the best interests of each better served by cooperating or cheating the other?

- More generally, discuss what (if any) moral issues are raised by law enforcement agencies doing favors for known criminals in exchange for potentially valuable information.

Source: William Allman, *The Stone Age Present: How Evolution has Shaped Modern Life—From Sex, Violence, and Language to Emotions, Moral, and Communities* (New York: Touchstone, 1995).

The notion of "self-interest" may thus be broader, more robust than we might imagine. Short of extreme forms of egoistic behavior that lead us to engage in moral wrongdoing for personal gain, perhaps "looking out for number one" involves or even requires what we might describe as altruistic or moral behavior. In other words, being a good person and doing the right thing may, rather than standing in opposition to self-interest, actually *promote and further* our own interests.

RECIPROCITY

Even if we were to accept the proposition that human beings are egoistic by nature, we are still left to explain the widespread existence of altruistic or, at least, cooperative behavior between people. Whether we are capable of genuinely selfless acts may be less relevant than the reality that people often do engage in behavior that seems to benefit others even with some corresponding cost to the actor. The more important question from an ethical standpoint, then, is why we commonly are and should be willing to incur some cost to ourselves for the sake of being moral or in taking account of the welfare of others. As we have suggested, the answer may be that morality and cooperative behavior more generally accommodate and are beneficial to self-interest. In other words, perhaps "morality pays." As we will see, there are many ways of interpreting the mechanisms by which altruistic and otherwise moral behavior occurs, and some of these allow for compatibility between the interests of self and other.

Kin Selection or Inclusive Fitness

One proposed answer to the puzzle of moral behavior in self-interested beings draws upon the notions of genetic relatedness or genetic kinship. Some other-regarding behavior—particularly in species such as bees and ants—can easily enough be explained by drawing attention to the expansion of self-interest to our immediate circle of close relatives. The notion of *inclusive fitness* is that our own genetic interests are furthered by aiding those with whom we share genes. The stronger the genetic relation, the more of our self-interest we are willing to sacrifice. Inclusive fitness would explain why we are willing to endure tremendous cost to ourselves for the sake of our children, grandchildren, and others with whom we share genetic relatedness. In that we share genes and have at least a biological interest in those genes being passed to future generations, the interests of my children, grandchildren, siblings, nieces and nephews *are* my own interests.[4]

Reciprocal Altruism

While some moral behavior can be explained adequately by inclusive fitness, most cannot. The majority of cooperative behavior among human beings in large societies such as the

United States occurs between people who are not closely related. Another possible source of and motivation for oral behavior is **reciprocal altruism**, or the idea that we sometimes set aside our own interests for the sake of others *with the expectation that others will do the same for us.* In short, moral behavior may be motivated by an "I'll scratch your back if you scratch mine" mentality.[5]

Reciprocal altruism may have explanatory power especially in those scenarios wherein we are likely to have future interaction with a person or group of people. Reciprocation of kindness need not occur immediately and, thus, it may make good sense for me to sacrifice now if I can expect a return act of consideration in the future. This is especially true of the circle of people with whom we have regular interaction (e.g., friends, roommates, neighbors, classmates, professional partners). It is important in law enforcement, for example, that partners look out for another—that they "have each other's backs." The same is true of law enforcement's cooperative relationships with other departments—Fire/EMS/Rescue, social service agencies, and so forth. Even where cooperating costs in the present, it may well pay in the future.

Reciprocal altruism appears not only to explain why and how morality developed in human communities but also to provide an important source of motivation for moral behavior. While being uncooperative and acting for personal gain at the expense of others can be attractive, it is not often the best option. Perhaps the best evidence of this comes from political scientist Robert Axelrod, who utilized computer simulations to test the notion that reciprocal altruism is more beneficial to self and other than purely self-regarding motives. In essence, his simulations consisted of numerous iterations of the Prisoner's Dilemma utilizing different strategies of cooperation and "defecting" (i.e., cheating, not cooperating). While taking advantage of the kindness of others for personal gain sometimes provided short-term benefit, those simulated players who elected this strategy eventually all died out. In every simulated "competition," the players whose interests were best served over the long run were those programmed to utilize a strategy termed, "*tit for tat*"—a cooperative approach in which players would always first cooperate, and then reciprocate the move of the other player. Thus, cooperative relationships were maintained with other cooperators, and those who cheated harmed themselves and were slowly pushed out of the simulated society.

Axelrod's findings have several important implications for our understanding of human nature, cooperation, and, indirectly, morality. Notably, when our decisions have an impact on the welfare of others, the approach which best serves the long-term interests of ourselves *and* others is that which is *nice* (i.e., kind, cooperative). Even if we are inherently motivated to pursue self-interest, we do best for ourselves not by cheating or exploiting the kindness of others, but by acting for the mutual benefit of all involved. Importantly, since kindness opens us up to the possibility of exploitation by others, it is necessary to be prepared to cease cooperating with—and even punish—cheaters, as well as to forgive those who have been punished and are willing to again become participants in a cooperative community.

Indirect Reciprocity: The Importance of *Reputation*

A related explanation and motivation for moral behavior is that of **reputation**. Whether personally or professionally, conducting oneself in ways that are honest, responsible, fair, etc., has the beneficial effect of increasing the number of people with whom one has the opportunity to form cooperative relationships in the future. Reputation is critical, for instance, in the business community wherein an established reputation for integrity, hard work, and so forth can generate not only continued business from current clients but also increased business from new clients. On a personal level, consider the importance of one's credit report—in effect, an electronic financial reputation—for future cooperative endeavors. Where we honor our financial obligations in the present, others are more likely to enter into new arrangements with us in the future; where we fail to honor those obligations, we are likely to find it difficult to find new cooperators in the future.

Within criminal justice, consider the importance that reputation plays within the police–community relationship. Where law enforcement officers have gained a reputation for dishonesty, discrimination, and the like, relationships with the community become strained, citizens less likely to be cooperative, and, consequently, law enforcement personnel are less able to perform their professional duties effectively. Positive interactions between law enforcement and the community can build trust and respect, making each side more likely to be cooperative in the future and thus creating conditions for a police–community relationship which is mutually beneficial (see Box 6.3). A law enforcement officer may incur short-term costs by, for instance, being more thorough on a routine call for service, but the opportunity to establish a positive reputation in the community may produce tremendous benefit in the future.[6]

We could certainly think of hundreds of additional examples of the ways in which reputation is crucial to personal and professional well-being. This is particularly in the twenty-first century, where ratings of professors, reviews of medical doctors, complaints about businesses, and appraisals of individuals are posted on the Internet for public consumption. The point is that, even if ultimately motivated by self-interest, we have every reason to treat people fairly, justly, respectfully, and kindly; to honor our obligations and commitments; and to embody honesty, responsibility, and otherwise-virtuous character in our interactions with others.

BOX 6.3

Crime Prevention and Community Safety: An Ethic of Police–Citizen Trust

Neighborhoods riddled with crime impact not only the residents who inhabit them, but also the officers who patrol them. In recent years, criminal justice agencies are more carefully considering how they can prevent crime while simultaneously promoting harmony and well-being within communities. Some suggestions include community policing strategies, neighborhood block watch efforts, and the notion of collective efficacy. While there are important differences among these approaches, each intervention is based on the value of *trust*. *Community policing* strategies require that officers be a part of the communities they patrol, working to assist residents in various ways that might have little to do with crime and delinquency. *Neighborhood block watch* strategies invite residents to be active participants in preventing or controlling crime by forming citizen patrol groups that operate in conjunction with local law enforcement personnel. The goal of *collective efficacy* is the (re)formation of safe and secure communities built upon resident cooperation. Collective efficacy seeks, with the assistance of law enforcement officers, the reestablishment of agency and power among residents of drug and crime-infested neighborhoods through the collective—and peaceful—reclamation of the streets.

In each of these instances, an ethic of police–citizen trust accounts for the quality and type of crime prevention and community safety that will eventually emerge in a given neighborhood experiencing pervasive violence and criminality. Thus, much like the notion of mutual aid suggests, when the inherent human qualities of cooperativeness, kindness, civility, compassion, etc., are allowed to develop, morality (i.e., being good and doing the right thing) is no longer dependent on laws, religion, or rules. Instead, morality resides within people motivated to act accordingly, given their intrinsic prosocial inclinations to express these healing tendencies. These tendencies can represent a source of fellowship and collective good—an ethic of community, citizenship, and justice for all.

Source: Gordon Hughes (Ed.), *Crime Prevention and Community Safety: New Directions* (Thousand Oaks, CA: Sage, 2002).

Strong Reciprocity and Altruistic Punishment

Thus far we have reviewed several explanations as to why cooperative systems are persistent features of human civilization. The difficulty is that kin selection, reciprocal altruism, and indirect reciprocity (i.e., reputation) become less powerful explanations of moral behavior where individuals are unrelated, unlikely to have future interactions with one another, and where reputation is not affected or not of concern—precisely the conditions that become more widespread as societies increase in size and complexity. So how are we to explain moral behavior involving unrelated strangers unlikely to have future contact with one another?

One solution to the problem of explaining and motivating cooperative behavior under the conditions described above is what is described as *strong reciprocity*. Where individuals within groups, communities, and societies benefit from collectively abiding by social norms, those individuals are inclined to themselves obey those norms and to punish those who would violate them. Abundant research suggests that human beings are prepared to engage in **altruistic punishment**—to willingly accept some personal cost in order to ensure that those who would violate the norms of cooperative society suffer consequences for their behavior (consider, for instance, how much taxpaying citizens in the United States willingly sacrifice for purposes of seeing law violators brought to justice and punished for their offenses). This is different from suggesting that those who have been personally victimized seek revenge against those who have harmed them—referred to as *second-party punishment*. Altruistic or *third-party punishment* involves punishing someone who specifically victimized someone else, but whose behavior generally undermines the social norms that are regarded as important within a cooperative community.

Altruistic punishment is regarded as an evolved and largely effective means of enforcing social norms and promoting cooperative and mutually beneficial social relations. It is perhaps the best means that communities have of expressing collective disapproval of actions that run contrary to the interests of the larger whole. While most civilized Western societies have developed institutionalized third-party punishment (i.e., systems of law and criminal justice), the most common (and arguably most effective) sanctions are those imposed informally by family members, peers, organizations, etc.—from simple disapproving glances to social exclusion.

The importance of the idea of strong reciprocity is not, however, its description of sanction as a basis for cooperation. As discussed in the previous chapter, the threat of sanction in and of itself is largely ineffective and in many ways undesirable as a source of motivation for moral behavior. Further, most of us do regularly act cooperatively and out of concern for others even in the absence of threats of punishment. The idea of strong reciprocity encourages us to consider the ways in which our commitment to social and moral norms derives from our recognition that those norms are mutually beneficial. Even if we do not expect direct reciprocation for our contributions, we recognize that the very system of cooperation itself benefits us in numerous ways. We are motivated to avoid pursuing our own advantage exclusively or excessively because we recognize that we would not want others with whom we share communities to pursue their own advantage exclusively or excessively.

NON-ZERO-SUM: COMMON INTEREST AND MUTUAL ADVANTAGE

We have thus far noted that human beings often do act from self-interest, often do act out of concern for others, and that self-interest and concern for others may not be mutually exclusive. It may be that human nature is egoistic *and* cooperative, and that cooperation is in fact an essential

It should also be noted that the relationship between a nominal variable and an ordinal variable is usually described by Lambda or tau-y. Although Wilcoxon's coefficient of differentiation, or theta, is especially suited for studying this kind of relationship, it does not have the exact PRE meaning.

Describing associations at the interval level. For the purpose of measuring the association between two variables, the interval level of measurement is the highest requirement seen in research practice. Unlike the "rank-order correlation" discussed above, the possible corresponding idea of "interval correlation" involves an important complication and limitation. That is, the linearity of the relationship between two variables. The most frequently used measure of association at this level is Pearson's product-moment correlation coefficient, or γ. The term "product-moment" is a mechanical metaphor of a mean-related quantity. Pearson's γ only deals with linear rather than any kind of curved joint distributions of two variables.

Generally speaking, the notion of linearity is very important since it represents a traditional focus of analysis and sets the limit for many state-of-the-art statistical techniques. In analytical geometry, a linear relationship between variable X and variable Y can be represented by a straight line on a plane determined by these two variables as coordinates. And the linear equation $Y = a + bX$ has become most familiar to us. In distributions considered by statistics, the relationship between two variables will not be so neatly laid out by such a deterministic linear equation. In other words, the geometric representation of the relationship will not be a straight line but a scattergram with a "strap" shape and varied width. To predict one variable based on the other using the linear equation, there will be an error whose size is the main concern of our analysis here. The probabilistic linear equation becomes deterministic and the "strap" becomes a straight line only when a measure of association like Pearson's correlation coefficient γ takes the value of 1. If γ is 0, there will be no linear relationship at all in the joint distribution of the two variables in the plane coordinates system. And the linear equation will be completely invalid. As a principle, you must make sure that there is a fairly high linear correlation between two variables before you attempt to establish a linear equation to link them.

When talking about "gamma," you should not confuse Pearson's γ with Goodman and Kruskal's G (Gamma). The meaning of γ is more complicated than G in terms of the PRE logic. Predicting the value of Y by its own mean (i.e., using the mean to represent all the possible values of Y) would have a total error of $E_1 = \Sigma|Y_i - M|$ (M is the mean of Y). Now, suppose we know the values of part of furthering one's own interests. If this is the case, then the question, "Why be moral?" is answered by appealing to the notions of *common interest* or *mutual advantage*.[7]

Think of any number of recreational games (e.g., checkers, poker, basketball). Why, for instance, is it considered wrong to cheat at poker? Why are there dozens of rules and regulations that govern the game of basketball? The answer, of course, is to ensure fairness and to promote the opportunity for everyone participating to play to the best of their ability and to enjoy themselves in the process. The rules and regulations that govern checkers, poker, and basketball are intended to prevent players from causing unnecessary and unjust harm or suffering to other participants, to resolve in an orderly and agreeable fashion any number of conflicts or disagreements that might arise during the course of the game, and to enhance the experience of the sport or the entertainment value for everyone involved.[8]

However, in some respects, recreational or athletic competitions are not the same as the game of life. Indeed, as Hospers explained, "[n]one of us is forced to play baseball or billiards, but the game of life is one which we all have to play in one way or another."[9] Each of us not only has to participate in the "sport" of living, but we have to play it together as well. Thus, the question becomes, what arrangements, values, principles, and rules create the most favorable conditions and relationships for everyone involved? Are there certain values and principles that create conditions within which each of us can pursue our own interests as much as possible, while allowing others to pursue theirs? Moreover, are there certain values and tendencies that *assist us* in pursuing our own interests and *also assist others* in their own quest for happiness?

Perhaps the most significant implication of research on reciprocity involves our very approach to living a good life. Too often, we approach life as if it were a *zero-sum game*—one in which there is a fixed quantity of rewards, such that one can get ahead only if someone else absorbs a loss. Imagine, for instance, if there were a fixed sum of money available in the world, and no new money would be created. In such a case, the only way for one person to acquire more money is for someone else to lose it. Other examples might include cutting a birthday cake, a game of poker with a fixed pot, and athletic competitions in which one team's success necessarily entails the other team's failure or loss.

Fortunately, complex human societies feature very few such games (other than those played for recreation); rather, our social world provides numerous opportunities for "win-win" outcomes, and life itself is perhaps best regarded as a *non-zero-sum game*. As William Allman suggests, "[p]erhaps the biggest obstacle to fostering cooperation is that people sometimes fail to recognize the nature of the game they're playing." Part of what cooperation and, by extension, morality entail is adopting an outlook of common interest and mutual advantage. In other words, our approach should not be to come out ahead of other people, but to cooperate such that everyone comes out better off. In other words, vices such as envy and greed and decisions motivated by them ultimately leave one worse off. In most cases, we "do better ourselves if other people do better, too." *We have a better opportunity to live a good life in a just society if others are able to do the same.*

Cooperative relationships that feature duties and obligations to one another and that are anchored by kindness, trust, and honesty thus operate to the mutual advantage of everyone involved.[10] While we might be tempted to derive personal benefit from cheating at a friendly game of poker, it is in the best interests of everyone concerned if we do not. By being honest poker players, for instance, we earn the trust and respect of others, we encourage other participants not to cheat, and we contribute to an overall climate of fairness and hospitableness that enables everyone to enjoy the experience. By the same token, if we are honest people in our personal and professional lives, our honesty not only benefits us personally, but positively enhances the well-being of others with whom we interact.

MORAL INTUITION AND MUTUAL AID

If we accept that human beings are genetically and/or psychologically "selfish," it may be that the best response we can offer questions about why people are and should be moral is that of mutual advantage, perhaps incorporating some threat of punishment from an external or divine authority for pursuits of self-interest that harm others or violate formal norms of human social behavior. By giving voice to the welfare of others, however, the notions of reciprocity and the common good (of which we are a part) move us beyond the more narrow positions explored in the previous chapter that rely exclusively on personal reward and punishment as incentives. As we will see shortly, notions of cooperation and reciprocity are foundational assumptions of the *social contract* tradition within moral and political philosophy—a tradition which comprises part of the foundation for modern government, along with its laws, law enforcers, and systems of punishment and correction.

Another possibility, however, is that the egoistic portrait of human nature is not entirely accurate. Perhaps human beings are motivated to be moral not (or not exclusively) for our own personal good, but because we have innate dispositions that sensitize us and incline us to act in light of the welfare of others. Consider the fact that most of us are happy when others are happy. We smile and laugh when others are smiling and laughing. Similarly, we become upset when others are upset. We may cry when others cry, or, at the very least, we may feel something stirring deep within us that compels us to reach out and help or want to comfort them. None of us enjoys seeing pictures or video footage of people suffering from criminal victimization, starvation, disease, homelessness, or other tribulations. Thomas Hobbes' egoistic interpretation of "pity" notwithstanding, many of us experience what could be taken as genuine concern when tragedy befalls another and, as we have noted, many of us do act in what seem to be altruistic ways in response. These thoughts and feelings, as well as the behaviors that stem from them, might be better understood as natural human tendencies. Our aid and assistance to those who are suffering or struggling in some capacity may not be motivated by the promise of reward, the fear of punishment, expectations of reciprocity, or even duty or obligation; instead, our altruistic behavior might be stimulated by inborn moral "reflexes" that make concern for the welfare of others a natural human characteristic and which, by extension, make morality possible (see Box 6.4).

Human Universals

In Chapter 3 we considered the possibility that morality is relative to culture, time period, and perhaps even individuals. Despite descriptive evidence that there are significant differences between cultures on questions of values, customs, and behavioral norms, recent research in the psychology of moral behavior suggests that there are several key tendencies that are characteristic of all human beings or social groups. **Human universals** are traits, values, or patterns of behavior that are (or appear to be) shared by all human beings, regardless of the culture in which they live. They are, in other words, elements not of culture but of human nature. In the context of morality, the existence of such universally shared values and norms suggests that there may be something like a universal *moral sense*. In his *Human Universals*, for example, anthropologist Donald Brown suggests that all human groups prohibit harmful acts such as murder, rape, and other violence, punish engagement in those acts, make distinctions between right and wrong, have concepts of fairness and justice, feature empathic understanding, value generosity, and other prosocial behaviors.[11]

The innate capacity for empathic understanding may be especially critical for morality and cooperation generally. Empathy allows us to consider the perspective of others as if we were they. Rather than making decisions from a purely egocentric vantage point (i.e., that of our own wants,

BOX 6.4
Empathy and Scientific Jury Selection

Psychologically, compassion and empathy require *identification* with another person. To empathize, we must put ourselves "in another's shoes"—we must "imagine ourselves in the other's place." If we understand compassion and empathy in the same egoistic light in which Hobbes interpreted pity, we might conclude that we are better able and more likely to empathize with those who are more like "us." At the same time, we would be less able and likely to empathize with those who are unlike ourselves in important ways. We would experience more compassion and a greater desire to aid others suffering misfortunes that could easily enough befall us.

One example of how identification and empathy might impact the practice of criminal justice involves the psychology of jury decision-making. Research on jury decision-making suggests that jurors are more likely to favor defendants who are demographically or socially similar to themselves. This phenomenon is referred to as the **similarity-leniency hypothesis**. Jurors are more likely to favor those with whom they share characteristics, presumably because they can more easily identify with them. By this same logic, jurors will be less likely to favor defendants with whom they share few characteristics. This would be particularly true if they share more characteristics with the *victim* than with the defendant.

Given this phenomenon, attorneys might predict that jurors who are similar in one or more ways to the defendant will be more likely to favor the defense; conversely, jurors who are similar in one or more ways to the victim (or different in some ways from the defendant) would be likely to favor the prosecution. In theory, attorneys could utilize this social science knowledge to help select favorable juries during jury selection.

- If jurors are more or less likely to experience "pity"—or a lack of pity—toward one or the other side in a criminal or civil trial, how does this impact the struggle for a fair trial? Does this phenomenon lend greater support to the need for a "representative" jury of one's peers?
- Does "scientific jury selection" have implications for fairness and justice in the legal system? Is it morally appropriate for attorneys to utilize such social science research to select favorable juries?
- What are some others ways in which difficulties empathizing with those who are not like us could create injustices within criminal justice or the wider society? How might we seek to remedy those problems?

Source: Murray Levine and Leah Wallach, *Psychological Problems, Social Issues, and Law* (Boston, MA: Allyn & Bacon, 2002).

needs, welfare), our empathic "sense" thus allows for awareness of the interests of others and integration of those interests into our own moral decision-making. We will have much more to say on empathy in future chapters; for now, it is worth noting that notions such as the "Golden Rule," "interchangeability of perspectives,"[12] "reversibility," "Categorical Imperative," and other principles that have proven central to moral philosophies throughout history all find the source of morality in this very element of human nature.

Moral Intuition

Psychologist Jonathan Haidt has argued that certain moral themes are common across peoples and cultures and represent the foundation of **moral intuition**—those morally relevant ideas, feelings, and judgments that arise in our consciousness without our being aware of how or why they arose. Our moral intuitions are those "gut feelings" that we should, for instance, help someone in need, avoid causing harm, or that certain kinds of behaviors are reprehensible. While there may be variation in how these basic intuitive themes are prioritized and applied,[13] their universal nature suggests that they emerge not from socialization, but from an "innate preparedness" for moral thought, feeling, and action.[14] Two of these themes that appear most prominently and carry the most moral weight in Western cultures are as follows:

- *A sensitivity to harm and the suffering of others* which stems from our empathic awareness, triggers compassion and gives rise to kindness and caring behaviors, as well as an impulse to refrain from causing harm, a dislike for those who would cause harm, and a desire to protect others from harm; and
- *Expectations of reciprocity* which give rise to a sense of fairness and justice, as well as to anger and a desire to punish those who would cheat or violate the norms of social cooperation.

While we have spent considerable time in this chapter discussing the latter of these two universal themes, the former has been noted by many as an important source of and motivation for morality. Social and political philosopher Jean-Jacques Rousseau (1712–1778), for instance, argued that it is "compassion that hurries us without reflection to the relief of those who are in distress . . ."[15] It is "natural compassion" that prevents us from harming others, while simultaneously inclining us to assist people in need. Further, these basic tendencies toward nonharm and benevolence, as mutual aid theorist Peter Kropotkin (1842–1921) offered, " . . . [do] not depend on presuppositions, concepts, religions, dogmas, myths, training, and education. On the contrary, [they] reside in human nature itself . . ."[16]

Rather than imagining human beings as egoistic, competitive creatures involved in a continual struggle for individual survival (as Hobbes and others had implied), perhaps we are naturally sociable, cooperative beings involved in a continual struggle to be well as a human community—to secure health and happiness not only for ourselves, but for others with whom we are interconnected and upon whom we depend.[17] Morality is thus not only mutually advantageous, but is also the realization of our compassionate nature, connecting us to others through kindness, caring, and generosity.[18] As some would argue, we do not need laws, rules, religions, and so forth to motivate us to be good and to do the right thing; instead, morality is something that is already within us.[19] Compassion, benevolence, kindness, and cooperation are natural dispositions that need only conditions that *allow* for them to develop and flourish.

INTEGRITY AND INNER BALANCE

At the beginning of the last chapter, we recounted Plato's tale of Gyges as a catalyst for our examination of moral motivation and its relevance to criminal justice decision-making. Plato's own response to the question, "Why be moral?" is worth our consideration. For Plato, being moral is having a well-ordered, balanced, harmonious soul—possessing a certain "inner balance" which allows us to avoid falling victim to selfish desire.[20] When we fail to embody virtue or good moral character, our choices and actions are too often driven by greed, pride, intemperance, selfishness, callousness, and other vices. We become precisely the types of people we ourselves would likely seek to avoid.[21] On the other hand, embodying virtue not only earns the respect of others, but in doing so we earn our own respect as well. Virtue and moral character supply the foundation for a psychologically healthier, happier, life characterized by fulfilling relationships with others and which contributes to a better sense of community, civility, and humanity. If we are compassionate, we will tend toward choices motivated by compassion, and acts of kindness and care stemming from compassion. We will take others' needs and interests into consideration before choosing and before acting, creating, as we have seen, a social climate that is beneficial to all.[22]

In some ways, Plato's depiction of moral character is close to what we mean by *integrity*. When we live and work with integrity, we embody a certain "wholeness" or "completeness" which is difficult to articulate in words. We have a conception of the "good life," justice, and awareness that our choices and behaviors should reflect that conception. We choose and act with a certain consistency which has important personal and interpersonal functions. We can count on ourselves to overcome temptation, and others can count on us to do the same.[23]

JUSTICE AND THE SOCIAL CONTRACT

Most of us would agree that we would not want to live in a community or a society (or to work in a professional setting for that matter) where people routinely lied, cheated, stole, harmed others, or always put their own needs or wants above all other considerations. If this were the case, we would all be at a mutual *dis*advantage and life—especially life together—would be exceedingly difficult. As we have seen, this is the logic underlying various forms of reciprocity and their importance in morality and social order. It is in everyone's best interest to agree upon certain rules that will allow each of us to pursue a good life, while not infringing upon the interests that others have in doing the same. We noted in Chapter 1 that the purpose of morality is to enable us to live a good life in a just society; importantly, our pursuit of a good life can be helped or hindered by the extent to which conditions of morality and justice characterize society. We all could be said to have a vested interest both in the existence of moral rules and in following those rules—even when we could selfishly benefit from doing otherwise.

This logic, in conjunction with several ideas discussed thus far—the tension between self and common interest, reciprocity, and mutual advantage—is the root of what is known as the **social contract**—that "set of rules, governing how people are to treat one another, that rational people will agree to accept, for their mutual benefit, on the condition that others follow those rules as well."[24] Where human beings are both self-interested and social by nature, living well together arguably requires that we accept some implicit arrangement whereby we forgo certain benefits to ourselves in exchange for the opportunity to accumulate greater benefit in the long run through cooperation. As we have seen, reciprocal altruism and reputation are important motivating factors where our social encounters and cooperative endeavors occur with others with whom we are likely to have repeated interactions. Direct and indirect reciprocity no doubt function to motivate cooperation in work settings, small groups, and even small communities in which we interact with the same people on a regular basis. And while the notion of strong reciprocity perhaps explains much of our incentive to be moral in other instances, in larger societies such as the United States the likelihood of people taking advantage of the *informal* system of cooperation by acting for personal gain at the expense of others is presumed to justify and require the presence of a *formal* arrangement of rules and sanctions.

Where social systems are susceptible to this kind of threat, the implementation of explicitly stated laws and rules that dictate what we can and cannot do in the course of our interaction with others, and which provides for sanctions for violating those laws and rules may be necessary. As Hobbes offered, "[T]here must be some coercive power to compel men . . ."—"the terror of some punishment."[25] Following this logic, it is often argued that societies need explicit rules and enforcers of those rules; in other words, we need government—including its enforcers of law, courts, and system of corrections—to apply and execute the social contract. In short, large-scale societies need some mechanism by which to punish those who would defect from their moral and social obligations, and the system of criminal justice is just such an authority.

For Hobbes and other social contract theorists, cooperation, trust, altruism, compassion, and any other prosocial qualities and practices are possible only when we have some sense of security—one not promised by morality alone, but which depends upon the existence of some form of political authority with the capacity to enforce established rules of social living.[26] The social contract—including the laws, enforcers of laws, and systems of courts and corrections to which it gives rise—can thus be thought of as *making possible* the existence and embodiment of moral values and principles. Once we no longer have to worry about our own safety and welfare, we can afford to be moral—we can afford to care about others.[27] Even if altruistic behaviors are a product of human nature, it could be argued that they become widespread only under the security offered by government.

The Importance of Justice

Social contract theory thus takes reciprocal altruism and strong reciprocity a step further; if morality is grounded in and perhaps explained by a natural and/or shared understanding that cooperation and trust are mutually beneficial, then the existence of laws and systems of justice are grounded in and explained by the pessimistic (but perhaps realistic) assumption that people will sometimes violate that trust. Even if one does not accept the assumptions that underlie the notion of the social contract, we must nevertheless acknowledge that the hypothetical contract itself encapsulates the very purpose of law and the criminal justice system. Contractualism justifies the state, its laws (i.e., codified moral rules), and mechanisms of social control (e.g., law, policing, courts, corrections) by arguing that those must exist to prevent society from regressing into a "state of nature" wherein theft, violence, and other social problems would run rampant.

As for those who would violate formal laws? They are *necessarily* punished. Criminals have violated the basic terms of reciprocity as presumed by the social contract—"we recognize the rules of social living as limiting what *we* can do only on the condition that others accept the same restrictions on what *they* can do . . . by violating the rules with respect to us, criminal release us from our obligation toward them and leave themselves open to retaliation."[28] It is not only morally *permissible* to punish offenders of the social contract, but perhaps morally *obligatory* that we do so.

There is at least one crucial concern with the theory and application of such a contract—including the ways in which it informs our assumptions about crime and our treatment of criminal offenders. In short, the contract must be *fair*. Cooperative social living must occur under conditions of *justice*. The idea of a social contract presumes that cooperative arrangements produce benefits for all involved parties. Our "acceptance" of the social contract might depend upon us feeling as though it *is* in our interests to accept the burdens of the contract (i.e., restrain our egoistic pursuits and even sacrifice something of ourselves) in exchange for its benefits. Yet what if the conditions within a society are such that significant numbers of people are expected to share burdens, but *do not benefit* from existing rules and arrangements?[29]

Let us again use the example of a friendly game of poker for purposes of analogy. If everyone participating is given $100 with which to start, your losing badly and walking away with nothing may be an undesirable outcome, but you will likely regard it as a fair outcome assuming that everyone else played by the rules. On the other hand, suppose you are given $10 with which to play, while all others are given $100. If you were to again lose and walk away with nothing, not only would the outcome be undesirable from the perspective of your interests, but you would likely also consider it to be unfair. Further, because of the disadvantage in which you found yourself, you may have had significantly less of an incentive to abide by the rules; in other words, you may even feel that you *needed* to cheat to have some opportunity to benefit from the outcome of the game.

A "fair" social contract requires that the system of cooperation enforced by law and criminal justice benefits everyone (or, at the very least, that everyone has more or less equal opportunity to benefit from it). This assumption arguably becomes problematic when we consider that not all people enter into that contract with the same advantages and opportunities, particularly in societies characterized by inequalities of class, race, ethnicity, gender, age, etc. Consider the following:

- In early 2011, in the midst of the United States' slow economic recovery, the unemployment rate for the white (non-Hispanic) population was 8.0 percent, while for blacks it was 16.2 percent[30].
- In a report released in 2010, the Insight Center for Community Development notes that the median wealth for single black women is $100, while for single white women it is over $41,000. Nearly 50 percent of all single black and Hispanic women have a negative net worth.[31]
- In 2008, the median income for white (non-Hispanic) families was over $52,000, while for black families it was less than $35,000.[32]
- The percentage of black families living in poverty in 2009 (25.8 percent) was nearly three times that of white non-Hispanics (9.4 percent).[33] In 2009, approximately 17 percent of white children lived in poverty, while the percentage of black children living in poverty was approximately 35 percent.[34]
- Racial and ethnic minorities now represent more than 60 percent of the prison population. On any given day, over 12 percent of black males in their twenties are in jail or prison.[35]

With considerations such as these in mind, we might ask ourselves whether the "rules of the game" truly create a situation of mutual advantage for everyone expected to abide by them. If existing arrangements are such that certain people or groups are not granted the same opportunities, rights, and liberties as others, or do not benefit from the same safety and security others experience, we are arguably "*demanding that they accept the burdens imposed by the social arrangement even though they are denied its benefits.*"[36] It becomes necessary to either justify those inequities, or change the "rules" (or laws, policies, etc.) to better ensure conditions of mutual advantage.

Reconsidering Justice

The very notion of a social contract, and the existence of laws and institutions designed to enforce that contract, raises a concern which is vital to moral, social, and political philosophy: that of *justice*. In Chapter 1, we briefly considered the centrality of justice in both ethics and in the study and practice of criminal justice. Morality not only entails some concern for our own choices and actions but also the extent to which the cooperative arrangements within the communities and societies in which we live and work are fair. Law, politics, economics, education, health care, and other institutions that help shape these arrangements have a vast and substantial impact on the prospects of individuals to pursue good lives. As such, we should seek always to embody an awareness of and concern for justice as we pursue good personal and professional lives. As criminal justice practitioners, for example, our obligation is not only to the enforcement of laws within our jurisdiction, but also to the greater concern of justice within our communities. This latter concern requires that we enforce those laws in ways that are fair (e.g., without prejudice, discrimination, and with respect for the rights of citizens), and also entails a consideration of the fairness of those laws themselves:

- Do the laws unfairly disadvantage certain groups of people?
- Do all people enjoy equal protection of law?

- Do all citizens, regardless of class, race, gender, age, sexual orientation, etc., have fair access to the justice system and its protections and services?
- Are the laws being *applied* in a way that respects the rights and liberties of all people equally?
- Is there prejudice or discrimination in the application or enforcement of those laws?

Where the terms or conditions of the social contract are unjust, it could be argued that our moral duty as citizens and as professionals is one of promoting necessary social change in the interest of justice. As we have seen, however, our commitment to justice should not be construed only as a moral duty; rather, we should recognize that unfairness in rules and procedures undermines the rules and procedures themselves, loosening our (and others') commitment to them. In working toward just conditions, we strengthen cooperative relationships and, consequently, help create conditions of mutual advantage that are more conducive to leading good lives in a just society (see Box 6.5).

BOX 6.5
What Is Justice?

To work toward conditions of justice within our communities and societies, we must first have some understanding of what justice is. Although there have been a great many responses to this question, perhaps the most influential conceptualization of justice comes from political philosopher John Rawls (1921–2002). With other social contract theorists, Rawls assumes that we are self-interested, rational beings motivated to select laws, rules, and ways-of-life that are most advantageous to ourselves. In light of this, he asks us to entertain the question of justice with a thought experiment he calls the *original position*. Imagine that you were participating in the creation of a new social contract with other members of society. However, you must work from behind a *veil of ignorance*. No one knows ahead of time what their place in society will be—who they will be, to what race, class, gender, and age group they will belong, where they will live, how intelligent they will be, and so forth. With uncertainty about our place in the world, we are prevented from approaching the question of justice from a position of personal bias. We are forced to be objective in our creation of the laws and rules that constitute the contract, as well as in our approach to how they are implanted and enforced. Recognizing that we are just as likely (in fact, more likely) to be poor than rich, disadvantaged rather than advantaged, our rational self-interest will persuade us to adopt rules and principles that are impartial and thus fair.

Rawls' conclusion is that there are two basic principles that define a "just" society. All rational people operating from within the original position would choose a society in which the following were featured:

1. **The Liberty Principle**. Every person should enjoy an equal and extensive set of basic liberties that are compatible with a similar system of liberty for all. In other words, we should all be willing to agree to a system of rules which guarantees each person the free exercise of basic liberties (e.g., speech, political participation) short of interfering with others' freedom to do the same.
2. **The Difference Principle**. Social and economic inequalities, to the extent that they exist, must be arranged so that they: (a) benefit the least-advantaged members of society; and (b) are attached to offices and positions that are open to everyone of similar qualification (i.e., fair equality of opportunity).

In a cooperative society in which the social contract is intended to be of benefit to all, the laws and rules that make up that contract should be fair from the perspective of everyone involved. Fairness from the perspective of all involved requires first that we each have equal basic liberties, secondly that we each have

(continued)

equal opportunity to compete for offices and positions that allow us to pursue good lives and, lastly, that inequalities can be perceived as fair and beneficial even from the perspective of those lacking advantage. While much could be (and has been) said about Rawls' principles, it may be helpful to consider several of its implications:

- Inequalities can justifiably exist only if everyone (but *especially* the least-advantaged members of society) is better off because of it (principle 2.a.). The rich can get richer if, in so doing, the poor are benefitted. Those with wealth and power, for instance, cannot morally strive to acquire more at the expense of or without benefit to those without wealth and power. Can you think of ways in which the least-advantaged members of society (or an organization, company, etc.) might benefit from the gains made by those at the top?
- Basic liberties such as those to free thought, speech, and religion, those to political participation, and those protecting citizens from unwarranted interference with their person or property are essential to a just society (principle 1). Can you think of existing laws, policies, or practices within law enforcement, courts, and/or corrections that contradict this principle? That protect the rights or liberties of some people or groups at the expense of others? That fail to respect basic rights or infringe upon basic liberties of some people without good reason?
- The difference principle (2.b.) would disallow laws, policies, and practices that deny access to offices and positions to people because of class, race, gender, age, sexual orientation, religious preferences, etc. In what ways is the principle of equality of opportunity relevant to criminal justice in the twenty-first century?

Source: John Rawls, *A Theory of Justice* (Cambridge, MA: Belknap Press, 1971; revised 1999); John Rawls, *Political Liberalism* (New York: Columbia University Press, 1996; revised 2005).

Summary

At the beginning of the last chapter, we posed the question of why we *should* be moral (especially if moral wrongdoing serves to bring personal benefit). Over the course of that chapter and the present one, we have explored a number of possible reasons or motivations for doing the right thing and being a good person:

- Fear of punishment, either by law or some divine entity
- Expectation of reward, either in this life or another
- Because God says so
- Kin selection
- Reciprocal altruism
- Indirect altruism
- Strong reciprocity
- Intuition
- Integrity and character

We argued that fear of punishment and the promise of reward are not, in and of themselves, entirely effective or even desirable motivations for moral behavior, and that the notion of Divine Command should not be employed without caution. In the present chapter, we have considered the possibility that the basis of and motivation for morality might reside in our nature as human beings. More specifically, we are social beings whose own welfare largely depends upon that of others; thus, proceeding in ways cooperative and altruistic is mutually advantageous. Moreover, we are perhaps naturally compassionate beings, our virtues aroused by the suffering of others. Importantly, these responses are not mutually exclusive; they are perhaps better regarded as a collective portrait of why morality develops in human cultures and how and why we, as individuals, might contribute to its dynamic. Indeed, we might have different reasons for being moral in different kinds of situations. Even if there is no single reason or motivation for moral behavior which applies to all people in all situations, we should keep in mind that, for those people and within those situations, some reasons are better than others. With this in mind, in the next chapter we explore how and why morality develops in *individuals*, and whether some motivations for moral behavior are more "advanced" than others.

Key Terms and Concepts

Altruistic (altruism) *104*

Altruistic punishment *109*

Ethical Egoism *103*

Human universals *111*

Moral intuition *112*

Prisoner's Dilemma *102*

Psychological egoism *102*

Reciprocal Altruism *107*

Reputation (indirect reciprocity) *107*

Similarity-leniency hypothesis *112*

Social contract *114*

Discussion Questions

1. What is psychological egoism? How is it related to ethical egoism? To what extent is self-interest permissible, necessary, and/or desirable in our personal and professional lives? Discuss several ways in which both psychological and ethical egoism might influence the perceptions, choices, and/or behaviors of persons working within the criminal justice system.

2. Thomas Hobbes offers some interesting observations on the reinterpretation of motives (Box 6.1). Imagine that a parole officer during the course of his site-visit work confronts a client selling marijuana. The parolee, a mother of three preschool children, lives in poverty. She does not possess a high school diploma and professes to have no marketable skills. Your parolee explains that she sells the drug in order to feed her family and to pay her bills. Would you take "pity" on this parolee? If so, what are your motivations? Are they different from those articulated by Thomas Hobbes? Explain your response.

3. At a citizen review board charged with examining complaints regarding police misconduct, an officer describes the reasons why he "planted" evidence to convict a suspect. The officer points out that the suspect reportedly was responsible for the rapes of at least ten preadolescent girls. In fact, the suspect's alleged actions resulted in permanent physical and profound psychological injuries to at least three victims. Regrettably, despite the best efforts of the police, there remained insufficient evidence to arrest, prosecute, and convict the suspect. Everyone on the force knew who was responsible for the crimes and everyone wanted this particular suspect caught. So, in order to prevent future acts of sexual abuse, the officer under review planted blood samples at the latest crime scene. The officer concluded that he felt an obligation and a duty to act this way, given the serious harm the alleged offender had caused several innocent victims. In this case, to what extent could the officer be said to have a duty to the public? The victims and their families? To justice? Did the officer do the "right" thing?

4. Recently, the fledgling local newspaper in your community ran a story describing the release of a man convicted

of murder. The man had served fifteen years in prison. Throughout this ordeal, he professed his innocence. Many residents in your hometown did not believe that the man was telling the truth; in fact, people recalled that the person was never particularly honest in anything he said or did. However, testing from new DNA technology revealed that the man was telling the truth all along. The newspaper saw the story as an opportunity to capture some public attention and bolster its circulation. It also felt that, given the lack of support the town displayed toward the convicted man over the years, it could help correct any injustice the town had committed against this person by not believing him. What motivation(s) informed the newspaper's decision? Given these motivations, was the action taken by the newspaper moral or not? Justify your response.

5. Following Hobbes, laws and moral rules create a social climate of mutual advantage in which our natural tendencies to be competitive, self-interested, and take advantage of others are held in check. But is this how things work in all facets of everyday life? Consider the world of business and corporate crime. Enron, for instance, grew to become America's seventh largest company in just fifteen short years. Its investments and holdings involved forty different countries; its workforce consisted of approximately twenty-one thousand employees. However, the success of Enron involved an elaborate hoax. In short, the firm lied about its profits to stockholders and to the government. This deception led investors and creditors to pull away from the company, believing that retreating sooner was far better than losing more money later. The company filed for bankruptcy and thousands of pensioners, stockholders, and other investors lost millions in revenue savings. Is Enron merely an exception to the rule, or are there other cases in which businesses and corporations lie, cheat, and exploit others for their own advantage? Do various types of corporate crime illustrate the ineffectiveness of the idea of mutual advantage? If some corporations are not motivated to "play by the rules," what might be done to reduce their harmful actions?

implement the research design as proposed. The first tasks may include instrumentation, sampling of the research population, and organization of the research team. You may get to know the importance of a pilot study and understand why and how researchers test their measurement instruments. You may also become familiar with some of the practical issues in sampling, which you probably will never think of or fully appreciate when taking related courses in research methods. Such experience will let you envision the later modifications you may need when planning your own research project.

(3) How to collect data. Among all the research activities, data collection involves probably the most intensive use of manpower. In other words, it provides a learning opportunity for a relatively large number of student research assistants. Data collection is very important since it generates the raw material - the facts - for research and analysis. The experience in data collection will help you to design your own research with a down-to-earth approach. Some intricate and subtle issues are associated with particular data collection procedures and can only be seen in the real research process. It is hard to imagine that a person who has never been an interviewer would fully appreciate the skills required for a good interview and the characteristics that define a good interview tool. Of course, if this person becomes a principal investigator, it is unlikely that she will envisage all the issues in data collection and apply needed quality control accordingly.

(4) How to manage and analyze the data. Data collection provides a relatively large number of research assistant jobs, whereas data management and analysis supply more stable and lasting research positions. To manage and analyze the data you need to familiarize yourself with the use of computers. You should also get conversant with various kinds of computational software, including such statistical packages as SPSS and/or SAS. This kind of skill is becoming more and more important nowadays. It is to your advantage to spend time preparing yourself for these sorts of tasks, even if you plan to hire someone later to manage the data and carry out the analysis for your own project (assuming such assistance is legitimized). You will be blinding yourself if you do not appreciate how different ways of handling the data (that often appears to be "trivial" and boring) would affect the results. The time needed to clean and to organize your data may also go well beyond your budget. As a matter of fact, the process of data manipulation and analysis is often tied to the process of creative thinking and writing. Since your thesis/dissertation is so important to you, you certainly want to succeed in all these crucial tasks. And your experience is extremely

another variable X and that X is linearly correlated with Y. To predict the value of Y (Y_i) by the linear equation $Y = a + bX$ the total error would be $E_2 = \Sigma |Y_i - Y|$. The reduction of error, therefore, is $E_1 - E_2 = \Sigma |Y_i - M| - \Sigma |Y_i - Y| = \Sigma |Y - M|$. And PRE $= (E_1 - E_2)/E_1 = \Sigma |Y - M| / \Sigma |Y_i - M|$. The operation of taking absolute values in mathematical calculation and derivation, however, has been felt to be inconvenient. Like we mentioned before, this has lead to the use of another frequently used approach in mathematics, that is, having the differences squared before summing them up. The result is called "coefficient of determination" (in the sense of determining the linearity of the relationship), i.e., $\gamma^2 = \Sigma (Y - M)^2 / \Sigma (Y_i - M)^2 = [\Sigma (X_i - M_x)(Y_i - M_y)]^2 / [\Sigma (X_i - M_x)^2 \Sigma (Y_i - M_y)^2]$. Here M_x is the mean of X and M_y the mean of Y. The significance of the end product should be highlighted, though the details of the derivation process is omitted here.

The above treatment is very similar to the measure of dispersion in univariate analysis in terms of the derivation of the variance (S^2). As a matter of fact, the coefficient of determination can be represented by the variances of the two variables as well as their covariance. The variance S^2 can be specified as Var(X) for X and Var(Y) for Y, and their covariance can be written as Cov(X,Y). By using these denotations, the above formula can be put as $\gamma^2 = \text{Cov}^2(X,Y)/[\text{Var}(X)\text{Var}(Y)]$. Pearson's product-moment correlation coefficient is the square root of the coefficient of determination: $\gamma = \text{Cov}(X,Y)/[\text{Var}(X)\text{Var}(Y)]^{1/2}$. It may range from -1 to +1 and treats the relationship symmetrically. Here we can see that the correlation coefficient is actually the ratio of the covariance of two variables to their variances. The quantities of the variance and the covariance have extensive use in statistical analysis. It is to your advantage, therefore, if you could feel at ease translating from the correlation language to the variance-covariance language, and vice versa. We will further touch on this when we proceed to the more general topic of analysis of variance.

It is obvious that neither the coefficient of determination γ^2 nor Pearson's product-moment correlation coefficient γ has the exact PRE meaning under conventional understanding. Nevertheless, they reflect the degree of association in different ways and determine the capability and applicability of a linear equation in describing a joint distribution of two variables. The larger the absolute value of γ and the size of γ^2, the closer the joint distribution approaches a straight line, and the more useful the linear equation. In such a sense, some authors would consider that γ still follows a PRE logic.

In SPSS, you can use the CORRELATION procedure to obtain statistical measures of association. Similar to the computation of the mean and the standard

Endnotes

1. See, e.g., Len Fisher, *Rock, Paper, Scissors: Game Theory in Everyday Life* (New York: Basic Books, 2008).
2. Donald Borchert and David Stewart, *Exploring Ethics* (New York: Macmillan, 1986), p. 2; Kurt Baier, "Egoism." In Peter Singer (Ed.), *A Companion to Ethics* (Malden, MA: Blackwell, 1993), p. 197.
3. James Rachels, *The Elements of Moral Philosophy* (New York: McGraw-Hill, 1986), pp. 54–56.
4. William Hamilton, "The Evolution of Altruistic Behavior," *American Naturalist*, 97, 354–356 (1963); William Hamilton, "The Genetical Evolution of Social Behavior," *Journal of Theoretical Biology*, 7(1), 1–52 (1964).
5. Robert Trivers, "The Evolution of Reciprocal Altruism," *Quarterly Review of Biology*, 46(1), 35–57 (1971).
6. See, e.g., Gary Cordner, "Community Policing: Elements and Effects." In Roger Dunham and Geoffrey Alpert (Eds.), *Critical Issues in Policing: Contemporary Readings*, 6th ed. (Prospect Heights, IL: Waveland, 2010).
7. John Hospers, *Human Conduct: An Introduction to the Problems of Ethics* (New York: Harcourt, Brace & World, 1961), pp. 189–191.
8. Ibid.
9. John Hospers, *Human Conduct: Problems of Ethics* (Belmont, CA: Wadsworth, 1995), p. 189.
10. For example, Will Kymlicka, "The Social Contract Tradition." In Peter Singer (Ed.), *A Companion to Ethics* (Malden, MA: Blackwell, 1993).
11. Donald Brown, *Human Universals* (New York: McGraw Hill, 1991); see also, Steven Pinker, *The Blank Slate: The Modern Denial of Human Nature* (New York: Viking, 2002).
12. Steven Pinker, "The Moral Instinct," *New York Times* (January 13, 2008).
13. Jonathan Haidt, "Liberals and Conservatives Rely on Different Sets of Moral Foundations," *Journal of Personality and Social Psychology*, 96(5), 1029–1046 (2009).
14. Jonathan Haidt and Craig Joseph, "Intuitive Ethics: How Innately Prepared Intuitions Generate Culturally Variable Virtues," *Daedalus*, 133, 55–66 (Fall 2004).
15. Jean-Jacques Rousseau, *Discourse on the Origins of Inequality* (Indianapolis, IN: Hackett Publishing, 1992), p. 76.
16. Peter Kropotkin, *Mutual Aid: A Factor of Evolution* (Manchester, NH: Porter Sargent Publishers, 1976), pp. 148–149.
17. For a recent application of Kropotkin's Mutual Aid Ethic in Crime and Justice Studies, see Christopher R. Williams and Bruce A. Arrigo, "Anarchaos and Order: On the Emergence of Social Justice," *Theoretical Criminology: An International Journal*, 5(2), 223–252 (2001).
18. Ibid.
19. Larry Tifft, *The Struggle to Be Human: Crime, Criminology, and Anarchism* (London: Cienfuegos Press, 1976).
20. Ibid., p. 88; Nicholas P. White, *Companion to Plato's Republic* (Indianapolis, IN: Hacket Publishing, 1979), p. 44.
21. Christopher Falzon, *Philosophy Goes to the Movies: An Introduction to Philosophy* (New York: Routledge, 2002), pp. 88–89.
22. Nickolas Pappas, *Plato and the Republic* (New York: Routledge, 1995), p. 69.
23. Robert Nozick, *The Nature of Rationality* (Princeton, NJ: Princeton University Press, 1993), p. 9.
24. Ibid. (emphasis in original).
25. Ibid.
26. Rachels, *The Elements of Moral Philosophy*, p. 125.
27. Ibid.
28. Ibid., p. 130
29. Ibid., p. 134.
30. Bureau of Labor Statistics, "Employment Situation Summary," (June 3, 2011). Available at http://www.bls.gov/news.release/empsit.nr0.htm (retrieved August 9, 2011).
31. Insight Center for Community Economic Development, "Diverging Pathways: How Wealth Shapes Opportunity for Children," (2011). Available at http://www.insightcced.org/uploads/CRWG/DivergingPathwaysReport-InsightCenter.pdf (retrieved August 9, 2001).
32. U.S. Census Bureau, *2011 Statistical Abstract*. Available at http://www.census.gov/compendia/statab/ (retrieved August 9, 2011).
33. U.S. Bureau of the Census, "Income, Poverty, and Health Insurance Coverage in the United States: 2009," (2010). Available at http://www.census.gov/prod/2010pubs/p60-238.pdf (retrieved August 9, 2011).
34. Child Trends, *Children in Poverty* (2010). Available at www.childtrendsdatabank.org/?q=node/221 (retrieved August 9, 2011).
35. The Sentencing Project, "Racial Disparity." Available at http://www.sentencingproject.org (retrieved August 9, 2011).
36. Ibid. (emphasis in original).

7

Becoming Ethical: The Development of Morality

"In Europe, a woman was near death from a special kind of cancer. There was one drug that the doctors thought might save her. It was a form of radium that a druggist in the same town had recently discovered. The drug was expensive to make, but the druggist was charging ten times what the drug cost him to make. He paid $200 for the radium and charged $2,000 for a small dose of the drug. The sick woman's husband, Heinz, went to everyone he knew to borrow the money, but he could only get together about $1,000 which is half of what it cost. He told the druggist that his wife was dying and asked him to sell it cheaper or let him pay later. But the druggist said: 'No, I discovered the drug and I'm going to make money from it.' So Heinz got desperate and began to think about breaking into the man's store to steal the drug for his wife." Should Heinz steal the drug? Why or why not?[1]

The "Heinz Dilemma" portrays a man faced with a profound moral dilemma, his wife's life, the druggist's interests, and his conscience (among other things) in the balance. Consider the ways in which the following might be important considerations:

- The alleviation of suffering
- The protection of life
- Honoring property rights
- Helping others
- Avoiding harm
- Laws prohibiting stealing
- Heinz's love and care for his wife
- Whether stealing would bring about more good than bad for everyone affected

The ethical significance of the Heinz dilemma and others like it is not so much in our conclusion about what Heinz should do, but in the process of moral reasoning which leads us to that conclusion. As we have noted on several occasions, morality is not simply about doing the right thing, but about doing the right thing for the right reasons. Presumed by this statement is that some reasons are "better" or "more advanced" than others. For instance, if Heinz chooses not to steal the drug out of respect for the law, can he be said to be more or less moral than another man who *would* steal the drug out of care and compassionate concern for his wife? Is it possible to know which kinds of reasons for moral behavior are superior to others?

MORAL DEVELOPMENT

The notion of **moral development** implies that conceptions of morality and types of moral reasoning are not static across the life span. Instead, to suggest that morality is subject to development is to suggest that it changes and evolves over time. What this means is that some beliefs, values, and ways-of-thinking are, in a manner of speaking, "better" or more desirable than others because they reflect a higher level or more advanced form of ethical judgment. Thus, it is important to consider *how* moral development occurs and *how* different stages of moral development appear. In other words, the question becomes what modes of reasoning, expressions of motivation, and types of moral principles, values, and ideals are characteristic of people at more advanced stages of moral development? And, how is it that people do or can reach such evolved stages of ethical choice-making and action?

While philosophers have always been interested in moral development, most recently our comprehension of it has been furthered by researchers in the field of developmental psychology. Among the more influential works stemming from the psychological study of moral behavior are those of Lawrence Kohlberg (1927–1987).[2] Kohlberg's pioneering work during the 1960s, 1970s, and 1980s was responsible for tremendous growth and progress involving the theory of, research on, and knowledge about the evolution of morality and moral behavior. Kohlberg was particularly interested in the moral reasoning of children and adolescents; that is, the thought processes characteristic of young people in relation to moral dilemmas.

Through his research on moral development, Kohlberg suggested that morality and moral reasoning proceed through a series of "stages." More accurately, Kohlberg argued for an elaborate developmental sequence consisting of three levels, with each level involving two developmental periods. Kohlberg maintained that individuals progress through these six phases in a fixed order; that is, without skipping a stage. Following Kohlberg, what this suggests, then, is that there are (more or less) universal stages of moral growth linked to developments in human cognition. In other words, types of moral beliefs, motivations, choices, and actions will be characteristically different in relation to the stage of cognitive development or intellectual maturity individuals have attained.

For Kohlberg, motivations for moral choices and behaviors are based in thinking and reasoning rather than in affect or emotion. Consequently, good moral reasoning and good moral choices require us to be sound thinkers and to have refined *cognitive* (thinking as opposed to feeling) skills. Cognitive skills that are central to morality and moral development include such abilities as imagination, conceptual thinking, the recognition of similarities and differences between (comparable) moral situations; and general reasoning ability that corresponds to the capacity for abstract and logical thought.

To illustrate, the capacity for imagination is essential to empathy (imagining oneself in another's position); and empathy, as many would argue, is central to moral reasoning and behavior. In order for any one of us "to put ourselves in another's shoes" we must utilize our powers of imagination. Theoretically, persons with more developed imaginative capacities are better able to empathize and, presumably, are more inclined to recognize the needs and feelings of others. When we recognize the needs and feelings of others, we are more likely to consider these interests in our moral reasoning, in the choices we make given that reasoning, and, ultimately, in our actions toward others.

KOHLBERG'S MORAL STAGES

Before we explore Kohlberg's stages of moral development in greater detail, it should be noted that very few people are thought to ever reach the highest stages (5 and 6). This is not necessarily because they *can't*; rather, higher stages of moral development represent ideal phases that

TABLE 7.1	Kohlberg's Stages of Moral Development

- *Level 1: Preconventional Morality*
  Stage 1: Punishment and Obedience
  Stage 2: Instrumental Purpose and Exchange
- *Level 2: Conventional Morality*
  Stage 3: Interpersonal Expectations and Conformity
  Stage 4: Law and Order/Social System Maintenance
- *Level 3: Postconventional Morality*
  Stage 5: Social Contract/Utility/Rights
  Stage 6: Universal Ethical Principles

require more than simply the natural evolution of cognitive skills. As previously noted, Kohlberg proposed that moral development occurs in a series of stages that are linked with the more general development of cognitive skills or intellectual faculties. More specifically, Kohlberg's research led him to conclude that there exist three levels of moral growth, with each level having two stages. The levels and stages form a developmental sequence in which no one can "skip" a stage (see Table 7.1).

Level 1: Preconventional Morality

At the preconventional level of morality, children (ages one to ten years) approach moral issues purely from the perspective of *self-interest*. Preconventional morality is *self-focused* morality, prior to any conception of social convention or shared norms. Moral values are regarded as external to the self; that is, they do not reside in any internal processes, but exist "out there." The child experiences these values through the enforcement strategies or regulation efforts undertaken by authority figures. At this stage of development, the child abides by rules; however, they are understood only in terms of the consequences that attach when following or failing to follow them (e.g., punishment by parents or teachers). Thus, what matters most during this period of moral development are the *consequences* stemming from one's (potential) actions.

For example, during their early years of psychological growth, many children will share toys with other children while playing. However, when this activity occurs it is not because they recognize that sharing is the morally "right" thing to do or because they understand cognitively that sharing is ultimately in their own best interest. Rather, the motivation for sharing is better understood as *fearing the consequences* of not sharing. Thus, preconventional morality is a rule-following form of morality, but one in which the underlying function of those rules is not yet comprehended.

During Stage 1—the **punishment and obedience orientation**—moral thinking is characterized by *perceptions* of right and wrong that are based on obedience to authority and shaped by the *threat of punishment* or the *promise of reward*. Actions for which the child receives praise are understood as right; actions for which the youth is censored are understood as wrong. Within this phase, then, moral thinking does not extend beyond the association of certain behaviors with particular rewards and/or punishments. As such, the child fully submits to an authority figure's definition of right and wrong: The youth is concerned only with the consequences that attach to the behavior and *not the behavior itself.*

The child is motivated to do what is "right" in order to avoid punishment. This motivation stems from his or her cognitive inability to understand the reasons underlying (perhaps justifying) the rules that have been imposed on the youth. However, what the child does understand is that other people have the power to dispense negative consequences on those who fail to follow the rules defined by these authority figures. Moreover, the child recognizes that these rules must be followed in the interest of avoiding such consequences. Thus, at the punishment and obedience stage, the needs and interests of other people are largely irrelevant. For instance, stealing is not wrong or bad because of its victimizing effect on the person from whom one stole; rather, the child identifies the activity as wrongful because the youth understands that she or he will be punished for stealing.

During Stage 2—the **instrumental purpose and exchange orientation**—moral thinking is characterized by egoism or self-interest. The aim of persons at this phase is to advance their own desires; the pursuit of self-interest (for oneself and/or for others) is understood as "right." Thus, whatever is effective in satisfying the child's self-regarding needs or wants is defined as right or moral.

"Moral" actions are undertaken purposefully and instrumentally: They are *used* only to further one's self-interest. Additionally, at this stage, a greater degree of concern for other people is noted. However, the logic of this behavior is purely egoistic as well. Finally, children operating within this period come to understand the basic notion of reciprocity. Reciprocity entails an exchange of goods and services. For example, person "1" engages in activity "X" in return for person "2" engaging in activity "Y." During Stage 2 of preconventional morality, children do not agree to reciprocity based on some reasoned assessment regarding the idea of justice, fairness, gratitude, and so on. Rather, reciprocal activities are undertaken because children recognize the self-serving benefits of doing so (e.g., "I'll scratch your back if you scratch mine").

Level 2: Conventional Morality

The level of conventional morality implies a concern for social rules and shared norms. Beginning around the age of ten years, children begin to recognize that right and wrong are in some ways tied to the interests of other people and to society as a whole. Persons at this level become invested in maintaining conventional order, meeting the expectations of others—be they a family, peer group, community, or country. In contrast to the preconventional focus on consequences and self-interest, the conventional level of morality is characterized by *conformity*.

At Stage 3—**interpersonal expectations and conformity**—the child's orientation turns toward approval from others or an interest in pleasing others. Sometimes called the "good boy/nice girl" orientation (approval from others is often attained by being "good" or "nice"), Stage 3 thinking defines morality in terms of what should be done to win the support of others. Children begin to understand what is expected of them by their parents, teachers, and friends, and morality is interpreted as doing what is necessary to achieve these expectations. As distinguished from Stage 4, the approval that is characteristically desired during the interpersonal expectations and conformity orientation period is limited in scope.

During Stage 4, the spectrum of concern begins to expand beyond the mere expectations of family, friends, and other close intimates. Termed the **law and order orientation**, this period of moral development is characterized by an interest in laws, codes, and commandments and a corresponding respect for authority. Unlike Stage 1 where fear of punishment or other sanctions is the primary motivating force, persons benefiting from Stage 4 growth exhibit some awareness about the need for laws. Moreover, at the same time, this recognition of law is tied to an understanding that social order must be maintained. Thus, persons within this phase of moral maturity display a respect for law and authority, recognized as legitimate and necessary tools that help further and maintain social order.

When people reach Kohlberg's Stage 4 development, then, their moral reasoning reflects an effort to abide by laws, codes, fixed rules, and social obligations. Additionally, by this stage, they have developed some understanding of the function of laws, codes, and other rules. Consequently, they possess some heightened sense of what is morally "right," that morality is related to their participation in the existing social order and that, through this participation, they help to ensure the system's stability and maintenance.

Stage 4 is an important milestone in Kohlberg's model of moral development for several reasons—particularly as it contrasts with higher (postconventional) phases of growth. Perhaps most significant among these reasons is that, for the majority of people, this is the highest stage of maturity they will experience in their lifetimes. Stages 1 through 4 reflect *natural* developmental processes. In other words, education, socialization, training, and other influences are thought by Kohlberg to have little, if anything, to do with the evolution of moral reasoning throughout the first four phases. Moreover, according to Kohlberg, the developmental process through Stage 4 represents a *universal* pattern of cognitive development (i.e., a process of growth that is the same for all people, everywhere). Consequently, almost everyone (regardless of class, race, religion, society, culture, etc.) should reach this stage. Interestingly, the *content* of morality may differ from culture to culture or from time period to time period (because laws and norms vary across societies). Moreover, the length of time it takes to reach certain stages may differ culturally and/or temporally. However, the *process* of moral reasoning exhibited through Stage 4 is presumed to be the same universally. In theory, while almost everyone advances to Stage 4, considerably fewer people ever advance past the law-and-order orientation into more progressive types of moral reasoning (perhaps 20–25 percent of adults in contemporary society).[3] (See Table 7.2).

There is a second characteristic of Stage 4 development that differentiates it from its Stage 5 and Stage 6 counterparts. In brief, while persons in Stage 4 demonstrate a "law-and-order" orientation, they do not question the legitimacy of those laws (or codes, commandments, etc.). In other words, there is no critique regarding the *content* of those laws, only a concern for conformity to them. Having reached Stage 4 development, many people internalize societal and institutional (e.g., religious, legal) rules regarding moral behavior; however, their adoption of these rules occurs *without having considered the underlying principles involved.* For example, the law-and-order orientation is exemplified in such reasoning as, "it is wrong to kill *because it is against the law*"; or, "abortion is wrong *because the Bible says so*" (see Box 7.1). Interestingly, these cases fail to offer any

TABLE 7.2	Summary of Kohlberg's Stages of Moral Development	
Stage	**Who Reaches It**	**When Reached**
Punishment and Obedience	Everyone	1–5 yrs.
Instrumental Purpose and Exchange	Everyone	5–10 yrs.
Interpersonal Expectations and Conformity	Everyone	10–16 yrs.
Law and Order	Everyone	16 yrs.–mid-20s, for most the remainder of life
Social Contract/Rights	20–25%	Mid-20s, at least
Universal Ethical Principles	Very, very few	(Some suggest middle age)

BOX 7.1
Moral Reasoning and the Ethics of Abortion

Abortion is and has always been a highly contentious issue in the United States. There are few moral (and political) issues that generate stronger emotional reactions for many people. Troublingly, much discourse on abortion consists of more name-calling than reasoned argumentation. Positions on abortion range from radical pro-life advocates who argue that a moral "right to life" exists from the moment of conception, to radical pro-choice advocates who argue that a woman's "right to choose" and "right to privacy" are always primary.

Indeed, abortion was illegal in most states prior to the 1973 case of *Roe v. Wade* in which the Supreme Court concluded that laws prohibiting abortion are unconstitutional in that they violate the fundamental right to privacy. Even then, the Court did not find abortion to be an absolute right. Under some circumstances, the right may be overridden. The Court ruled that states may not interfere with a woman's choice during the first trimester of a pregnancy. During the second trimester, however, states may impose limitations in the interest of protecting the pregnant woman's health. Finally, during the third trimester, the state may justifiably interfere with a woman's decision for purposes of protecting potential human life (the beginning of the third trimester is the time of viability—that point at which the fetus is capable of surviving outside of the mother's womb).

We should keep in mind that the Supreme Court rules on the legality and constitutionality of issues, not their morality. The Court's decision in *Roe v. Wade* was not a ruling on the moral desirability or acceptability of abortion, but an effort to sort out a complex constitutional issue. Thus despite the Court's legal findings, the morality of abortion remains a pressing concern. The following is a list of questions that might be helpful when contemplating the abortion debate. Each of these is a difficult question that must be answered before reaching any reasoned conclusion about the morality of abortion:

- For moral and legal purposes, are unborn children *persons?* Most people will agree that fetuses are *human*, but some argue that being human is different from being a person. Mary Anne Warren, for instance, suggests that "personhood" requires

the following characteristics: (1) consciousness, (2) reasoning, (3) self-motivated activity, (4) the capacity to communicate, and (5) self-awareness. Because a fetus's brain is not sufficiently developed for these characteristics, some have argued, it is not a person and therefore does not enjoy the same moral rights as people (e.g., the right to life).

- If unborn children are not persons, is the fact that they have the *potential* to become persons enough to justify a right to life? Even those who argue that fetuses are not persons will generally recognize that they are potentially persons. Nevertheless, some would argue that a potential person is still not a person and therefore does not enjoy moral and legal rights.

- Should women (or, for that matter, all persons) have absolute rights over their own bodies? In other words, on what—if any—grounds can we morally invade the most private possessions (i.e., mind and body) that people have?

- If abortion is killing, is killing always wrong? We saw in Chapter 1 that many forms of killing are considered justifiable (e.g., war, self-defense). Even if we admit that killing is generally wrong, is it necessarily always so?

- Some sexual relations that result in pregnancy are not voluntary. If abortion should be illegal, should we make exceptions for women who become impregnated through rape or incest?

- In extreme cases, if a woman faces a significant risk of death if she continues to carry a fetus, does her "right to life" trump that of the unborn child's? If so, how significant must that risk be to justify terminating the pregnancy?

Now consider the following reasons for *having* an abortion. As you read through them, ask yourself, (1) whether the reason is a morally good one; and (2) which of Kohlberg's stages of moral development is reflected in the reason provided:

- The mother is a teenager
- The sex of the child is undesirable
- The mother is mentally ill or developmentally disabled

- The mother is physically disabled and will be unable to care for the child
- The mother is a fourteen-year-old who was coerced into having sex by a twenty-five-year-old man
- The child will be severely mentally retarded
- The mother is poor and will not be able to provide well for the child
- The child will interfere with the mother's career plans

Source: Emmett Barcalow, *Moral Philosophy: Theories and Issues,* 2nd ed. (Belmont, CA: Wadsworth, 1998), pp. 266–277; Mary Anne Warren, "On the Moral and Legal Status of Abortion." In T. Mappes and J. Zematy (Eds.), *Social Ethics,* 3rd ed. (New York: McGraw-Hill, 1987); Wendy Simonds, *Abortion at Work: Ideology and Practice in a Feminist Clinic* (Piscataway, NJ: Rutgers University Press, 1996).

thoughtful or sophisticated consideration of the fundamental values and principles from which the laws or rules themselves are formed. Instead, there is only a concern for their authority as laws and rules and a felt need to conform to them because they issue from established powers.

What this means, then, is that through Stage 4 moral development does not require any *independent* thought on the part of the subject. We come to embrace societal and institutional laws, norms, and values as part of a natural development of reasoning skills, not because we have carefully considered them and determined, for ourselves, that they are legitimate and necessary. For this reason, adopting societal and/or institutional norms and abiding by them (e.g., living ones' life as a law-abiding citizen) is regarded as but a natural and expected outcome of moral development and not a reflection of advanced moral sensibilities.

Level 3: Postconventional Morality

Postconventional morality is characterized by an understanding of mutuality, the common good, and a genuine concern for the interests and welfare of other people. At this point, morality is *post*conventional because individuals (now at least in the mid-20s) no longer rely exclusively on social conventions, norms, or laws as the basis for understanding. Instead, postconventional moral reasoning reflects some effort to determine desirable moral values and principles apart from everyday, shared understandings, and to live on the basis of those unique values and principles. This is not to suggest that these morals are necessarily different from customary interpretations; only that the process by which they come to be accepted is different. Postconventional morality is arrived at independently through critical reflection. Ultimately, it is *internalized.* In other words, concepts such as justice, fairness, civility, and community develop from *within us* rather than being derived from sources external to us (e.g., parents, law, religion, social norms).

Persons having reached Stage 5—**social contract/legalism**—demonstrate an understanding of morality that emphasizes the social good and the principles by which it is achieved. Values such as individual rights (e.g., freedom, citizenship, autonomy) are understood as those that a "healthy" civilization should uphold and those that make a society "good." At this stage, moral thinking becomes more abstract and conceptual, rather than a literal interpretation of laws, rules, and regulations. For the most part, right and wrong are still defined in terms of codes and other institutionalized rules and regulations; however, the individual acknowledges the under lying merits of these laws—that is to say, the individual comes to have some fundamental and critical understanding of *why* they are valuable to society.

In Stage 4, people are interested in an orderly society and in "playing their part" to maintain this order through obedience to rules, procedures, commandments, and so forth. During Stage 5, people recognize that following established laws or shared norms is not always good.

Simply because certain rules promote social order does not mean that the form this order takes is good or healthy. For instance, a totalitarian society can be orderly and can function well. At the same time, though, it may also leave much to be desired in terms of promoting or securing moral ideals (e.g., justice, fairness, rights).[4] Kohlberg concluded that persons at Stage 5 generally believe that a good society is best conceptualized as a *social contract* in which everyone agrees on two basic principles: (1) that all people should have basic *rights* such as life and liberty; and (2) hat there should exist *democratic* procedures for making and changing laws and for making society a better place.[5] While persons at Stage 5 may very well conform to established laws, principles, and commandments, adherence to them is based on the recognition that these rules are fairly and justly created, thereby fulfilling a greater ethical purpose. As we will see in the next chapter, the sort of morality Kohlberg has in mind during Stage 5 is consistent with *utilitarian* conceptions, while his position in Stage 6 is best represented by the moral philosophies of Kant and Rawls (see Chapter 9).[6]

What we have by Stage 5, then, is a developmental process in which a significant qualitative change in moral reasoning occurs. The social contract/rights orientation involves, for the first time, a *critical* dimension—that is, a willingness to evaluate and assess those with whom one identifies.[7] Conversely, Stages 1 through 4 largely are characterized by an unthinking association with the values and interests of those social groups to which one belongs (e.g., friends, community, political or religious affiliations, or society more generally). By contrast, Stage 5 persons are committed to certain moral values and principles and are willing to regard as wrong or unethical those behaviors that are inconsistent with these values and principles. They adopt this point of view no matter who thinks or how many people act otherwise. Thus, Stage 5 is the first time in one's moral progression that *moral courage* becomes important (recall the discussion in the previous chapter regarding Plato's threefold soul, the virtue of courage borne of the spirited part, and inner balance). As we will see, courage is more fully developed and becomes a defining feature of one's Stage 6 moral growth; however, by Stage 5, there is some willingness to maintain and defend moral beliefs that are at odds with larger social groups, as well as society as a whole.

Stage 6—**universal ethical principles**—is the most advanced period of moral development, theoretically representing the highest level of moral reasoning. Very, very few people are thought to ever reach this stage (attained, perhaps, during midlife). Kohlberg suggested that because Stage 5 moral reasoning can still produce injustices, there must be some point of development that stands above the social contract/legalism orientation. Laws, for instance, can be created and enforced democratically; however, they nonetheless can result in unjust outcomes. In a democracy, the influence of the majority can work to have legislation passed that is opposed to the interests of the minority. However, persons at Stage 6 recognize that while laws may be enacted fairly and democratically, this is not necessarily the same as doing what is, in fact, fair and just. Democratic procedures, the rule of law, religious principles, and codes of conduct (including criminal justice codes) are regarded as less authoritative than higher ethical values and principles. However, individuals at Stage 6 acknowledge that transcendent principles (e.g., multiculturalism, mutual respect, inclusiveness, dignity, autonomy, community) are the foundation of a just and good society (see Table 7.3).

One issue that exemplifies that distinction between Stages 5 and 6 moral reasoning is **civil disobedience**.[8] Civil disobedience involves a peaceful refusal to obey existing laws that are felt to be unjust—a conscientious disrespect for laws that conflict with one's commitment to higher ethical principles.[9] These principles include such things as humanism, justice, equality, and respect for the dignity of other persons. Once having acquired the insight of Stage 6 moral development, persons typically adopt the wisdom of these *universal* ethical principles as a basis for their reasoning, judgment, choices, and actions. For these "enlightened" individuals, this

TABLE 7.3	Motivations for Moral Behavior at Each Stage of Development

Stage 1:   avoiding punishment

Stage 2:   advancing one's own interests

Stage 3:   expectations of others

Stage 4:   what the law says is right or wrong

Stage 5:   greatest good for the greatest number of people

Stage 6:   reversibility; empathic understanding

orientation to everyday life replaces what they believe to be the perpetuation of injustice built on a foundation of blind obedience to the authority of law. Because persons at Stage 5 demonstrate a commitment to changing unjust laws through democratic processes, they are less inclined to endorse civil disobedience. In other words, their criticism of the "system" is not an outright rejection of it. However, by Stage 6, commitments to higher ethical principles trump what are believed to be limited (and flawed) regulations, laws, and codes.

Civil disobedience toward or peaceful noncompliance of unjust laws exemplifies the *independent* and *self-chosen* nature of moral values, principles, and commitments characteristic of Stage 6 development. Thus, for example, respecting the dignity of all human beings (and all nonhuman living things) may be recognized as more important than the legal provisions that pertain to our treatment of them. Additionally, the law may allow for—even demand—slavery (consider cultures where slavery is still practiced); however, persons at this advanced period of ethical reasoning embody the principle of respect for the dignity of others and embrace the freedom to exceed the demands of law or to otherwise renounce formal rules in forthright and virtuous ways. Consequently, such open-minded persons may refuse to keep slaves, perhaps even helping to liberate them despite potential adverse consequences. In this respect, then, moral reasoning at this point in an individual's life demonstrates the courage to adopt and live by one's own ethics, notwithstanding the harms that might result (e.g., ostracism, imprisonment, death). For instance, a person drafted during a time of war who refuses to fight for one's country could be subjected to imprisonment. However, at this stage of moral development, the person would likely accept these consequences because her or his opposition to a war deemed unjust is more important than any legal obligation or negative sanction.

What is the process of reasoning that underlies Stage 6 moral development? Kohlberg referred to it as *second-order Golden Rule role taking.*[10] Essentially, this process entails two steps: (1) making an effort to understand how each person involved in a given situation perceives it; and (2) imagining how every person participating in the situation would feel if they were placed in each other's position. In short, the reasoning process is imaginative, *empathic*, and aimed at finding a "reversible" solution. By "reversible" solution, Kohlberg is referring to *a remedy that would be equally fair and just from the perspective of everyone involved in the situation*. This requires that we treat the needs and interests of all parties impartially, respecting the dignity of each individual and attempting to come to a resolution that would be agreeable for all concerned.[11]

Implications of Kohlberg's Moral Psychology

Kohlberg's theory is grounded in human cognitive processes. Consequently, what is most important is not necessarily the beliefs, values, or even choices we ultimately subscribe to or make. Instead, what is of fundamental importance is the method of reasoning by which we come to adopt these deviation in univariate analysis, the calculation of correlation coefficients does not require you to collapse or categorize interval or ratio variables to suit such nominal level treatments as cross-tabulation. The procedure is actually more suitable for those variables that are often considered as continuous (e.g., age by year, and income by dollar), for it will render more accurate results than a lower level procedure such as CROSSTABS. In exploratory data analysis, it is usually helpful to put all your key continuous variables in the CORRELATION procedure and the computer will immediately produce a "correlation matrix" for you. This will show linear relations between all pairs of the important variables and thus give you a good hunch as to how to proceed with your linear analysis. In such multivariate procedures as multiple regression, you must first run this procedure to determine your analytical model.

Suppose you have obtained a considerable γ and want to predict the change of one variable based on the change of the other variable. How can you construct a linear equation to accomplish this? Obviously, it is not that any kind of linear equation will achieve the same effect. You want the total error of the prediction through the equation to be as small as possible. Ideally, the actual PRE represented by γ or γ^2 (if indirectly) should approach the maximum and the linear equation should eventually realize this PRE. Conceivably, the derivation of the linear equation will have much to do with the logic of the correlation coefficient. In real terms, the specification of the main parameter of a linear equation is very similar to the calculation of the correlation coefficient. The difference is that the relationship of the two variables in the equation is asymmetrical, and the main parameter does not limit its variation within the range between -1 and +1.

Let us start over on this. Geometrically, you can draw a line to represent the scattergram of X and Y (you can instruct the computer to produce the scattergram for you by using the PLOT procedure in SPSS). Then you can use it to predict the values of Y (dependent variable) according to the values of X (independent variable). Since the mean of Y on each value of X is the best prediction of Y, we call the line constituted by the means of Y a "regression line." The regression line, however, is rarely straight and thus very difficult to represent with an algebraic equation. Further treatment, therefore, has been developed based on the idea of linearization, that is, to use a linear regression line in place of the original regression line. The simple linear equation representing the straight line can be written as: $Y' = a + bX$. Here Y' may be different from the actual value of Y due to the possible error in prediction. Geometrically, a is the intercept of the line

TABLE 7.4	To Steal or Not to Steal

Stage 1: I should not steal because I will get in trouble (i.e., be punished).

Stage 2: If I can get away with it, I should steal because it's an easy way to get something want.
I should not steal because I might bring great harm to myself if something goes wrong or if I get caught.

Stage 3: I should steal because my friends will think I'm "cool."
I should not steal because my parents, teachers, and friends will not think of me as a good person.

Stage 4: I should not steal because it's against the law.

Stage 5: I should not steal because it is in the best interest of my community and society. Not stealing from others is a basic principle that is necessary to allow people to live good lives in a just society.

Stage 6: I should not steal because I know how I would feel if someone stole from me.
I should steal if doing so rectifies a fundamental injustice—(e.g., I am fighting oppression, inequality, and helping to make the world a better place).

values and beliefs. However, following Kohlberg's insights on moral development, are some principles "better" than others? (See Table 7.4.)

Upon closer inspection, the answer appears to be, "maybe." While Kohlberg's model suggests that higher-order values including dignity, community, and fellowship are more enlightened than several others (thus challenging relativist arguments as described in Chapter 4), what is more explicit is that some *reasons* for our choices and actions are, in fact, better than others. Thus, two people can have contradictory beliefs concerning capital punishment, racial profiling, Internet pornography, and any number of criminal justice controversies. While Kohlberg's theory does not necessarily allow us to determine which view on any ethical controversy is correct (based on our values/principles), it does allow us to assess which perspective is more "moral" by determining which of them is grounded in "better" reasoning.

Let us consider the example of volunteering at a homeless shelter. Suppose that three different persons (John, Paul, and Laurel) each volunteer at the shelter twice a week—John to fulfill community service obligations that are a mandate of his probation; Paul because his girlfriend will act more positively toward him; and Laurel because she recognizes that impoverished persons have certain needs and interests they cannot address on their own. Each person is *doing* the same thing (i.e., volunteering). However, based on Kohlberg's model, each individual represents a different level of moral development. Laurel is clearly the "most moral" of the three: Her motivation for volunteer work reflects a commitment to higher level ethical principles. John is motivated by an effort to avoid undesirable consequences (punishment) that would result from his failing to fulfill the conditions of his probation. Paul is motivated by self-interest. Though all three are engaged in morally desirable behavior, they do not exhibit the same degree of ethical maturity. As noted in Chapter 1, morality is not simply about "doing the right thing." In the context of ethics, what is important are the reasons underlying one's choices and actions.

Perhaps the most important implication of Kohlberg's model is his insistence that being a morally good person—possessing ethical maturity—requires that an individual *develop* moral reasoning skills. As we have seen, through Stage 4 this progression is thought to occur naturally and in spite of social and cultural influences (e.g., parenting, education, class, ethnicity). However, development beyond this stage is not natural to the process of cognitive development. Instead, evolution or maturation to Stages 5 and 6 requires several things. Assuming that morality does develop, it becomes important to consider *how* it develops; that is, how do we *become* good moral thinkers and decision makers, exhibiting higher-stage characteristics of virtue and integrity?

If postconventional morality represents a more advanced and, thus, desirable level of moral development, we should have an interest in pursuing such advances. However, we cannot simply "choose" to exhibit Stage 6 reasoning and ethics. We may admire the character, qualities, and achievements of a Gandhi or a Jesus of Nazareth. We may even make an effort to model our own lives after such exemplary historical figures. Still, our admiration for these "enlightened" individuals, particularly as symbols of morality, does not necessarily mean that we can so easily embody the level of moral development they exhibited. Following Kohlberg's model, this is because we must first acquire and then grow the sort of reasoning and other cognitive skills characteristic of great moral leaders. Consequently, it is not so much a matter of *imitating* the moral qualities or behaviors of Gandhi, but of understanding *why* Gandhi adopted the values and principles that he did; that is, of thinking and reasoning like Gandhi.

Most of us are by now familiar with popular slogans such as, "What would Jesus do?" or "What would Buddha do?" From a developmental perspective, the question, actually, is not what Jesus or the Buddha would do, but *how they would think about what to do.* We may acknowledge that several great moral figures throughout history engaged in forgiveness and that, as such, we should make an effort to forgive in similar situations. However, if we do not understand *why* mercy, compassion, and forgiveness are desirable traits, we are not embodying the same degree of moral wisdom and insight featured by past ethical leaders.

Thus, what is implied in Kohlberg's model is the notion that good moral behavior is not a matter of attempting to emulate persons of good moral fiber. Instead, it is a matter of *internalizing* the reasoning processes these persons employ. What this means is that ethical maturity is not so much about internalizing moral content (e.g., learning certain values and principles) as much as it is about developing cognitive skills and thinking about moral dilemmas in more advanced ways. Once we have developed the sort of advanced reasoning talents characteristic of great moral figures, we will not have to make a conscious effort to think about what they would do when faced with the moral problem confronting us. Instead, sound moral choices will emerge naturally for us by virtue of the ways in which we have come to think about complicated moral situations.

Kohlberg also recognized that sometimes there is a discrepancy between thinking and doing that characterizes our choices and behaviors in the face of moral concerns. In short, people do not always act as they think. While we may show evidence of advanced moral reasoning when asked about a moral predicament, in practice we may act in a way that reflects a lower level of moral development. For instance, we may agree that assisting the needy or the underprivileged is important, but choose not to make charitable contributions, fail to volunteer our time, or refuse to support tax increases even when earmarked for additional social programming (some of us may even go to great lengths to avoid paying taxes!).

HOW DOES MORALITY DEVELOP?

So, how do we acquire and nurture reasoning skills characteristic of higher stages of moral development? As previously indicated, according to Kohlberg, moral development through Stage 4 proceeds independently, absent any particular socialization or training. Fear of punishment (Stage 1), self-interest (Stage 2), concern for approval/disapproval from others (Stage 3), and the internalization of group and societal norms (Stage 4) are age-related occurrences that are thought to happen universally. We advance through these stages simply by being exposed to life experiences that encourage us to utilize and develop various cognitive skills. These experiences enable us to think about ourselves, other people, and various life situations.

In short, Kohlberg argued that children (and, at postconventional phases, adults) progress through different stages of moral development *from their own thinking about moral concerns.*[12] Various interactions we have over the course of the lifespan promote moral development by stimulating cognitive processes, thereby encouraging the refinement of reasoning skills essential to morality.[13] For example, becoming engaged in discussions or debates with others—especially those whose views differ from our own—can challenge us to reconsider our beliefs and encourage us to develop a more comprehensive position or to consider a variety of perspectives.[14]

Suppose that Marc (Stage 4) argues that we should obey the law under all circumstances because it is central to ensuring social order. In response to Marc's position, Sandra indicates that laws are not always moral, nor are they always in the best interest of the collective good. She uses the example of Nazi Germany, which was characterized by rules most people today would find morally objectionable, especially since these laws were opposed to the interests of a great number of people (e.g., the extermination of Jewish people, persons of color, gays, and various ethnic groups). Theoretically, Marc will recognize the inadequacy of his own view, experience some cognitive tension, and resolve this tension by modifying his own perspective to account for this inconsistency. In other words, Marc's debate with Sandra encourages him to move closer to Stage 5 development.[15]

Kohlberg suggested that when we are challenged to recognize the inadequacies of our existing reasoning, we are forced into a situation that motivates us to formulate better positions.[16] This sort of critical thinking about ethical issues is especially relevant at more advanced (postconventional) phases of moral development. Postconventional morality seems to depend upon the evolution of critical, independent thought and reasoning skills that require, for most people, considerable life experience, exposure to different cultural values and belief systems, emotional maturity, and/or education and training aimed at developing improved thinking skills. We will return to the importance of independent thought and critical thinking skills in significantly greater detail in Chapter 11.

Additionally, though, Kohlberg indicated that *role-taking opportunities* can provide worthwhile occasions for moral development by inviting us to reflect on the views of others.[17] Considering the perspective, needs, and interests of people is integral to Stage 6 moral development, and role-taking opportunities represent a context in which to increase these capacities. At the same time, however, a significant amount of research has been carried out in recent years questioning the ways in which our present system of education inhibits rather than promotes the development of empathy and role-taking.[18] As some have argued, the current educational system encourages social differentiation and competition more so than empathy, compassion, and cooperativeness.[19] Many educational theorists have called for a reconfiguration of the learning process built on alternative, prosocial values in which caring, interpersonal knowing, openness to different viewpoints, and a sense of community are emphasized.[20] In this replacement model of learning, the educational process would be restructured such that it sought to expose students to connections between learners rather than accept the barriers that follow from artificially constructed differences.[21] This is best achieved by providing opportunities for supportive participation, "community" problem solving, and role-taking interactions that promote a genuine receptiveness to the viewpoints and experiences of others. As we become more open to the views of people, not only do we develop our capacity for empathy, we also grow our connection to others, thereby establishing a corresponding sense of respect for and responsibility toward our fellow human beings (see Box 7.2).

BOX 7.2

Moral Development, Education, and the Criminal Justice Practitioner

Given the importance of moral decision-making in criminal justice, it could be argued that those invested with the discretion and authority to make and enforce laws and policies will, ideally, demonstrate advanced levels of moral reasoning. As we have seen, however, progression to higher stages of moral reasoning does not occur as part of a natural developmental process. Kohlberg emphasized that morality develops in large part from being exposed to challenging moral scenarios and being forced to think critically about those dilemmas. For the current or future criminal justice practitioner, this process of critical inquiry can encourage a more robust understanding of moral concerns and their application to professional situations.

Partly for this reason, college courses in ethics have become increasingly popular in criminal justice, business, and other disciplines for which developed moral sensibilities are an important prerequisite for entering the workplace. Ideally, these courses encourage students to critically reflect upon moral values, principles, and issues while giving special attention to those that are central to their respective discipline. As we have seen, Kohlberg suggested that advancement to higher stages of moral development occurs largely as a result of opportunities that expose us to moral controversies, allow us to analyze them from the perspective of all people involved, challenge our current thinking about those issues, and encourage us to understand and consider various alternative solutions to moral conflicts. While these opportunities can and often do emerge as we confront real-life situations, they also arise through exposure to issues and controversies and the more general atmosphere provided by *higher education*.

To illustrate the importance of higher education for criminal justice professionals and its potential link to moral development, we might consider the ways in which college education seems to impact *police attitudes*. Over the past several decades, the influence of college education on police attitudes and performance has become a developing area of research within

criminal justice. As more and more law enforcement agencies are requiring at least some higher education, this research is not only timely, but also important. Though this area of research is still in the developmental stage, several themes have emerged. Compared with police officers who have no college education, research suggests that those who do generally:

- Have more open belief systems
- Are more flexible in their thinking
- Are more aware of social problems
- Are more aware of and sensitive to racial and ethnic tensions
- Have greater acceptance of minorities
- Better understand the psychological and sociological bases of human behavior
- Are better able to empathize
- Are better able to communicate
- Are better able to adapt to complex situations
- Demonstrate greater tolerance toward others
- Are more ethical

Many of the characteristics highlighted above are arguably crucial to the law enforcement profession, particularly as practitioners carry discretionary powers into complex situations. Of course, the impact of college education on current and future law enforcement officers may vary depending upon the type and quality of that education. Based on Kohlberg's model of moral development, if courses—whether specifically on the topic of ethics or otherwise—are structured to expose students to controversy, to multiple points of view, and to encourage critical, independent thinking with regard to those issues, they would be more likely to have the desired effect. Even beyond specific courses, however, the college experience more generally would seem to expose students to diversity, conflict, and other situations that may benefit their moral development. As the research in this area continues to develop, we will no doubt attain a better understanding of the impact of education on law enforcement practitioners and other criminal justice professionals.

Gender Differences? Gilligan's Ethics of Care

A number of researchers have taken exception to Kohlberg's model of moral development. One of the more potent criticisms comes from Carol Gilligan (1936–), a former research assistant to Kohlberg and Harvard University Professor. Gilligan's work on moral development led her to

TABLE 7.5	Gilligan's Stages of Moral Development		
Stage	**Description**	**Goal**	**Notes**
Preconventional	Self-interest	One's own needs and interests are of exclusive importance	Similar to Kohlberg; egoism and "me-first" reasoning
Conventional	Self-sacrificing	The needs of others are more important than one's own	In most cultures, women are socialized to nurture and care for others, therefore "self-sacrifice" is part of being a "good" friend, mother, wife, etc.
Postconventional	Care ethics	Balance between one's own needs and those of others; Synthesis of justice and care approaches	Recognizing value of self as a unique person worthy of respect (and self-respect); attention to both needs of self and others, as well as justice-based issues of equality

conclude that there are significant *gender differences* in the ways men and women respond to moral dilemmas (see Table 7.5). Gilligan argued that Kohlberg's model was constructed almost exclusively from interviews with privileged white men and boys and, consequently, reflected a male-centered orientation that was biased against women.[22] Moreover, in Kohlberg's model, the higher stages of moral reasoning focus on justice, rights, rules, and other abstract principles. However, as Gilligan explained, these abstract notions are more characteristic of men and not women. Indeed, as she discovered, what distinguishes morality for women is a concern for human relatedness and caring.[23] Thus, rather than relying on formal rules and procedures, women tend to approach and resolve conflict through "a process of ongoing communication and involvement that considers the needs, interests, and motivations of all involved"[24] (see Box 7.3).

Given these differences, women tend to score at Stage 3 when utilizing Kohlberg's model of moral development (emphasis on interpersonal relationships and helping/pleasing others). However, the implication is that they are somehow less moral than men because of their gendered focus on these, rather than other, male-centered values (e.g., rights and justice). While some researchers claim that Gilligan exaggerates the extent of these gender differences,[25] an interesting possibility nonetheless emerges.

Essentially, Gilligan suggests that morality may very well develop out of more than a single orientation: one focusing on justice, rights, and logic (for men)[26] and another on interpersonal relationships, compassion, and care (for women). Gilligan argues that each orientation should be valued equally. Moreover, if there are two different models of psychological and moral development, then, perhaps, these perspectives could become *integrated* such that each gender became more responsive to the other's viewpoint.[27] Ideally, men would become more attuned to the value of compassion, care, and responsiveness toward people; women would become more attentive to the principles of individual rights and rules. Imagine, for a moment, how the world might be quite different if legislators, judges, police officers, and military leaders were concerned about justice and fairness while, at the same time, were committed to caring for and responding to the welfare of others. We will have more to say about Gilligan's work, the ethic of care, and its implications for criminal justice in Chapter 10. For now, consider the ways in which her three stages of moral reasoning in women differ from Kohlberg's (which are arguably applicable primarily to men).

BOX 7.3

The "Heinz Dilemma"

Gilligan presented eleven- and twelve-year-old boys and girls with the "Heinz dilemma" which we reviewed at the outset of the chapter. Recall that Heinz has a terminally ill wife and the only means of helping (saving) her is with a drug owned by the local pharmacist. Unfortunately, the drug is priced too high for Heinz to afford, and the pharmacist refuses to lower the price. Should the husband steal the medicine?

Male responses tended to focus on impartial principles and rules, as well as abstract considerations of justice and rights (e.g., stealing is morally prohibited; we have a duty to prevent people from dying; everyone has a basic right to life; the pharmacist has a right to his property). Female responders tried to find alternative solutions that considered the needs of all parties involved—can Heinz borrow the money? Can Heinz and the pharmacist work out a payment arrangement? Can Heinz appeal to the pharmacist's sense of compassion and encourage him to give her the medicine?

Given the care perspective's focus on relationships and sensitivity to the needs of all affected parties, there are other matters of concern leading to questions that would be crucial from a care perspective, but that would factor less significantly into traditional (justice/rights) approaches to moral decision-making.[28] For instance,

- How will Heinz's wife feel if he steals the medicine?
- How will Heinz feel if he doesn't steal the medicine and his wife dies?

- How will the pharmacist feel if Heinz's wife dies after he has refused him the medicine?
- Do Heinz and his wife have children and/or other relatives who would be affected if she dies? What happens to them? How is their well-being affected by each alternative?

With this difference in mind, consider this variation on a classic ethical dilemma. Suppose that ten people are stranded on an island after their tour boat has engine problems. They call for assistance, but it will take four days for anyone to reach them. The stranded tourists remove all available food and water from the boat before it sinks. They realize, however, that they only have enough for ten people to survive for three days. With only nine people, however, their supplies will last until help arrives. In a scenario such as this, is it morally justifiable to take the life of one of the tourists? If so, how should it be determined whose life is lost? Justice-based reasoning might demand that the person whose life will be taken is chosen by random selection, otherwise the tourists might unjustly single out the person they like the least, who is least attractive, contributes the least to society, and so forth. How, if at all, would an ethic of care differ in the kinds of questions it asks in approaching this and similar dilemmas?

Source: Carol Gilligan, *In a Different Voice: Psychological Theory and Women's Development* (Cambridge, MA: Harvard University Press, 1982); Emmett Barcalow, *Moral Philosophy: Theories and Issues*, 2nd ed. (Belmont, CA: Wadsworth, 1998), pp. 214–216.

MORAL DEVELOPMENT AND THE CRIMINAL JUSTICE SYSTEM: MAKING AND BREAKING LAWS

Moral development and its related concepts are pertinent in a variety of ways to the criminal justice system. As we saw in Chapter 1, individuals employed within criminal justice—whether as makers or enforcers of law, as attorneys or correctional officers—are expected to demonstrate a heightened degree of moral judgment. Decisions about when and how to exercise the authority and discretionary powers with which criminal justice practitioners are often invested are ideally informed by advanced moral reasoning skills. Beyond its application to criminal justice practice, the notion of moral development may also shed light on the processes of *lawmaking* and *lawbreaking*. Firstly, the notion of a "higher" morality and universal ethical principles may serve as a guide for lawmaking and as a means of judging the morality of existing laws. Secondly, differences in moral development may help us to understand motivations—good and bad—for violating criminal laws and, perhaps, to make distinctions on this basis. To illustrate the ways in which the concept of moral development can aid us in understanding these various facets of law, crime, and justice, we conclude this chapter by briefly exploring how it might further our regard for the making and breaking of laws. We begin by exploring the notion of natural law and its relation to justice and postconventional morality.

Justice, Natural Law, and Postconventional Morality

Natural law is an ethical theory, dating more than two thousand years to the ancient Greeks, that grounds morality in "nature" (or, more specifically, *human* nature). Its primary theme is that there exists a "higher" law or justice that transcends or stands above human-made law (i.e., *positive law*). It is through reference to this higher law that we are able to judge the morality and justice of human conventions—including those that have become part of written law. This higher, unwritten law has always existed, will always exist, and can never be superseded by human law. It consists of and promotes universal moral principles that protect and apply to all people, everywhere (e.g., those upholding basic human dignity and universal human rights—we will look more closely at natural or human rights in Chapter 9).

A widely discussed example of invoking natural law in the face of an unjust human law is one that we were briefly exposed to in Chapter 1. At the Nuremberg trials, judges appealed to natural law as a means of bringing Nazi leaders and war criminals to trial. The actions committed under the Nazi regime presented a challenging legal scenario, as they were not "crimes" under German law. Further, they did not occur within the legal jurisdiction of any other government. On what grounds, then, could Nazi leaders and war criminals be prosecuted and punished if they had violated no written law? Ultimately, the United Nations tribunal appealed to natural law in arguing that the Nazis had committed **crimes against humanity**—violations of universal moral standards. The tribunal generated a list of standards of justice that were held to transcend any human authority, thereby acknowledging that there are standards of justice that are more important than and supersede the authority of any nation or local government. By 1949, more than two hundred Nazi war criminals had been tried under these newly formed universal standards—with 131 found guilty and 37 sentenced to death.[29]

Natural law suggests that any human code of law must ultimately be consistent with this higher sense of justice. Justice and the universal moral principles it entails are the standard against which we measure human codes. In what ways can human laws be unjust? Judith Boss suggests that a law may be unjust if it has one of the following characteristics:

- *It is degrading to humans* (e.g., laws that permit slavery or torture)
- *It is discriminatory* (e.g., the Fourteenth Amendment gave men, but not women, the right to vote; laws that support apartheid in South Africa and the caste system in India)
- *It is enacted by an authority that is not truly representative*
- *It is unjustly applied* (e.g., search and seizure laws employed to harass political dissidents or other groups of people)

While there are certainly other ways in which human law can be unjust, the above examples illustrate that while human laws may be consistent with "natural" law, in some cases they contrast. Where there is a conflict between natural and human law, the former renders null and void all human laws that conflict with it. Because of this, natural law may justify knowing *violations of human authority* in the interest of justice. If human law is determined through natural law to be unjust and immoral, natural law may *demand* that we take illegal action—even if those actions bring negative consequences (e.g., prosecution and punishment). Natural law thus not only holds violations of human law to be morally justifiable in some cases, but may impose a *moral requirement* of noncompliance for the sake of justice.

As we saw earlier in this chapter, acts of *civil disobedience* characteristic of Kohlberg's universal ethical principles orientation are often justified by appealing to natural law or some higher sense of justice or morality. To exemplify the universal ethical principles orientation, Kohlberg referenced great moral leaders such as Gandhi and Martin Luther King Jr.—both of whom, not coincidentally, are recognized for employing strategies of civil disobedience as means of changing unjust laws, policies, and practices. Both Gandhi and Martin Luther King Jr. practiced peaceful noncompliance with existing power brokers because of their belief in and commitment to higher ethical principles. Gandhi did this during the British occupation and control of India, and King during the Civil Rights movement of the 1960s.

In his *Letter from a Birmingham Jail*, for instance, Martin Luther King Jr. argued that " . . . there are two types of laws: just and unjust. I would be the first to advocate obeying just laws. One has not only a legal but a moral responsibility to obey just laws. Conversely, one has a moral responsibility to disobey unjust laws."[30] Practicing what he preached, King engaged in nonviolent acts of disobedience in Alabama, Mississippi, South Carolina, and Georgia to challenge the law's unmistakable denial of equal opportunity for persons of color in education, employment, and housing, as well as in general social life (e.g., separate bathrooms, separate seating in buses and restaurants). Although repeatedly imprisoned for his "criminal" behavior, for King (as well as for many others), the pursuit of a higher sense of justice and morality justified—even required—the intentional defiance of human law.

While critics have expressed concerns with the implications of Kohlberg's model, it does provoke more critical consideration of lawbreaking behaviors. While some have pointed to the dangers of people placing their own principles above respect for the law and the social order, we are at least encouraged to question the relationship between lawbreaking, motivation, and moral development.[31] Although the social desirability of postconventional morality remains open to debate, we cannot simply assume that morality and legality go hand in hand.

Lawbreaking and Moral Development

Gandhi, Martin Luther King Jr., Henry David Thoreau, and other nonviolent activists exemplify the ways in which violations of human law might be justified on moral grounds. In Kohlberg's model of moral development, they illustrate a recognition of and commitment to a "higher" or "natural" law, morality, and sense of justice consisting of universal ethical principles (e.g., equality) that serve as basic standards of moral behavior—whether for persons, organizations, institutions, or entire nations. Yet not all lawbreaking is motivated by a commitment to higher moral principles. How might Kohlberg's model of moral development help us make sense of motivations for lawbreaking?

Many people presume that criminality somehow reflects immorality or, at least, is an indication of lower levels of moral development. As we have seen, this is not always the case. That persons who have reached higher stages of moral development may violate human laws in light of a commitment to higher moral principles suggests that at least some instances of lawbreaking may reflect moral development that is more advanced than persons who abide by the law. Depending on the motivation and circumstances, obeying human laws may actually reflect a lower level of moral development. Because Kohlberg's model suggests that reasons or motivations for behavior are of more significance than the behavior itself, there are more and less advanced reasons for following the law, and more and less advanced reasons for violating the law. As we saw in Chapter 1, morality is not simply about doing the "right" thing or avoiding the "wrong" thing. Instead, what matters most is the reasoning that informs the choices we make and the actions we undertake.

To illustrate the ways in which different stages of moral development can provide different motivations for violating or respecting the law, consider the following motives for and examples of criminal behavior as they correspond to different stages of development:

Kohlberg's model suggests that rather than criminality being directly equated with immorality, it may be better to understand the relationship between lawbreaking and morality as a continuum. Toward one end of the continuum are behaviors that violate the law and

Stage	Motive(s) and Possible Examples
Punishment and Obedience	fear of greater harm to oneself; obeying or respecting power and authority; obedience to leader/authority figure with power to impose sanctions for disobedience (e.g., organized crime, gangs, "pimps")
Instrumental Purpose and Exchange	pleasure, material gain, vengeance, drug use (e.g., joyriding, shoplifting, revenge or street justice for personal harm)
Interpersonal Expectations and Conformity	reputation, status, peer pressure or conformity to peer group (e.g., fights, fire-setting, thefts to look "cool" or "tough" within one's peer group; drug use within groups)
Law and Order	maintaining law and social order; punishing people who break laws or disrupt social order; while people at this stage generally respect and obey the law, some may take law into their own hands in an effort to maintain social order and punish lawbreakers (e.g., vigilantes)
Social Contract/Rights	protecting freedom and individual rights
Universal Ethical Principles	fighting injustices and advancing causes such as life and equality (e.g., environmental terrorism, Robin Hood–type thievery; draft-dodging)

represent lower levels of moral motivation; toward the other end are behaviors that violate the law but are motivated by higher levels of moral reasoning. A provocative question is whether the system of law and law enforcement should, on any level, make distinctions between crimes motivated by more or less moral interests. For instance, should we consider persons who violate the law for moral reasons less reprehensible and thus less legally blameworthy than others? Should motivation and moral reasoning be considered in the sentencing process such that crimes motivated by higher-level moral interests are subject to lesser types or degrees of punishment? If so, who determines what moral interests justify more lenient treatment?

As a concluding exercise, consider the following hypothetical cases involving lawbreaking behaviors. Which, if any, of these behaviors are immoral? Based on Kohlberg's model, at what level and stage of moral development would you place the persons in the following scenarios?

- A recently laid-off husband and father of five steals several food items from a local grocery store to feed his hungry children.
- A concerned mother drives 80 miles-per-hour in a 55-mile-per-hour zone to get her child to the hospital. The child has a 104-degree fever.

- A new law is passed that requires all citizens in a community to keep a firearm in their house. A couple who has recently moved into the community refuses to do so, citing their moral opposition to firearm possession.
- A research laboratory is conducting biomedical experiments on small animals. A group of animal rights activists breaks into the laboratory, releasing the animals back into nature.

Now consider the following *legal* behaviors. Which, if any, would you consider to be immoral? Given Kohlberg's model of moral development, at what level and stage would you place the actor in question?

- Passing by a dark alley late at night, a young man witnesses what appears to be a rape in progress. As he is unsure what is happening and somewhat afraid to get involved, he chooses to simply continue on his way.
- A young couple has managed to accumulate $50 worth of late charges at a local video store. Upon their next visit, the store manager informs them that there has been a computer malfunction, resulting in the store losing track of all late charges on customer accounts. The manager asks them if they had any outstanding charges, to which the couple replies, "no."
- A large corporation, though acquiring $400 million in profits last year, manages to avoid paying *any* taxes through a variety of legal loopholes.

Of the seven scenarios described above, which are the most morally reprehensible (if possible, rank-order them from most to least reprehensible)? Which, if any, of the seven cases described should result in charges of criminal wrongdoing? Of those, which should be subjected to the harshest punishment? As a final consideration, ask yourself whether your responses are similar to or different from a purely legal approach to these questions.

Summary

Over the course of the last several chapters, we explored a number of concerns pertinent to moral psychology. Whether human nature is inherently egoistic, most of us assume that we have some capacity to act in a moral fashion. To the degree that we *can* act morally, we are left to consider *why* we are inclined to act morally, noting especially the prosocial benefits that follow from engaging in such behavior (e.g., reciprocity, mutual aid).

However, the issue of moral development as presented in this chapter considered *how* morality progresses, given the status of our cognitive skills. For example, we saw that the expectation of reward and the fear of reprisal leave much to be desired as motivations for moral behavior (Stage 1). In fact, Kohlberg identified obedience and punishment as reflecting the lowest level of cognitive development. Conversely, one's appeal to universal and transcendent ethical principles indicates more advanced moral reasoning capabilities (Stage 6). Additionally, however, this chapter noted that the acquisition of these more advanced skills was not necessarily the same as being moral. Ethics is about "doing" what is right for the "right" reasons. Consistent with this logic, Kohlberg explained that postconventional moral reasoning entails thinking critically and independently, questioning or, at least, seeking to understand the underlying reasons for laws, codes, and other formal ethical guidelines, and then moving to reasoned, empathic, justice-based action.

Interestingly, support for Kohlberg's perspective on moral development is not universal. For example, with the Y axis, and b is its slope. Since the mean of variable Y (M_y) and the mean of its predicted value Y' ($M_{y'}$) should be the same to satisfy the accuracy requirement, a can be determined as this: $a = M_y - bM_x$. Here the mean of Y (M_y) and the mean of X (M_x) can be calculated from the measurement results of an actual sample. Yet the key issue is, how to calculate b?

The original idea guiding the computation of b might be called the least errors criterion. Similar to the calculation of dispersion in univariate analysis, the total error of predicting Y using the linear equation $Y' = a + bX$ would be $\Sigma|Y - Y'|$. For reasons similar to those that have shifted the measurement of dispersion to the calculation of the variance in univariate analysis, we may have the errors squared before summing them up. Finding the best-fitting line is then equivalent to the operation of finding the minimum value of the squared errors. This is called the least squares criterion in linear regression analysis. The result of the operation is the general formula of what is called the regression coefficient b: $b = [\Sigma(X_i - M_x)(Y_i - M_y)]/\Sigma(X_i - M_x)^2$. Here M_x is the mean of X and M_y the mean of Y.

Compared with the formula of γ, the calculation of b is the same except that it leaves out the variance of the dependent variable while squares the role of the variance of the independent variable. The formula can be rewritten as: $b = Cov(X,Y)/Var(X)$, which treats the relationship asymmetrically and may take on any value to allow Y a broad range of variation. Here we can see that the regression coefficient is actually the ratio of the covariance of two variables to the variance of the independent variable.

In practice, behavioral and social science researchers seldom use linear equations to actually predict the values of the variables. Regression and correlation are both used to describe the relationship between variables. If the correlation coefficient turns out to be too small, you should not even spend time on constructing the linear equation model. Rather, you need to explore whether there is a nonlinear relationship that may be considerable even if γ is close to 0. If this is the case, a curved regression line may fit the scattergram. The scattergram is a powerful tool for guiding regression and correlation analysis. The analysis of nonlinear relationship, however, is difficult, and one of the approaches is still based on the idea of linearization. You can substitute the variables with certain functions in the hope to transform the original distributions into more linear shapes. For the variable X, for instance, you may try to use $Z = \log X$, $1/X$, or X^n to substitute it, and plot the joint distribution of Y and Z to see if it has been linearized from the original distribution of Y and X. This may

Carol Gilligan indicates that women's morality is based on an ethic of care, compassion, and intimacy rather than the logic of rights, judgments, and rules. Given these gender-based psychological differences, Gilligan recommends that both models be valued—particularly when it comes to understanding the development and use of moral reasoning.

In Part III of this book (Chapters 8, 9, and 10), normative ethics is featured. Normative ethics formulates standards or guidelines for ethical behavior. In short, normative ethics addresses such questions as, "What should I do?" or "How should I be?" As we will quickly discover, the answers to these concerns are not so easily arrived at, especially within the realm of criminology/criminal justice. However, depending on the type of normative ethics in use (i.e., consequentialist, deontological, or virtue-based), a blueprint for moral reasoning, decision-making, and action is supplied. Normative ethics provides "tools" for ethical analysis—tools that can be employed when responding to moral dilemmas that most assuredly emerge for the criminal justice practitioner.

Key Terms and Concepts

civil disobedience *128*

crimes against humanity *136*

instrumental purpose and
    exchange orientation *124*

interpersonal expectations and
    conformity orientation *124*

law and order orientation *124*

moral development *122*

natural law *136*

punishment and obedience
    orientation *123*

social contract/legalism *127*

universal ethical principles *128*

Discussion Questions

1. Stage 6 moral development requires looking at ethical problems empathically; that is, impartially and from the perspective of all parties concerned. In the following situation, consider what the relevant needs and interests are of the participants, giving equal attention to their various perspectives.
   • A second-time convicted pedophile has just completed a mandatory fifteen-year term in prison. The ex-offender is now living in your local community. Some residents are outraged that this man resides in this family-oriented neighborhood. The leadership of your home owner's association calls for a "special" meeting. The purpose of the meeting is to discuss how the community should respond to the presence of a "pedophile roaming their streets." At the meeting, some insist that the police should be contacted and that they should handle the situation; others suggest that any pedophile—even if "reformed"—is mentally unbalanced and, consequently, should be involuntarily hospitalized for psychiatric care; still others believe that the man should be completely shunned by all those who reside in the neighborhood because this will protect their children from the man.

   • How do you interpret this moral dilemma? What is the ethical thing to do here? Given Kohlberg's levels and stages of moral development, how would you interpret the respective positions taken by your neighbors?

2. To the best of your ability, indicate which of Kohlberg's stages of moral development might best explain the moral reasoning involved in the following:
   a. Waging war to protect or further economic interests.
   b. Engaging in a self-defensive war, having been attacked by another country.
   c. Waging war to retaliate against another country.
   d. Executing convicted murderers to serve vengeance.
   e. Executing convicted murderers to protect the public from further harm.
   f. Avoiding paying taxes to further one's profits.
   g. Refusing to pay taxes as a means of protest against injustice.

3. To the best of your ability, indicate how the following ethical dilemmas might be resolved based on *each stage of Kohlberg's model of moral development*: use Table 7.4 as a guide.
   a. Speeding versus not speeding
   b. Lying versus telling the truth
   c. Cheating on an exam versus doing honest work

Endnotes

1. Lawrence Kohlberg, "Stage and Sequence: The Cognitive Developmental Approach to Socialization." In D. A. Goslin (Ed.), *Handbook of Socialization Theory and Research* (Chicago, IL: Rand McNally, 1969), pp. 347–480.
2. Lawrence Kohlberg, *The Philosophy of Moral Development: Moral Stages and the Idea of Justice* (New York: HarperCollins, 1981); Lawrence Kohlberg, *The Psychology of Moral Development: The Nature and Validity of Moral Stages* (New York: HarperCollins, 1984).
3. Anne Colby and Lawrence Kohlberg, *The Measurement of Moral Judgment, Volumes 1 and 2* (Cambridge, MA: Cambridge University Press, 1987).
4. William C. Crain, *Theories of Development* (Upper Saddle River, NJ: Prentice Hall, 1985), p. 21.
5. Ibid.
6. Among other things, Kohlberg has been criticized for his assumption that utilitarian conceptions are somehow less advanced. See, e.g., Edmund V. Sullivan, "A Study of Kohlberg's Structural Theory of Moral Development: A Critique of Liberal Social Science Ideology." In Bill Puka (Ed.), *The Great Justice Debate: Kohlberg Criticism* (New York: Garland, 1994), p. 46.
7. Ibid.
8. See, e.g., Hugo Bedau, *Civil Disobedience: Theory and Practice* (New York: Pegasus, 1969).
9. The classic work on civil disobedience and an ethic of moral dissent is, Henry David Thoreau, *Civil Disobedience* (Bedford, MA: Applewood, 2000).
10. Kohlberg, *The Philosophy of Moral Development*, 1984.
11. William Crain, *Theories of Development*, 5th ed. (Upper Saddle River, NJ: Prentice Hall, 2005), p.122.
12. Ibid., p.124.
13. Ibid.
14. Ibid.
15. Ibid.
16. Ibid., p. 125.
17. Ibid.; Kohlberg, *The Philosophy of Moral Development, Vol. 1–2*, 1981.
18. See, e.g., Carol Gilligan, Janie Victoria Ward, and Jill McLean Taylor, *Mapping the Moral Domain: A Contribution of Women's Thinking to Psychological Theory and Education* (Cambridge, MA: Harvard University Press, 1990); Martin L. Hoffman, *Empathy and Moral Development: Implications for Caring and Justice* (Cambridge, MA: Cambridge University Press, 2002), p. 21.
19. Carol Gilligan, Nona P. Lyons, and Trudy J. Hanmer, *Making Connections: The Relational Worlds of Girls at Emma Willard School* (Cambridge, MA: Harvard University Press, 1990).
20. Carol Gilligan, *In a Different Voice: Psychological Theory and Women's Development* (Cambridge, MA: Harvard University Press, 1982).
21. Gilligan, Lyons, and Hanmer, *Making Connections*.
22. Gilligan, *In a Different Voice*.
23. Ibid.
24. See, e.g., Carol Gilligan, "In a Different Voice: Women's Conceptions of Self and of Morality." In Bill Puka (Ed.), *Caring Voices and Women's Moral Frames: Gilligan's View* (New York: Garland, 1994), p. 1.
25. Christina Hoff Sommers, *The War Against Boys: How Misguided Feminism Is Harming Our Young Men* (New York: Simon and Schuster, 2001).
26. Crain, *Theories of Development*, p. 136; see Gilligan, *In a Different Voice*, chap. 6.
27. Crain, *Theories of Development*, p. 136.
28. Emmett Barcalow, *Moral Philosophy: Theories and Issues*, 2nd ed. (Belmont, CA: Wadsworth, 1998), pp. 214–216.
29. Judith Boss, *Ethics for Life*, 2nd ed. (Mountain View, CA: Mayfield Publishing 2001), p. 134.
30. See, e.g., Martin Luther King, Jr., *The Martin Luther King, Jr. Companion: Quotations from the Speeches, Essays, and Books of Martin Luther King, Jr.* (New York: St. Martin's Press, 1998).
31. Crain, *Theories of Development*, 5th ed., p. 135.

PART THREE

Normative Ethics:
Theory and Application

8

Means and Ends: The Importance of Consequences

On Christmas Eve 1968, Robert Anthony Williams sexually assaulted and murdered a ten-year-old girl in the bathroom of a YMCA in Des Moines, Iowa. Having wrapped her body in a blanket and placed it in his car, he fled from the scene and disposed of the body in the wilderness. Two days later, Williams contacted an attorney in Davenport, Iowa, indicating his desire to surrender to law enforcement. As part of an agreement reached between his attorney and the Davenport police, the officers who would transport him from Davenport back to Des Moines were not to question him. Williams had indicated he would provide details of the offense once in the presence of his attorney in Des Moines. During the subsequent transport, however, one of the police officers accompanying him gave Williams what has come to be known as the "Christian Burial Speech." Knowing that Williams was a deeply religious man with a history of serious mental illness, the officer (addressing Williams as "Reverend") stated:

> I want to give you something to think about while we're traveling down the road . . . They are predicting several inches of snow for tonight, and I feel that you yourself are the only person that knows where this little girl's body is, that you yourself have only been there once, and if you get a snow on top of it you yourself may be unable to find it . . . the parents of this little girl should be entitled to a Christian burial for the little girl who was snatched away from them on Christmas [E]ve and murdered.[1]

Following the speech, Williams led the officers to the young girl's body. He was later tried and convicted of murder—a verdict which was upheld on appeal, despite claims that the evidence uncovered during the trip from Davenport to Des Moines should not have been admitted.

Although this case raises important legal questions concerning the admissibility of evidence and Sixth Amendment right to counsel, it also provokes crucial ethical questions about police interrogations, agreements and contracts, and the desirability of employing questionable means to achieve a desired (and desirable) end:

- Was the officer's appeal to Williams' conscience simply a case of good police work?
- Does it matter that Williams was mentally ill and easily manipulated?

- Does it matter that the officer violated an agreement or promise not to question Williams during the automobile ride?
- Does it make a difference that the behavior of the officer ultimately led to success in finding the girl's body and, thus, critical evidence?

To answer questions such as these, we need a means of identifying what is ultimately important, and how what we regard as important applies in principle to particular instances. As discussed in Chapter 2, we need to know what we *value,* and how decisions and actions promote or fail to promote what we regard as valuable. Is there some sense in which finding the young girl's body should be prioritized over procedural rules? Does our respect for individual rights take priority over what we regard as the best interests of the victim's family and the community?

When we introduced the ethical importance of good decision-making in Chapter 2, we noted that our decisions and beliefs should be informed by good reasons, and having good reasons is often a matter of identifying and prioritizing key moral values and principles and the ways in which they apply to the issue or situation in question. We also noted that the subfield of ethics known as *normative ethics* consists of theories or frameworks that attempt to identify and prioritize moral values and, in so doing, provide guidelines for moral decision-making. Different ethical frameworks, however, prioritize different values, thus promoting different principles and pulling us toward different conclusions about moral issues and dilemmas: *consequentialist* theories focus on the consequences that our decisions or actions bring about; *deontological* theories focus on conforming our decisions and actions to relevant moral duties and obligations; and *virtue ethics* encourages us to develop good moral character, seeking to embody virtue while avoiding vice.

Given the importance and usefulness of these three basic ethical frameworks, we explore each of them in greater detail over the next three chapters. We begin in the present chapter with an examination of consequentialist theories—those that have us ask, "What will happen of I do X?" "Who will be affected and how?" and "How might other alternatives produce different outcomes?"

CONSEQUENTIALISM

According to **consequentialism**, actions are "right" so far as they have beneficial *consequences.* Thus, actions, laws, policies, etc., are morally right to the degree—and only to the degree—that they produce some good or some useful *outcome.*[2] Actions themselves are neither inherently right nor inherently wrong; rather, moral worth attaches only to what decisions and actions bring about, not directly to the decisions or actions themselves. Some consequentialists, for example, would argue that there is nothing inherently wrong with an act of torture; instead, the moral permissibility of torture should be judged only by the good that it yields (or is expected to yield) relative to all other possible courses of action. In other words, the "means" can be justified by the "end."

For a particular decision or action to be morally appropriate, then, it must on balance generate better consequences than all other available courses of action. If all available options produce both good and bad consequences, then the morally preferred one is the action that yields more overall good than harm.[3] The desirability and permissibility of pretrial release policy, plea bargaining, determinate sentencing, capital punishment, and many other issues and dilemmas within criminal justice can be determined using the basic orientation of consequentialism: if, relative to other reasonable options, the overall benefits of the policy or practice outweigh the overall harm, then it is a "good" policy or practice.

While seemingly straightforward and intuitively appealing, several critical questions need to be addressed with respect to the logic and implications of consequentialist moral theory, each of which will be explored over the remainder of the chapter:

- What constitutes a "good" or desirable outcome?
- For whom should the outcome be beneficial?
- Should we focus on actual consequences? Expected consequences? Intended consequences?
- Are consequences really the only thing that matters morally?

GOOD AND DESIRABLE CONSEQUENCES

What if we could substantially decrease the overall amount of physical pain in the world by giving everyone a "universal" vaccination which guards against almost all illnesses and diseases, but has the inescapable side effect of dulling emotions and permanently limiting our experience of joy? Would we willingly give up our experiences of joy for the sake of remaining in good health? What if we could completely eradicate crime in society, but doing so would require each of us to live under constant surveillance? Would we be willing to give up our experience of privacy and freedom for the sake of living without fear of criminal victimization?

To answer either of these questions, of course, we need to know whether we place greater value on health or on joyful emotions, on privacy and freedom or protection from criminal harm. If morality requires that we bring about good consequences through action or policy, we need to first know what things are *good*—in other words, what we *value* most. In and of itself, the idea that we should act so as to produce the best overall consequences does not answer this question for us. We need an additional "theory" of the good. We need to determine what matters.

By far the most widely discussed and influential variation of consequentialism is *utilitarianism*. Originally outlined by Jeremy Bentham (1748–1832) and John Stuart Mill (1806–1873), **utilitarianism** argues that actions are morally right so far as they maximize good consequences and/or minimize bad consequences; more specifically, however, classical utilitarianism understands only one thing to be ultimately "good" or valuable—*happiness*. Every human being desires happiness, and each of us understands happiness to be the greatest possible kind of good. In John Stuart Mill's words, "The utilitarian doctrine is that happiness is desirable, and the only thing desirable, as an end; all other things being desirable as means to that end."[4] In other words, wealth, status, food, love, knowledge, and many other things commonly understood as "goods" can only be understood as such because they are means by which we attain the more primary end of happiness.

Mill's quote employs the distinction we made in Chapter 2 between values and goods that are *intrinsic*, and those that are *instrumental*. Recall that intrinsic goods are those things that are good in and of themselves or for their own sake; instrumental goods are those things that help us attain intrinsic goods. Thus, money is generally understood to be an instrumental good because its value lies in its ability to help us attain other things that are intrinsically good—by itself, money is of limited worth or utility. Happiness, however, is not a means to anything—we do not *use* it to get other things that are desirable. Instead, we desire happiness because the state of being happy is, by itself, something we consider to be good. Knowing that happiness is the highest of goods, we are in a better position to determine what constitutes good consequences, as well as what kinds of decisions and actions are morally permissible and desirable.

Whereas happiness is intrinsically valuable, honesty, legal rights, and other moral values and principles must be thought of as valuable only instrumentally—only to the extent that they aid in realizing the ultimate goal of producing happiness. It may be the case that having legal rights aids in producing a more just society in which people are better able to pursue good lives. In this respect, legal rights may be morally desirable. However, the instrumental nature of legal rights also means that they can be trumped by other considerations in some situations. Rights to privacy, for instance, might be justifiably violated if doing so brings to light information that could potentially save many lives, thereby generating more happiness than unhappiness on the balance.

The Principle of Utility: Seeking the Greatest Happiness

Consider the following: Would it be morally permissible for local law enforcement to infringe upon privacy rights by surreptitiously monitoring the phone conversations of suspected drug dealers? For the U.S. government to do the same of suspected terrorists? In both examples, producing good consequences requires that we also cause harm. How do we resolve moral dilemmas such as these? We need a rational, overriding principle by which to guide our decision. According to utilitarianism, where we have a choice such as that between respecting privacy rights (a moral good) and protecting the community from harm (also a moral good), it is not only morally permissible but perhaps morally *obligatory* to choose that action or policy which has "the best overall consequences for everyone affected."[5] Because we know that "good" consequences are defined in terms of happiness, we can say that our decisions should be guided by an effort to bring about the "greatest happiness for the greatest number of people."

The rational, overriding principle promoted by utilitarianism is thus the **principle of utility** or **greatest happiness principle**, which holds that:

- Actions are right to the extent that they promote *happiness*, and wrong to the extent that they produce unhappiness; and
- Because more than one "party" will be affected, the action which is "right" is that which produces the happiness *for the greatest number of people* (or, conversely, "eliminates pain for the greatest number of people").

Actions (or laws, policies, practices, etc.) are morally justifiable only if they have a tendency to produce happiness or eliminate pain for the greater number of people relative to other courses of action.[6] In some instances, the best overall consequences for everyone involved may include doing what is necessary to protect the well-being of the group, community, or the country, even if that course of action also causes harm in other respects. The goal of utilitarian decision-making is to produce the greatest *balance* of happiness over unhappiness. Thus, with respect to the questions posed at the beginning of this section, utilitarian logic may support infringing upon people's privacy rights if, in so doing, we are bringing about a greater good for a greater number of people. Again, "means" such as wire-tapping might be justified by an "end" such as community safety.

Agent Neutrality: Consequences for Whom?

Thus far we have seen, according to the principle of utility or Greatest Happiness Principle, that: (1) actions are to be judged right or wrong only (or at least primarily) with reference to their *consequences*; (2) in considering consequences, what is important is the amount of *happiness or unhappiness* that is brought about; and (3) we must take into consideration the happiness and unhappiness experienced by *all people affected by the decision*. This last point is particularly important and worth emphasizing further, as it separates utilitarianism from another common form of consequentialism—that of *ethical egoism* (see Box 8.1).

BOX 8.1
The Rationale for Ethical Egoism

Ethical egoism suggests that self-interest is not a psychological motivation but a *moral principle*. We act rightly whenever we act out of consideration for our own interests, and wrongly whenever we do not. On its face, ethical egoism seems objectionable. Thus, on what basis or by what reasons might we legitimately support such a principle? The most common justifications for ethical egoism are as follows:

- We know what is in our own interests, while we can know the needs and interests of other people only imperfectly. If we attempt to look after the needs and interests of others, we may well do more harm than good. If we limit our concern to ourselves, we are more likely to "get it right."
- Looking out for other people's interests is akin to invading their privacy. We should "mind our own business."
- Aiding or assisting others is *degrading* to them—it is an assault to their dignity and self-respect. In a way, it suggests that others are incapable of meeting their own needs and caring for their own interests. In taking care of others, we may even be fostering a cycle of passivity and dependence, discouraging them from being or becoming self-reliant.
- Each of us has one—and as far as we know *only* one—life to live. Thus, we have a single opportunity to find success, fulfillment, or happiness. Altruism would have us sacrifice that opportunity (or parts of it) for the sake of other people or the common good. Consequently, altruistic obligations inhibit the development of outstanding individuals and, because great societies are achieved through the work and insight of great individuals, we should allow space for outstanding individuals to flourish.

As an example, consider cases such as mandated drug treatment or involuntary mental health intervention. These paternalistic practices involved are premised upon the notion that educated and trained professionals are in a position to understand the interests of others and assist them in overcoming their maladies. As we have

seen, however, ethical egoism questions whether we can ever know the needs and interests of others. Consequently, not only might paternalistic practices be misguided and unfruitful, they may also be construed as invasions of privacy and affronts to the dignity of those whom we are attempting to aid. Ethical egoism might raise the following concerns:

- Treatment services are not based on the patient's expressed wants, needs, or desires, but on the professional's "expert" knowledge of what the patient needs. In effect, experts presume to know patients' needs and interests better than the patients themselves do. Are these assumptions accurate, or might they do more harm than good?
- Some have argued that patients who are treated against their will eventually come to appreciate the services they have received. The argument is that persons who are mentally ill or drug dependent are not—because of their illness—in a position to know what is in their best interests. Because of this, they may initially resist treatment. Once they are "better," however, they come to realize that treatment was in their best interest and are grateful for the intervention. Would you agree that persons who are drug dependent or suffering from a mental disorder such as major depression or schizophrenia are incapable of knowing their own interests because of their "illness?" Do you agree that many people who are treated without consent might eventually be thankful for the intervention?

Source: Ellen Frankel Paul, Fred D. Miller, Jr., and Jeffrey Paul (Eds.), *Self-Interest* (Cambridge, MA: Cambridge University Press, 1997), pp. 286–307; James Rachels, *The Elements of Moral Philosophy* (New York: McGraw-Hill, 2002); Ayn Rand, *The Virtue of Selfishness* (New York: Signet, 1964); Alen A. Stone, *Mental Health Law: A System in Transition* (Washington, DC: U.S. Government Printing Office, 1975); J. Beck, and E. Golowka, "A Study of Enforced Treatment in Relation to Stone's 'Thank You' Therapy," *Behavioral Sciences and the Law*, 6(4), 559 (1988).

Recall from Chapter 6 that ethical egoism demands that our decisions be guided by self-interest that each of us should—indeed, is morally obligated to—act so as to satisfy our own best interests or maximize our personal welfare. Ethical egoism is consequentialist in that, like utilitarianism, it is concerned primarily with the consequences of our actions. However, where ethical egoism argues that what matter most are consequences for *ourselves*, utilitarianism holds that our decisions should produce the greatest happiness for *the greatest number of people*. The "all people affected" aspect of the principle of utility means that no one person's happiness is more important than anyone else's. In other words, *each person's welfare is equally important*. As John Stuart Mill wrote,

> The happiness which forms the utilitarian standard of what is right . . . is not the agent's own happiness, but that of all concerned. As between his own happiness and that of others, utilitarianism requires him to be as strictly impartial as a disinterested and benevolent spectator.[7]

Thus, utilitarianism requires that we weigh equally the happiness of everyone affected by our actions, without placing more or less importance on that of anyone (including ourselves). In fact, in some cases, the morally right action may be one in which *we* endure harm or pain in the interest of bringing about happiness or reducing suffering for a greater number of people. We cannot, then, consider our own happiness to be more important than anyone else's—much like we cannot (or should not) make distinctions on the basis of personal relationships, wealth, status, race, gender, age, or any other potential source of bias. Utilitarianism demands that we become "disinterested spectators" in making a rational assessment of what consequences will result from our actions and in determining which course of action will have the most beneficial consequences for everyone (see Box 8.2).[8] We are to be objective, unbiased, "neutral" decision-makers, with self-interest, the welfare of family, friends, colleagues, and so on granted no special moral attention.

BOX 8.2
Plea Bargaining and the Greatest Happiness Principle

The practice of plea bargaining is one that is widely employed in criminal justice, yet has been attacked from a variety of perspectives. In effect, a **plea bargain** is an agreement between a defendant and the prosecution whereby the latter reduces charges or recommends a reduced sentence in exchange for the defendant pleading guilty before (or, on occasion, during) trial. Plea bargaining became a popular means of resolving criminal cases in the early decades of the twentieth century and, today, over 90 percent of criminal cases are disposed of through plea bargains.

Utilitarianism would have us consider the consequences of plea bargaining for everyone affected by its practice. Morally "good" practices are those that produce the greatest happiness (or eliminate the greatest pain) for the greatest number of people. In the case of plea bargaining, we would need to consider the ways in which it affects the defendant, prosecution, victim(s), and the greater community. Because each of these parties will be affected, the morality of plea bargaining becomes a matter of whether it tends to produce the "greatest happiness for the greatest number of people" when compared with alternative responses (in this case, a criminal trial). What consequences—good and bad—are produced by the practice of plea bargaining? Do the "good" consequences sufficiently outweigh the "bad" such that plea bargaining can be morally justified on utilitarian grounds?

Following is a list of possible effects, both beneficial and detrimental, to each of the major parties

(continued)

significantly improve the results in a linear analysis aimed at finding the relationship between variables. The regression model may appear to be a linear equation, though essentially it is not, like: $Y' = a + bZ = a + b(\log X)$. If a single substituted item is not good enough to describe the relationship, you may introduce more items for the regression analysis. One approach is called polynomial regression, which allows you to include items of higher and higher power until the equation fits the ideal regression line: $Y' = a + b_1 X + b_2 X^2 + b_3 X^3 + \ldots$

    <u>Variables of different measurement levels.</u> The logic of the coefficient of determination γ^2 can be followed when one variable is categorical or measured at the nominal level. In such cases the analysis is often called group comparison of the other variable. Here the categorical variable is treated as an independent variable (X) and thus its correlation with the other variable (Y) is asymmetrical. Predicting the value of Y by its own mean (i.e., using the mean to represent all the possible values of Y) would have a total error of $E_1 = \Sigma|Y_i - M|$ (M is the mean of Y). Now, suppose we know the values of the categorical variable X and that X is in some way associated with Y. To predict the value of Y by its mean on each value of X (M_{xj}), the total error would be $E_2 = \Sigma|Y_i - M_{xj}|$. The reduction of error, therefore, is $E_1 - E_2 = \Sigma|Y_i - M| - \Sigma|Y_i - M_{xj}| = \Sigma|M_{xj} - M|$. And PRE $= (E_1 - E_2)/E_1 = \Sigma|M_{xj} - M|/\Sigma|Y_i - M|$. The operation of taking absolute values in mathematical calculation and derivation, again, has been felt inconvenient. This has lead to the use of another frequently used approach in mathematics, that is, having the differences squared before summing them up. The result is called correlation ratio or eta square, i.e., $E^2 = [\Sigma(Y_i - M)^2 - \Sigma(Y_i - M_{xj})^2]/\Sigma(Y_i - M)^2$.

    The E^2 is different from the γ^2 in that one variable here is at the nominal level. Therefore, it is asymmetrical, has no negative value, and does not involve the linearity issue. When two interval variables are suspected of having a nonlinear relationship, you may categorize one variable and use E^2 as a measure of association in place of γ^2 to avoid linearizing the relationship through complicated substitution. This "downgrading" treatment may also be applied to an ordinal variable in relation to an interval variable. On the other hand, comparing E^2 with γ^2 will not only tell you about the intensity but also the linearity or curved nature of the relationship. As mentioned above, the treatment of nonlinear relationship includes the strategy of linearization via substitution and downgrading via categorization. One way to categorize but remain at or legitimately upgrading to the interval level is to use "dummy variables," which are dichotomous variables with the codes of only 0 and 1. Dummy variables can be treated affected. As you read through them, weigh the costs and benefits and ask yourself whether the practice of plea bargaining on the whole passes the test of greatest happiness. If so, are there other reasons that plea bargaining might not be morally desirable?

- *Prosecution.* By most accounts, the party most positively affected by the practice of plea bargaining is the prosecution. Reaching a compromise with the defendant saves the prosecution countless hours of preparation, the time and monetary costs of trial, and ensures a conviction. This latter point is significant, as prosecutors often face strong administrative and political pressures to maintain a high conviction rate. This tension only increases where district attorneys are elected and must appease the public to secure reelection. Particularly in cases where the prosecution's case is weak, plea bargaining can serve a variety of interests with relatively few negative consequences.
- *Victim(s).* Critics have argued that plea bargaining often leaves victims feeling as though justice has not been done. Defendants often receive more lenient sentences than would have been imposed by a judge following a conviction. We might imagine how a rape victim would feel upon learning that the offender had pled guilty to a lesser sexual assault charge and will only serve a minimal amount of time in prison. On the other hand, victims are spared the pain of enduring— and perhaps participating in—a criminal trial. As well, even though a lesser sentence may be imposed, victims are not exposed to the uncertainty that comes with not knowing whether a jury will reach a guilty verdict. In other words, the victim is assured that the offender will be punished in some fashion and to some extent.
- *Defendant.* Although on the surface it may seem as if the defendant has the most to gain from plea bargaining (e.g., a lesser charge, reduced

sentence), the alleged offender may also be most negatively affected by the process. Defendants find themselves in the unattractive predicament of having to choose between pleading guilty and thus ensuring their own punishment, or braving the uncertainty of a criminal trial that may or may not bring a conviction on a more serious charge and/or a harsher punishment. This dilemma is especially troubling in cases involving *innocent* defendants who may fear being found guilty by a jury following an unsuccessful defense. Those defendants who are poor, represented by public defenders, and/or do not understand the legal process may be especially at risk. Critics have argued that plea bargaining exploits the fear and uncertainty that defendants feel, thereby *coercing* them into surrendering their constitutional (Sixth Amendment) right to a trial by jury.

- *Community.* In some ways, plea bargaining serves the interests of the community. Firstly, the costs associated with criminal trials are shouldered by taxpayers. If most criminal cases went to trial, the financial burden on taxpayers would increase substantially. As well, in those cases involving defendants who present a continued danger to the community (e.g., violent offenders, drug dealers), plea bargaining offers a more certain means of ensuring public protection—even if for a shorter period of time. On the other hand, if the public feels that criminals are "getting off easy" and/or that innocent persons are being coerced into pleading guilty to crimes they did not commit, pubic confidence in and respect for the legal system may be undermined.

Source: Jeff Palmer, "Abolishing Plea Bargaining: An End to the Same Old Song and Dance," *American Journal of Criminal Law,* 26 (3), 505–535 (1999); Michael Gorr, "The Morality of Plea Bargaining," *Social Theory and Practice,* 26 (1), 129–151 (2000); Kenneth Kipnis, "Criminal Justice and the Negotiated Plea," *Ethics,* 86 (2), 93–106 (1976).

MEASURING HAPPINESS: QUANTITATIVE HEDONISM

If our guiding moral principle is one which obligates us to attempt to maximize the happiness of everyone affected by our decisions and actions, we need to know a bit more about what "happiness" is and how we are to "measure" it for purposes of choice-making. Although the answer to each of these questions is a matter of continuing dispute within ethics, it may be valuable to consider the responses of Bentham and Mill themselves.

HEDONISTIC GOOD   Bentham defined "good" not simply as happiness, but more specifically as *pleasure*. What is "good" is happiness, and what makes people happy is pleasure. Bentham's position on this matter followed a philosophical tradition dating as far back as the ancient Greeks known as hedonism (*hedone* = a state in which pleasure is present or a quality that produces pleasure). **Hedonism** is a simple and popular theory which suggests that pleasure and pain are the only things we can say are intrinsically good or intrinsically bad.[9] Everything that we normally consider good is good only because it in some way produces pleasure; while anything bad is bad because it produces pain. Thus, pleasure is considered central to human motivation, choice, and action—including moral considerations. While there has been long-standing disagreement about what kinds of things are pleasurable, all hedonists favor the basic idea that pleasure—whether linked to good food, wine, sex, or to family and friendship, tranquility, or knowledge—is the "ultimate good" in life and the only thing worth pursuing.

Bentham's utilitarianism fits squarely within this broader tradition of hedonism. More fundamentally, Bentham's moral philosophy assumes that human beings are *by nature* hedonistic or pleasure-seeking. Indeed, all human behavior ultimately is motivated by pleasure and/or pain alone. Thus, we naturally seek to maximize pleasure while avoiding pain. This is the principle of **psychological hedonism**: the claim that the pursuit of pleasure is a fact of human nature. As Bentham famously wrote, "Nature has placed mankind under the governance of two sovereign masters, pain and pleasure. It is for them alone to point out what we ought to do . . ." In terms of normative implications, psychological hedonism suggests that we can determine what we *should* do by appealing to what we naturally seek—happiness in the form of pleasure (see Box 8.3).

THE FELICITY CALCULUS   How do notions of happiness and pleasure assist us in making moral decisions? Bentham argued that we can make moral decisions by considering the amount of pleasure or pain that our actions bring. More specifically, he believed that we can *quantify* such pleasures and pains along a number of dimensions. Bentham described this process of categorizing and measuring pleasures as the **felicity calculus** (also sometimes referred to as the "hedonic calculus," "calculus of pleasures," or simply the "utilitarian calculus"). To aid our moral decision-making, pleasure can be measured by seven dimensions:

- **Intensity** of pleasure—how strong is it?
- **Duration** of pleasure—how long does it last?
- **Certainty** of pleasure—how sure are we that it will be experienced?
- **Proximity** of pleasure—how soon will it be experienced?
- **Fecundity**—will the pleasure lead to or produce other pleasures as well?
- **Purity**—how free will the pleasure be from pain?
- **Extent**—how many people are affected?

Bentham suggested that whenever we are contemplating an action, we should analyze its consequences in terms of these seven dimensions of pleasure, contrasting it with alternative courses of action.[10] For instance, suppose you are trying to decide whether to stay home and study for a midterm exam tonight or go out with friends. In making your decision, you should consider how intense the pleasures of studying versus going out with friends are, how long those pleasures will last, how certain you are that these respective pleasures will occur, how soon you will experience them, whether they will lead to further instances of happiness, how free from pain either or both will be, and whether they each will bring pleasure to other people as well. Your felicity calculus might look something like Table 8.1 (numbers in parentheses are "*hedons*" or

BOX 8.3

Hedonism, the "War on Drugs," and "Noble-Cause" Corruption

Though remaining within the tradition of hedonism, Bentham made some important modifications. In particular, his utilitarianism represents a variation of *social hedonism* (as distinguished from egoistic hedonism). **Social hedonism** regards pleasure as the ultimate good, but demands that we consider the pleasures and pains of *others* in our moral contemplations. In fact, utilitarianism demands that, at times, we place the interests of others *above* our own if in so doing the result is happiness to a greater number of people. Indeed, the Greatest Happiness Principle demands that our actions bring the greatest amount of pleasure to the *greatest number of people*. This is the social and altruistic element of utilitarianism, and this is what distinguishes it from the tradition of *egoistic hedonism* in moral philosophy.

One prominent issue in criminal justice ethics that is an interesting illustration of this difference is police corruption—particularly as it intersects with the "war on drugs." Indeed, drugs are a significant force in police deviance, with as many as half of all convictions in police corruption cases involving drug-related crimes. As we saw in Chapter 5, much corruption in law enforcement, courts, and corrections can be explained through egoism—selfish desires for personal gain. In other cases, however, corruption might be better understood as stemming from *socially hedonistic* incentives; that is, a desire to produce good consequences for others. In their discussion of drug-related police corruption, for instance, Kappeler, Sluder, and Alpert describe four types of corruption that can be linked with drugs:

- **Use corruption** occurs where police officers *use* illegal drugs. In one study, as many as 20 percent of officers admitted to smoking marijuana.
- **Economic corruption** occurs where officers use their power and discretion for personal

monetary gain, such as by keeping drug money confiscated from offenders.
- **Police violence** may occur in the context of extracting confessions or information from drug suspects.
- **Subjugation of a defendant's rights** occurs where police commit perjury or plant drugs on a suspect in the interest of obtaining a confession or getting a conviction.

While the first two of these forms of corruption would seem to be explicable in terms of egoistic hedonism (i.e., self-interested pursuit of pleasure or personal gain), the latter two (use of violence and subjugation of rights) might be linked to what is sometimes called **noble-cause corruption**. Rather than a purely egoistic form of corruption, noble-cause corruption occurs when police officers violate ethical and legal obligations in the interest of achieving the "good" ends of police work. Getting the "bad guys" and protecting communities and potential victims are seen as more important than ethical and procedural restrictions on police conduct. Planting evidence at a crime scene, for instance, may result in the apprehension and conviction of a notorious offender who has avoided criminal prosecution and continues to present a significant danger to the community. While "noble-cause" corruption is by all accounts still unethical and often illegal, would you consider the latter two types of drug-related corruption to be less morally reprehensible than the first two?

Source: Roy Roberg, Kenneth Novak, and Gary Cordner, *Police and Society*, 3rd ed. (Los Angeles, CA: Roxbury, 2005), pp. 304–305; Victor Kappeler, Richard Sluder, and Geoffrey Alpert, *Forces of Deviance: Understanding the Dark Side of Policing*, 2nd ed. (Prospect Heights, IL: Waveland, 1998), pp. 166–173.

"happiness units" along a ten-point scale with the score of "1" representing very low happiness and the score of "10" representing very high happiness).

Admittedly, the above example is drawn from decision-making in everyday life rather than from moral choice-making; however, the same "calculus" applies to the decisions we make that have ethical implications. To illustrate, if you were considering whether to lie to a friend in order to protect that person's feelings, to have an abortion in order to not be subjected to parenting as a

TABLE 8.1	Bentham and Measuring Pleasure	
	Studying for the Exam	**Going Out with Friends**
Intensity	Not intensely pleasurable; perhaps even more painful than pleasurable (2)	Moderately to very intense, depending upon the specifics of the evening (7)
Duration	Potentially long lasting; though studying is short lived, the knowledge you gain will last indefinitely (9)	Short lived; likely lasts only a few hours (2)
Certainty	Not very certain that it will be pleasurable; in fact, more certain that it will be painful (3)	Fairly certain that you'll have a good time (7)
Proximity	More than likely, you won't experience the pleasure until later in life, although doing on the exam could be pleasurable in the near future (4)	Pleasure will be experienced in the very near future (9)
Fecundity	There are many additional benefits that come from studying: knowledge, wisdom, better career prospects, income, etc. (9)	Probably will not lead to other pleasures, although you could meet new friends, contacts, learn new things, etc. (2)
Purity	Probably not free from pain, unless you really enjoy the subject (2)	Could lead to some pain (e.g., arguments with friends, hangover), but overall probably more pure than not (7)
Extent	In the near future, studying probably only benefits you; but it is possible that your knowledge could benefit many other people in the future (4)	May bring pleasure to your friends as well, but mostly affects your happiness (5)
Score	33	39

teenager, or to take sick leave from work when not sick (a type of "stealing") in order to have some time off from a stress-filled period in your life, you could apply the same formula. To be clear, however, there are some obvious problems with this approach. One of these problems is that Bentham focused on the *quantity* of pleasure as opposed to its *quality*. In the above example, the felicity calculus would have you go out with friends rather than study for your exam. For at least some people, this would seem unsettling. So, what is missing from the formula?

Quality of Pleasure: Quantitative versus Qualitative Hedonism

Bentham's utilitarianism describes "good" in terms of *pleasure* and, more specifically, the quantity of pleasure that results from our actions. As we have seen, this is consistent with the doctrine of hedonism—that pleasure and pain are the only things that we can say are intrinsically good and bad, with everything else being in some way dependent on or secondary to pleasure and pain. However, even within the tradition of hedonism, there has been some debate regarding the interpretation of happiness and pleasure for purposes of moral decision-making.[11] Perhaps the most notable detractor from Bentham's original formulation of utilitarianism was his disciple, John Stuart Mill (Mill's father was a friend of Bentham's and a key figure within his intellectual circle). Though working within the utilitarian tradition established by Bentham, Mill sought to rework what he understood as several problematic dimensions of Bentham's original formulation. In particular, while Bentham saw pleasure as good and pain as bad, John Stuart Mill argued that there are *degrees of goodness* associated with different types of pleasures. In other words, we should understand some pleasures as *better* than others.

Given the formulation of the felicity calculus put forth by Bentham, we could easily conclude that we should go out with friends rather than study for our examination, or that watching reality television is better than pursuing knowledge in the arts and sciences. These sorts of prospects were especially troubling to Mill. In fact, he believed that utilitarianism needed to be reworked in order to demonstrate that certain pleasures (e.g., reading Shakespeare) were more important than, better than, or of a *higher quality* than other pleasures. As Mill saw it, the problem was that the felicity calculus was purely quantitative in nature, with no regard for qualitative differences in types of pleasures. In turn, Mill claimed that our concern should not be with the quantity of pleasure, but with its *quality*.[12]

Mill argued that some kinds of pleasures are of higher quality than other kinds. Thus, "lower" pleasures such as eating, drinking, and sexual activity are qualitatively different from the "higher" pleasures of intellectual, creative, and spiritual activity.[13] The pleasure of studying for and doing well on an exam is of a higher quality than that of going out with friends and having a few drinks; the pleasure of reading classic literature is greater than that of reading a sports magazine; and the pleasure of doing volunteer work to help persons in need is of a higher quality than that of going fishing. In cases such as these, Mill argued that there are important differences between types of pleasures, and that these differences are a function of the quality of enjoyment being experienced: "It is quite compatible with the principle of utility to recognize the fact that some kinds of pleasures are more desirable and more valuable than others."[14]

As an example, Mill suggested that, "anyone who has experienced the pleasure of solving a mathematical equation will attest to the fact that it is indeed superior in kind to the pleasure of eating an exquisite meal." Even though the "lower" pleasure of eating an exquisite meal may be more *intensely* gratifying, the "higher" pleasures tend to be of more benefit in the long run. As most of us have experienced, the pleasure associated with eating a good meal comes and goes in a matter of hours. Even though it may be intensely pleasurable during the time we consume the food, it does not offer any long-term pleasure—and may even produce long-term pain (e.g., overeating, weight gain). "Higher" pleasures—though not always immediately and intensely experienced—are capable of contributing to our *continued* happiness.

Although Mill accepted the basic principle of hedonism (i.e., that pleasure is the basis of determining what is good), he clearly believed some pleasures were *better* than others.[15] The question then becomes, *"By what or whose criteria are we to make such determinations?"* For Bentham, pleasure is "measured" in terms of duration, certainty, fecundity, and as forth. However, for Mill "better" pleasures are those that possess a higher quality.[16] With quality of pleasure in mind, Mill essentially reformulated the Greatest Happiness Principle from "greatest happiness for the greatest number of people," to the greatest quantity *and quality* of happiness for the greatest number of people. The problem with this reformulation is that many people do not know which qualities are desirable and valuable and, thus, are unaware of those qualities that should be taken into consideration in the Greatest Happiness Principle. So, how should qualities of pleasure be judged?

In response, Mill claimed that "Of two pleasures, if there be one to which all or almost all who have an experience of both give a decided preference . . . that is the more desirable pleasure."[17] In determining which types of pleasures are of higher quality, we must rely on the opinions of those who have experienced various types. In other words, establishing the quality of a pleasure requires a judge or an "expert" on the subject. This person can distinguish between them. Thus, for example, we cannot expect a person who has never solved a complex mathematical equation to be able to distinguish the happiness derived from it versus the pleasure experienced while watching football. Following Mill's utilitarian theory, anyone who has experienced both of these types of pleasure clearly should recognize that solving a difficult arithmetic problem produces happiness that exceeds the pleasure experienced from watching football. Of course, many people have no point of reference when it comes to deciphering complicated mathematical equations. As such, they are not in a position to make a distinction between the quality of happiness that follows from doing this successfully versus enjoying an athletic event on television. In fact, given the choice, we might suspect that most people would choose the pleasure of watching football. For Mill, this possibility was the source of considerable concern. The "uncultivated cannot be competent judges of cultivation," he argued, as their preference for "lower" desires and pleasures may lead to the eventual degeneration of entire cultures.

The Problems with Utilitarianism

Bentham's utilitarianism is intuitively and practically appealing: there is one—and only one—principle to apply in all situations. This simple rule pertains equally to personal and professional scenarios; to love, friendship, and acquaintance relationships; to law, crime, and justice decision-making; and to environmental, economic, and health care policy. In all cases, we are to maximize happiness or pleasure, and/or minimize suffering or pain. What is more, Bentham offered a means of quantifying pleasure and pain such that in any given instance we can calculate and impartially apply our measurements to the issue or situation in question in order to determine what we should do. Additionally, some have argued that utilitarianism is valuable in that it "seems to get at the substance of morality."[18] Following utilitarianism, morality is not simply a formal system of rules and principles, but has a function or end to which it should aim. Ultimately, this end is about promoting happiness and alleviating suffering. Morality, then, is not so much about following rules as it is about helping people and doing what we can to alleviate the misery in the world. Utilitarianism seems to recognize this feature of morality. It asks us to consider the happiness we can cause and the suffering we can reduce by way of our (quantitatively and qualitatively calculated) choices and actions.

However, despite its appeal, utilitarianism is certainly not without its shortcomings. The three most significant criticisms leveled against utilitarianism include: (1) its requirement that we predict the future; (2) its focus on happiness as the only consequence of importance; and (3) its exclusive regard for the consequences of our actions.[19]

THE PROBLEM OF PREDICTION Utilitarianism has been accused of asking—or requiring—us to do that which we cannot possibly do: *know* what the consequences of our actions will be.[20] Bentham's felicity calculus requires us to make a *prediction* about the intensity, duration, extent, and so on of pleasure brought about by certain courses of action. Yet, none of us can ever know the consequences of our actions—especially including the more long-term effects.

Recall the decision to stay at home and study for an exam or go out with friends. Now suppose that in choosing to go out you run into an ex-lover, have a heated argument, go home upset, stay up all night thinking about the encounter, and miss your exam. Conversely, suppose you choose to stay home and study when, had you gone out, you would have met your future husband/wife or would have made an important contact resulting in your career being launched upon your graduation. The point is that there are an infinite number of possible events that could follow whatever choice you make. And while each of these events represents a possibility, none can be predicted with any degree of success. Given all of these possibilities, how can we possibly be expected to make an informed decision?

In response to this difficulty, supporters of utilitarianism distinguish between *real* consequences, *expected* consequences, and *intended* consequences.[21] Since it is impossible to determine what the actual or real consequences of our actions will be, the moral "rightness" of our choices must be based on what we *reasonably expect* the consequences to be. The best we can do—and that which we should do in any situation—is to use whatever information we have at our disposal to make a choice that any reasonable person would, anticipating that it will result in the best possible (most pleasurable) outcome.[22] If our actions fail to produce the expected consequences, perhaps even causing more pain than happiness, we cannot be said to have made a poor choice. So long as we do what a reasonable person would do in light of the expected consequences, we are fulfilling utilitarian requirements. Since we cannot predict the future, we simply need to do what "reason judges to be the best act based on likely consequences."[23]

ONLY HAPPINESS?   Utilitarianism simplifies morality in that it reduces "good" to happiness or pleasure. However, in doing so, arguably it *oversimplifies* morality. While most of us would not deny that happiness is intrinsically good and that it is worth pursuing, the more important question is whether happiness is the *only* thing that is good in itself, worthy of consideration in our moral decision-making. The notion that happiness is the one ultimate good and the only thing worth considering when faced with ethical choices is problematic on a number of grounds.

Consider the following illustration from James Rachels. Your neighbor insists that he is your friend and so you believe him. However, in actuality he ridicules you behind your back. Not one of the other neighbors discusses this with you, so you believe the person who professes to be your friend.[24] By hedonistic standards, this situation is *not* a concern because you were never caused any unhappiness. However, in evaluating this situation, most of us know or at least feel that something *is* wrong here. You are led to believe that someone is your friend when, in fact, that person is just using you as a source of humor for himself and others. On utilitarian grounds, the problem is that because you do not know this, you are not caused any unhappiness and, consequently, do not suffer in any way. At the same time, as a good source of humor you unknowingly bring happiness to a group of people. Clearly, because no harm is being caused and a good amount of happiness is taking place, the situation is not a moral predicament, according to utilitarianism. In fact, happiness is produced for everyone involved, and, moreover, "the truth would hurt."

However, for many people there is something deeply disturbing about the situation as it exists, despite the happiness it brings. What seems to make it disturbing is that we value other things in addition to happiness. We value truth, honesty, and fairness. Moreover, we are generally upset by people who use or exploit others for their own benefit, despite the considerable pleasure that materializes because of it. Thus, in cases like this, many of us would likely determine that ridiculing a person for the sake of so many people's happiness is not the morally right decision to make.

ONLY CONSEQUENCES?   The most fundamental principle of utilitarianism is that, in making moral decisions, we should attend to what will happen as a result of our doing one thing or the other. While being considerate of the consequences of our actions seems like a good rule of thumb, utilitarianism's *exclusive* focus on consequences carries with it several limitations. Suppose, for instance, that we are troubled by overpopulation. We might then define beneficial consequences as those that reduce overpopulation in the world. Any number of questionable actions (e.g., suicide, abortion, euthanasia, murder) might have to be defined as "good" because they bring about the beneficial consequence of reducing the world's population. Of course, undertaking these sorts of actions would be a problem for most people. However, if we focus *only* on the consequences of our actions—to the exclusion of other considerations—they must be regarded as good in that they bring about desired consequences (see Box 8.4).

BOX 8.4

Are We Utilitarians? The Trolley Problem

Utilitarianism is normative theory which provides a framework for what we *should* do. However, we can also ask a descriptive question about moral decision-making; namely, *are* we often inclined to make moral decisions on the basis of expected consequences. Several researchers of moral psychology have sought to provide relevant insight into this question. Consider the following classic scenario—referred to as the "trolley problem"—initially presented by moral philosopher Philipa Foot:

> *A trolley is running out of control down a track. In its path are five people who have been tied to the track by a mad philosopher. Fortunately, you could flip a switch, which will lead the trolley down a different track to safety. Unfortunately, there is a single person tied to that track. Should you flip the switch or do nothing?*

Most research subjects presented with this dilemma will choose to flip the switch and save five lives at the expense of one—a decision we would be *obligated* to make by utilitarian principles. Yet consider whether you would respond differently if we were to change one significant detail, as originally posed by Judith Jarvis Thomson:

> *As before, a trolley is hurtling down a track towards five people. You are on a bridge under which it will pass, and you can stop it by dropping a heavy weight in front of it. As it happens, there is a very fat man next to you—your only way to stop the trolley is to push him over the bridge and onto the track, killing him to save five. Should you proceed?*

Fiery Cushman, Liane Young, and Marc Hauser presented just such a dilemma to over 200,000 people representing various religious backgrounds, nationalities, and educational levels. In response to this second variation of the trolley problem, most people are *not* willing to push the man to his death to save five lives. Why this is the case is a matter of debate. In fact,

when asked to explain why they would pull the switch but not push the man, most people couldn't provide a reasoned response. Importantly, however, the logic is precisely the same—make a decision which leads to the death of one person but saves the lives of five others. If we are operating under the principle of the "greatest good for the greatest number," the good of five people clearly outweighs the good of the one. It would seem that we are utilitarians with respect to some things, but not others.

- First, consider what you would do in each of the two scenarios. Would you, like most people, choose to flip the switch? Would you, also like most people, choose not to push the man?
- To add a twist to the dilemma, would your own response change if the one person you would have to sacrifice to save the five lives was a person of importance? The President of the United States? A scientist close to finding a cure for a deadly disease? Your best friend? Your child?
- In general, why do you suppose that people make different decisions when the scenario is changed?
- Joshua Greene suggests that human beings might share an innate revulsion to "hands-on" killing or harming of other people. Do you believe that there is some truth to his conclusion? Might such a revulsion help explain why it is easier to pull a trigger than murder someone with bare hands? Might it help explain any of the relationship between homicide rates and handgun availability?

Source: Philippa Foot, *The Problem of Abortion and the Doctrine of the Double Effect* in *Virtues and Vices* (Oxford: Basil Blackwell, 1978); See Judith Jarvis Thomson, "The Trolley Problem," *Yale Law Journal*, 94 (6), 1395–1415 (1985); Judith Jarvis Thomson, "Killing, Letting Die, and the Trolley Problem," *The Monist*, 59, 204–217 (April 1976); See, e.g., Joshua Greene, "The secret joke of Kant's soul." In W. Sinnott-Armstrong (Ed.), *.Moral Psychology, Vol. 3: The Neuroscience of Morality: Emotion, Disease, and Development* (Cambridge, MA: MIT Press, 2007).

Utilitarianism has been criticized for precisely this reason. In addition to utility, what other considerations should be important when determining what actions are morally right? Critics have pointed to several. For example, *justice* requires that people be treated fairly, according to what they need or deserve.[25] If consequences are the only consideration deemed important when making moral decisions, then injustices might be warranted by appealing to their beneficial effects. Additionally, critics of utilitarianism's consequences-only approach object that it can lead to *violations of rights*.[26] According to utilitarianism, these infractions may be morally permissible if they serve the greater good (see Box 8.5). Again, the example of the neighbor who professes to be your friend when, in fact, he privately ridicules you, undermines your "right" be treated decently and honestly. Finally, a third objection to the idea that only consequences are of moral importance is that the theory does not allow for "*backward-looking reasons*."[27] Utilitarianism is future directed. It demands that we consider what *will* happen as opposed to what *has* happened. The problem with this reasoning is that most of us believe that the *past* is important, or at least certain types of past actions (e.g., promises we have made) should be regarded as important for purposes of determining what we should do in the present.

BOX 8.5
Ethics, Crime, and the Internet

As technology continues to evolve at a rapid pace, lawmakers and law enforcers are faced with increasingly novel challenges. "Computer crime," "internet crime," "cybercrime," and similar terminologies are relatively recent additions to the vocabulary of crime and justice—though they refer to what are by now recurrent themes within media and scholarly accounts of crime and justice. Only within the past decade or so have "crimes" and emerging issues such as child pornography, cyberstalking, cyberbullying, cyberhomicide, and theft of identity and other confidential or private information begun to warrant serious attention from the criminal justice community. As new crimes and new techniques of criminal behavior emerge, new strategies of social control are devised to combat them. Generated within this cycle are a host of issues of moral relevance. Consider the following, particularly with respect for the interplay of "means and ends," and the ways in which rights and justice might be balanced with the interests of the community:

- There is much content on the Internet that might be regarded as obscene or offensive to many readers/viewers. In only some cases is such material illegal. What are the moral implications of allowing the following to be accessible by choice: hate speech; politically radical speech; pornographic images? To what extent should

people have the freedom to express their views online, when those views are potentially inflammatory? In some cases, people are exposed to offensive materials, not by choice, but by accident or malicious intent on the part of the author. Generally, should the rights of persons to express their "speech" and "art" take priority over the potential harm caused to the public?

- **Online predators** are those who utilize the Internet (e.g., chat rooms, e-mail, message boards) to exploit children for sexual purposes. Some parents have turned to utilizing software to track where their children go and to what they are exposed on the Internet. Is there any sense in which such parental behavior could be regarded as a violation of the privacy interests of children? If so, are these justifiable violations? To what extent do parents have a right or *responsibility* to track the online behavior of their children?

- A number of organizations have emerged with the goal of combating online predators. Perverted Justice, for example, is a vigilante organization (featured on the television program, *To Catch a Predator*) that lures online predators from chat rooms to the homes of underage children for what they believe will be sexual encounters. In less than a decade, Perverted Justice claims to have helped police capture hundreds of potential child sex offenders. Specifically, adult volunteers pose as children in chat rooms and wait for messages from adults with explicit or implied sexual content. Striking up a relationship, the volunteer eventually sets up an in-person meeting where law enforcement officers will be waiting to make an arrest. Ethically speaking, a number of critical issues are raised, including:

- Is it morally permissible for volunteers to pose as children, or do such deceptive techniques raise moral red flags?
- The approach of these organizations is *preventive*, meaning they act to intervene before any actual (in-person) illegal contact occurs between the adult and the child. Is it morally permissible to take action in such cases under the assumption that a crime would have been committed?

- Is there any sense in which organizations such as Perverted Justice invade the privacy interests of adults, particularly when they have yet to be convicted of any crime?
- Is it morally permissible for spouses and family members to be called and/or information posted for public consumption labeling that adult a "predator" or "pedophile" (again prior to any conviction)?
- What other ethical issues are raised by such vigilante efforts?

Source: Yvonne Jewkes, *Crime Online* (Cullompton: Willan, 2006); Matthew Williams, *Virtually Criminal* (New York: Routledge, 2006); Janis Wolak, David Finkelhor, Kimberly J. Mitchell, and Michele L. Ybarra, "Online Predators and Their Victims: Myths, Realities, and Implications for Prevention and Treatment," *American Psychologist*, 63 (2), 111–128 (2008).

CONSEQUENTIALISM AND THE CRIMINAL JUSTICE SYSTEM: MEANS AND ENDS IN POLICING

All varieties of consequentialist ethics ultimately raise questions about the relationship between *ends* and the *means* used to achieve those ends. As we have seen, consequentialism holds ends to be more important than means, such that actions that might otherwise be considered immoral (e.g., lying) become moral so long as they serve to bring about good ends. In the next chapter, we will see that varieties of deontological ethics generally hold means to be the more important moral consideration, such that immoral or illegal means are never justifiable—even if they lead to morally good or desirable outcomes.

This tension between means and ends is one that criminal justice practitioners are forced to confront and work within on an everyday basis. In the context of criminal justice practice, this tension is perhaps best summarized by Carl Klockars' question, "When and to what extent does the morally good end warrant or justify an ethically, politically, or legally dangerous means for its achievement?"[28] In other words, can the "good" ends of police work ever justify the use of morally questionable means to achieve them? If so, when and under what circumstances are we willing to accept or at least overlook immoral or illegal law enforcement practices? To illustrate this tension as it applies to criminal justice work, we focus on two important—and interrelated—ethical controversies in policing, linking them to ethical utilitarianism as discussed earlier in the chapter.

The Dirty Harry Problem

The "Dirty Harry" problem is titled after a series of films in which the protagonist "Dirty" Harry Callahan (played by Clint Eastwood) employs a variety of questionable and sometimes outright objectionable means to "get the bad guy." Callahan's techniques involve everything from illegal stops and searches, to intimidation and coercion, to the use of torture to obtain the whereabouts of a kidnapped girl. As the hero, Callahan's methods are presented as justifiable—"dirty" but necessary methods of getting the job done in a society plagued by dangerous criminals who prey on innocent victims.

as interval variables, and even nominal variables may be coded this way.

Downgrading is a useful strategy in measuring association, and may avoid a lot of complication only at the expense of a little mathematical delicacy. On the other side, researchers often treat an ordinal variable as an interval variable and apply Pearson's γ and even regression analysis to the description of the association between such variables. Strictly speaking, the results can only be regarded as some kind of analogy or approximation. Yet such upgrading in measuring association is largely regarded as practical and useful.

It should be underscored that a correlation coefficient does not tell you which variable is the cause and which is the consequence. This is solely a matter of theoretical reasoning. We will discuss the logic of causal modeling later, which further involves the idea of statistical control and introduces such new concepts as different orders and dimensions in the measurement of associations.

Statistical inference

So far our concern has been the reduction of data for the purpose of effectively and efficiently describing the characteristics of a research sample. Descriptive statistical results, however, leave us with the question as to whether or not they also apply to the research population at large. Although we have used the term "parameter" frequently in preceding discussions, in statistics a number computed from the sample data can only be formally referred to as a "statistic." A parameter, on the other hand, is a number used to describe the population, which is usually unknown. Inferential or inductive statistics is concerned with drawing conclusions about population parameters based on available sample statistics. This is done through hypothesis testing and parameter estimation. From the viewpoint of measurement, sample statistics enable the researcher to pursue the internal validity of various measures of variables and associations, whereas statistical inference deals with the issue of external validity of such measures. Essentially, inferential statistics is based on the need of sampling, though sampling does not necessarily lead to the use of inferential statistics.

The logic of a statistical test begins with a research hypothesis suggesting the presence of a condition of a variable or a relation between two variables of the research population. Its antithesis is called a null hypothesis, implying a zero result, or the non-presence of the condition or relation suggested by the research hypothesis. In analytic logic, it is much easier to dismiss a null hypothesis than

Outside of popular film, "dirty" methods are regularly practiced and assume a number of forms in everyday police interactions. Nearly any legally or morally questionable police practice undertaken to achieve the "good" end of preventing or controlling crime can be made to fit the moral dilemma raised by the Dirty Harry Problem. For our purposes, the **Dirty Harry Problem** can be outlined as follows:

- A police officer is in a situation in which a morally good or desirable outcome may be accomplished.
- The officer believes that the only way (or, at least, the most certain way) to accomplish this end is through the use of techniques that would otherwise be considered morally questionable or even illegal (e.g., falsifying probable cause to make a stop, manufacturing a false arrest to justify an illegal search, using deceptive interviewing and interrogation techniques).
- The officer believes that the good brought about by accomplishing the desirable outcome outweighs the evil done through the use of immoral or illegal techniques.

The moral dilemma of this scenario is contained in the third statement above; namely, can good ends ever justify immoral or illegal means? According to utilitarian varieties of ethics, the answer to this question may be affirmative. Of course, as Carl Klockars points out, there are other considerations:

- How certain is the good outcome? As critics of consequentialism suggest, we cannot predict the future and thus can never be certain of any outcome. When a police officer is in a situation in which she or he believes that a desirable outcome may be accomplished, the officer is necessarily dealing only with probabilities. With this in mind, how certain must one be that the outcome will be accomplished in order to justify the use of dirty means? If an officer believes that there is a 10 percent chance that a suspect knows the whereabouts of a kidnapped victim, does this justify the use of intimidation, coercion, force, and even torture to try to extract that information? What if the officer is 50 percent certain? 99 percent certain?
- Are dirty means necessary? How certain are we that dirty means are the only—or only reasonable—method of achieving the good end? If dirty means are simply the easiest or most convenient means of accomplishing the end, this may dramatically change the extent to which they are justifiable. How certain is the officer that she or he has considered all alternatives and all possible nondirty means?
- Because the consequences of our actions are unpredictable, the question is not only whether a given action will bring about the desired end but also whether that action might bring about other, unintended or undesirable outcomes. In other words, what if the use of dirty means accomplishes the good end, but at the same time has the effect of causing other harms that were not predicted? While the good of the end might outweigh the evil of the means, can the good of the end outweigh the evil of the means *and* the additional evil consequences that are brought about by the means?

Deceptive Interrogation

Deceptive interrogation strategies present intriguing ethical questions. While brutal or otherwise physically coercive means are no longer commonly used by police officers to obtain confessions, officers regularly use deception as an interrogation strategy. Jerome Skolnick and Richard Leo suggest that "psychological persuasion and manipulation" are "the most salient and defining features of contemporary police interrogation," as officers are "instructed to, are authorized to—and do—trick, lie, and cajole to elicit so-called 'voluntary' confessions."[29] The ethical question is on what, if any, moral grounds the use of deception as an interrogation strategy is justifiable.

Skolnick and Leo offer a typology of interrogatory deception which is worth briefly reviewing as we consider the ethics of ends and means. As you read through each type of deception, consider whether it is a justifiable means of reaching the desired end.

- *"Interview" versus "interrogate."* By telling a suspect that she or he is free to leave at any time and having her or him acknowledge the voluntariness of the encounter, police can sidestep *Miranda* requirements that would apply to a suspect taken into custody. An interrogation becomes, for legal purposes, a noncustodial interview.
- *Miranda warnings.* Police cannot deceive a suspect into waiving her or his *Miranda* rights, although some officers consciously recite the warnings in such as way (e.g., as if they are merely a bureaucratic ritual) as to increase the likelihood of obtaining a waiver.
- *Misrepresenting the nature or seriousness of the offense.* This particular strategy comes in several varieties. For instance, police may tell a suspect that a murder victim is still alive, hoping she or he will then openly talk about her or his role in the lesser offense (e.g., assault); exaggerate the seriousness of the offense, hoping the suspect will then admit to a lesser role in the offense to "save" herself or himself; or suggest to a suspect that they are interested in her or his role in one crime, when they are in fact investigating another (e.g., suggest that they are interrogating a suspect for possession of stolen property when, in fact, they are hoping the suspect will admit to participating in a robbery which involved a homicide).
- *Role-playing: Manipulative appeals to conscience.* Interrogators may project sympathy, compassion, and understanding to "play the role" of the suspect's friend, brother or father figure, or therapeutic/religious counselor to elicit a confession. Doing so may produce an "illusion of intimacy between the suspect and the officer while downplaying the adversarial aspects of interrogation."
- *Misrepresenting the moral seriousness of the offense.* This common strategy involves an officer offering excuses or justifications for the offender's conduct by providing an "external attribution of blame that will allow [the suspect] to save face while confessing." The officer may, for instance, suggest to a rape suspect that the victim was "asking for it" or is somehow responsible for the incident. Doing so displaces moral guilt, encouraging the suspect to think of herself or himself as justified or less morally responsible for the offense.
- *The use of promises.* While officers cannot legally make direct and specific promises of leniency, they can make vague and indefinite promises. Officers may suggest to a suspect that they will "inform the court of [her or his] cooperation," that showing remorse will be a mitigating factor, or that they will do whatever they can to aid the suspect if she or he confesses. In each case, officers are creating implicit expectations of leniency that will not be met.
- *Fabricated evidence.* This strategy involves confronting a suspect with false evidence of guilt through one of several deceptive techniques: (1) falsely informing a suspect that an accomplice has identified her or him; (2) falsely state that physical evidence (e.g., blood, fingerprints) exists that confirms her or his guilt; (3) falsely suggest that a victim or eyewitness has identified the suspect; (4) staging a lineup in which a false witness identifies the suspect; or (5) have the suspect take a lie detector test and suggest that its results confirm her or his guilt.

The various types of deceptive interrogation outlined by Skolnick and Leo are morally problematic in that they involve the intentional use of deception or dishonesty to accomplish the aim of a confession (or the revealing of other desired information). As you may have realized, many—if not all—of these strategies *could* be legitimized or justified on utilitarian grounds. In each case, the use of deceptive means may allow law enforcement officers to accomplish the "good" end of a confession or the obtaining of information that may lead to solving a crime. The larger question, however, is whether deception, deceit, and dishonesty are ever justifiable on moral grounds—despite the "goodness" of the outcome they may produce. As you read through the next chapter on deontological ethics, consider how the moral legitimacy of these practices might be more questionable when approached from an alternative ethical perspective.

Summary

This chapter examined the normative theory of consequentialism, especially as a basis or a set of "tools" for engaging in ethical choices and moral actions. Our focus was on utilitarianism, which suggests that what matters morally are the consequences for *everyone affected* by our actions. Although utilitarianism offers considerable insight into how to make choices and undertake actions that are moral—including decisions within criminal justice—it is not without significant and varied limitations. Although utilitarianism has many supporters (and may be the "default" moral framework in everyday life), we need to critically examine at least two other forms of normative theory. In the next chapter, we explore how duties, rights, and obligations represent another normative basis for ethical reasoning, decision-making, and behavior, mindful of several ethical problems posed in the realm of crime, law, and justice.

Key Terms and Concepts

consequentialism *145*
deceptive interrogation *160*
Dirty Harry Problem *160*
felicity calculus *151*
hedonism *151*

noble-cause corruption *152*
plea bargain *149*
Principle of Utility
   (Greatest Happiness
   Principle) *147*

psychological hedonism *151*
social hedonism *152*
utilitarianism *146*

Discussion Questions

1. Suppose that a person regularly watches another person undress by peeping through a small hole in an adjoining wall. Suppose further that the voyeur has planted a small camera in a second hole with which photographs to be taken. Address this scenario using a utilitarian approach to moral decision-making.

2. A police officer close to retirement is training a rookie cop. Their shift is over and they are returning to the precinct. Suddenly, they spot several teenagers smoking marijuana. Relying on utilitarianism, explain how the officers' choice *not* to pursue the matter is (or is not) consistent with moral principles.

3. An overworked and underpaid public defender is assigned to represent a prostitute who has no prior arrests and "works" to support a drug habit. What arguments from consequentialism might the attorney utilize when discussing this case with the assistant district attorney prosecuting the matter? Would these arguments change if the prostitute had been previously arrested and/or convicted? Explain your response.

4. A successful *Fortune* five hundred company manufactures tires. In an effort to make the tires more affordable for and more readily available to the general public, several modifications to the tires are proposed by the marketing division of the company. The automotive engineering division objects, arguing that the changes will likely produce an increase in accidents and fatalities. The proposed changes are approved by the company's corporate board of directors. An increase in accidents and fatalities occurs. Explain how this decision *is* ethical based on insights from consequentialism.

5. To illustrate Mill's concern with the uncultivated making poor decisions, consider the following example. Your state government determines that it has a budget surplus of $5 billion that it must spend before the end of the fiscal year. So, the legislature puts the following to a popular vote: *ALL* citizens currently residing in the state are entitled to *either* (1) a free college education; *or* (2) a free lifetime supply of beer. Because the "uncultivated" among you may not be able to distinguish between the "lower" good of free beer and the "higher" good of free education, do you believe that the majority of citizens would choose the beer? In what, if any, ways might decisions such as this lead to the eventual decline of the cultural and intellectual life of your state? Mill argued that we should implement a requirement that people be "competent" judges, familiar with differences, before they could vote. Do you agree? If so, how should we determine who is competent or who is not?

Endnotes

1. *Brewer v. Williams*, 430 U.S. 387 (1977); Phillip Johnson, "Return of the 'Christian Burial Speech' Case," *Emory Law Journal*, 32, 349–381 (1983); see also Ronald Standler, "'Christian Burial Speech' in *Brewer v. Williams*," (2010). Available at http://www.rbs2.com/cbs.pdf (retrieved August 9, 2011).

2. S. Jack Odell, *On Consequentialist Ethics* (Belmont, CA: Wadsworth, 2003).

3. Ibid., p. 1.

4. Ibid., p. 91.

5. James Rachels, *The Elements of Moral Philosophy* (New York: McGraw-Hill, 1986), p. 80.

6. Ibid., pp. 80–81.

7. John Stuart Mill, *Utilitarianism* (Indianapolis, IN: Hackett, 2002), quoted in James Rachels, *The Elements of Moral Philosophy* (New York: McGraw-Hill, 2002), p. 90.

8. Ibid.

9. Ibid.

10. Donald Palmer, *Does the Center Hold? An Introduction to Western Philosophy*, 2nd ed. (Mountain View, CA: Mayfield, 1996), p. 256.

11. Michael Flocker, *The Hedonism Handbook: Mastering the Lost Arts of Leisure and Pleasure* (Cambridge, MA: De Capo Press, 2005).

12. Palmer, *Does the Center Hold?* pp. 257–258.

13. Ibid., pp. 258–261.

14. Quoted in Ibid., p.259.

15. Ibid., p. 261.

16. Ibid.

17. Ibid.

18. Louis Pojman, *Life and Death: Grappling with the Moral Dilemmas of Our Time,* 2nd ed. (Belmont, CA: Wadsworth, 2000).

19. Rachels, *The Elements of Moral Philosophy*, pp. 91–97.

20. Pojman, *Life and Death*, pp. 40–41.

21. Ibid., p. 40.

22. Ibid., p. 41.

23. Ibid.

24. Rachels, *The Elements of Moral Philosophy*, p. 92.

25. Ibid., 94.

26. Ibid.

27. Ibid.

28. Carl Klockars, "The Dirty Harry Problem," *The Annals of the American Academy of Political and Social Science*, 452, 33–47 (1980).

29. Jerome Skolnick and Richard Leo, "The Ethics of Deceptive Interrogation," *Criminal Justice Ethics*, 11(1), 3–12 (1992).

9

Respecting Persons, Respecting Rights: The Ethics of Duty

Suppose that you are sitting on your front porch one afternoon when a woman suddenly runs past you, dives behind some bushes, and quietly hides herself from view. After a moment, you approach the woman and ask her what she is doing. She proceeds to tell you that someone is trying to kill her and asks if you would please leave so she can remain hidden. After a moment, you return to the front porch and make yourself comfortable again. A couple of minutes later, a man approaches with a knife in his hand and asks if you have seen a young woman run by this way. Assuming on her word that the man probably intends to kill the young woman, should you lie to him or tell him the truth?[1]

In response to the dilemma of the "Inquiring Murderer," most people have little difficulty concluding that lying to the man is the best course of action. Informing the man as to the whereabouts of the woman may well result in him taking her life, whereas if we are dishonest, he may continue searching unsuccessfully and the woman will live. In other words, we should lie because doing so is likely to produce the best outcome for all but perhaps the inquiring murderer. Indeed, approaches to ethical decision-making such as those explored in the last chapter would almost certainly have us violate the moral prohibition against dishonesty in these kinds of situations. However, it could be argued that the focus on consequences proposed by frameworks such as utilitarianism tends to devalue, if not altogether ignore, features of morality that we cannot justifiably disregard simply for the sake of generating some desirable result. Indeed, by appealing exclusively to beneficial effects, consequentialist variations of ethics would often justify violating moral concerns for duty, rights, obligations, and justice that some would prioritize over matters of self-interest, social welfare, or general happiness.

In this chapter, we will examine several approaches to ethics that place diminished importance on consequences, arguing instead that the decisions we make and the actions we undertake should be informed by relevant *moral duties*. Ethical theories of this sort are called **deontological** (Greek *deon* = "duty"). In holding good outcomes to be largely irrelevant moral concerns, deontological ethics shifts attention away from the effects of our actions, placing the focus squarely on the *actions themselves*. As such, the question to examine is not what consequences might result from those actions, but whether a given action conforms to relevant moral duties, such as those prohibiting lying, killing, and dishonesty. Over the course of this chapter, three schools of thought consistent with the deontological tradition will be featured. These include the following:

- *Kantian Ethics*—what matters morally is whether our actions conform to relevant duties and absolute moral laws (i.e., those that cannot be violated).
- *Prima Facie Duties*—what matters morally is whether our actions conform to relevant duties and moral laws, though these duties can sometimes be overridden by other duties that are more significant in a given situation.
- *Rights-Based Ethics*—there exist certain basic moral guarantees that all ethical subjects enjoy and which should not, under any circumstances, be violated.

KANTIAN ETHICS

For most people, the case of the "Inquiring Murderer" which opened the chapter is one in which a typically immoral act such as lying might be permissible in light of its overall results. Yet there is another angle from which to contemplate that same dilemma. Immanuel Kant (1724–1804), widely considered one of the most important philosophers in the history of Western civilization, asks us to consider that morality is grounded in *absolute moral rules*. Kant argues that there exist moral rules that we must adhere to under *all* circumstances—rules that *must be followed*—no matter what consequences may befall an individual, a group, a social institution, and/or society more generally. One such moral rule is the prohibition against lying. For Kant, lying is morally forbidden under any and all circumstances, including those from which "good" consequences might result. Even in extreme cases such as that of the "Inquiring Murderer," we are still morally obligated to be honest. Even if lying to the inquiring murderer leads to the death of the young woman, we can still be said to have done the morally "right" thing (more on this in a moment). Kant rejected outright the notion that consequences should be an appropriate measure of right and wrong. Instead, acts are only considered right when they are performed in accordance with *duty* (e.g., the moral duty not to lie).

Hypothetical and Categorical Imperatives

To get a better sense of Kant's moral philosophy, we can begin by distinguishing between what he termed, "hypothetical imperatives," and what he termed, "categorical imperatives."[2] An *imperative* is a command. More specifically, it is a command that we perform or not perform some action. Various forms of "oughts" are imperatives that govern much of what we do in all areas of our daily lives. For instance, if we claim that we ought to study or that we ought not to lie, we are making use of imperatives. However, the imperative that we "ought to study" is in an important respect different from the contention that we "ought not to lie."

By stating that we ought to study we are really saying that we ought to study *if* we wish to bring about some desired consequence. In other words, *if* Joe wishes to receive an "A" in geometry, he "ought" to study. Similarly, *if* Jane wishes to make the basketball team, she "ought" to practice this summer. In both illustrations, we are claiming that we ought to do this or that *if* (and only if) we wish to achieve some end.[3]

Much of our everyday conduct is informed by precisely these ways of "if-then" thinking. We realize that in order to get what we want there are certain courses of action we should follow. Consequently, we conclude that we ought to follow that course of action in order to reach one or another desired state of affairs. The types of imperatives at issue here are what Kant called *hypothetical* or *conditional* imperatives.

A **hypothetical imperative** is a command that we ought to follow *if we have certain desires* that we wish to achieve or realize.[4] If Joe did not care about getting an "A" in geometry or if Jane did not care about making the basketball team, they would have no reason to abide by those respective commands or imperatives. Hypothetical imperatives, then, have no binding moral force. To avoid adhering to them, all we need to do is renounce the wish or desire that they are intended to produce.[5] Thus, escaping the force of hypothetical imperatives—"getting out of" the obligations they entail—is as simple as foregoing our desire for certain consequences.

Moral obligations, however, are not conditioned by or dependent on any particular desire or the realization of any particular outcome. For Kant, moral obligations are *categorical.* **Categorical imperatives** are *absolute* commands that we ought to follow, *period!*[6] A conditional imperative might consist of the moral principle that we ought to respect others if we want them to respect us. However, a categorical imperative would indicate that we ought to respect others regardless of what we want or desire from them, including their respect. For Kant, categorical imperatives are the basis of morality. We have certain moral duties and obligations that we cannot avoid or escape even when abandoning our wants or desires, and that *must* be followed irrespective of the consequences they bring about for us or for others. Categorical imperatives are thus more difficult for and demanding of us than conditional duties.

Maxims and Universal Laws

From where do these duties or commands come? Kant suggested that categorical "oughts" are a product of human reason alone. As he argued, they are derived from a single principle that *every rational human being must accept.*[7] Once we understand this basic principle, we have a formula or procedure by which we can infer a number of more specific moral oughts. Since all categorical oughts are derived from this one basic principle, our obligation to abide by them should be clear to any sensible person. While there are several variations to or formulations of this principle, Kant suggested that they are all similar in nature. He termed this principle the *Categorical Imperative.* In its first formulation, the Categorical Imperative can be stated as follows:

> *Act only according to that maxim by which you can at the same time will that it should become a universal law.*[8]

Through the Categorical Imperative, Kant effectively proposed a procedure that we should use when determining whether any given act is morally permissible or morally right. When contemplating a given action, we should first ask ourselves what *maxim* we would be following in so doing. By **maxim**, Kant simply was referring to a moral rule—whatever rule we would be adhering to is the *maxim* of the act.[9] For instance, if we determine that we should lie to our best friend in order to avoid hurting that person's feelings, the maxim we would be following is: "We should lie to our friends whenever telling the truth stands to hurt another's feelings." Once we figure out the rule or maxim we are adopting, the next step is to ask ourselves whether we would be willing to make it a *universal law.* By **universal law**, Kant meant a rule that would be followed by everyone, all of the time. Thus, in the above example, we would need to ask ourselves whether we would want all people, all of the time, to lie to their friends whenever telling the truth would hurt their feelings. If we answer "yes" to this question, then the act is morally right or permissible. If we answer "no"—that we would *not* be willing to have everyone follow this principle on all occasions—we must conclude that the maxim is not a universal law and, as such, is not morally permissible.

All moral principles that we could wish to become universal laws are categorically imperative—they are principles that we must, in all situations, follow irrespective of our desires or the consequences that may issue forth from them. At the same time, all such principles that we could not wish to become universal laws are those that we ought not to adopt, again regardless of our desires or the potential consequences. Kant's most notable examples on this subject include borrowing money and charity.

BORROWING MONEY   Suppose you need to borrow money. Further, suppose you know that no one will lend it to you unless you promise to repay it. Finally, assume that you know that there is no way you will ever be able to repay the loan. Given this, the question becomes whether you should promise to repay the money, knowing full well that you will never be able to do so, in order to persuade someone to financially assist you. The maxim of the act would be as follows: When a person needs a loan, one should promise to repay that loan even though the person knows he or she will not be able to do so. Can we say that this maxim becomes a universal law? Kant indicates that the answer is "no." His reasoning is as follows: If everyone who needed a loan promised to repay it, despite knowing that they could not, then no lenders would believe any such promises and no borrowers would ever be granted the money.[10] Obviously, this would be self-defeating—the entire practice of loan making would be jeopardized if not altogether undone.[11] Consequently, we cannot will that this maxim should become a universal law and, moreover, we are categorically bound to abide by the moral principle that we should not make promises that we know we can never keep.

CHARITY   Suppose that Scott refuses to help people who are in need, claiming that its not any concern of his. In Kant's words, "What concern is it of mine? Let each one be as happy as heaven wills, or as he can make himself . . . to his welfare or to his assistance in time of need I have no desire to contribute."[12] Can Scott will that this maxim—that we should not concern ourselves with others who are in need—become a universal law? Again, Kant says "no." Such a maxim would contradict itself because there may be future cases in which one "would need the love and sympathy of others, and in which he would have robbed himself . . . of all hope of the aid he desires."[13] In other words, because we, at some point in the future, may ourselves be in need, we clearly cannot will a maxim by which we do not assist others in distress to become a universal law.

Moral Duties and Absolute Rules

According to Kant, then, ethics is about following absolute moral rules, derived from the Categorical Imperative. These imperatives are universal in that they must be followed by all persons, all of the time. Strictly adhering to these rules—applying them without exception in all situations—is our *duty* as rational, moral human beings. **Duties** are things we *must* do (*positive duties*)—or must *not* do (*negative duties*)—no matter how we feel, how we or others might be affected, and no matter the peculiarities of the situation in which we find ourselves. In short, duties are obligations that *must* be fulfilled.

While we have numerous specific moral duties, each of them is derived from the general moral principle of the Categorical Imperative. One of Kant's most notable examples of a specific duty is not to lie. As he suggested, lying could not be a universal law and, thus, would not pass the test of the Categorical Imperative. Lying would be self-defeating in that if we fail to tell the truth, we must be willing to wish that all other people do so as well. If this were the case, we would all soon enough stop believing what other people said. If none of us could trust what others said, social living would be exceedingly difficult.[14]

Recall the "Case of the Inquiring Murderer" discussed at the beginning of this chapter. Kant held that even in a situation where undesirable consequences plainly might result (e.g., the death of another person), we were morally bound to uphold our duty—we were still obligated to abide by the universal law not to lie. The problem for Kant is that he supposed that by telling the inquiring murderer the truth, we endorsed a universal law that prohibits lying. However, there are other potential interpretations or formulations of this general law that might be applicable in this case.

For instance, suppose that by lying the moral rule we followed was not that it is permissible to do so but, rather, that it is acceptable only when doing so saves someone's life.[15] Many of us probably *would* be willing to have this latter formulation become a universal law. Thus, when put to the test of the Categorical Imperative, the potential universal law that "it is permissible to lie when doing so saves the life of another" seems defensible and justifiable. This action would rescue or salvage lives and, more than likely, would not result in a situation in which none of us believed anything anyone else said. Because circumstances in which people lie in order to save another person's life would be extremely rare, especially in the context of our everyday realities, we would have no reason to cease trusting the word of other people.

Changing the maxim on lying as delineated above represents a basic problem with Kant's ethical approach on the whole; namely, "for any action a person might contemplate, it is possible to specify more than one rule that he or she would be following."[16] Anytime we posit certain moral rules or laws as absolutes, we can "get around any such rule by describing our action in such a way that it does not fall under that rule but instead comes under a different one."[17]

Exceptions and Consequences

In his own analysis of the Case of the Inquiring Murderer, Kant suggests that:

> . . . whoever tells a lie, however well intentioned he might be, must answer for the consequences, however unforeseeable they were, and pay the penalty for them.[18]

Suppose that you lied to the inquiring murderer, believing that doing so would save the woman's life. Not knowing that the woman is hiding in the bushes, the would-be murderer proceeds to continue about his search, leaving your porch step and making his way around the back of your house. In the meantime, however, the woman has decided to find a more secure place in which to hide. She has quietly removed herself from the bushes, called the police, and sought shelter in a storage shed in your backyard. Unfortunately, the storage shed is the next place the inquiring murderer looks. He finds her in hiding and, before the police can arrive to apprehend him, kills her. At least to some degree, Kant would argue, you were responsible for the woman's death. In lying to the potential murderer, you encouraged him to search elsewhere, which eventually led him to locate her and, in so doing, to take her life. Of course, you could not have known that this would happen, but this is precisely Kant's point. Had you told the truth, it is possible that the man would have wasted time searching in the bushes, thus giving the police time to get to the scene and thereby preventing the woman from being murdered. On the other hand, she might still have been hiding in the bushes and your honesty would have led him directly to her, resulting in the woman's untimely death.

But these various conditions help to make Kant's argument even simpler: "*We can never be certain what the consequences of our actions will be.*"[19] Though we may often consider lying, cheating, stealing, and so forth in order to prevent evil or bring about good consequences, we can *never* know exactly what the results of our actions will be. This is a considerable problem for all approaches to morality that emphasize consequences—consequences require us to *predict the future*, something which cannot always be done by any of us with a sufficient degree of accuracy (recall the limitation of utilitarianism on this point as discussed in Chapter 8). Even if we are motivated to lie (or to tell the truth) in order to bring about good (e.g., preventing a murder), we can never be certain that our actions will, in fact, bring about that good. It is at least possible that the results of our action would be much worse than those that would have resulted had we told the truth.

In the Case of the Inquiring Murderer, there are several important considerations that might factor into our decision about whether we should lie:

- In telling the truth, we are *avoiding* a *known evil* (lying), which might:
    1. bring about good consequences (preventing a murder), or
    2. bring about evil consequences (causing a murder by leading the assailant to his victim)
- In lying, we are *committing* a *known evil* (lying), which might:
    1. bring about good consequences (preventing a murder), or
    2. bring about evil consequences (accidentally causing a murder)

Though we can never be certain what the consequences of our actions will be, we *can* be certain that lying would be committing an evil, and that telling the truth would be avoiding an evil. Whether good or bad consequences follow is largely beyond our control. What *is* in our control is whether we intentionally commit an act that we know to be an evil. Kant argues that in every situation, the best policy is to "avoid the known evil . . . and let the consequences come as they will."[20] On the chance that bad consequences arise from our telling the truth, they are not our fault. We have abided by the moral law not to lie, and this is as much as we can do.[21] So long as we have done our duty we cannot control the consequences nor should we be held accountable for them (see Box 9.1).

Respect for Persons

Kant also offered us a second variation of the Categorical Imperative. This alternative formulation has slightly different but equally important implications:

> Act so as to treat humanity, whether in your own person or that of any other, as an end and never as a means only.[22]

This version of the Categorical Imperative entails a key component of Kant's moral philosophy—and arguably a key feature of any moral philosophy. In brief, Kant argued that *all* human beings have *intrinsic worth* or *dignity*.[23] Because of this, we have a moral imperative to treat all human beings with respect—to affirm, through the way we treat others, the inherent dignity of every person. This imperative or absolute exceeds any self-interested gain or loss we might experience as a consequence of so doing. Moreover, it transcends any personal feelings we might have or might not have for individuals. The very basis of morality, then, is to demonstrate—through our intentions and actions—a respect for the inherent value or worth of others.

to prove the original research hypothesis. Therefore, the statistical test of a research hypothesis is usually carried out in the form of trying to reject the corresponding null hypothesis, although the effect is far weaker than directly proving the original research hypothesis.

You do not have to have a hypothesis in order to conduct statistical inference. You can directly estimate a population parameter by using available sample information. Hypothesis testing and parameter estimation follow the same logic, though they are often conducted in different forms. It should be noted that hypothesis testing can be both univariate and relational; so can parameter estimation although occasionally the term "parameter" is used solely in the univariate sense.

How do you use the sample data to infer to the situation of the population? In order to understand the procedures as well as the results of statistical inference, you must know what is meant by a "sampling distribution." This is one of the hardest topics in statistics, although it may be taken for granted by some authors of statistical texts.

Let us start from where we are. In the discussion of sampling strategies, we gained the understanding that the use of random sampling is to ensure that every case of the research population has an equal chance to be selected. However, this does not mean that every case will actually be chosen. For a specific case, there is no lead at all about the outcome beforehand, and being eventually selected or not is a totally different result. For a particular sample, there is no lead at all about its composition beforehand either, and the cases that are eventually selected could be rather different from one sampling process to another. Since each sample appears to be so singular from one another, it seems rather inadequate to base your conclusion about a population on any of its particular samples. This is true if you just look at the difference among the results when you repeat the same sampling procedures again and again (this can be done easily by computer simulation).

The difference in the composition of the samples, however, is not the point of our concern. As a matter of fact, if the same cases are always selected, the rule of equal chance as embodied in the random sampling process should be doubted. The question is, when you look at a specific variable, does the sample statistic vary or stay the same even though the samples are different?

The answer is, unfortunately, that the statistic of every variable will vary when different samples are used. This fact is known as sampling variability in repeated random sampling. Probably you are now feeling at a loss again: How could you

BOX 9.1

Policing and the Duty to Tell the Truth

You are a police officer called to testify at a murder trial. Through your investigation of the case, you and your partner collected enough physical evidence to ensure a conviction, including the murder weapon with the defendant's fingerprints, an audiotape of the defendant confessing the crime to a cellmate, and a videotape showing the defendant entering the victim's apartment building shortly before the time of the offense. However, you also know that the murder weapon was obtained through an unconstitutional search of the defendant's place of residence, and that the audiotape was acquired in such a way that, if truth be told, it would likely not be admitted at trial as legally obtained evidence. Upon taking the stand, you are directly questioned concerning the constitutionality of the search and the acquisition of the tape.

Kantian ethics would ask that you consider the following: (1) if you lie, this will likely (but not certainly) result in the conviction of a known killer; (2) if you tell the truth, this will likely (but not certainly) result in the case against a known killer being dismissed for lack of evidence. Importantly, Kant's deontology would remind you that there are other potential consequences that you cannot possibly predict as well. Suppose that having lied, the truth comes out through some other means—either during the trial or sometime thereafter. If this happens, not only will a known killer be found not guilty (or released on appeal), but you and your partner will likely be brought up for disciplinary action and reprimand, face criminal prosecution, and/or lose your jobs. Moreover, the case would bring national media attention, making you, your partner, your department, the chief of police, and your entire city look bad in the eyes of the public. Though it is likely that the criminal trial will be dismissed for lack of evidence if you tell the truth, it is also possible that the defendant may be found guilty anyway—perhaps he unwittingly confesses at trial, or there is additional testimony from witnesses, friends of the defendant, and so on, of which you are unaware. Even if the case were to be dismissed, perhaps new evidence would emerge sometime in the near future and the defendant would then be convicted legitimately.

Whatever the consequences of lying or telling the truth might be, Kant reminds us that we cannot ever know for sure. The best we can do is to pursue our moral duty and let the consequences come as they may. In this instance, our moral duty is to tell the truth. If the criminal case against the murderer is dismissed because evidence is lacking, this is certainly not your fault—no one can blame you for abiding by your moral duty to tell the truth.

More specifically, Kant presented this ultimate law of morality as an imperative to never treat others "as a means only." In other words, we should never "use" others purely as a means to some end—whatever the end is or its importance might be.[24] For instance, some of us may have friends who we do not truly respect as human beings; however, we are willing to spend time with them in order to benefit from something they possess or could get for us. Maybe we date someone because the person has money; maybe we invite someone out with a group of our friends because the individual has physical qualities that attract members of the opposite (or same) sex; maybe we associate with a co-worker because the person's parents are season ticket holders to the football games played by our city's professional team.

In each hypothetical case, we are using someone because of what that person can do for us. Missing in these interactions is any genuine regard for the individual's inherent worth as a human being. Kant reminds us that in none of these cases would we be acting morally. Of course, this does not mean that we can never benefit in various ways from others. Instead, it is simply to say that our treatment of others—whether they are friends, stockbrokers, convicted criminals, or the clerk at the checkout counter from the local convenience store—should reflect a genuine respect for that person's inherent and *ever-present* importance as a human being.

By "ever-present," we mean that dignity is not something that people must earn or that people will lose through their actions; rather, it is something that each of us possesses *by virtue of being human.* This sense of worth and respect endures so long as we are alive. In many cases, it remains long past our time on this earth.

What, more specifically, does this innate respect for and call to value others mean, especially in terms of our treatment of them? According to James Rachels,

> we have a strict duty of beneficence toward other persons: we must strive to promote their welfare; we must respect their rights, avoid harming them, and generally 'endeavor, so far as we can, to further the ends of others.'[25]

Given the above observations, there is yet another implication embedded in the second formulation of the Categorical Imperative. Kant believed that the inherent worth of human beings stems from their nature as *rational* creatures—as "free agents capable of making their own decisions, setting their own goals, and guiding their conduct by reason."[26] As such, treating people as "ends" requires that we *respect their rationality.* In part, this clearly entails assigning value to the capacity of others to make free, autonomous choices about their own welfare through the exercise of their reason. As Kant insisted, we should never select courses of action *for* others or influence their choices through manipulation, deceit, or trickery. Manipulating people or otherwise using people to satisfy our own needs or to achieve our own goals—no matter how significant or valuable those needs and goals might be—fails to respect the rationality of others and, consequently, fails to conform with the moral imperative to always treat others as ends. By treating people as "things," we are regarding them as beings without the capacity for reason and autonomy. Reason is what differentiates human beings from other "things" in the world. Thus, following Kant, our moral duty is to respect that difference.[27]

Returning to the example of pursuing a loan, Kant asks us to consider the following: If we were to ask for the money, promising to repay it even though we knew we could not, we would be manipulating someone for purposes of getting financial assistance (i.e., using the lender as a means or as a way to achieve our own ends). On the other hand, if we told the truth—that we needed money but would not be in a position to repay it—the lender would be in a better position to assess whether to grant the loan or not. In short, by being truthful we allow the lender to utilize his or her own capacity for reasoning and autonomous decision-making as this person endeavors to determine whether financial assistance in our case is warranted. In doing so, even though we would still be relying on that individual as a means to get money, we would be respecting that person's rationality and, thus, dignity in the process.[28]

To be clear, Kant did *not* claim that we could never use people as a means; instead, he argued that we should not use them this way exclusively. To illustrate, we cannot avoid "using" our stockbroker as a means to purchase stock (or to make money); we cannot avoid "using" the waitress at our favorite local restaurant as a means to obtain food and drink; and we cannot avoid "using" our teachers as a means to gain knowledge or a degree. However, in doing so, we can still treat these persons as human beings with intrinsic value and dignity. In all such situations, then, Kant reminds us that in order to be ethical we should recognize and respect people's capacity for reason and autonomous choice, fully acknowledging them as unique and valuable individuals with their own needs, wants, and goals (see Box 9.2).

BOX 9.2

Means, Ends, and Intimate Relationships: The Case of Mary Jo Laterneau

Consider the following: Is there a difference between "using" one's spouse or someone with whom one is involved in an intimate, caring relationship to meet one's sexual needs versus "using" a person one has just met at a nightclub for purposes of satisfying one's own sexual desires? The answer, of course, is that there most often *is* a significant difference.

Intimate, caring relationships are (hopefully) founded upon a genuine respect and concern for the other person and recognition of that person's value as a unique human being. As spouses, girlfriends, boyfriends, etc., we not only respect the other person as a human being, but value the fact that the individual has unique wants and interests. Moreover, we should do whatever we legitimately can to help that person satisfy those needs and interests.

Conversely, "one-night stands" and other short-term sexual relationships are often characterized by one or both parties using the other purely to fulfill selfish desires. As Kant would remind us, this is especially the case—and especially morally problematic—when manipulation or deceit is involved. Making false promises or implicit false promises (e.g., the pledge of a long-term relationship when this is not intended) or offering false compliments (e.g., "you have the most beautiful eyes I have ever seen") are ways of manipulating the other person for one's own ends. In doing so, Kant would argue that we fail to allow that other person to make a free and rational choice about whether to engage in the relationship. Instead, that person's decision is—at least in part—influenced by the promises, compliments, or other falsehoods we

have offered. Kant would suggest that we should always be completely honest and up-front with the other person, allowing the consequences to come as they may.

Now consider the case of Mary Jo Laterneau. Mary Jo was a schoolteacher. She found her "Romeo" in a twelve-year-old boy whom she had initially met and taught while he was in second grade. At the age of thirty-five, Mary Jo entered into a "consenting" and ongoing sexual relationship with the boy when he was fourteen years of age. She had a child with him and the case erupted into a national debate about responsibility and intimacy. To make matters more complicated, Ms. Laterneau's affair occurred while she was married with children of her own. Although eventually resigning from her place of employment; separated and divorced from her husband (losing custody of her children); and prosecuted, convicted, and sentenced to a prison term, Mary Jo professed deep and abiding true love for the boy. After serving a term in prison, Ms. Laterneau defied a court order upon her release requiring her to terminate all contact with the boy. Ms. Laterneau resumed the relationship with her "Romeo" and had a second child with her lover. The boy, now an adult, and Ms. Laterneau recently were married. Following the ethical insights of Kant, the only obligation in life one has is to be true to oneself and those others with whom one interacts. Despite our likely repulsion concerning this story, would you agree that this is precisely what happened in the case of Mary Jo Laterneau, especially given the nature and quality of the intimate relationship she established?

PRIMA FACIE DUTIES

One of the key concerns with Kantian ethics—as with absolute moral rules more generally—is that it provides no resolution for or guidance in the face of *conflicting duties*. Most of us have confronted or will face situations in which we are forced to choose between doing "A" and doing "B," where both "A" *and* "B" are governed by moral imperatives. Returning again to Kant's Case of the Inquiring Murderer, suppose there are two absolute moral rules at issue: (1) it is wrong to lie; and (2) it is wrong to permit the murder of an innocent person.[29] If both of these as maxims are absolute, then each of us is morally obligated to follow them in all situations. However, the inquiring murderer presents a dilemma: we cannot *both* not lie *and* not permit the murder of an innocent person. The coexistence of two equally weighty imperatives seems to have created an irreconcilable ethical quandary.

While the Case of the Inquiring Murderer is not likely to occur in "real life," there are certainly other situations in which conflicts between absolute moral duties can and do arise. For instance, think of prisoners of war who are forced to choose between revealing government secrets and watching an innocent person be executed as a consequence of their refusal to cooperate with the enemy. Assuming that there is an absolute moral duty to be loyal to one's country *and* an absolute moral duty not to permit the murder of innocent people, a moral dilemma arises that seemingly cannot be reconciled simply by appealing to absolute moral rules. Whatever choice is made, one or the other moral rule will be violated. Thus, it appears as if Kantian ethics and the notion of absolute moral duties are seriously flawed. Or are they?

In situations where we are forced to choose between multiple moral duties (i.e., imperatives), we have no ethical basis for making such a choice. W. D. Ross (1877–1971) recognized this problem with traditional Kantian ethics. In response, he argued for an ethics of **prima facie duties**.[30] "Prima facie" duties—also called *conditional* duties—are different from those of the absolute variety that are central to Kantian ethics. While prima facie duties should be followed in most circumstances, they can be *overridden* by other duties that are more imperative in a given instance. In situations where more than one prima facie duty is at issue, we should "study the situation as fully as [we] can until [we] form the considered opinion . . . that in the circumstances one of them is more incumbent then any other. . . ."[31] In other words, certain duties can and should be violated if, given the situational factors in play, we determine that other duties override them.

This is the key difference between prima facie duties and absolute moral duties—the former are not absolute in the sense that they must always be followed. So, how would conflicting prima facie duties function in an everyday context? Let us return to the inquiring murderer, supposing that we have both a duty not to lie *and* a duty not to permit the death of an innocent person. If our duty not to permit the death of an innocent person outweighs (or is more important than) our duty not to lie, then we may—with good conscience—violate our moral duty not to lie in favor of saving someone's life. If the duty not to lie is a prima facie duty—one that is not absolute but can be overridden—we are allowed the possibility of violating it if the circumstances demand that we do so.

The Role of Prima Facie Duties

While Ross offers a tentative list of prima facie duties (see Box 9.3), we are still faced with the question of how to determine which prima facie duties override others. This question is not easily addressed. In part, Ross attempts to respond by focusing on those concerns that emerge from Kant's emphasis on absolute moral duties. Again, these are imperatives that we all must adhere to no matter what the situation is or the "good" consequences that follow. We can use prima facie duties to determine what we should do in any given situation. Remember, these types of imperatives *are* binding or obligatory *unless* they are superseded by other duties. For example, we have a prima facie duty of fidelity that includes keeping the promises that we make. Thus, we are morally obligated to keep our promises *unless* there are other, stronger moral considerations that override or "trump" that duty in a particular situation.

However, we should keep in mind that by "other, stronger moral considerations," we are not referring to consequences. Similar to Kant, Ross provides us with a deontological variation of morality. Our ethical choices should be based on whatever prima facie duties apply to the situation at hand. Unlike Kant, Ross recommends using conditional duties to address moral

BOX 9.3

A Brief List of Prima Facie Duties

Exactly what are prima facie duties? In response to this question, W. D. Ross offers an "incomplete," though useful, list of major types:

Duties arising from our own previous acts:

- *Duties of Fidelity*—These include duties that stem from our own previous promises, contracts, or other agreements. Prima facie duties of fidelity can be explicit or implicit. The duty not to tell a lie is a prima facie duty arising from an implicit promise that we make to others upon entering a conversation, writing a book, etc. The duty not to lie can also be an explicit prima facie duty of fidelity arising from the oath we take as a witness in a criminal trial or the pledge of faithfulness that we make when getting married.

- *Duties of Reparation*—These are duties that issue forth from our own previous wrongful acts. We have prima facie duties to make reparations for harms or damages that we have caused previously. Examples include criminal conduct, school bullying, gossiping.

Duties issuing from the previous acts of others:

- *Duties of Gratitude*—These are duties that surface, given the previous acts of others. Prima facie duties of gratitude require that we be grateful for the assistance of others, returning that aid or kindness whenever possible. Examples include buying lunch for a friend who has done the same for you in the past; volunteering your time at a rape counseling or drug abuse center, given that others have done the same for you previously.

Duties that emerge from an imbalance between the distribution of happiness (or the means by which to attain happiness) and the merit of the people concerned:

- *Duties of Justice*—These duties require that we act so as to distribute benefits and burdens in a fair and equi-table manner. We have a prima facie duty to prevent an unfair distribution of goods, or to disrupt an existing unfair pattern of distribution. Work-place inequities (e.g., salary discrimination, scheduling imbalances) based on race, gender, ethnicity, age, disability, etc., illustrate this principle.

Duties arising from the notion that there are other individuals in the world whose condition we can improve:

- *Duties of Beneficence*—Doing good deeds for others such as aiding their health, happiness, welfare, etc.

Duties stemming from the fact that we can improve our own condition:

- *Duty of Self-Improvement*—This entails the duty to promote our own good—our health, security, wisdom, happiness, virtue, etc.

Duties that can be summarized as not injuring others:

- *Duty of Nonharm or Nonmalfeasance*—This duty entails not harming others—physically, emotionally, or otherwise. Examples include avoid causing harm to the health, safety, character, happiness, etc., of others. The duty of nonharm has also been interpreted to include the duty to prevent harm to others.

Source: W. D. Ross, *The Right and the Good* (Oxford: Clarendon Press, 1993).

dilemmas involving more than one imperative. In other words, if the application of duty "A" conflicts with the application of duty "B" in the *same* situation, we are not obligated to follow both unconditionally or absolutely. Rather, we can violate one in favor of the other, *provided* the one we select to follow is more imperative.

So, which conditional duties are more imperative than others? Regrettably, Ross' theory does not offer a precise way for us to determine which ones take precedence over others or which ones serve as "trump cards" in particular situations. In short, he does not offer a ranking of prima facie duties nor does he suggest that one exists. Each situation must be judged uniquely.

RIGHTS: THE "OTHER SIDE OF DUTY"[32]

In contemporary American culture and society, the idea of "rights" plays a crucial role in the consideration of moral behavior, as well as in our response to contentious social, political, and legal issues. Examples such as the "right" to have an abortion, the "right" to bear arms, the "right" to punish criminal offenders or to utilize animals and the natural environment as we see fit, all convey this point.[33] Similarly, discussions surrounding rights *violations* inform our views on such matters as torture, poverty, and slavery.[34] What this suggests, then, is that the idea of rights is especially important when addressing various topics in law, crime, and the justice system.

For instance, the significance of procedural rights tends to be one of the first topics to which students and practitioners of criminal justice are exposed in their educational and professional careers.[35] Along these lines, we commonly hear stories of the rights of criminal suspects, defendants, or prisoners being in some respect violated by persons working within the criminal justice system.[36] The appellate court system operates for precisely this purpose—it hears arguments and makes rulings on these sorts of infractions. What all of this suggests, then, is that irrespective of how we might feel about rights or certain types of rights (e.g., for defendants, for victims, for those criminally confined, for women, for minorities), the reality is that we cannot easily escape their consideration.[37] This is as true in ethics as much as it is in criminology and criminal justice.

In the context of ethics, rights are important in that their existence *justifies* behavior and *places limitations* on behavior. They factor into determinations about what is morally required, permissible, or forbidden. Where rights are prioritized over other moral considerations, we may be required to respect a person's right to privacy; we might assert that an act of self-defense was morally permissible given our right to protect self and/or property against harm from others; or we may be forbidden from violating the bodily integrity of another person. In each case, rights regulate what we can and cannot do, how we treat others, and how we expect others to treat us. In this light, rights share an important relationship with moral duty.

Rights and Duties

In the last section, we were introduced to Kant's deontological or duty-based claim that there exist absolute moral imperatives that each of us is obligated to follow, irrespective of consequences, contexts, and desires. In this approach, our moral duties spring forth from universal maxims or laws. Similarly, the tradition of rights also can be regarded as deontological in the sense that it argues for moral duties. However, the duties that stem from moral rights do not emerge from universal moral laws but, instead, they arise from the moral rights themselves.[38] How so?

First, consistent with deontology, the notion of rights implies that consequences are irrelevant moral considerations. If you have a "right" to own a handgun, then your possession of it has nothing to do with the consequences that might arise from your doing so. If a criminal defendant has a "right" to an attorney, there is no suggestion that having counsel should depend, in any way, on what the consequences will be for the defendant, the prosecution, the victim, or the criminal justice process overall. Thus, the various rights that we enjoy are not contingent upon whatever effects may or may not result. The same can be said for the sorts of absolute moral rights that underlie other duties. Your right to be treated with respect and dignity stems alone from your status as a human being. Each of us can be said to have a moral duty to respect your status as a person and, therefore, to revere your moral right to be treated as such.

BOX 9.4

The Right to Refuse Treatment and Competency to Be Executed

Just because rights and duties are correlative does not mean that this relationship is supported in all situations or with all ethical dilemmas. One such example is the problem of treatment refusal invoked by mentally ill persons on death row. Complicating this matter is the process of competency restoration. Typically under these conditions, returning one to a state of mental fitness involves the forced administration of drug treatment over the confined person's objection. The goal is to restore competency such that the individual is cognizant of his or her imminent execution. Clearly, there are ethical concerns about physicians forcibly administering mind-altering drugs to psychiatrically ill death row offenders who object to them, particularly when the expressed purpose is execution and nothing more. To some extent, the court has addressed this matter. However, the issue at hand is one of respecting the rights of individuals as a moral duty, notwithstanding the individual's psychiatric condition.

In the instance of treatment refusal for persons on death row, this is difficult to assess. Part of this difficulty relates to whether a person can exercise a right to refuse treatment knowingly and voluntarily. After all, if someone does not know what she or he is requesting and/or does not make such a decision freely, it remains to be seen whether the exercise of this right should be respected and honored at all. Ethically speaking, the absence of both (awareness and volition) may very well erode one's duty to adhere to the request.

Perhaps one way to gauge whether one's treatment refusal is undertaken freely and knowingly is to consider whether the mentally ill death row inmate's position changes after competency is restored. Some have suggested that if a person's competency is restored and the individual still insists that the forced medication remains objectionable, that the person was, at the least, *competent enough* prior to the restoration to have had their right respected in the first place. Unfortunately, this "after the fact" sort of proof does not value the person's deontological right and the corresponding duty that should have been adhered to initially. At best, the right to refuse treatment and competency to be executed demonstrate how the politics of mental illness and fitness for death can trump the fundamental rights of citizens, despite disability.

Source: Bruce J. Winick, *The Right to Refuse Treatment* (Washington, DC: American Psychological Association, 1997); Bruce A. Arrigo and Christopher R. Williams, "Law, Ideology, and Critical Inquiry: The Case of Treatment Refusal for Incompetent Persons Awaiting Execution," *New England Journal on Criminal and Civil Confinement*, 25 (2), 367–412 (1999); Kursten Hensly, "Restored to Health to Be Put to Death," *Villanova Law Review*, 49, 225–251 (2004).

Second, rights are often said to be *correlative* with duties. The **correlativity of rights and duties** means that the rights of people imply duties that others must acknowledge and value.[39] To illustrate, if you have a right to privacy, then people (including the government) have a duty to respect what you define as intimate or confidential. If you possess a right to refuse unwanted and invasive medical treatment, this right implies that others have a duty not to interfere by imposing or forcing it on you, even if it is deemed therapeutic (see Box 9.4). If you have a right to worship as you see fit, this means that others have a moral duty to respect your right by not interfering in any way with your religious preferences or practices.

Natural Rights Ethics

Rights are generally understood as either natural or derived from duties.[40] The idea of *natural rights* has its conceptual basis in a type of moral universalism. Recall from Chapter 4 that ethical universalism refers to the notion that there exist moral principles or standards that can and should be relevant to everyone, everywhere, in all situations. To say that such principles or standards are universal is to suggest that they are true of and applicable to all people in all cultures and all time periods. Thus, we are obligated to recognize and utilize them in all cases in which those principles or standards are pertinent. Moreover, that which is identified as universal supersedes all other considerations (e.g., cultural, historical, situational contexts).

The doctrine of natural rights suggests that all human beings enjoy certain basic rights irrespective of their membership in a particular political society.[41] In this sense, then, rights are enjoyed universally and apply globally. The natural rights that all people benefit from are not derived from laws or granted by governments; rather, they stem from human nature. That these rights stem from human nature means that: (1) they do not need to be earned; and (2) they cannot be taken away. Thus, natural rights function as universal moral laws or principles that must be respected regardless of circumstances. What are these principles and what implications do they hold for morality?

In short, the tradition of moral rights maintains that each "moral subject" has a right to "a kind of integrity."[42] This "kind of integrity" implies that each individual has moral worth wherein the individual is endowed with certain rights that cannot be taken away and which must be respected in all instances. These rights are said to be shared by all citizens, irrespective of who, where, what, or when they are, and irrespective of consequences, motivations, situational factors, and so forth.

The universality or absoluteness of moral rights has its roots in the tradition of *natural law* (see Chapter 7 for more on natural law). This tradition emerged in antiquity and, more specifically, in the writings of ancient Greek philosophers such as Aristotle and the Stoic philosopher, Chrysippus.[43] The Greeks routinely distinguished between *nomos*, or human law, and *phusis*, or laws of nature. Human laws included established practices such as customs, and "positive" or human-constructed written laws that varied by time and place. Consequently, they were subject to change. Because they were variable and changeable, human laws were understood to be fallible; that is, they could be unjust or misguided. In contrast, *phusis* represented a general term referring to what was unchangeable, such as the laws of physics. Thus, as philosophers reasoned, there must be some moral equivalent to the laws of nature—an unchanging moral order that was, like the laws of physics and biology, part of the natural world. This natural law was thought to exist independently of human laws and codes, applicable to everyone, everywhere.

The *ethics of human rights* begins with the natural law assumption that there is a certain universal moral order that exists apart from social, cultural, and historical conditions—a moral order which supersedes or "trumps" the "man-made" laws and socially constructed moral principles that are particular to civilizations and time periods.[44] Within this all-encompassing order exists a universal moral community that includes all human beings (and, by some accounts, all living things). By virtue of being connected to this global community, all human beings enjoy equal moral worth and status. This standing cannot be removed by others, and we are all morally obligated to honor it. In some important respects, the tradition of natural law is not unlike the laws of God or the sorts of universal laws that are found in many religions. However, the difference is that the natural law tradition does not depend on any conception of a supernatural being; instead, the source of its laws are derived from the natural order of the universe and apply to all human beings who are a part of that order.

While the concept of "rights" was not specifically discussed by Aristotle, the Stoics, and other early Western philosophers, the notion of natural law that emerged from Greek antiquity would later generate the idea of **natural rights**. Natural rights refer to the notion that basic guarantees exist and that all people possess them simply by virtue of being human.[45] For example, the eighteenth-century philosophers argued for the existence of a number of **negative rights** (or *liberty rights*) that were understood as *limitations* impacting the treatment of citizens by governments or political authorities.[46] More recently, the idea of rights has come to include **positive rights** (i.e. *welfare rights*) as well—rights *to* various things as well as rights against unjust interference by lawmakers. Unlike earlier conceptions that worked to restrict government, subsequent variations justified the expansion of the state. Rights to education, health care, housing, and so forth, all justify increased government involvement in the lives of its citizens. Examples of natural rights include those of life, liberty, and property, as well as the right to be treated fairly and equally no matter one's class, race, gender, political or religious affiliation, and the like.

Legal and Moral Rights

In many cases—including several of those noted above—discussions of rights revolve more specifically around various **legal rights**. This is especially true in criminal justice where the notion of rights typically refers to legal protections that people enjoy when interacting with representatives of the justice system. For instance, the right to the presence of an attorney in a criminal trial and the right to humane treatment are specific legal protections. Moreover, as an indication of the importance that legal rights assume in criminal justice, consider the decision in *Miranda v. Arizona* (1966). In this case, the U.S. Supreme Court guaranteed criminal suspects a right to *be informed of* their protections under the law. The aim was to ensure that such citizens, although thought to be responsible for criminal wrongdoing, were not treated unfairly. However, the legal rights that are so crucial to criminal justice are different in an important sense from the broader notion of **moral rights**. To be clear, moral rights are of greater concern when it comes to ethics.

When Thomas Jefferson (1732–1799)—writing under the influence of British philosopher John Locke (1632–1704)—authored the U.S. Declaration of Independence, he claimed a "right" to life, liberty, and the pursuit of happiness for all citizens. Clearly, the Declaration of Independence is not concerned with outlining legal rights that U.S. citizens have or should have in relation to these basic goods. This was the function of the Bill of Rights. However, what Thomas Jefferson and others did have in mind with the Declaration was basic, fundamental guarantees that each of us should enjoy irrespective of our backgrounds, statuses, or positions within society. In this respect, then, this document is similar to a variety of more recent provisions on rights, including the Universal Declaration of Human Rights (1948), the European Convention on Human Rights (1954), and the International Covenant on Civil and Economic Rights (1966).[47] What each of them has in common is a profound conception of rights in which certain "inalienable" liberties and protections possess deeper and more enduring significance than any formal rights that might or might not be created by government. In other words, the *moral rights* enumerated or implied in these declarations attach to people simply by virtue of their being human and this is why they are considerably more fundamental than the articulated legal protections.

It is worth noting that there is often an overlap between moral and legal rights. For example, many legal rights—such as those derived from the U.S. Constitution—are themselves traceable to some more elemental conception of human and moral rights. To illustrate, the notion of a right to life gives rise to a number of more specific legal guarantees including those pertaining to self-defense; the right to liberty gives rise to a variety of specific legal protections against unjustified interference with our pursuit of happiness. In many cases, then, human or moral rights (to life, to liberty) ground the drafting of legal rights.

However, what is more important in the context of ethics are the ways in which legal and moral rights differ. Notwithstanding the overlap, not all legal guarantees originate from moral rights, and many moral rights exist apart from an appeal to legal assurances. To be clear, *moral* rights exist *prior to* and *independent of* any legal considerations. And, as we have seen, some interpret moral rights as being derived from a universal moral order that precedes social and historical conditions—a moral order that applies to all human beings, everywhere, in every time period. Whether the legal system recognizes them, all human beings are said to have certain needs and interests, and corresponding moral rights that exist to protect and further these needs and interests. For instance, governments that deny political participation to ethnic or racial groups (whether the groups represent majority or minority constituencies) may do so legally; however, the moral "rightness" of political participation cannot be denied to people because of one's heritage or skin color. Similarly, slavery in the United States was deemed objectionable because its practice violated certain moral rights pertaining to humanness and personhood, even though existing laws made slavery entirely permissible.

What the above observations make evident is that moral rights possess binding force, irrespective of whether they are translated into law. Under these circumstances, even if laws exist requiring us to violate a particular moral right, it is unethical to do so. This is because in those situations where the law and moral rights come into conflict, our ethical duty is to obey the moral order rather than the formal law. Thus, moral rights transcend and "trump" human law. After all, human law can be, and some times is, constructed in error. Perhaps most importantly, the presence of moral rights suggests that laws made by people are subject to *limits* that emerge because of moral rights. In other words, precisely because moral rights are not derived from legal guarantees or from a Constitution, it is possible for existing laws and constitutional protections to be in violation of moral rights (see Box 9.5).[48]

BOX 9.5
The Scope of Moral Rights and International Criminal Justice

As we have seen, moral rights are said to be possessed by all people, everywhere, and in equal degree. Thus, irrespective of class, race, religion, nationality, or any other social distinction, each person enjoys the same basic moral rights simply because he or she is a human being. At the same time, though, this implies that all persons have a duty to protect and promote the moral rights of everyone else, regardless of whom these individuals are or where they might live.

Notwithstanding our personal moral responsibility to protect and promote the moral rights of others, in practice this duty often falls upon nations and international governments. According to some, government is best situated to effectively undertake these actions. Indeed, we need such institutions to protect rights for two reasons: (1) as individuals we tend to place higher moral priority on persons close to us (e.g., family, friends, community); and (2) our ability to exercise our duties with regard to the protection and promotion of moral rights is often limited by our personal circumstances (e.g., financial, geographical). To illustrate, it might be difficult for individuals in the United States to intervene in rights violations taking place in countries on the other side of the globe. If we consider various claims to rights that we are said to possess (e.g., the

right to an adequate education; protection against cruel and unusual punishment), it seems necessary to have some form of governmental body to ensure that these rights are promoted. But how do these rights translate into actions that countries and political authorities can and must ensure ethically?

- Generate a list of rights that you believe to be fundamentally important in the context of crime and justice.
- With the rights you have identified, ask yourself whether they should also be protected in foreign lands, or if there is room for cultural variability.
- Moreover, ask yourself whether and to what extent the United States has a duty to ensure that these crime and justice rights be enjoyed by all citizens in other countries. Would you argue that the United States has an affirmative obligation to ensure these rights exist in other countries even if the result is war? In what ways are these rights moral imperatives?

Source: Philippe Sands (Ed.), *From Nuremburg to the Hague: The Future of International Criminal Justice* (New York: Cambridge University Press, 2005).

justify the use of information from a particular sample to draw any general conclusion about the population? There is indeed no way to draw such a conclusion, unless the behavior of a sample statistic is predictable. The question, therefore, becomes whether or not there is a comprehensible behavioral pattern of the sample statistic, based on which an inference could be made with regard to the population parameter. This requires you to obtain and examine descriptive statistics for any key variable not only from one sample but from all possible samples drawn from the same population. The work is now made possible by computer simulation, which can render you at least a sufficiently large number of different sampling results on the same variable. For that specific statistic, the different values derived from different sampling results will form a distribution, from which a pattern of the behavior of the statistic may be discerned.

A sampling distribution is nothing distinct from the distribution of an ordinary variable in that it can be described by all kinds of measures of central tendency and dispersion. And a frequency histogram can be used to show the sampling distribution of the sample statistic. If there is anything special about a sampling distribution, it is because the variable that constitutes the distribution is not confined to one sample but based on all possible samples. And the "cases" are not the original analytic units but different samples. In real terms, this has to do with one of the measures of central tendency and dispersion of a number of samples or sampling results whose values constitute the special variable. In this respect, a sampling distribution is different from the distribution of a variable among a single sample. The former is the distribution of a sample statistic, which as a variable does not come from the ordinary source, i.e., direct measurement of the research subjects. It is a variable at a higher level; each of its values is a statistic (e.g., mean or standard deviation) of the entire distribution of an ordinary variable among a particular sample. The number of the values of the statistic as the variable of a sampling distribution is the number of different samples repeatedly drawn from the same population.

The standard deviation (SD or S) of a sampling distribution is called standard error (SE). In the case of a mean, it is determined by the standard deviation of the same variable in the population divided by the square root of the size of the samples. Yet the standard deviation in the population is usually unknown. In statistical practice, this is substituted with the standard deviation of the actual sample (with modification if necessary). That is, $SE = S/N^{1/2}$, which is called the estimated standard error in more accurate terms. The standard error helps to determine the potential degree of discrepancy between the sample mean and the

DEONTOLOGY AND THE CRIMINAL JUSTICE SYSTEM: THE MORALITY OF LEGAL PUNISHMENT

To illustrate the significance of deontological ethics for criminal justice issues, as well as to demonstrate how it differs from consequentialist perspectives, we turn in the remainder of this chapter to a common but morally controversial criminal justice practice—that of punishing lawbreakers. In Chapter 1 (Box 1.1), we were exposed to the *moral problem of punishment.* In short, the problem is one of *justifying* punishment. In other words, because punishing people involves inflicting pain and suffering—things we typically should not do—we must have some ground upon which we can claim that it is morally appropriate to impose punishments upon criminal offenders.[49] To find this ground, we must turn to normative ethical theories. Although many justifications for punishment have been proposed, most of them can be classified as either utilitarian or deontological. As normative moral frameworks, both utilitarianism and deontology offer ethical recommendations for how we *should* or *ought* to treat people who violate criminal laws. As we will see, however, utilitarian and deontological justifications for punishment are largely incompatible; that is, we cannot have both. Importantly, the ethical perspective we employ to justify punishing criminals will have important implications for why, how, and when we punish.

Utilitarianism and Criminal Punishment

As we saw in the previous chapter, utilitarian ethics holds the morality of actions to be a function of whether they bring about good consequences to all affected parties. As you might imagine, whether punishment of any sort is justifiable from a utilitarian perspective depends upon whether it brings about good or desirable consequences for the people who are affected by it. While the offender herself or himself is most directly affected by punishment, the positive (or negative) effects of punishment also indirectly impact the larger community and society. Because punishment typically causes pain and suffering to those individual offenders who are subjected to it, utilitarianism would have us look to its beneficial impact on the greater community to find moral justification.

What are the "good" consequences of criminal punishment for the community? In what ways can these benefits be said to outweigh the pain caused to those who are punished? While we will shortly see that there are several ways in which punishing criminals arguably benefits the greater good, all of them are said to have the same basic positive effect—*preventing* future crime. From a utilitarian standpoint, we punish lawbreakers *so that* future crime is prevented (and *only* for this purpose). As you may anticipate, if punishment practices fail to achieve the intended effect of preventing future crime, then they cannot be morally justified on utilitarian grounds.[50]

From a utilitarian standpoint, then, the negative consequences for the punished lawbreaker are "smaller evils" that may be outweighed by the greater moral good that is the prevention of future harm to others. In other words, *if* punishment can prevent many future victims from suffering the effects of crime, the gain in public safety is enough to justify the harm caused to individual offenders. It is important to keep in mind, however, that there are various types of punishment available in any given case (e.g., fines in various amounts, probation, imprisonment). As a general rule, utilitarianism holds that punishment should entail as little harm as is necessary to achieve the desired goal of prevention. If, for instance, a sentence of probation can effectively prevent an individual from committing future crimes, then any more severe punishment would cause harm above and beyond what is necessary and therefore morally justifiable. It is in part for this reason that utilitarians often *oppose* the practice of capital punishment. If an offender can be prevented from committing further crimes by imposing a life sentence, then capital punishment causes harm above and beyond what is necessary to achieve the goal of crime prevention.[51]

While crime prevention is the overriding utilitarian goal of punishment, there are several ways in which this goal can be accomplished. Each of the following is a purported beneficial effect of punishment that, from a utilitarian standpoint, serves to justify its practice:[52]

1. *Disablement.* Commonly referred to as *incapacitation*, **disablement** prevents future crime by *physically disabling* the offender. The most common form of punishment that serves the goal of disablement is *incarceration*. The imposition of a jail or prison term makes it physically impossible for the offender to victimize persons outside of that immediate environment. *Mutilation*, or physically dismembering or disfiguring an offender (e.g., removing the hand of a thief or the penis of a rapist), may also prevent certain offenders from repeating certain types of offenses (see Box 9.6). Finally, disablement can occur where a person (e.g., public official, medical or mental health professional, accountant) is simply removed from her or his position. In these instances, eliminating access to resources needed to commit future crimes can physically prevent the offender from repeating her or his offense.

BOX 9.6
Chemical Castration as Disablement

A contemporary controversy involving "mutilation" is that surrounding the practice of *chemical castration* for sex offenders. While surgical castration has never found popularity in the United States, beginning in the late 1990s a number of states proposed laws that would require qualified convicted sex offenders to submit to chemical castration. In 1996, California made chemical castration a condition of probation for certain offenders, and Montana, Iowa, Wisconsin, Louisiana, Oregon, and Florida have since implemented their own variations of chemical castration statutes.

Specifically, chemical castration involves weekly injections of medroxyprogesterone acetate (MPA) (commonly known as female contraceptive Depo-Provera). In effect, MPA administration in males fools the brain into believing that there are sufficient levels of circulating testosterone in the body, thereby inhibiting natural testosterone production and, in theory, lowering sex drive. Metaphorically "cutting off" an offender's sex drive will thus disable him from committing future sex crimes. While the use of MPA has been successful with some—perhaps even the majority—of sex offenders, it is not universally so. As well, it carries side effects such as loss in bone density, weight gain, fatigue, and depression—though the majority of such effects are thought to be reversible upon cessation of treatment in most men.

The reasoning behind chemical castration laws is clearly utilitarian in nature. Castration of sex offenders is performed in the interest of rehabilitation and protection of the public (especially children) from dangerous criminals. The advancement of these utilitarian goals is held to justify the practice of chemical castration on moral grounds. If, however, castration fails to work, then there is no corresponding gain in public safety. For those offenders for whom chemical castration is ineffective, the practice may be unjustifiable on utilitarian grounds. In addition, critics have raised a number of other legal and moral concerns about the practice of castration:

• The U.S. Supreme Court has held that competent adults—including prisoners and the civilly committed mentally ill—maintain a constitutional *right to refuse medical treatment*. This right may be subject to limitation, however, where there is a compelling government interest at stake (e.g., preserving prison safety). Where chemical castration is *required* as a condition of release for convicted sex offenders, the right to refuse medical treatment has in effect been taken away. Does the state's interest in protecting the public from known sex offenders outweigh an offender's constitutional right to refuse treatment? If so, does it matter that some drugs—including MPA—have known side effects?

• An implied *right to privacy* under the Fourteenth Amendment generally protects autonomy and bodily integrity with regard to decisions concerning childbearing and contraception.

(continued)

Forced castration could be interpreted as a violation of an offender's reproductive autonomy—the fundamental civil right to procreation that we all enjoy. Again, does the state's interest in protecting the public morally justify infringing upon an offender's autonomy and bodily integrity with regard to reproductive decisions? Does it matter that the effects may be reversible?

- Several states require that an offender's crime/s be against a child for chemical castration to be imposed. Others have no age requirement. Should chemical castration, if practiced, be limited to or mandated for offenders with certain victim types?
- Some states (Iowa, Louisiana, California, Florida) still allow for, but do not mandate, physical

castration as an alternative to a longer prison sentence and/or chemical castration. What are the moral implications of the practice of surgical castration and why, if at all, is chemical castration a "more moral" option?

Source: Elizabeth Tullio, "Chemical castration for Child Predators: Pra`ctical, Effective, and Constitutional," *Chapman Law Review*, 13 (1) (2009); Charles L. Scott and Trent Holmberg, "Castration of Sex Offenders: Prisoners' Rights Versus Public Safety," *Journal of the American Academy of Psychiatry and Law*, 31 (4), 502 (2003); Stone T. Howard et al., "Sex Offenders, Sentencing Laws, and Pharmaceutical Treatment: A Prescription for Failure," *Behavioral Sciences and the Law*, 18 (1), 83–110 (2000).

2. *Specific Deterrence.* The aim of **specific deterrence** is to prevent an *individual offender* from committing future wrongdoings by instilling in her or him *fear* of punitive consequences. To "deter" is to "discourage" or even "scare away." Recall that utilitarianism views humans as free-willed, rational beings, motivated to pursue pleasure and avoid pain. In the context of criminal motivation, lawbreakers will choose the pleasures of crime when they outweigh its associated pains. Contrarily, potential lawbreakers will choose law-abiding behaviors if the painful consequences of crime outweigh its pleasures. One such painful consequence is that of legal punishment, whether it be in the form of a fine, community service, probation, incarceration, etc. As we have discussed on several occasions throughout this text, many persons choose to follow the law because they fear such consequences. It is this fear by which deterrence operates and through which future crime is arguably prevented. Punishment in all forms, then, serves as an example or reminder *to the individual offender* of the "evil" that will be inflicted if she or he should choose to violate the law again in the future.

3. *Reform.* Importantly, deterrence does not eliminate the *desire* to engage in wrongdoings; rather, it simply makes a potential offender afraid to commit them for fear of consequences. The goal of **reform** or *rehabilitation*, on the other hand, is to *change the inclinations, motives, habits, and character of the offender* so that the offender no longer desires to engage in criminal activities. For example, a prisoner who is released back into the community after serving a five-year term may refrain from committing future crimes because she or he fears going back to prison. While it would be accurate to suggest that the offender has been effectively deterred by her or his previous punishment, she or he cannot be said to have been rehabilitated. In principle, reform efforts should be tailored to fit the individual offender's needs and therefore may occur in a variety of settings and may include treatment for drug and alcohol problems, education and job training, psychological or spiritual counseling, and participation in other programs designed to aid in the offender's rehabilitation.

4. *General deterrence.* Whereas disablement, specific deterrence, and reform all seek to prevent crime by modifying the behavior of *specific offenders* who have already violated the law, **general deterrence** seeks to prevent crime by deterring people "in general." The underlying principle of general deterrence is the same as that of specific deterrence; namely, people will choose law-abiding behavior where the negative consequences of crime outweigh any pleasure it might bring. The key difference between specific and general deterrence is that, in the latter, punishing criminals serves as an example *to others* of the negative consequences of lawbreaking.

Deontology and Criminal Punishment

From a deontological ethical perspective, a number of objections to utilitarian justifications for punishment can be raised. One such objection was noted above; namely, because utilitarianism justifies punishment by appealing to the beneficial end of preventing crime, it fails to justify punishment if *the means don't achieve the end*. If it can be shown that punishment fails to prevent crime (e.g., incapacitate, deter, and/or rehabilitate criminals), then by utilitarian standards we have no grounds on which to punish. In short, it could be argued that punishment *does not work* and we are therefore inflicting harm on persons without any corresponding "greater good." If punishment fails to achieve its utilitarian objectives, then it becomes an exercise in increasing the amount of suffering in the world without the increase in happiness that would be necessary to justify it.[53] As support for this claim, many have pointed to high rates of *recidivism* as evidence that deterrence and reform efforts are ineffective. For the utilitarian, however, this is merely a practical problem. It is not, for instance, that criminals cannot be rehabilitated, but that the system has been ineffective in doing the job of rehabilitating criminals.[54]

A second deontological objection to utilitarian grounds for punishment is one that Kant alluded to on a number of occasions. Recall that Kantian ethics holds *human dignity* to be of fundamental moral importance. With this in mind, Kant claimed that utilitarianism ignores human dignity. More specifically, justifications for punishment that appeal to beneficial consequences—incapacitation, deterrence, and rehabilitation—violate Kant's second variation of the categorical imperative ("treat others as an end and never as a means only"). When punishment practices are grounded in a concern for the incapacitation, deterrence, or reform of offenders, we are *using* offenders as a means to an end. While the objective of preventing crime may be worthy, using people—treating them as a means rather than an end—is fundamentally incompatible with the deontological commitment to and respect for human dignity.[55]

- *Incapacitation*. If we imprison an individual to secure the well-being of the community, we are *using* that offender to benefit others.
- *Deterrence*. Philosopher Georg Wilhelm Friedrich Hegel once wrote, "to base a justification of punishment on threat is to liken it to the act of a man who lifts his stick to a dog. It is to treat a man like a dog instead of with freedom and respect due to him as a man."[56]
- *Rehabilitation*. Reform or rehabilitation would have us treat others as "unfree, immature being[s], whose behavior may legitimately be reshaped by others in accordance with their notions of what is good, desirable, and socially acceptable."[57] Rehabilitation can thus be criticized as an attempt to mold people into what *we* think they should be. For Kant, this violates respect for *autonomy*—if we are to treat others as free, rational beings, then we must recognize that they are entitled to decide for themselves what sort of people they wish to be.

If incapacitation, deterrence, and reform are not moral grounds for punishing lawbreakers, how are we to justify punitive practices? Rather than justifying punishment by appealing to *future* consequences, deontology looks *backward*. The moral basis for punishment is not in future consequences, but is the offense which has been committed and for which justice must be done. Offenders should be punished because—and only because—they have committed a crime.[58] Further, where an offense has been committed, punishment of the offender *must* occur—irrespective of consequences. We punish the guilty because that is what is demanded of us by justice. If it so happens that good consequences result, then so much the better. Yet consequences, whether positive or negative, should have no bearing on our decision to dispense justice.

The principle of justice found in the practice of punishment is that of **desert**—giving people what they *deserve*. Punishment is "just" because it entails treating offenders the way they deserve to be treated in light of their offenses. The justification for punishment is thus **retribution**, or the principle that the state should "pay back" the offender for her or his offense.[59] Importantly, the notion of desert implies that punishments must be *proportionate* to the seriousness of the offense. **Proportionality**— the principle that the "punishment should fit the crime"—is crucial to deontological justifications for punishment. If an offender has been convicted of rape, for instance, he deserves to be punished for his crime. He does not, however, deserve to be punished with death. In this case, the severity of the punishment would unjustly outweigh the seriousness of the crime. On the other hand, while utilitarianism does not generally allow for the imposition of capital punishment, deontology can justify the punishment of death where—and only where—it is proportionate to the offense (e.g., murder).

Deontologists would argue that utilitarianism potentially violates both of these key principles (that punishment *must* be administered following a conviction, and that the punishment *must* be proportionate to the offense). In this respect, they argue, utilitarianism fails to account for justice and, in fact, would have us commit injustices if doing so would bring beneficial consequences. The focus of utilitarianism is on preventing crime, not ensuring that offenders get what they deserve. Consequently, there are several scenarios in which utilitarianism might allow for persons to receive something less, more, or other than what is deserved in relation to their actions.[60]

There is nothing, for instance, in utilitarianism that limits the amount of punishment that can be imposed. Utilitarianism could allow for *disproportionately harsh or disproportionately lenient penalties* if their imposition would achieve the desired end of crime prevention. A ten-year prison sentence for speeding may be effective in deterring crime, but would be arguably unjust in that the severity of the penalty would be undeserved in relation to the severity of the crime. Conversely, the experience of killing an innocent pedestrian while driving intoxicated and having to apologize to the victim's family may be enough to deter an offender from ever again driving drunk, yet without further punishment many would argue that the offender received less than was deserved and, thus, that justice had not been done (see Box 9.7).

As well, there is nothing in utilitarianism that prevents innocent persons from being punished, or guilty persons going unpunished. In all of those cases where punishing an offender would do more harm than good, utilitarianism commits us to refrain from punishment. On this note, Kant once asked, "What then are we to think of the proposal that the life of a condemned criminal should be spared if he agrees to let dangerous experiments be carried out on him in order that the doctors may gain new information of value . . . ?" Justice, Kant notes in response to this question, "ceases to be justice if it can be bought at a price."[61] Similarly, in those cases where punishing the innocent may bring about good overall consequences, utilitarianism may allow for it to be introduced. In both cases, although the punishment (or nonpunishment) has passed the test of utility, many would argue that justice has been compromised.

How is it that retribution, unlike incapacitation, deterrence, and reform, *respects human dignity*? Kant tells us that to treat others as ends involves treating them as rational beings, responsible beings. In punishing offenders, we are respecting their freedom and rationality, holding them responsible for what they have done, and treating them as they deserve to be treated. In other words, we are allowing *their conduct*—rather than the system's objectives—to determine how they will be treated.

In sum, the deontological justification of criminal punishment suggests that: (1) the state has a moral *right* to punish offenders on the basis of what they have done; (2) the state has a moral *duty* to punish offenders in the interest of justice; (3)that punishments must be proportionate to the offense committed; (4) that punishment serves to rectify or "even out" the harm of the offense; and (5) offenders have a moral right to be treated by respect and, therefore, punishment is a moral *right of the offender*.[62]

BOX 9.7
Mandatory Sentencing Laws: The Case of California

On June 30, 1992, Douglas David Walker and friend Joe Davis attempted to rob eighteen-year-old Kimber Reynolds of her purse in the Tower District of Fresno, California. Kimber resisted and, during the ensuing struggle, was shot and killed by Davis—who himself was later killed in a shootout with police. Subsequent investigation revealed both Walker and Davis to have long histories of criminal conduct. Davis had two prior felony convictions and Walker—who entered a plea agreement to avoid murder charges—had a criminal record dating to age thirteen.

On October 1, 1993, twelve-year-old Polly Klaas was kidnapped from her home just a few hours from Fresno in Petaluma, California. The perpetrator crept into the Klaas household and abducted Polly at knife-point as her family slept not far away. In late November, after a troubling investigation, police arrested Richard Allen Davis for the murder of Polly Klaas. Davis' criminal record revealed that he had twice been convicted and sentenced to prison for prior attempted kidnappings.

The tragedies of Kimber Reynolds and Polly Klaas generated public outcry and political pressure to "crack down" on habitual criminal offenders. In 1994, California voters passed Proposition 184—California's "Three-Strikes Law"—by an overwhelming 72 percent majority vote. Under California's new legislation, offenders who were convicted of three serious crimes would, following their third "strike," receive a lengthy mandatory prison sentence (often twenty-five years to life). California allows for a variety of offenses to count as strikes, and for *any* felony to count as the third strike. Many offenders incarcerated under California's law have been convicted of nonviolent and often nonserious offenses (though, in 2000, Californians amended the statute to allow for those convicted of

drug offenses to be mandated to treatment rather than life in prison).

Over the next decade, more than half of the states in the United States (as well as the federal government) would pass similar legislation. Proponents of Three-Strikes Law and other habitual felony statutes appeal to their purported *deterrent* effect for justification. The threat of severe punishment is, in theory, enough to convince those with felony records to refrain from committing any additional offenses. The morality of mandatory sentencing laws is thus justified on utilitarian grounds—harsh penalties pass the test of utility if they bring about good consequences (i.e., reduction in crime). To date, however, studies of the effects of mandatory minimum sentencing practices on crime rates have shown mixed and inconclusive results.

On the other hand, critics have argued that the severity of punishments handed out under mandatory sentencing laws are *disproportionate* to the severity of the offenses for which they are imposed. From a deontological perspective, sentences of up to life imprisonment for crimes as minor as shoplifting violate the imperative that the punishment must fit the crime (though, in 2003, the U.S. Supreme Court upheld as constitutional California's statute by a 5–4 margin).

Source: Peter W. Greenwood, *Three Strikes and You're Out: Estimated Benefits and Costs of California's New Mandatory Sentencing Law* (Santa Monica, CA: Rand Corporation, 1994); Paul G. Cassell, "Too Severe: A Defense of the Federal Sentencing Guidelines (and a Critique of Federal Mandatory Minimums)," *Stanford Law Review*, 56 (5), 1017–1032 (2004); Shamica Gaskins, "Women of Circumstance: The Effects of Mandatory Minimum Sentencing on Women Minimally Involved in Drug Crimes," *American Criminal Law Review*, 41, 1533–1554 (2003).

Summary

This chapter examined the deontological approach to the choices we should make and the actions we should undertake. Central to this approach are a focus on duties, rights, and obligations. As we have seen, deontological ethics binds us in ways that transcend laws, rules, codes, and procedures. Although this brand

of ethics is difficult to uphold in our daily lives, it attempts to establish universal principles of doing what is good for others, for ourselves, and for society more generally. Deontological ethics commits us to concerns for personhood, fairness, dignity, and worth for all people everywhere, regardless of timeframe or historical period. Whether in the context of personal responsibility or international accountability, these types of concerns are woven into the operation of criminal justice practices and are crucial to decision-making in criminal justice contexts. While the deontological approaches entertained in this chapter offer several strategies for advancing ethical conduct, there remains one further normative approach warranting consideration. Unlike consequentialist or deontological ethics that emphasize what it means to *do* good, *virtue ethics* stresses what it means to *be* good. This topic is the focus of review in the subsequent chapter.

Key Terms and Concepts

categorical imperative *166*
correlativity of rights and
   duties *176*
deontological (deontology) *164*
desert *184*
deterrence (specific and
   general) *182*
disablement (or incapacitation) *181*

duties *167*
hypothetical (or conditional)
   imperative *166*
legal rights *178*
maxim *166*
moral rights *178*
natural rights *177*

negative rights *177*
positive rights *178*
prima facie duties *173*
proportionality *184*
reform (or rehabilitation) *182*
retribution *184*
universal law *166*

Discussion Questions

1. Explain the difference between hypothetical and categorical imperatives. Provide three examples of each, taken from the field of criminal justice. How might this distinction be used to explore the practice of correctional facilities placing violent prisoners in solitary confinement?

2. A citizen is held up at gunpoint. A second person is a witness to this crime. The second person has a permit to carry a weapon and is in possession of this handgun. The second person reasonably believes that the attacker is likely to shoot and kill the citizen. Given these circumstances, the second person is trying to determine what course of action is ethically justified. Following the observations on prima facie duties, how would you reconcile this dilemma? Are there any conditional duties in operation here? Explain your response.

3. Explain the relationship between rights and duties. Identify three rights that help to understand a particular problem in crime and justice. Identify what corresponding duties attach to these rights and who is responsible for these corresponding duties.

4. Explain the concept of natural rights. Apply your definition to the following situation. A suspect is seen fleeing the scene of a crime. The suspect, brandishing a handgun, allegedly shot a police officer. A second police officer is in pursuit. The second officer firmly instructs the suspect to stop. The fleeing suspect does not adhere to the officer's command. The officer repeats the instruction a second time, but the suspect does not yield. The officer fires at the suspect, killing him instantly.

5. What is the difference between human rights, legal rights, and moral rights? Rely on a criminal justice ethical dilemma to substantiate your perspective.

Endnotes

1. James Rachels, *Elements of Moral Philosophy* (New York: McGraw-Hill, 2002).
2. Immanuel Kant, *Foundations of the Metaphysics of Morals* (Indianapolis, IN: Bobbs-Merrill, 1959), pp. 30–31.
3. Ibid., pp. 31–33; Rachels, *Elements of Moral Philosophy*, p. 105.
4. Rachels, *Elements of Moral Philosophy*, p. 105.
5. Ibid.
6. Ibid.

7. Ibid., p. 106.
8. Kant, *Foundations of the Metaphysics of Morals,* p. 39.
9. Rachels, *Elements of Moral Philosophy*, p. 106.
10. Kant, *Foundations of the Metaphysics of Morals,* p. 40.
11. Rachels, *Elements of Moral Philosophy*, p. 106.
12. Kant, *Foundations of the Metaphysics of Morals,* p. 41.
13. Ibid.
14. Rachels, *Elements of Moral Philosophy*, p. 107.
15. Ibid., p. 108.
16. Ibid.
17. Ibid., p. 109.
18. Quoted Ibid.
19. Ibid., p. 109 (authors' emphasis).
20. Ibid.
21. Ibid.
22. Kant, *Foundations of the Metaphysics of Morals,* p. 47.
23. Rachels, *Elements of Moral Philosophy*, p. 114.
24. Ibid., p. 116.
25. Ibid.
26. Ibid., pp. 115–116.
27. Ibid., pp. 116–117.
28. Ibid.
29. Ibid., pp. 110–111.
30. William David Ross, *The Right and the Good* (Oxford: Clarendon Press, 1993).
31. Ibid., p. 216.
32. Judith Boss, *Ethics for Life* (Mountain View, CA: Mayfield, 2001), p. 355.
33. John Finnis, *Natural Law and Natural Rights* (New York: Oxford University Press, 1980).
34. Lee Epstein, *Constitutional Law for a Changing America: Rights, Liberties, and Justice* (Washington, DC: CQ Press, 2004).
35. Ronald J. Allen, *Criminal Procedure: Investigation and Right to Counsel* (New York: Kluwer Law International, 2005), p. 33.
36. Ibid.
37. See, e.g., Barbara Rafel Price and Natalie J. Sokoloff (Eds.), *The Criminal Justice System and Women: Offenders, Prisoners, Victims, and Workers* (New York: McGraw-Hill, 2004).
38. Boss, *Ethics for Life*, pp. 372–374.
39. Ibid.
40. Ibid., p. 361.
41. Finnis, *Natural Law and Natural Rights.*
42. Ibid., p. 17.
43. See, e.g., Knudd Haakonssen, *Natural Law and Moral Philosophy: From Grotius to the Scottish Enlightenment* (New York: Cambridge University Press, 1997); Ellen Frankel Paul, Fred D. Miller, and Jeffrey Paul (Eds.), *Natural Law and Modern Moral Philosophy* (New York: Cambridge University Press, 2001).
44. Haakonssen, *Natural Law and Moral Philosophy.*
45. Finnis, *Natural Law and Natural Rights.*
46. Frankel, Miller, and Paul, *Natural Law and Modern Moral Philosophy,* p. 9.
47. Henry Steiner and Philip Alston, *International Human Rights in Context: Law, Politics, and Morals* (New York: Oxford University Press, 2001).
48. Boss, *Ethics for Life,* p. 359.
49. Igor Primoratz, *Justifying Legal Punishment* (Atlantic Highlands, NJ: Humanities Press, 1989).
50. Ibid.
51. Jonathan Glover, *Causing Deaths and Taking Lives* (New York: Penguin Books, 1977); see, generally, Gertrude Ezorsky (Ed.), *Philosophical Perspectives on Punishment* (Albany, NY: SUNY Press, 1972), pp. 249–280.
52. See Primoratz, *Justifying Legal Punishment*, pp. 18–22.
53. Ibid; see also, Ted Honderich, *Punishment: The Supposed Justifications* (New York: Penguin, 1984).
54. Ibid., pp. 33–35.
55. Ibid.
56. Quoted in Primoratz, *Justifying Legal Punishment*, p. 35.
57. Ibid.
58. Immanuel Kant, "The Right of Punishing." In Gertrude Ezorsky (Ed.), *Philosophical Perspectives on Punishment*, pp. 103–104.
59. Edmund Pincoffs, *The Rationale of Legal Punishment* (New York: Humanities Press, 1966), pp. 2–16.
60. See Primoratz, *Justifying Legal Punishment*, pp. 35–61.
61. Kant, "The Right of Punishing," p. 104.
62. Primoratz, *Justifying Legal Punishment,* p. 12.

10

The Virtuous and the Vicious: Considering Character

Psychologists, criminologists, and others who study criminal behavior have, for some time now, dedicated substantial attention to a certain subgroup of offenders: those often described in everyday language as the embodiment of *evil*. While we suggested in Chapter 2 that the majority of "evil" in the world results from well-intentioned people making poor choices as they go about their everyday activities, there remain inexplicable acts of harm and cruelty that can only be described as wicked acts of *bad people*. The label psychologists typically reserve for the worst of such people is that of the *psychopath*—those described by Robert Hare as "social predators . . . [c]ompletely lacking in conscience and in feelings for others, they selfishly take what they want and do as they please, violating social norms and expectations without the slightest sense of guilt or regret."[1]

Fortunately, psychopaths are rare, accounting for only about 1 percent of the population, and up to 25 percent of jail and prison inmates,[2] and news-making crimes commonly associated with psychopathic offenders, such as serial homicide and sadistic sexual assault, represent only a very small percentage of all criminal offenses. However, there is at least one important parallel between our moral evaluations of the heinous crimes of some psychopathic offenders and far more common instances of schoolyard bullying, callous property offending, or manipulative heartbreaking. In both kinds of cases, we tend not only to negatively assess the action, but also the *person* engaging in that action. We say not that the bully is a good person who made a poor choice or didn't fully consider the consequences of his actions; rather, we are more apt to assume that the bully is a certain *type of person*—one with enduring personality characteristics that lead to him to consistently demonstrate selfish behavior patterns, disregard for the welfare of others, and so forth. For most, there is an important relationship between evil deeds and evil persons. Our discussion of normative ethics, then, must account not only for actions and consequences, but also for *types of people*.

In the previous two chapters, we explored normative ethical theories that concentrate on the consequences of our actions and on our actions themselves. Consequentialist ethics asks that we consider the results of our actions, with those that produce the greatest benefit (i.e., good consequences)—for oneself and/or others—being the "right" ethical choice in a given situation or with regard to a particular issue. Deontological ethics, in turn, asks that we consider relevant duties and principles, making choices and engaging in actions that are consistent with those duties and principles. What each has in common is an emphasis on *doing*. The overriding question of both types of theories is, "What should I do?"

The importance of actions and consequences notwithstanding, what each of these types of theories fails to consider is the types of people we should *be*. When we shift moral focus from our actions and their consequences toward the notion of good moral *character*, we begin asking questions common to the third major tradition of normative ethics—that of *virtue ethics*.

Virtue ethics is the eldest of all ethical traditions, having its roots in the ancient Greek and Roman moral philosophies of Plato, Aristotle, the Stoics, and Epicureans, as well as a storied history in Eastern philosophical traditions such as Buddhism, Taoism, and Confucianism. Each of these philosophers and philosophical traditions shares an interest in examining what it means to lead a "good" life, with the "goodness" of our lives having much to do with the kinds of people that we are. In short, they are each concerned with our being *virtuous* people. The principal question asked and contemplated by the virtue tradition is, "What kind of person should I be?" Consequently, our goal or task as moral people is to develop into and continue to be that type of person; that is, to develop certain types of character traits (i.e., virtues), while seeking to "avoid or extinguish" others (i.e., vices).[3] In this third and final chapter on normative ethics, we explore this eldest of all ethical traditions and the crucial questions it poses about what it means to *be* a moral person.

VIRTUE AND VICE

Think of the people that you most admire ethically—people that can and do commonly serve as ethical role models or after whom you pattern (or try to pattern) your own moral behavior. Now, consider if you will what all of those people have in common. Most likely, it is not that they were all skilled at considering the consequences of their actions. It is also probably not that they were steadfastly committed to certain ethical imperatives and always placed their duty to abide by certain moral laws above all else. While they may have demonstrated one or both of these qualities, it is more likely that what they all have in common is that they are all certain *types of people*. Perhaps the people that came to mind are historical figures such as Jesus, the Buddha, Mother Teresa, or Martin Luther King Jr.; perhaps they are parents, family, friends, or teachers. In any case, what the people we most admire as exemplars of moral goodness seem to share is usually not so much about what they *do*, but the types of people they *are*. They tend to be caring people, compassionate, forgiving, merciful, respectful, and considerate of the needs and interests of others. In short, when we think of ethical or moral people, we probably think of what moral philosophers would call *virtuous* people.

Virtue and Character

When we talk about the types of people that we or others are, we usually do so in terms of character traits. A **character trait** is "a tendency to behave in certain ways in certain circumstances."[4] Character traits can dispose us toward moral or immoral behaviors; they can encourage us to be honest, responsible, and considerate of the needs and interests of others, or incline us to be dishonest, deceptive, fraudulent, irresponsible, or indifferent to or harmful toward others. What is important about character traits is not only that they define us as people, but that they dispose us to act in certain ways when we encounter certain types of situations.

When taken together, character traits define a person's character. By **character**, we mean a collection—a "cluster, or perhaps system"—of character traits as they appear in a given person.[5] Thus, a person who possesses the individual traits of honesty, integrity, humility, and self-respect possesses an overall character that is constituted by these dispositions. Ultimately, as we will see, being a "good" or virtuous person requires more than simply possessing a few population mean. Therefore, it has important uses in certain statistical tests.

Having discussed all the above, you might be intimidated by the amount of work involved in obtaining different samples, calculating the values of each statistic, examining the sampling distribution, and figuring out an appropriate way to infer to the population parameter. Fortunately, mathematicians have done the work and are able to show that there are some general patterns of sampling distribution with regard to such sample statistics as the mean. The general patterns are not influenced by the particular content of the original variable based on which the sample statistic is obtained. The mathematicians have also worked out some general procedures of testing a hypothesis, which have greatly facilitated the work of social scientists.

In the following, we will use a basic univariate statistic, i.e., the mean, to exemplify the idea of statistical inference. According to the central-limit theorem in probability and statistical theory, the sampling distribution of the means of large samples ($N>30$) will approach a normal distribution as the number of samples obtained increases; and the mean of the sampling distribution will approach the mean of the population for any variable. This is very important and produces great convenience, since what we need is to thoroughly study the normal distribution (also called Z distribution when standardized). It is easy to calculate that there are 68.26% of all cases whose value on the normally distributed and standardized variable will fall within an interval centered at the mean with a width of 2SE. For a sampling distribution with a mean of M and standard error of SE, that means there are 68.26% of all possible samples that will have a mean between M-SE and M+SE. Similarly, 95.46% of all possible samples will have a mean between M-2SE and M+2SE, and 99.37% between M-3SE and M+3SE. Apparently, in statistical estimation and testing, if we allow an error range of M±2SE or M±3SE, we will have a great chance to make correct inferences from the sample to the population based on the normal distribution.

Statistical inference, including parameter estimation and hypothesis testing (in both univariate and relational senses), is based on this simple belief in probability. For the sampling distribution of the population mean (M) of any variable, it is known that 99% of all possible samples will have a mean between M-2.58SE and M+2.58SE, or only 1% of all possible samples will fall outside that interval, which can be looked up in a Z distribution table. If we use such an interval (called confidence interval) of a sample mean to make an estimation of the population mean, we will have a 99% confidence level and would ignore the 1% chance of making a mistake. In testing the hypothesis about the population mean

---

BOX 10.1

Virtue and Leadership

As Judith Boss points out, people tend to emulate those who are at a higher stage of moral development. Because of this tendency, placing virtuous persons in *leadership roles* can have a positive moral impact on an entire organization, community, or society. Think of persons you know who are in leadership roles—presidents, legislators, judges, police chiefs—and discuss whether those people serve as good moral role models by exhibiting virtue. What virtues *should*

persons in such positions embody? What, if any, *vices* should they embody? What are the dangers of embodying different virtues and vices for each of the following positions?

- The President of the United States
- Legislators in your state
- Judges and Supreme Court Justices
- Chiefs of Police

---

individual character traits; rather, it is about possessing a collection of traits that work together to generate a moral character that is typified by its collective "goodness" (see Box 10.1).

While it is common in everyday language to refer to "character traits," moral philosophers have historically used the more specific terms *virtue* and *vice* to refer to traits of character that are regarded as "good" or "bad" in moral contexts. Good character traits such as honesty and integrity are considered *moral virtues,* while traits such as selfishness and arrogance are regarded as *moral vices.* Most generally, then, **moral virtues** are traits of character that dispose a person to act in a moral fashion, while **moral vices** are traits of character that dispose a person to act in an indifferent or harmful fashion. In the remainder of our discussion of moral character, we will typically use the terms "moral virtues" and "moral vices" rather than the more generic term "character traits." Here are but a few character traits that are widely regarded as virtues:[6]

Benevolence	Compassion	Courage
Faithfulness	Generosity	Gratitude
Honesty	Humility	Integrity
Justice	Kindness	Loyalty
Mercifulness	Modesty	Nonharm
Open-mindedness	Patience	Politeness
Prudence	Reliability	Responsibility
Self-control	Self-respect	Sincerity
Tactfulness	Tolerance	Trustworthiness
Unselfishness	Wisdom	

VIRTUE, CHARACTER, AND BEHAVIOR

Moral virtues are thus dispositions to act, out of habit, in ways that benefit self and others.[7] Compassion, generosity, and tolerance, for instance, are most always cited as examples of virtue—as character traits that, when motivating action, stand to benefit all those affected by the action. Persons of virtuous character are those who are disposed to act in ways compassionate, generous, and tolerant in situations that demand such actions. Importantly, to say that we act *out of habit* or in light of virtue is different from saying that we act on principle or in consideration of consequences. Instead, dispositions and habits are part of who we are as people. As we will see, however, this does not mean that we somehow either have these virtues

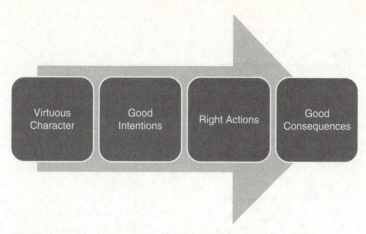

FIGURE 10.1   Correlativity of Character, Action, and Consequences

or do not (e.g., as a function of personality); rather, virtue is something that, through regular *practice*, one *comes to* and continues to embody.

The exercise of virtue, then, does not follow from rational reflection or a desire to conform to duty; rather, it simply emanates from the person herself or himself. In other words, persons who demonstrate prudence through their choices and actions tend to *be* prudent people. This does not, however, mean that we should regard virtue as independent of actions and consequences. Rather, it is important to realize that there is a strong *correlation between character and behavior*. Though admittedly oversimplified, on the whole we can think of the relationship as depicted in Figure 10.1

In other words, virtuous character gives rise to good intentions which lead to right actions which produce good consequences. Part of the reason that right actions and good consequences are less significant in the virtue tradition than character is that the former tend to follow automatically from the latter. In other words, if we are virtuous people, we will almost invariably engage in right actions and right actions, in turn, often lead to good consequences. It would be difficult, for instance, for the kind person *not* to act kindly; it would be difficult for she or he who is compassionate to act other than compassionately. Virtue ethics recognizes that if we focus on character, ethically sound choices and behaviors will often follow (see Box 10.2).

Virtue and Negative Emotions

Virtues are not only tendencies to act in certain ways in certain situations, they are also tendencies to *think, feel, believe,* and *desire* in certain ways.[8] Humility, for instance, has much to do with how we think about ourselves, our accomplishments and importance, while tolerance has much to do with how we think and feel about others. Having moral character is not simply a matter of being disposed to have good intentions and engage in right actions, but also concerns the psychological states that give rise to intentions and that inform our choices and behaviors.

Especially problematic within the virtue tradition are incentives for human action that stem from "negative emotions"—often referred to as *vices*. Whereas virtues are dispositions to act in ways that benefit self and others, *vices* are traits of character or dispositions to act in ways that are *indifferent toward* or that *harm* oneself and/or others. In other words, vices are those characteristics that interfere with our capacity to be moral and that dispose us toward

BOX 10.2
Actions and Intentions

Consider the following two scenarios:

> Ralph is independently wealthy. Several years ago, he sold a company that he owned for a hefty $400 million. As part of that deal, he continues to receive an annual "payment" of $4 million per year. Yesterday, Ralph donated $1 million to Cure for Cancer—a charitable organization. His donation, of course, is tax deductible. In addition, Cure for Cancer has decided to use the money to open the "Ralph Research Center."

> Louisa is a seventy-two-year-old widow who is currently unemployed and lost her entire retirement savings in an investment scandal. She has no savings, no checking account, no investments, and about $20 in her purse to last her until next week. While walking downtown yesterday, she came upon a homeless person who seemed tired, hungry, and suffering a good deal. After talking with him for several minutes, Louisa took her last $20 to the grocer on the corner and bought the homeless person food and a warm jacket.

Looking at the stories of both Ralph and Louisa, who would you consider to be the most virtuous?

Why? The difference between the two is not the *action*, nor is it the *consequences* of those actions. Ralph's donation might be regarded as a right action with overall good consequences—particularly for himself. Louisa also performed what would likely be considered a moral action. The consequences of her charity, however, will not have the large-scale impact that Ralph's did.

This, however, is where virtue ethics differs somewhat from Kant's ethics and from utilitarian ethics in particular. Virtuous persons act on the basis of an "underlying disposition of concern for the well-being of others and themselves." Louisa's actions, it would appear at least, were motivated by just such a concern—she acted, in short, out of compassion. One might have difficulty, however, saying the same of Ralph's actions. More likely, Ralph donated to the Cure for Cancer Foundation not out of compassion for persons with cancer, but largely from self-interest. While Ralph's actions have far-reaching consequences, most of us would likely consider Louisa to be the more virtuous (and, therefore, *moral*) of the two. If we were interested only in consequences, we would be logically forced to regard Ralph's actions as of higher moral quality. This is a function of something to which utilitarian moral philosophers do not attend; namely, the role of *intention*.

Source: Jupith Boss, *Ethics for Life* (Mountain View: CA. Mayfield, 2001). Quote is from p. 405.

indifference or harm rather than morally desirable behavior. Below is a list of *some* character traits that are widely regarded as vices or "ways-of-being" that are in some ways harmful to oneself and/or others:[9]

Arrogance	Callousness	Cowardice
Cruelty	Dishonesty	Disloyalty
Envy	Faithlessness	Greed
Ignorance	Impatience	Imprudence
Ingratitude	Insincerity	Intolerance
Irascibility	Irresponsibility	Jealousy
Laziness	Manipulativeness	Mercilessness
Prejudice	Promiscuity	Rudeness
Selfishness	Servility	Shamelessness
Tactlessness	Unreliability	Untrustworthiness

BOX 10.3
Crime, Anger, and Forgiveness

In a recent essay on the role of virtue in criminal justice, Williams argues that the vice of *resentment* has come to define the American public's attitude toward criminal offenders and, consequently, has come to play an important role in many criminal justice practices (e.g., determinate sentencing, capital punishment). Problematically, he argues, the embodiment and expression of resentment and related desires for vengeance, retribution, and punishment more often lead only to further harm. Virtues such as forgiveness and mercy are crucial in helping us to overcome the negative emotions of resentment and the passion for revenge and punishment.

The emotional experience of anger, Williams suggests following Aristotle, is not one and the same with the belief that the offender should endure harm as a consequence of her or his offense. The experience of anger is justified; in fact, ignoring, overlooking, or forgetting about harms caused would be equally *vicious* (a deficiency indicative of an absence of proper anger). Yet the desire to *express* anger through harming the offending party is a *learned* response to those initial feelings. Alternatively, the virtue of forgiveness asks not that we cease to feel anger, but that we overcome the desire to cause further harm that often issues from our emotional experience of anger. In this case, forgiveness "checks" anger, encouraging us to feel it with proper intensity and for the right length of time. Excessive anger can easily lead to hatred and the desire to respond excessively to an offense, causing more harm that what is called for.

Do you feel that the American criminal justice system is built upon resentment or the desire for vengeance and retribution? What practices demonstrate this? What practices are at odds with this claim? What role do you feel forgiveness plays in our current system of criminal justice? What role can or should forgiveness play?

Source: Christopher Williams, "Toward a Transvaluation of Criminal 'Justice': On Vengeance, Peacemaking, and Punishment," *Humanity and Society*, 26 (2), 100–116 (2002); reprinted in Joseph L. Victor (Ed.), *Annual Editions: Criminal Justice 05/06* (Dubuque, IA: McGraw-Hill).

Part of the importance or value of virtue is that it enables us to *overcome* these sorts of negative emotions, desires, and tendencies. Contemporary virtue ethicist Philippa Foot suggested that virtues are *corrective*—they "correct" our tendencies toward indifference or harm.[10] The virtues of compassion and forgiveness, for instance, help us to overcome tendencies toward anger, hatred, and the desire for revenge; open-mindedness can help us overcome tendencies toward prejudice; and humility and modesty can help us overcome arrogance and excessive pride. Virtues not only have the positive function of disposing us to do good, but have the negative function of aiding us in overcoming tendencies to think, feel, and act in ways that are immoral or otherwise demonstrate a lack of moral goodness (see Box 10.3).

VIRTUE AND THE GOOD LIFE

Ancient Greek philosopher Aristotle (384–322 B.C.E.) is perhaps the most widely recognized and widely discussed of virtue ethicists. Some would argue, in fact, that his *Nichomachean Ethics* (titled in reference to his son, Nichomachus) is the most important book ever written on ethics and morality. In any case, it is a text of crucial significance in philosophy, ethics, and virtue ethics more specifically. While some of Aristotle's conclusions have since been the subject of controversy, his general theses about morality, virtue, and the "good life" are mainstays in discussions of ethics. In what follows, we outline several ideas that play a central role in the *Nichomachean Ethics* and that are vital to our discussion of virtue and its importance.[11]

The Purpose of Human Life

Aristotle begins the *Nichomachean Ethics* by offering a simple but significant point—every action and every pursuit aim at some end or good.[12] In other words, all actions are done for a reason or purpose. Why do we wake up in the morning? Eat breakfast? Brush our teeth? Go to school or work? To each of these questions we could no doubt offer one or more reasons (e.g., because we want to be healthy, because we want to make money or earn college credit). For Aristotle, however, each of these reasons has a further aim or purpose—we want to earn college credit so that we can get a job, we want a job so that we can earn money, we want to earn money so that we can . . . and so on. Ultimately, Aristotle tells us, all of these aims are motivated by one overriding aim or purpose. What is this ultimate aim or "highest good" toward which all of our actions in some way lead?

ARISTOTLE'S TELEOLOGY In asking what we *aim at* in life, Aristotle was ultimately concerned with what makes a life worthwhile or "good." Answering this question, however, requires some understanding of the ultimate *purpose* of human life. It is only once we know the purpose of human life that we can begin to talk about what a "good" human life would be. This notion of "purpose" is fundamental to Aristotle's ethics and his philosophy more generally. Aristotle has a **teleological** (*end, purpose, goal*) view of the world, meaning that he understands behavior to be goal-directed or aimed at achieving some purpose or end. Everything in the world—from inanimate objects such as knives, to plants and animals, to human beings has some "inborn" purpose. Knives cut, flowers blossom, caterpillars turn into butterflies, and so forth. If we know that the purpose of knives is to cut, then we can deduce that a "good" knife is one that cuts well; if we know that the purpose of a flower is to blossom, we might say that a flower which has blossomed has in some sense lived a good, meaningful life in that it has fulfilled its purpose.

INTRINSIC GOODNESS Aristotle applies this same logic to human purpose and existence. What is the highest human good or ultimate purpose of human existence? Before looking more closely at this idea of "purpose" as it relates to human life, we need to revisit an idea we were exposed to in Chapter 2 and again in Chapter 8. In our discussion of values, we briefly discussed the distinction between *intrinsic* and *instrumental* goods and values—the former being those things that are good in themselves, and the latter being those things that are good only because they allow us to get some higher or more important good. Money, status, and power, for instance, are instrumental goods in that they are valuable only to the extent that they allow us to achieve or maintain other things that are more intrinsically valuable or desirable. Other things such as health and knowledge are regarded by many to have intrinsic value. Even if health and knowledge may help us to achieve or maintain other goods (in fact, they may even be necessary to achieve or maintain certain other goods), they are valuable in and of themselves. The purpose of health, for instance, is simply to be healthy. The value or "goodness" of health and knowledge do not disappear even if they are not used for anything in particular.

THE HIGHEST GOOD You may recall that we mentioned in this same context that, for many of the ancient Greeks, the *only* thing that was intrinsically good was *happiness*. Happiness was the "highest good" and, ultimately, all other goods, values, and human pursuits could be reduced to means or efforts to attain or maintain a "happy" existence. Indeed, Aristotle makes precisely this claim in the *Nichomachean Ethics*. His answer to the question of what we aim at in life is that we aim at *happiness*. This, for Aristotle, is the "highest good"—the good toward which all other goods lead. Leading a "happy" existence, in fact, is the very purpose of human life—it is what we aim for in life, what we naturally strive to achieve, and what all of our other pursuits are ultimately about. If we think about why we do anything at all, our answers will eventually lead us to realize that everything we do is done to further our pursuit of happiness. Consider the following example:

Why do I wake up in the morning?
I wake up in order to go to school.

Why do I go to school?
I go to school in order to get a degree.

Why do I want a degree?
I want a degree in order to get a job.

Why do I want a job?
I want a job in order to make money.

Why do I want money?
I want money in order to buy a house, food, etc.

Why do I want these things?
I want these things so that I can have shelter, nourishment, etc.

Why do I want these things?
Ultimately, I want these things because they allow me to pursue a "happy" existence.

Although your answers to the above questions may vary, Aristotle would argue that eventually we are led to conclude that everything we do is ultimately done as a means for achieving the highest human good—*a happy existence*. All other goods are good only in that they allow us to pursue or maintain happiness, and all other values are valuable only in this same sense. Yet what exactly is "happiness"? How are we to achieve it? We will return to these concerns shortly. Before we judge Aristotle on this claim, however, we should understand that what Aristotle means by "happiness" and "happy existence" is a bit different from how we might use these terms in everyday conversation.

The Fulfilled Life

"Happiness" has a particular meaning for Aristotle (and the ancient Greeks more generally), and one that is central to understanding his ethics. The term Aristotle uses to describe the "good life" is *eudaimonia*—a Greek term that is often translated as "happiness" or "well-being" but, for Aristotle, means something closer to "*flourishing*." To be "happy" or to "flourish" is to live a *fulfilled life*. When flowers blossom and caterpillars become butterflies, they are flourishing in that they are fulfilling their ultimate purposes. In an important way, they are living "good" or "happy" lives. To know the "good life," we must know in what the fulfilled life would consist; and to know the fulfilled life, we need to know something about the function or ultimate purpose of that life.

BEING EXCELLENT   So far, we know that the highest good for human beings is happiness, that happiness consists in flourishing, that flourishing has to do with living a fulfilled life, and that fulfillment has something to do with our ultimate purpose as human beings. What is a realized or fulfilled life for human beings? To answer this, we need to consider Aristotle's conception of human *function*. Before doing so, however, we need to consider one more concept that appears prominently in Aristotle's ethics—that of "*excellence.*"

For Aristotle, "function" is closely linked with the notion of "excellence" or "virtue." The "good" or "fulfilled" life requires the embodiment and exercise of excellence (or virtue) in relation to function (i.e., performing one's function with excellence). Thus, a knife is good to the degree that it excels at the function of cutting, while a medicine is good to the degree that it excels at its intended function of healing or alleviating symptoms of illness. By knowing the function of something, we can know what it means to be an "excellent" or virtuous thing of that sort. Generally, to exercise excellence or virtue is to do something "in such a way that one's skill, or virtue, is expressed in the way it is done."[13] The degree to which someone or something acts or performs its function with excellence or virtue, in turn, is the degree to which we can attribute "goodness" and "fulfillment" to that person or thing.

The excellences or virtues that are of primary concern for Aristotle are those that belong to one's *moral character.* Courage, for instance, might be regarded as a moral excellence, and the exercise of moral excellence or virtue would entail doing something in such a way that one's courageousness is expressed in how it is done. Again, moral excellences or virtues are traits that would allow for human beings to flourish in pursuing their ultimate function or purpose as human beings. To talk about moral virtues, then, we need to ask questions about the function of human beings, the purpose of human existence, and the qualities and characteristics that allow for human beings to fulfill those functions and flourish with respect to those purposes.

HUMAN FUNCTION AND PURPOSE   Aristotle would thus suggest that when we talk about the virtue, excellence, or goodness of a thing, we should understand it in relation to the function of that thing (i.e., what the thing is *for*). "Excellences" or virtues are traits that enable things to flourish in performing their intended functions or in fulfilling their purposes (e.g., a knife is *for* cutting and the sharpness of a knife is an excellence or virtue that assists in the performance of that function). If we know that the function of ears is to hear and the function of teachers is to impart knowledge, then we can deduce whether someone's ears are excellent and whether a given teacher is excellent. Both ears and teachers are excellent or virtuous to the extent that they fulfill their function. Logically, if we can know the function of human beings, we can know what it means to be an excellent or virtuous human being. What does Aristotle suggest is the function of human beings?

If we are looking for an answer that is provocative, controversial, or entertaining, we are not going to find it in Aristotle. However unsatisfying it may be to some, Aristotle's answer to this question is nevertheless an important one. Specifically, he claims that the function and purpose of human being, and thus the characteristic feature of human excellence, is *rational activity.* Our capacity to reason is what distinguishes us from all other living (and nonliving) things. Unlike pleasure and procreation (other common answers to the question of human purpose), higher-level reasoning is a characteristic that human beings do not share with other animals. Thus, the good or excellent human life must have something to do with making use of this distinctive capacity. Being excellent or virtuous is thus about utilizing and expressing our rational potential in our choices and actions.

For Aristotle, then, virtue is a kind of *practical use of reason,* whereby we utilize our specifically human capacity for reason and rational reflection to determine what choices to make and what actions to undertake. We will see shortly that the exercise of virtue is not as simple as being a certain way in a certain situation. For Aristotle, there are no easy answers to what types of choices or actions are virtuous in a given context. Instead, we have to "figure it out"—we must use *judgment.* In so doing, we are employing **practical wisdom** or *moral rationality.* When we lead our lives in such a way that we exercise practical wisdom or moral rationality, we are acting with virtue and we are living a fulfilled or "happy" human life.

THE ACTIVITY OF VIRTUE   In other words, for Aristotle, the fulfilled life is a life in which our specifically human capacity for rational activity is put to good use. We are well, happy, and flourish when we exercise virtue. Importantly, happiness and flourishing are *ways of doing things.* They are *activities.* Excellence or virtue, well-being and happiness are not about possessing something or attaining a certain condition or state of affairs; rather, they are about living our lives a certain way. A flourishing life is a life of *virtuous activity.* More specifically, flourishing involves the exercise of reason or practical wisdom as we make the choices that we do and engage in the actions we undertake while experiencing our lives. Before we turn to a closer examination of virtue and practical wisdom, let us conclude here with several summary points about Aristotle's conception of the "good life."

- The good life involves the possession of *good character*
- More specifically, the good life further involves living in such a way that one *expresses one's good character in one's choices and actions*
- Expressing virtue (moral character) in our choices and actions is the *foundation of well-being, happiness, and flourishing* (i.e., *eudaimonia*)
- Well-being, happiness, or flourishing is ultimately *what we aim at in life* (i.e., the highest good)
- In living a life according to virtue, we are flourishing and, in so doing, we are *fulfilling our very function or purpose as human beings*

VIRTUE AND HUMAN FLOURISHING

We have seen that, for Aristotle, everything in the world has some "inborn" purpose. Just as flowers blossom and caterpillars turn into butterflies, all things strive to fulfill their purpose—including human beings. Once we have identified these purposes, we can then talk about *what traits enable them to flourish* in fulfilling that purpose. Once we recognize that the purpose of a knife is to cut, for instance, we can ascertain that the trait of "sharpness" is that which allows it to excel at that purpose. In the context of human life, once we understand human purpose and what we aim for in life (i.e., the highest good), we can begin to talk about what *traits of character* and what types of behaviors are necessary for helping us live purposively. Virtues become moral excellences that enable humans to function well, and vices become precisely the opposite. In other words, we can redefine *virtue* and *vice,* respectively, as traits of character that promote human flourishing, and those that hinder it.

Consider, for instance, how embodying the virtue of courage might assist a person in living a good life (earning respect from peers, doing well in academic and athletic pursuits, interviewing for and getting a job); alternatively, consider how lacking the virtue of courage might inhibit a person in these same pursuits. Some traits of character clearly aid us in living a good life, while others such as envy and jealousy clearly interfere with this purpose.

Human Flourishing

Aristotle was interested in offering a generalized portrait of human well-being, happiness, and flourishing that applies to *all* people *everywhere*. In other words, Aristotle believed that, despite individual differences, all human beings are similar in certain respects. It is not differences between people that tell us something about human happiness and flourishing; rather, it is the similarities that we share as human beings that can help us to understand what it means to be well, flourish, and be happy. Though we depart somewhat from Aristotle's conception of human flourishing here, we might consider more recent philosophical and psychological insights into human well-being. Our interest in this section is in outlining what we can call "universal conditions of well-being, happiness, and flourishing"—those elements of being well, happy, and flourishing that are characteristic of and sought after by all people and, consequently, represent a foundation for thinking about virtues and vices, good and evil in relation to human life.

BIOGENIC NEEDS   At a most fundamental level, all human beings have basic biological needs that must be met as a *precondition* for the possibility of further well-being, happiness, and flourishing. How, for instance, can we expect the homeless person who struggles for food and warmth to spend time developing traits of character that will enable him to flourish? What we might call **biogenic needs** are those linked with the maintenance of life.[14] These include such universally necessary and desired goods as food, housing, clothing, clean air, adequate medical care, and exercise and physical recreation. To this we might also add goods such as safety and security that are necessary for biological survival (animals will go days without even food and water if they feel their physical safety is at risk). Each of these goods must necessarily be met *before* one can pursue higher goods. It will do little good, for instance, to encourage the homeless, starving, and physically ill person to pursue a life of compassion, justice, and generosity.

COOPERATION   Fulfillment of biogenic needs is, however, not sufficient for well-being, happiness, and flourishing. As psychologist Erich Fromm (1900–1980) reminds us, "man does not live by bread alone."[15] Indeed, simply having one's basic biological needs fulfilled does not make for the "good life" in the sense in which Aristotle discussed it. In large part, this is because human beings also share another universal feature—in addition to being biological entities, we are also *social beings*. Our nature as human beings demands that we live in communities, cooperating with and depending upon one another—not merely for survival, but also to be well, happy, and flourish.

Aristotle recognized that human beings, like many other species of beings, are **social animals.** In other words, we are not best suited for solitary lives independent of other human beings. We live in *groups* because we must live in groups to survive and to have better opportunities for being well and flourishing. As *interdependent* creatures, our needs and desires are best met or satisfied by *cooperating* with others. If John is a good farmer yet knows nothing about managing finances or building houses, Liz has exceptional money-management skills yet knows little about farming and building houses, and Jane is adept at building houses but not so good with farming or money, then each stands to benefit from the others. Liz's financial talents do little for her flourishing if she has no house in which to live and no food to eat. The same logic applies to John and Jane. Although this is obviously an oversimplified example, it demonstrates Aristotle's point that human beings must live in groups if we are, collectively, to survive and flourish.

CONNECTEDNESS   Because we are social animals, destined to live interdependently and cooperatively in groups, we have other types of social needs that emerge from these living circumstances. We seem, for instance, to have needs for affection, love, friendship, and family, as well as those for belonging and to be "connected" in meaningful ways with other people. We thus depend on other people not only for survival and for purposes of meeting basic biological needs, but also to meet social and psychological needs.

The necessity that human beings live in groups to flourish creates consequent needs. While French existentialist philosopher Jean-Paul Sartre once suggested that "hell is—other people!"[16] there is a sense in which life without other people would be equally hellish. Imagine, for instance, having to live the rest of your life on a deserted island or in solitary confinement in a prison.[17] Even if your basic needs were met, chances are you would not consider it a life of well-being, happiness, and flourishing. Humanistic philosopher Carliss Lamont once suggested that " . . . people experience their deepest and most enduring joys, not as solitary hermits on some mountain top or desert isle, but in association with their peers, their friends, or their family."[18]

The Value of Virtue

Healthy, cooperative, and caring relationships with other people thus become necessary elements of the "good life." Much as life as social animals provides us with opportunities to flourish that we would not otherwise enjoy, it also creates difficulties that we would not experience in solitary circumstances. In short, group life means that we must be able to "get along" with one another. We must cooperate with one another, respect one another, care for one another, and be considerate of one another's interests; we must reach compromises with others, be willing to sacrifice our own wants and desires for the sake of the needs of others; we must be able to resolve conflicts—ideally in constructive, nonviolent ways—when they arise; on the whole, we should be able to be well, happy, and flourish ourselves while contributing to the well-being, happiness, and flourishing of others. This, we might suggest, is precisely where the value of virtue is to be found.

Imagine, for instance, the difficulties that might arise in a family, organization, community, or society in which members are disposed toward selfishness, prejudice, envy, and intolerance. Not only will such persons be unhappy themselves, as Aristotle suggested, but their dispositions will give rise to a host of interpersonal conflicts and problems. In such a situation, we would no doubt find a family, organization, community, or society in which the possibility of well-being, happiness, and flourishing for *all* people would be substantially diminished—in fact, nearly impossible. Part of the value of the virtues is that they can assist us in overcoming these vices, thus allowing for meaningful, productive human relationships that benefit the well-being of all involved. Dispositions toward compassion, care, and concern for others, for instance, not only give rise to positive relationships (thus augmenting our own pursuit of happiness), but also create a foundation for group life wherein all people have a better opportunity to realize their own potential and thus flourish as human beings.

Virtues, then, are not valuable in that they can get us money, status, power, or other instrumental goods; rather, virtues are good in that they allow us to pursue the ultimate or highest "good" of human existence—happiness or flourishing. The embodying and practice of virtue (and the avoidance or elimination of vice) will, in turn, provide the greatest opportunity to live a life of wellness, flourishing, and happiness and, simultaneously, provide the same sorts of opportunities for others. Thus virtues can be understood as all of those traits that in some way contribute to human well-being and flourishing, while vices are those traits that interfere with human well-being and flourishing or make them less likely.[19] With this in mind, let us look more specifically at the types of character traits that are typically regarded as virtues.

M, on the other hand, we can reject the hypothesis if the mean of the actual sample falls outside the interval of M-2.58SE and M+2.58SE (these two values are called critical values, and the outside area the critical region). We know that the chance of being wrong, which is called significance level for a critical value, is no more than 1% or 0.01. Social research rarely tolerates more than 5% risk of error, or uses a confidence interval smaller than M±1.96SE. The belief or the rule of making such judgments essentially says "small probabilities are impossible." The kind of risk involved is called Type I error, which occurs when a rejected hypothesis is actually true. Since the rejected hypothesis (null hypothesis) is usually the antithesis of the real research hypothesis, this also means the kind of error of claiming a research hypothesis as being possibly true when it is actually false.

There is another kind of error called Type II error, which refers to the failure of rejecting a false null hypothesis or accepting a true research hypothesis. The lower the risk of Type I error, the higher the risk of Type II error. The probability of Type I error is simply and arbitrarily chosen by the researcher, and therefore its value is always known. The calculation of the risk for Type II error, on the other hand, is a complex matter, and in many occasions and to many investigators (especially novice researchers) it is actually unknown. Generally speaking, our ability to infer from the sample statistics to the population parameters depends on the representativeness of the sample, which entails the use of random sampling procedures. There is no general measure of the representativeness of a sample, however. The question can only be answered with reference to some specific variables that are most important to a study. For different distributions of the key variables in a research population, the representativeness of a random sample with a given size may vary considerably. A quantity called statistical power can be calculated on each key variable, which gives some indication of the representativeness of a random sample in that particular aspect. Statistical power is related to Type II error by the following equation: Statistical power = 1 - Type II error. Statistical power is an important concept. It shows the probability for a non-zero random sample statistic to successfully pass a statistical test and qualify for representing a parameter of the research population. For a variable with a given degree of dispersion or variation (variance), the statistical power for testing the random sample statistic on that variable depends on the size of the sample. Conversely, statistical power can be used to determine and calculate the desired sample size in research design. We have mentioned earlier that (under a given variance) the sample size can also be determined solely by confidence or

VIRTUE, WISDOM, AND THE "GOLDEN MEAN"

Of moral virtue, Aristotle suggested that it, "is concerned with feelings and actions, and these involve excess, deficiency, and a mean."[20] One of Aristotle's most widely discussed ideas on virtue is this notion of the **golden mean** (sometimes called the "doctrine of the mean"). Aristotle suggested that all virtues are *means between two extremes of deficiency and excess*. More specifically, he suggests of virtue that it is, "a mean between two kinds of vice, one of excess and the other of deficiency."[21] In any given situation and with regard to any given feeling or action, it is possible to have too much or too little of something. In both instances, what amounts is vice. In addition, we can find virtue by identifying these vices of deficiency and excess and finding the "middle road" between the two. It is possible, for instance, to feel too much anger, pity, or pleasure. It is equally possible to feel too little of these things. Virtue requires that we have such feelings, "at the right times on the right grounds towards the right people for the right motive and in the right way."[22] This "middle way" of feeling, he tells us, "is the mark of virtue."

For every type of feeling, Aristotle is suggesting, there is some form of it that would be considered excessive and some form of it that would be regarded as deficient. The same applies for every type of action:

- "For both excessive and insufficient exercise destroy one's strength, and both eating and drinking too much or too little destroy health, whereas the right quantity produces, increases and preserves it."[23]
- In cases where we face danger, being "cowardly" would constitute a moral deficiency, whereas being "foolhardy" would constitute a moral excess. The mean lying between the vicious extremes of cowardliness and foolhardiness is the virtue of *courage*.
- With regard to how we should feel about ourselves and our own accomplishments, we might recognize as vices the excessive trait of arrogance (thinking *too much* of oneself) and the deficient trait of servility (thinking *too little* of oneself). Somewhere between these vices of deficiency and excess lies a middle ground that entails "self-respect" and "self-esteem," or what Aristotle called "proper pride." Self-respect and self-esteem can benefit one's well-being, happiness, and flourishing, while traits such as servility and arrogance will have a detrimental impact on this pursuit.

The Golden Mean and Practical Wisdom

Recall that Aristotle suggested that virtue had to do with practical wisdom. This link with human reason and rationality is most evident in his conception of virtue as a mean. Supposing we know that courage is a virtue, what exactly is a courageous act? Aristotle in no way meant for his doctrine of the mean to serve as a "science" of ethical decision-making and behavior. In fact, he tells us that virtue and morality are in no way exact. Instead, they are *situational*—what may be courageous for one person may be cowardly for another, and what may be courageous in one situation may be cowardly in another.[24] The exercise of virtue demands that we exercise practical wisdom in any given situation.[25]

In other words, virtue requires *experimentation*. It requires that we *engage in life*. Persons of practical wisdom "have developed skills to make the right decision at the right moment and to act efficiently on those decisions."[26] A courageous act is one that a person of practical wisdom deems to be courageous at a given moment in a given situation. As there is no "quick and easy" definition of virtue and virtuous behavior that can apply to all persons in all situations, the exercise of virtue requires that we practice, learn from our experiences, and make an effort to continually develop our moral character. While some traits are inborn, the moral virtues must be developed.

They are *habits* of character, and habits are developed through *practice*. We learn the virtues by exercising them regularly. In Aristotle's terms:

> Anything that we have to learn to do we learn by the actual doing of it. People become builders by building and instrumentalists by playing instruments. Similarly we become just by performing just acts, temperate by performing temperate ones, brave by performing brave ones.[27]

Aristotle's Virtues

Aristotle named only a handful of virtues, including the "intellectual" virtues of wisdom and prudence, and the "moral" virtues of courage, temperance, liberality (i.e., generosity), magnificence, proper pride, gentleness, truthfulness, justice, patience, friendliness, modesty, and wittiness. In relation to these named virtues, his "golden mean" looks something like this:

Deficiency (Vice)	Mean (Virtue)	Excess (Vice)
Cowardice	*Courage*	Foolhardiness
Inhibition	*Temperance*	Overindulgence/intemperance
Miserliness	*Liberality*	Prodigality/extravagance
Shabbiness	*Magnificence*	Bad taste/vulgarity
Lack of ambition	*Proper pride*	Ambitiousness
Poor-spiritedness	*Gentleness*	Irascibility
Peevishness	*Friendliness*	Obsequiousness/flattery
Maliciousness	*Righteous indignation*	Envy
Sarcasm	*Truthfulness*	Boastfulness
Boorishness	*Wittiness*	Buffoonery
Shamelessness	*Modesty*	Shamefacedness

We can also think of vices of excess and deficiency as they appear in our attitudes toward ourselves and our attitudes toward others. Contemporary moral philosopher Lawrence Hinman gives us the following list:[28]

Attitude toward Self

	Vices of Deficiency	Virtues	Vices of Excess
Attitude toward Self	Self-deprivation; Servility	Proper self-love; Proper pride; Self-respect	Arrogance; Egoism; Narcissism; Vanity
Attitude toward Our Own Offenses	Indifference; Remorselessness; Downplaying	Agent regret; Remorse; Making amends; Learning from them; Self-forgiveness	Toxic guilt; Scrupulosity; Shame
Attitude toward Our Own Good Deeds	Belittling; Disappointment	Sense of accomplishment; Humility	Self-righteousness
Attitude toward Our Own Desires	Adhedonia	Temperance; Moderation	Lust; Gluttony

(continued)

Attitude toward Others

	Exploitation	Respect	Deference
Attitude toward Other People			
Attitude toward Offenses of Others	Ignoring them; Being a doormat	Anger; Forgiveness; Understanding	Revenge; Grudge; Resentment
Attitude toward Good Deeds of Others	Suspicion; Envy; Ignoring them	Gratitude; Admiration	Over-indebtedness
Attitude toward Suffering of Others	Callousness	Compassion	Pity; "Bleeding heart"

The Unity of Virtue

Finally, we should point out that, even though it is common to discuss the virtues as though they were individual traits, Aristotle reminds us that virtue is better regarded as an "overarching quality of goodness or excellence that gives unity and integrity to a person's character."[29] On this note, we can think of virtuous people not only as those who exhibit virtuous traits, but also as those who serve as examples to follow—as *role models for moral behavior*. They are people who can be "counted on to act in a manner that benefits others" and who show a "willingness to perform supererogatory actions—going beyond what is required by everyday morality."[30] Rather than a collection of personality traits, then, virtue is best thought of as a unifying concept.[31] A "good person" is virtuous in the sense of having a more global disposition to act in ways that benefit herself or himself and others.

THE ETHIC OF CARE

In Chapter 7 we were briefly introduced to Carol Gilligan's research on gender differences in moral development and moral reasoning. Gilligan's insights, along with those of Nel Noddings and others, are sometimes referenced as grounds for an alternative moral framework that emphasizes *care* and related virtues such as compassion, tolerance, and benevolence.[32] Though not identical to virtue ethics, an ethic of care shares much in common with the tradition of virtue.[33]

Based on her research, Gilligan suggests that there are two fundamentally different orientations toward moral scenarios—one more characteristic of, but not limited to, males; the other more characteristic of, but not limited to, females. The "male" orientation (termed the *rights/justice orientation*) is more consistent with the dominant mode of Western moral reasoning that perceives the world as comprised of isolated, independent, rights-bearing individuals. Through this lens, justice is a matter of impartially and universally applying laws, rules, procedures, and principles to the case at hand.[34] Importantly, the justice approach tends to dismiss or deny a role for emotions—even those that may be beneficial such as care, compassion, love. Each of the approaches to moral decision-making examined prior to this chapter— utilitarianism, duty- and rights-based ethics, social contract theory—encourage the application of abstract principles to moral dilemmas, often specifically cautioning against allowing emotions to bias our judgment.

Arguably, however, "cultivating appropriate feelings and emotions" is a key part of becoming ethical—"we should try to make ourselves more empathic, sympathetic, compassionate, loving, and caring and less indifferent, hostile, and prejudiced."[35] As an alternative to the justice mode of moral reasoning, an **ethic of care** stresses relationships, situational and contextual factors, and the unique needs and interests of affected parties as key considerations for moral issues and dilemmas. It conceives morality "contextually and in terms of interpersonal relationships and connections."[36] Rather than isolated, independent individuals, we are each fundamentally interdependent and connected to one another; rather than justice being linked with impartiality and universally applicable rules, it is best understood in relation to the situation and the particular or unique needs and interests of all parties involved;[37] and rather than asking questions about relevant moral duties or applicable general principles, we should ask, "What is the loving or caring thing to do?"[38]

Care should not be confused with a moral duty or principle which should or must be followed; rather, it has more in common with virtue—it is an attitude or disposition, a way of perceiving, experiencing, and responding to the world. Especially important to a caring disposition is that we be *mindful*—seeking to understand and know the needs and interests of others and take these into consideration in our moral reasoning. We must "take on the standpoint or role of others . . . We must imaginatively project ourselves into the emerging dramas of *their* lives . . . " Consider the problem of homelessness. Being mindful, compassionate, and caring might entail imagining what it would be like to be homeless and thereby becoming connected to the nature of that form of suffering; " . . . being upset, distressed, regretting the different aspects of [the] plight" of the homeless, and wishing that such suffering did not exist; and "giving thought to what might be done to alleviate" that suffering.[39] It is not so much that we feel a moral duty or obligation to aid the homeless, but that we perceive ourselves as being connected to them through their suffering, and this connection inclines us to act in benevolent ways and to avoid causing further harm or exploitation (see Box 10.4).

An ethic of care thus offers an alternative approach to moral issues and dilemmas which allows for greater sensitivity to the needs and interests of others. At the risk of oversimplifying, we might summarize by noting that an ethic of care:

BOX 10.4
Caring, Suffering, and the Perception of Desert

Especially important to an ethic of care is that we recognize that, despite our superficial differences, we are all similar in important respects. We are, for instance, "fellow sufferers"—we know, on some level, what it is like to suffer physically and emotionally. Whether we have limited food to eat, not enough money to pay bills, are victims of crime and abuse, grapple with a debilitating illness, or are shunned by friends, suffering is an experience to which all of us can relate. Because it is universal, suffering is perhaps the most fundamental way in which we are all connected to one another. Recognizing this connectedness allows us to increase our awareness of and sensitivity toward the pains and struggles of others.

Indeed, suffering is a fundamental human experience that cuts across social divisions such as race, class, gender, religion, and age. Moreover, it does not discriminate between those who deserve it and those who do not. However, we often perceive suffering as something experienced only by those who do not deserve to deal with the situation in which they find themselves—the undeserved suffering of innocent children, crime victims, persons afflicted with disease, and the like. In contrast, others are perceived as deserving of their condition and, consequently, may be considered less worthy of our care and sympathy. Aristotle made precisely this point in his discussion of the virtue, noting that our experience and exercise of compassion may be tied to our perception of whether a fellow sufferer *deserves* her or his suffering. In other words, our belief about whether suffering is justified may interfere with our capacity to relate to others in compassionate ways.

(continued)

In a study of contemporary American attitudes, for example, Candice Clark found that sympathy is less forthcoming when we perceive suffering to result from malfeasance, negligence, risk-taking, or when it is perceived as in some way being brought on by the sufferer's own actions. Poverty may be regarded as a deserved form of suffering if perceived in terms of personal responsibility rather than economic forces or "bad luck," and even sexual assault victims are sometimes regarded as provoking or precipitating their own victimization. In the context of criminal offending, of course, we regularly regard the suffering of legal punishment as deserved—even as "justice."

Even in such cases where persons "deserve" to suffer by most accounts, the absence of compassion is not justifiable from a care or virtue perspective. How are we to have compassion for a convicted criminal offender? As moral philosopher Lawrence Blum suggests, we can " . . . have compassion for someone in a difficult or miserable situation without judging his overall condition to be difficult or miserable." In other words, it is possible to regard the condition of imprisonment as just and deserved without losing our compassionate awareness for the suffering an offender endures as a consequence of that imprisonment (e.g., isolation, separation from family, victimization by other offenders).

How might we "care" in such a situation? If compassion inclines us to refrain from adding more suffering to those who already suffer, what policies and practices might we support (or oppose) within jails and prisons? As is often argued with regard to imprisonment, offenders are sent to prison *as* punishment, not *for* it. Combined with compassionate awareness, what implications might this logic have for how we treat incarcerated criminals?

Source: Candice Clark, *Misery and Company: Sympathy and Everyday Life* (Chicago, IL: University of Chicago Press, 1999); Lawrence Blum, "Compassion." In A. Rorty (Ed.), *Explaining Emotions* (Berkeley, CA: University of California Press, 1980).

- Values "compromise and accommodation";
- "Seek[s] solutions that will minimize pain and suffering for all involved";[40]
- Focuses on relationships between people, seeking to create, preserve, or strengthen relationships while addressing the needs and interests of all involved—particularly those with the least power, status, and thus the most vulnerability;
- Attends to "all of the concrete details of a situation in order to understand it in all of its individuality and specificity";[41] and
- Encourages us to *imagine alternative* solutions that we may not have considered—"focus[ing] less on deciding between given alternatives than on envisioning new alternatives . . . that we meet everyone's needs . . ."[42]

VIRTUE, CARE, AND CRIMINAL JUSTICE

As we have seen, virtue ethics emphasizes moral character, the embodiment of virtue in one's decisions and actions, and the avoidance of vice. The ethical codes and statements of principles developed by professional organizations in virtually every field of practice continue to emphasize traits of character that are regarded as necessary and beneficial within those professions. Within criminal justice, some virtues are conventionally regarded and commonly cited as critical. Examples include:

Honesty

- Law enforcement officers " . . . *shall be accurate, complete, and truthful in all matters.*" (International Association of Chiefs of Police, "Model Policy on Standards of Conduct");
- Lawyers "*shall not . . . engage in conduct involving dishonesty, fraud, deceit, or misrepresentation*" and "*shall not . . . use or participate in the use of any form of public communication*

involving a false, fraudulent, misleading, deceptive, self-laudatory or unfair statement or claim." (American Bar Association, "Code of Professional Responsibility").

Justice

- *"Corrections leadership . . . must ensure that employees are treated with righteous standards of fairness and justice . . . "* (American Correctional Association, "Declaration of Principles").

Wisdom/Knowledge

- *"Corrections must be committed to pursuing a continual search for new knowledge . . . "* (American Correctional Association, "Declaration of Principles");
- *"A lawyer is aided in attaining and maintaining his competence by keeping abreast if current legal literature and developments, participating in continuing legal education programs . . . and by utilizing other means."* (American Bar Association, "Code of Professional Responsibility").

Responsibility/Accountability

- *"Accountability is a keystone of sounds corrections practice; therefore, all those engaged in corrections activity should be held responsible for their actions and behavior."* (American Correctional Association, "Declaration of Principles");
- *"Officers shall accept responsibility for their actions without attempting to conceal, divert, or mitigate their true culpability . . . "* (International Association of Chiefs of Police, "Model Policy on Standards of Conduct").

Temperance

- *"A lawyer . . . should be temperate and dignified, and he should refrain from all illegal and morally reprehensible conduct."* (American Bar Association, "Code of Professional Responsibility").

Other virtues, however, appear less frequently in discussions of moral character and criminal justice. While bravery and courage are widely regarded as admirable qualities among criminal justice professionals, are compassion, mercy, and love desirable qualities for police officers, judges, prosecutors, prison guards, and others in the practice community? Moreover, is the "masculine" justice orientation to criminal justice policy and practice more desirable than its care-based alternative? Although the implications of caring as an ethic have not been fully developed within criminal justice studies, it raises some important questions about (and criticisms of) many current criminal justice policies and practices.

Justice and the Ethic of Care

As previously discussed, a key component of caring is having and utilizing the capacity to empathize—to consider the needs and interests of all people involved in a situation. Seeking to know others and project ourselves into their situations is not only the basis of caring, but arguably is crucial to justice as well. It is this element of the ethic of care that is perhaps most relevant to the resolution of conflicts, cases, and issues in the realm of criminal justice. Those promoting an ethic of care would point out that the American criminal justice system leaves little—if any—room for the types of considerations that are central to caring. The American legal system, for instance, operates largely according to the "rights/justice" approach. Judges are expected to decide cases with reference to the rule of law and legal precedent; to approach cases in an impartial, unbiased fashion and decide similar cases in a like-minded fashion. In other words, the same resolution (e.g., determination of guilt, sentencing decision) may be applicable in many different cases, so long as the *legal* facts of those cases are similar.

The ethic of care would seem to promote a radically different approach to the resolution of legal cases. Rule of law, legal precedent, and legal facts would be less important considerations than contextual or situational factors. As we have seen, the ethic of care centralizes contexts, situations, and relationships. Justice cannot follow from the application of universal rules and principles; rather, justice emerges when we attend to the uniqueness of human situations and of the people involved in those situations (see Box 10.5). Resolving conflicts in both criminal and civil spheres would require that judges come to know the details of a particular situation, the persons involved in and affected by that situation, and make a determination on the basis of those particulars—not, as traditional conceptions of law and justice would have it, on the basis of a law, rule, principle, or precedent that is meant to apply to all similar cases. In a criminal case, for instance, this may mean that judges would need to make an effort to "know" the defendant, consider her or his life circumstances and motives, and take these into consideration when making a ruling.

BOX 10.5
Restorative Justice

As an example of an alternative approach to criminal justice which focuses less on abstract legal principles and more on the needs and interests of all parties affected within a particular situation, consider the relatively recent movement toward restorative justice. **Restorative justice** is an approach to justice which focuses on repairing harms caused by criminal offending through programs that seek to involve the offender, the victim, and the community in the restorative process.[43] Rather than focusing on the individual offender and abstract principles such as those derived from law, restorative justice emphasizes relationships and the needs and interests of all parties affected by crime. As traditional approaches to criminal justice focus almost exclusively on the offender, restorative justice is argued to provide an alternative that allows for the forgotten victim as well as representatives from the community to become involved in forging a solution that benefits all parties involved.[44]

One of the more popular and widely used restorative justice programs is Victim-Offender Reconciliation. **Victim-Offender Reconciliation Programs (VORP)** bring offenders and victims together in a setting that promotes a healthy interaction between them. Under the guidance of a trained mediator, victims have the opportunity to explain the harm that was caused by the offender and the ways in which the criminal event has affected their lives. The offender, in turn, has an opportunity to explain her or his motivations to the victim. As John Fuller writes,

> Sometimes all the victim wants is to tell his or her story to the offender and receive an apology. Sometimes the offender welcomes the opportunity to confess his or her transgression without fear that the court will use it to impose a harsh sentence.[45]

Overall, as "each side learns more about the humaneness and circumstances of the other, they are able to craft solutions" that identify the injustice, make things right, and establish mechanisms for future action.[46]

Victim-Offender Reconciliation Programs, as well as other restorative justice programs such as *family group conferencing* and *victim-offender panels* seek to re-involve the victim and the community in a legal process that has lost sight of them. Justice, some have argued, requires that victims, offenders, and communities be healed, and that all involved parties are offered an opportunity to participate in the healing or restorative process.[47] Doing so not only repairs the harm caused, but arguably does much more for the prevention of future offending than traditional models of criminal justice.

A contemporary criminal justice trend that would seem to be at odds with this type of approach is the movement toward **determinate sentencing** schemes. Many states have now implemented sentencing guidelines that severely restrict the amount of discretion judges have in deciding sentences in individual cases. Consequently, judges are unable (or less able) to take situational and circumstantial factors into consideration. Instead, judges are forced to impose sentences within a limited range that is defined by legislatures. For example, an offender convicted of a residential burglary might be sentenced to twenty-three months in prison, as mandated by sentencing guidelines, regardless of the circumstances of the crime or the offender. In theory, determinate sentencing produces uniformity, proportionality, and equity in sentencing decisions. In addition, it prevents judges from considering the types of situational factors that an ethic of care might otherwise showcase.

Beyond judicial decisions, the ethic of care would seem to have relevance for a range of decisions and decision-makers in criminal justice settings. In policing, for example, caring would entail officers seeking to know the people and circumstances involved in the situations they confront on a daily basis. Approaching law enforcement scenarios in this way would require individual officers to make liberal use of discretionary powers, considering the needs and interests of all parties involved in a conflict or situation before resolving it. To illustrate, not all persons who violate the law would require arrest. In at least some cases, the needs and interests of lawbreakers, victims, and the public may be better served by *not* making an arrest (or *not* ticketing traffic violators, etc.). This is commonly referred to as **selective enforcement** of the law. Because situations and the people involved in them are unique, the same approach may not be desirable in all factually similar cases. In addition, critics of selective enforcement have argued that allowing officers to rely on their own judgment (including moral sensibilities) in deciding when to make arrests markedly increases the likelihood of discrimination, favoritism, and other undesirable influences affecting decision-making. In other words, discretion *might not always be used in the interest of care* (see Box 10.6).

Do the benefits of adopting a care orientation in judicial and law enforcement decision-making outweigh the potentially negative consequences of selective enforcement and individualized sentences? Should judges, juries, police and correctional officers, and others involved in the criminal justice system embody an ethic of care when deciding cases or making decisions? Do virtues such as compassion, mercy, tolerance, and benevolence have a place in criminal justice? From a care perspective, these are precisely the questions that we should be asking ourselves. Further, our answers to these and related questions might have a profound impact on the future of criminal justice practice.

BOX 10.6

Domestic Violence and Mandatory Arrest Policies

A good example of a conflict situation involving relationships and unique needs and interests—yet for which the breadth of officer discretion has been criticized—is that of *domestic violence*. Historically, domestic violence offenders were not always—or even often—arrested. Decisions about whether to arrest, separate the parties for a temporary "cooling off" period, attempt to mediate the dispute, refer the couple to counseling, or employ some other means of resolving the conflict were largely in the hands of the officer(s). In part because of concerns raised by victim's advocates, some police agencies have implemented **mandatory arrest policies** that *require* police officers to make an arrest wherever possible.

(continued)

Nonarrest often requires written justification, and failure to follow departmental policy may result in disciplinary action against the officer. Do such policies potentially undermine the possibility of exercising an ethic of care? Consider whether any or all of the following *should* influence how domestic violence scenarios are handled by law enforcement officers:

- Whether the couple is married, separated, divorced, etc.
- Whether the victim and offender are of the same sex

- The potential financial consequences of making an arrest (for one or both parties)
- Whether there is a history of prior incidents
- Whether alcohol or drugs are involved
- The emotional state of the victim
- The emotional state of the offender
- The extent of injuries
- The victim's expressed desires

Source: William Doerner and Steven Lab, *Victimology*, 2nd ed. (Cincinnati: Anderson, 1998), pp. 151–153.

Summary

Virtue ethics differs from consequentialist and deontological ethics in the very question with which it begins. Rather than asking the question, "What should I *do*?" virtue ethics insists that we ask a different normative question—"What kind of person should I *be*?" In so doing, the virtue tradition displaces emphasis on duties and consequences and shifts it to considerations of moral character—on "being" a certain kind of person instead of "doing" certain kinds of actions or bringing about certain types of consequences. *Character* is thus emphasized more than duties, principles, rules, or consequences. This is not to say, however, that we should understand character as entirely independent of actions and consequences. Many would argue that "being" certain kinds of people means we are disposed toward "doing" certain kinds of actions, while those kinds of actions, in turn, have a tendency to produce certain types of consequences.

Historically, it is this emphasis on *being* as opposed to *doing* that distinguishes virtue ethics from other moral theories. Importantly, people who embody virtues—those disposed to *be* kind, caring, compassionate, forgiving, respectful, generous, and just—act out of a genuine respect and concern for the well-being of themselves and others. Compassion, for example, does not stem from a commitment to the principle of compassion, conformity to a duty to be compassionate, or a thoughtful and rational consideration of the consequences of being compassionate. Instead, people who act out of compassion tend to *be* compassionate people. Mother Teresa—perhaps the quintessential exemplar of the compassionate character—was not exercising compassion in the interest of acting morally; rather, her compassion was a function of her character as a compassionate person. It is for this reason that the virtue perspective regards right actions and good consequences as less morally significant than developing good habits of character that dispose us to do the right thing or incline us to act in a certain fashion. If we are disposed, by way of our character, to be compassionate, caring, forgiving, and so on, our actions will naturally follow from these dispositions or traits of character.

Key Terms and Concepts

biogenic needs *198*

character *189*

character trait *189*

determinate sentencing *207*

ethic of care *203*

eudaimonia 195

golden mean *200*

mandatory arrest policies *207*

moral vices *190*

Discussion Questions

1. Describe in detail the difference between moral virtue and moral vice. As you think about criminal justice professionals (e.g., police officers, probation/parole officers, lawyers) list the five characteristics that you would argue are most typical of the character of these types of professionals. Are these characteristics virtues or vices? Finally, list five characteristics that you feel would be ideal or desirable for such professionals to embody.

2. Using an example from juvenile justice (e.g., teenage prostitution, underage drinking, waiver to the adult system, execution), explore how virtuous or vicious character might influence the decisions of all parties involved at all levels of the process, from the deviant behavior itself to disposition of the juvenile within the justice system.

3. Recalling the section of this chapter on virtue and the good life, what is the end to which criminal justice is directed? To what extent is this end consistent with the highest good as described by Aristotle? Use examples to explain and/or justify your response.

4. What is the function and purpose of the criminal justice system? To what extent are these functions and purposes consistent with Aristotle's notion of the "good life"? To what extent do these functions and purposes promote or fail to promote the good life for citizens? Be specific!

5. Explain the relationship between virtue and human flourishing. In what ways are biogenic needs, cooperation, and connectedness important to this relationship? Do you believe that the adult and juvenile justice systems are structured to support these values? If not, what does this tell you about virtue ethics and the overall criminal justice system?

6. As the ethic of care requires us to consider situational factors before making decisions, what types of situational factors might be important in determining whether an arrest needs to be made in the following cases: solicitation of prostitution, possession of small quantities of illicit substances, a simple assault stemming from a drunken verbal confrontation at a bar, public intoxication, loitering.

Endnotes

1. Robert Hare, *Without Conscience: The Disturbing World of the Psychopaths Among Us* (New York: Guilford Press, 1999), p. xi.

2. June Price Tangney and Jeff Stuewig, "A Moral-Emotional Perspective on Evil Persons and Evil Deeds." In Arthur Miller (Ed.), *The Social Psychology of Good and Evil* (New York: Guilford Press, 2004), p. 340.

3. Emmett Barcalow, *Moral Philosophy: Theories and Issues* (Belmont, CA: Wadsworth, 1998), p. 99.

4. Ibid.

5. Ibid.

6. Cf. Barcalow, *Moral Philosophy*, p. 107.

7. Judith A. Boss, *Ethics for Life* (Mountain View, CA: Mayfield, 2001), p. 402.

8. Barcalow, *Moral Philosophy*, p. 99.

9. Ibid., p. 107.

10. Philippa Foot, "Virtues and Vices." In Joram Haber (Ed.), *Doing and Being: Selected Readings in Moral Philosophy* (New York: Macmillan, 1993), p. 301. Originally published in Philippa Foot, *Virtues and Vices and Other Essays in Moral Philosophy* (1978).

11. Aristotle, *Ethics*, J. A. K. Thomson (trans.) (New York: Penguin, 1976).

12. Ibid, p. 63.

13. Gerald Hughes, *Aristotle: On Ethics* (New York: Routledge, 2001), p. 23.

14. Paul Kurtz, *Embracing the Power of Humanism* (Lanham, MD: Roman & Littlefield, 2000), pp. 25–34.

15. Erich Fromm, *Man for Himself: An Inquiry into the Psychology of Ethics* (New York: Fawcett, 1965), p. 55.

significance level, i.e., based on Type I error. Yet statistical power analysis further takes into account Type II error and thus may produce more precise results.

The concepts of Type I and Type II errors have significant implications for the understanding of empirical research results. Because we cannot get rid of the errors, we can never be too sure about the accuracy of the results of any particular empirical research project. Although the chances of being wrong are small for a "perfectly" designed study, there *are* chances of being totally wrong when the procedures are all right. Being skeptical is therefore a necessary quality of a good researcher, especially when most research designs are actually imperfect. If there is an absolute demand for precision, the best scientists can do is to conduct a sufficiently large number of studies with the same research question and design. Our confidence is built on scientific results as a whole, not simply on any particular project. The concept of Type II error is particularly important. It shows that the probability of achieving accuracy largely depends on our ability to acquire large-sized random samples.

In social sciences, statistical inference is mostly conducted in the form of hypothesis testing. This consists of several steps: (1) forming a research hypothesis about a population parameter (including association); (2) computing the corresponding sample statistic; (3) calculating the (estimated) standard error; (4) deciding significance level and calculating the critical value; and (5) determining whether or not to reject the null hypothesis.

There is another form of statistical inference called parameter estimation. Parameter estimation does not involve a hypothesis, thus the procedure is more straightforward than hypothesis testing. Normally, the steps would include: (1) computing a sample statistic; (2) calculating its (estimated) standard error; and (3) deciding the confidence level and interval for the sample statistic to represent the population parameter. Parameter estimation is seldom applied to associations between variables; and researchers generally seem to prefer statistical tests to statistical estimations.

The task of parameter estimation can be accomplished by using the following general formula: $M \pm \alpha \cdot SE$. M is the sample statistic on a specific variable, and SE is the standard error. For a normal sampling distribution such as that of the mean, $SE = S/N^{1/2}$. Here N is the sample size, S is the unknown standard deviation of the variable among the population substituted by the standard deviation of the sample. For a nonnormal sampling distribution, such as that of Person's γ, we can transform it into a new statistic with a normal sampling

16. Jean-Paul Sartre, *No Exit* (New York: Vintage Books, 1955), p. 47.
17. Barcalow, *Moral Philosophy*, p. 111.
18. Carliss Lamont, *The Philosophy of Humanism* (New York: Humanist Press, 1997), p. 273.
19. Barcalow, *Moral Philosophy*, p. 109.
20. Aristotle, *Ethics*, p. 101.
21. Ibid., p. 102.
22. Ibid., p. 101.
23. Ibid., p. 94.
24. Donald Palmer, *Visions of Human Nature: An Introduction* (Mountain View, CA: Mayfield, 2000), p. 56.
25. Ibid.
26. Ibid.
27. Aristotle, *Ethics*, pp. 91–92.
28. Lawrence Hinman, *Ethics: A Pluralistic Approach to Moral Theory* (Fort Worth, TX: Harcourt Brace, 2003), p. 280.
29. Boss, *Ethics for Life*, p. 402.
30. Ibid., p. 403.
31. Ibid., p. 426.
32. See also, Virginia Held, *The Ethics of Care* (New York: Oxford University Press, 2005).
33. Nel Noddings, "Caring as Relation and Virtue in Teaching." In Rebecca Walker and Philip Ivanhoe (Eds.), *Working Virtue: Virtue Ethics and Contemporary Moral Problems* (New York: Oxford University Press, 2007).
34. M. Kay Harris, "Moving into the New Millennium: Toward a Feminist Vision of Justice." In H. Pepinsky and R. Quinney (Eds.), *Criminology as Peacemaking* (Bloomington, IN: Indiana University Press, 1991), p. 89.
35. Barcalow, *Moral Philosophy*, p. 218.
36. Harris, "Moving into the New Millennium."
37. Ibid.
38. Barcalow, *Moral Philosophy*, p. 216.
39. Lawrence Blum, "Compassion." In A. Rorty (Ed.), *Explaining Emotions* (Berkeley, CA: University of California Press, 1980), p. 511.
40. Barcalow, *Moral Philosophy*, p. 215.
41. Ibid., p. 215.
42. Ibid., p. 221.
43. Gordon Bazemore and Mara Schiff, *Restorative Community Justice: Repairing Harms and Transforming Communities* (Cincinnati, OH: Anderson, 2001).
44. Michael Braswell, John Fuller, and Bo Lozoff, *Corrections, Peacemaking, and Restorative Justice: Transforming Individuals and Institutions* (Cincinnati, OH: Anderson, 2001).
45. John Fuller, *Criminal Justice: Mainstream and Crosscurrents* (Upper Saddle River, NJ: Prentice Hall, 2006), p. 561.
46. Ibid.
47. D. Van Ness and K. Strong, *Restoring Justice* (Cincinnati, OH: Anderson, 1997).

11

The Examined Life: *A Guide to Critical Ethical Thinking*

Morality is ultimately about the choices we make and the actions we undertake (or fail to take) as a result of our decisions. Whether our choices are informed by our character, our commitment to moral duties and principles, our obligations, or a rational consideration of the potential consequences of our actions, moral goodness is ultimately reflected in morally good choices. Yet what makes a choice "good"? For example, on what grounds can we say that one's decision to support the death penalty, to endorse racial profiling as a legitimate method of policing, or to promote the waiver of juveniles to the adult criminal justice system is, indeed, morally justified or "sound"? On what grounds can we say that one's decision to "rat on" a fellow police officer, to "look the other way" when stopping a friend for driving under the influence, or to accept bribes from drug dealers is morally unjustified? On what grounds can we claim that our choice to be truthful with a friend or colleague even though in doing so considerable harm comes to a third party was the "right" one? What *conditions* make decisions morally right or wrong, good or bad?

Recall from Chapter 1 that while "morality" has to do with *people's beliefs about right and wrong, good and bad, and the choices they make and the actions that they take as a result of those beliefs*, "ethics" has more to do with *critically reflecting on moral values, beliefs, choices, and actions*. As a process of critically reflecting on morality, ethics should not simply describe moral issues and present moral perspectives; rather, ethics should also offer us some *strategies* that can be *used* to determine what position we should take on moral issues and what choices we should make in given moral contexts. Determining what position to take on moral issues such as capital punishment, racial profiling, or abortion requires a thorough analysis of the issue, utilizing principles of reasoning as well as whatever evidence we have available. Determining how we should choose or what we should do in a given situation requires the same sort of analysis—in this case, not of the issue, but of the situation, its circumstances, and how moral values and principles might be *applied* in that situation.

In this portion of *Ethics, Crime, and Criminal Justice,* we outline a number of concerns with specific relevance to moral decision-making. In a way, we hope that readers will understand what follows as a collection of "tools" that can be used as aids in moral choice-making. Though admittedly not exhaustive, our aim is to assist crime and justice professionals as they confront any number of possible moral issues and dilemmas in their everyday personal and professional lives. The observations that follow might be thought of as a practical "guide" for ethical choice-making and behavior. The types of skills and tools emphasized are *essential* components of morality. They help us make sound moral judgments, and these judgments or choices become the basis for undertaking right actions. Arguably, if these skills and tools become a part of how the criminal justice professional approaches moral dilemmas, they help to ensure that the person will lead a life built on character, integrity, and virtue.

JUSTIFYING BELIEFS AND DECISIONS

This is perhaps the most important point to be made about moral beliefs and ethical decision-making. The ethical life requires that we make good decisions, and good decisions are *justified* decisions.[1] To say that a particular choice, decision, belief, action, law, policy, practice, punishment, or sentence is "justified" is to be able to show that *there are good reasons for it*. Beyond this, justification also requires that we be able to show that our "good reasons" are better than those for alternative decisions, policies, and so forth. While you may be able to produce good reasons for being dishonest at a court appearance, if there are better reasons for being honest, we cannot claim that dishonesty is a justified choice.

- *We cannot simply seek to develop reasons for our decisions; rather, we must assess reasons for all possible alternatives, choosing the alternative that is supported by the best reasons.*

Moral Reasons Are Different from Personal Reasons

Personal reasons for decisions are those that appeal to our personal needs, desires, emotions, and interests. Most of the everyday, nonmoral decisions we make can be justified by appealing to personal reasons. One might have chocolate ice cream for dessert rather than chocolate cake because it sounds more pleasurable, because it has fewer calories, or perhaps because it is the middle of summer and ice cream seems more refreshing.

- *What reasons can you provide for your position on gun ownership, abortion, or flag burning? How many of those reasons appeal to self-interest? Emotion? Personal needs and desires? How many of them are reasons you have adopted from parents? Friends? Religious teachings?*

Personal Reasons Are *Not* Sufficient Reasons for Moral Decisions

While perhaps justifying everyday (nonmoral) sorts of decisions, *personal reasons are not sufficient to justify decisions with moral implications*. We might support equal treatment of women because we recognize that equality is an important part of a just society, not because we are trying to impress our parents, pastor, or a romantic interest.

Good Reasons Are the Result of Careful, Rational, and Unbiased Consideration

While most of us can offer a variety of reasons for our beliefs and decisions, closer examination oftentimes reveals that our reasons are flawed in one or more ways. More often than not, this is a result of our tendency to accept beliefs and make decisions without having fully and carefully scrutinized them. Good ethical decision-making and sound ethical actions require that we spend some time considering *where* our beliefs and opinions come from, *how* and *why* we believe certain things or have certain opinions, and, most importantly, whether we are *justified* in having them.

Ethical Frameworks Can Serve as Bases for Thinking about Reasons

Moral reasons often stem from ethical frameworks.[2] Over the course of this text, we have been exposed to a variety of ethical frameworks, all offering reasons for moral decisions. Moral reasons may appeal to the consequences of our actions for other people, to moral duties or principles (e.g., it is wrong to take an innocent life), or to the value of virtue. The frameworks outlined in Chapters 8, 9, and 10 are good starting points for developing good reasons for moral decisions.

UTILIZING OUR CAPACITY TO REASON

The ethical life is not simply about "doing the right thing," it is about *doing the right thing for the right reasons.* When we talk about good or right reasons, we are stressing the importance of human *rationality* and the *capacity for reasoning* which it provides. Reasoning skills are and have always been considered an important—indeed necessary—part of the pursuit of the ethical life. When making choices in both personal and professional contexts, we must utilize our uniquely human capacity to *reason.*[3]

Defining Reasoning

Reasoning refers to *any process whereby we apply available information such as evidence or principles (i.e., reasons) to a question, issue, or dilemma in the interest of reaching a conclusion.* When we think critically about whether we should support capital punishment, whether we should lie to a friend when telling the truth could be harmful, or about what we should believe or do with regard to any issue or in any situation, we are engaged in reasoning.[4]

Broadly Speaking, There Are Two Basic Types of Reasoning

These include *theoretical or pure reasoning* and *practical reasoning.* Though there is some considerable overlap between the two, for our purposes they can be described as follows:[5]

- *Theoretical or pure reasoning involves deciding what we should or* ought *to believe. When we reason theoretically, we are not figuring out what we should do in a given situation, but attempting to reach conclusions about morally responsible beliefs. Thus, theoretical reasoning is what* guides our thinking.
- *Practical reasoning involves deciding what we should or* ought *to do. We involve ourselves in practical reasoning anytime we deliberate an action. Thus, practical reasoning is what* guides our actions.

Theoretical Reasoning Assists Us in Developing Good Moral Beliefs

As we will see shortly, an important part of becoming a moral person is critically reflecting on the values and beliefs we hold, the principles we follow, the policies and practices we support and uphold, and the ends toward which we strive. We do so in the interest of identifying desirable values and principles, distinguishing justified from unjustified beliefs, and determining good policies and practices.

- *Should the value of life outweigh the value of choice? Should the virtue of loyalty be held in higher esteem than that of honesty? Are the consequences of our actions more important considerations than our moral duties? Is the overriding goal of our system of punishment and corrections to deter would-be criminals? To rehabilitate convicted criminals? To exact vengeance? Are nonviolent strategies of conflict resolution more desirable than violent ones? How can we use ideas from moral theory (e.g., utilitarianism, Kantian ethics) to justify our answer?*

Practical Reasoning Assists Us in *Applying* Values, Beliefs, and Principles to "Practical" Issues or Situations

Practical reasoning is crucial when we are facing an issue or situation about which *something needs to be done.* It guides our choices and actions by aiding us in determining how best to achieve ends that we have determined to be good, how we should choose when faced with conflicting ends, and most generally how the insights we gain from theoretical reasoning can be *used* over the course of our everyday personal and professional lives.[6]

- *If rehabilitation is determined to be a desirable end or goal for our system of punishment and corrections, practical reasoning is necessary to determine the best method(s) by which to achieve this outcome.*
- *Law enforcement officers are sometimes forced to choose between being loyal to a fellow agent versus telling the truth in a court of law. This sort of ethical dilemma can materialize when concerns are raised about an officer's investigative techniques or respect for the constitutional rights of suspects. Reasoning helps to clarify and evaluate the options we possess, enabling us to make more informed (and hopefully "better") decisions.*
- *If nonviolent strategies of conflict resolution are more desirable than violent strategies, we need practical reasoning to tell us how to apply nonviolent strategies in a given situation or with regard to a given issue.*

The Ethical Life Thus Requires That We Make Good Use of *Both* Theoretical and Practical Reasoning Abilities

Morally, some "ends" are better than others, and some means are better than others for achieving those ends. Theoretical reasoning aids us in contemplating the goodness of ends, while practical reasoning assists us in determining what to do in the interest of attaining those ends. Assuming that equality, for instance, is a desirable end, theoretical and practical reason together may help us determine: (1) *that* equality is a desirable end or state of affairs; and (2) *what means* (e.g., laws, policies, personal or institutional practices, character traits) are best—practically and morally—for achieving the end-state of equality.

Effective Reasoning Requires That We Have *Skills and Tools* with Which to Work

Reasoning about ethics is not something we simply "do"; rather, it is something that requires knowledge, skills, tools, and a good bit of critical reflection. These skills and tools of reason are often discussed as those of *critical thinking.*

THINKING CRITICALLY

The ethical life certainly involves making good decisions and performing right actions on the basis of those decisions. Good decision-making in ethics, in turn, has much to do with being a good *critical thinker.* To be a good critical thinker is to clearly *possess and routinely use the knowledge, skills, and tools necessary to work through ethical dilemmas, and to effectively analyze laws, policies, practices, and other concerns of moral significance.* Knowing *how to think* provides us with a foundation for being ethical people, for making morally good choices, and for reaching justified conclusions on complicated moral issues. As we come to incorporate critical thinking strategies into various facets of our personal and professional lives, practicing them with regularity, this tendency to think critically and to make sound decisions becomes almost second nature.[7]

Critical Thinking Is the "Activity of Reason" or "Reason in Action"

It is the process by which we actively use our innate capacity for rational thought to make good choices or decisions, as well as to justify and carefully assess beliefs, principles, laws, policies, and the like.[8]

The Goals of Critical Thinking Include

(1) *understanding and evaluating reasoning*, including existing and proposed laws, policies, and court decisions; (2) *making well-reasoned choices* and decisions, both in our personal lives and in professional contexts; and (3) *being fair-minded, avoiding the traps or pitfalls of emotion, convention, and other problematic—though common—influences on moral judgments and decisions.*[9]

Accomplishing These Goals Requires a Good Mind-Set Coupled with an Understanding of How Reasoning Works and Where It Can Go Wrong

While we cannot hope to consider even most of what needs to be said in this context in a short chapter, we have identified some of what we believe are the most important points to be considered as you embark on the journey that is the ethical life. Attaining a good ethical mind-set and making good ethical decisions requires, in part, that we: (1) recognize uncritical thinking in ourselves and others; (2) be willing to explore ways unseen; (3) recognize and seek to avoid common errors in reasoning and judgment, including *assumptions*, *errors of relevance*, and *errors of evidence*; (4) be able, on at least a basic level, to evaluate our own reasoning and that of others; and (5) be able, on at least a basic level, to *apply* moral principles and ethical frameworks to issues, situations, and dilemmas of ethical relevance.

RECOGNIZING UNCRITICAL THINKING

In *The Republic*, Plato asks us to envision an underground cave with the mouth open toward the light of a fire. Within the cave are cave dwellers (i.e., prisoners) who are chained such that they are unable to move, seeing only the cave wall directly in front of them. The light from the fire illuminates the wall so that shadows of people and objects can be seen, but not the people and objects themselves. Because it is all they know—all they can see and experience—the cave dwellers come to equate these shadows with truth and reality, naming them and talking about them as if they were real. In other words, truth and reality for the prisoners are merely shadows of what is.

Plato suggests that if one of the cave dwellers were to escape or be allowed to leave the cave, he would realize that the shadows were merely reflections of a more complex reality. He would realize that what had been truth and reality for him and his fellow cave dwellers—what they had taken to be knowledge of the world—was flawed and distorted. Having experienced what exists outside of his imagined world, our escaped prisoner would never be able to live the old way—having seen the world outside, he would never be able to return to the cave and the world of images that he once took to be real. He would no longer be able to accept his confinement, and he would pity the ignorance of his fellow dwellers. If he were then to share his newfound knowledge with his fellows, he would be met with ridicule, derision, and mockery. To the prisoners, the images of the cave wall are a meaningful reality—far more meaningful than a world they had never experienced. Furthermore, because our once-released prisoner would be unable to resume life in the imagined world, he would be perceived by the others as dangerous. Consequently, they would come to believe the world outside to be dangerous, favoring their world of images only that much more. What lessons can we learn about critical thinking and ethical decision-making from Plato's "allegory of the cave"?

It Is Easy to Become Imprisoned by *Favored Ways of Seeing the World*

We too easily slip into *habits of thought, belief, opinion, preconception, prejudice, stereotype,* and the like. If we are not careful, we can become "trapped" in certain ways of thinking about or seeing the world, unable or unwilling to recognize alternative possibilities. When challenged, rather than critically assessing the value of alternative thoughts, opinions, policies, and so forth, we tend only to become even *more strongly attached* to our favored ways of thinking. Our thoughts come to take on a power of their own, exercising *control over us* and shaping—if not determining—the way we perceive, experience, and interpret the world.[10]

We Think "Uncritically" When We Accept Ideas, Opinions, and Beliefs without Carefully Assessing Their Merit

Plato's cave demonstrates the need to *think* rather than accept things as they appear or are given/taught/preached to us. For Plato, this kind of critical reflection is the path out of our metaphorical "imprisonment"—the means by which we escape the state of being confined in a "cave" of ideas and opinions that we have accepted but left unexamined.

Socialization and Experience Tend to Provide Us with a *Limited and Incomplete* Portrait of Ourselves, Others, and the World in Which We Exist

Beginning at a very young age, we unknowingly absorb the ideas and opinions that are presented to us. We are largely passive products of our socialization and environment, digesting almost everything our parents, teachers, religious leaders, and others tell us. As we mature, we are bombarded by the advertising industry, mass media, political officials, and other assorted "experts" telling (or "advising") us as to how to think, what to know, and how to be. This extended process, in conjunction with the personal experiences we have along the way, shape and largely determine the way we perceive and understand the world. Consequently, our understanding is often *limited* and *incomplete,* subsequently making it difficult to engage in objective, unbiased, careful, and critical examination of moral concerns.[11]

The Ethical Life Requires That We Develop Our *Own Reasons* for Beliefs, Opinions, Decisions, and Actions

The value of socialization and experience is not to be altogether dismissed. Much of what we are taught or exposed to, as well as that which we learn from personal experience, can have value. We should first simply recognize that we come to accept a good many ideas, beliefs, and opinions without ever having decided their merits ourselves. Whether we continue to accept them or decide to reject them after critical reflection is less important than developing our *own reasons for accepting or rejecting* them. Developing our own reasons is what thinking critically is all about.

The ethical life requires that we objectively weigh ideas, opinions, and arguments when presented to us and, *through this process*, reach sound conclusions.

Ways of Seeing Can Become *Ways of Not Seeing*

When we think in exclusive ways—as "Christians," "liberals," "women," "environmentalists," and so on—no matter how attractive those ways might seem and how much easier it makes understanding the world, we can be prevented from considering new methods of understanding or new ways of seeing existing problems. When this occurs, the process of intellectual growth and moral development is inhibited, and efforts to find desirable solutions to ethical dilemmas and moral issues are hindered. In short, our *"ways of seeing" become ways of not seeing.*[12]

- *Think, for instance, of how absorbed people can become in the beliefs and opinions of their political party or religion when discussing current issues such as crime or poverty. When trapped in such favored ways of seeing, they become unable (or simply unwilling) to consider alternative perspectives. Rather than talking with one another and engaging in reasoned discourse in the interest of a desirable and agreeable resolution, they simply talk past one another.*

Critical Ethical Thinking Requires That We Approach Issues in Unbiased, Unprejudiced, and Open-Minded Ways

When we engage an issue by *starting with a conclusion* or answer that is consistent with our feelings, politics, religious sentiments, etc., we trap ourselves into not seeing. Oftentimes, we make the critical mistake of *seeking out evidence or justifications to support our preestablished conclusion.* In so doing, we are likely not to see beyond the limits of our own point of view.[13]

- *If we strongly believe that executing juveniles under the age of sixteen is a morally acceptable criminal justice response to offender behavior and then proceed to search only for evidence that supports our position, we will never "get to the bottom" of the issue. More than likely, there are many important points to be considered and not all (or even most) of them will necessarily be consistent with what we already believe. What is important is that we consider all of these points, arguments, and sources of evidence. Only by approaching complex crime and justice issues in unbiased, unprejudiced, and open-minded ways can we hope to be good ethical thinkers and make sound, informed, and morally responsible decisions.*

Sometimes, Traps of Not-Seeing Can Have Their Basis in the Beliefs and Norms of Entire Cultures, Communities, or Organizations

Sometimes the traps of not-seeing are much broader in scale than we realize. They can stem from traditions that have existed for hundreds or thousands of years; they can stem from the largely shared beliefs or norms of entire countries or cultures. In these cases, ways of seeing or doing can seem perfectly "natural" and "normal." What is regarded as natural and normal, in turn, is often presumed to be the "right" or "correct" way of seeing or doing.

- *Consider, for instance, the ways in which the tradition of **patriarchy** impacts the organization and practice of law enforcement. Patriarchy is a form of social organization in which men and typically masculine values are granted priority over women and values that are customarily defined as feminine. Under these conditions, patriarchy becomes a cultural force that can serve as a conceptual prison. For instance, without our conscious awareness of it, patriarchy can encourage us to regard masculine values as somehow better, more important, or more desirable* *that feminine ways of knowing, being, and doing. One of the practical effects of patriarchy in law enforcement is that this profession has tended to structure itself around masculine values, with the majority of senior positions within precincts and departments occupied by men. Values such as aggressiveness, control, and forthrightness are deemed more desirable with in law enforcement than the values of human relating, compassion, and reconciliation. Interestingly, however, most police work is not physically demanding. In fact, aggressiveness is seldom a necessary characteristic for successful performance. Instead, the skills that are most useful to police officers include communication, negotiation, and nonviolent problem-solving. In many important respects, these skills are consistent with feminine ways of knowing, interacting, and being.*

EXPLORING WAYS UNSEEN

We noted earlier that good (justified) decisions require not that we develop reasons for our decisions, but that we assess reasons for all possible alternatives, choosing the alternative that is supported by the best reasons. As ethical thinking requires exploring and considering all possible ways of seeing an issue or situation, it requires that we always make a point to seek out and consider various explanations, reasons, forms of evidence, and the like. Doing so can go a long way toward helping us overcome the inevitable prejudices or selfish interests that often shape our reasoning about difficult moral issues. Problematically, many of us put up a good bit of resistance to this necessity. How willing are we to *explore ways unseen*?

- *Think of a moral issue that you feel quite strongly about (e.g., abortion, sexual abuse, murder, flag burning, or police use of lethal force). First, identify three reasons to support your position (some people have trouble even with this). Next, identify three reasons in support of the opposing position. When asked to do so, many people eventually realize that they are so committed to their own perspective that they cannot cite many (if any) reasons to support the contrasting viewpoint. Most often, what this indicates is a failure to adequately consider alternative possibilities.*

Living the "Examined Life" Requires That We Regularly *Take a Step Back* in Order to See What Is in Front of Us

The ethical life entails subjecting our beliefs, opinions, and ideas to critical scrutiny. Making ethical choices and undertaking ethical action (i.e., being moral) entails examining and continually reexamining these crucial elements of ourselves. Living the examined life means that we take a step back from our experiences, socialization, feelings, and other influences that are potentially bias-inducing, in order to assess thoughtfully the issue right in front of us. Failure to do so can result in making poor choices, including the support of laws, policies, and practices that are largely ineffective and, worst, directly harmful or counterproductive. Ethics helps not only to *clarify our thoughts and feelings* on many of these matters, but also enables us to *work through* those thoughts and feelings in the interest of critically evaluating their merit. In this respect, the ethical life is about carefully reviewing moral values, principles, and arguments that form the basis of our opinions and beliefs, as well as our decisions and actions.

The Examined Life Requires That We Maintain a Healthy Degree of *Skepticism*

Skepticism is the *willing suspension of belief pending investigation of reasons.* Thus, skepticism is an *attitude.* To be "skeptical" of something is not to deny its validity, truth, value, or desirability.

Rather, to be skeptical is to *doubt* and to *maintain that uncertainty* until we have *sufficiently investigated* and reflected on reasons that support or fail to support the validity, truth, value, or desirability of that which is at issue.[14]

- *It may be helpful to think of ethical reasoning like the process of critical thinking that occurs during a legal proceeding. In proceedings like a criminal trial, there are standards of proof, burdens of proof (that attach to the defense or the prosecution), and judges and/or juries who weigh the evidence presented to them. The evaluation of the evidence is undertaken in the interest of determining whether the relevant standards and burdens of proof have been success-fully met. Thus, when thinking critically about ethical issues, a healthy amount of skepticism should be maintained until such time as we are confident that we have sufficient information or evidence enabling us to believe, choose, or act a certain way.*

The Examined Life Requires That We Keep an Open Mind

Narrow-minded persons avoid thoroughly considering all possibilities or courses of action, often because they limit their considerations to preformed ideas about what is worthy of consideration. Narrow-minded persons are sometimes dogmatic and often adopt a defensive posturing— almost instinctively defending their preformed ideas rather than thoughtfully considering alternatives and challenges to their ideas. In all cases, the defining feature of narrow-mindedness is simply an unwillingness to open oneself to new ideas, learn from those new ideas, and, where appropriate, *change one's own ideas.* Remember, as soon as we believe we have found *the* answer or the *correct* way of being or doing, we close ourselves off to other possibilities and make growth and development nearly impossible.

- Willingness to change—*particularly in light of new evidence—is central to keeping an open mind. The ethical life should be thought of as a work-in-progress. We regularly have new experiences, attain new knowledge, and are exposed to new evidence and new alternatives. The ethical state of mind is one in which we demonstrate a willingness to incorporate these new experiences, knowledge, and alternative possibilities into our ways-of-thinking about the world.*
- *Clearly, it would be impossible—and detrimental—to be open to every idea and every possibility. The ethical life requires that, to some extent, we be discriminate. As a general rule,* be judicious and use reasoned judgment *when determining which ideas and alternatives may be valuable in a given context or with regard to a given issue. We run into problems, of course, when we discrim-inate against new ideas and possibilities simply because they are different from ideas we have already formed.*

The Examined Life Requires That We See Beyond Categories, Labels, Stereotypes, and Other Preformed Ways of Sorting and Separating

When we categorize people or ideas, we attach generalized and stereotypical characteristics to them *before* considering them on their own merit or as unique entities. Specifically, we (often subconsciously) attach the stereotyped qualities of the category to the individual idea or person, thus seeing the person or idea *through* the category. Categories such as race, gender, social class, ethnicity, and nationality are common ways of limiting our perspective on people and, consequently, preventing ourselves from seeing unique characteristics, circumstances, and possibilities. The same happens when we see people through labels such as "criminal," "convict," or "sex offender." At other times, we see ideas through categories, whether these be political, religious, theoretical, philosophical, or otherwise. Doing so prevents us from seeing ways unseen in the fullest light.

important in the preparation process.

(5) How to interpret the results and write research reports. Once you have invested enormous time and energy in your own research, you should fully grasp the meaning of your results. The experience of being a research assistant will help you obtain needed insights. Your "bosses," the principal investigator(s) and your advisor(s), could be the best tutors of statistics and/or other research techniques in the sense that they know best about the uses of different procedures in a particular research setting. They will show you how to look at the computer output and select the most meaningful results. If you take part in the report writing process, you will also be trained in how to present your findings. For students who are not really good at the language used, it would also be a unique opportunity for them to improve if they could digest the corrections and comments of their supervisors on the student drafts.

The research courses and readings

As a student you have the opportunity to take some introductory and advanced courses in research methods. Some courses might be required by your academic program; others might be taken as electives in your curriculum.

If you are taking the required research courses, you may be eager to learn about research, or you may just take it as another subject for academic credit. Or, for some reason, you may not like to hear the research "gobbledygook" at all, but you have to take the courses anyway. You should, however, realize that research is something that is worth spending extra time and tenacious effort to learn, to get familiar with and even fall in love with. To get the most out of a research course, you should carefully schedule your total course load and allow enough time for attending classes, reading, doing exercises, and probably also conducting a required research project. If you feel overwhelmed or your time is squeezed by some other courses, you may consider taking the research course another time. If you get the sort of "research phobia" in yourself, it will become harder for you to succeed in a research career.

When considering your elective research courses, be clear about your criteria of selection. Do you just like the credits, or do you really want to learn something? If you really want to learn something, there are courses that are more suitable for you than others, even though those credits might be harder for you to obtain. You need to have a vision about your future career directions and distribution. The calculation of the SE is only slightly different in such a case. The coefficient α is determined by the required confidence level; researchers customarily use 95% or 99% as the desired level. It also depends on the sampling distribution of the statistic. For the normal distribution, the values of α corresponding to the above confidence levels are 1.96 and 2.58 respectively. Depending on the nature of the research question, however, the normal distribution is not always applicable. Binomial sampling distribution is another frequently used base for statistical test and estimation, which is described in most statistics texts.

Although we have a list of the logical steps of a statistical test in the above, the practice of hypothesis testing may proceed in a modified fashion. The target sample statistic and the estimated standard error are usually incorporated along with the hypothesized parameter value into a special standardized test quantity, such as Student's t, F ratio, and X^2 (Chi-square). This test quantity can be directly compared to the critical region corresponding to the selected significance level of an applicable sampling distribution. Note that F, X^2, and binomial sampling distributions are not normal and thus have different ways of calculating the standard errors and significance levels. The link between the critical region and the selected significance level is provided by a statistical table of the specific sampling distribution. Such a table is available in most statistics texts. The application of computer-aided statistics, however, has made such tables nearly (if not absolutely) useless, although statistics instructors may still require their students to use them for exercises. If you are used to using the statistical tables for homework, you may get confused when you look at the computer output.

Different computer programs may work in different ways, and they all tend to deviate from the usual procedure of hand calculation. In most statistical software, for example, the test quantity further becomes a significance level (called *p*-value) given by the actual sample. What you need is a very simple judgment, that is, whether or not this is up to your expectation — the desired *p*-value or significance level of 0.05 or 0.01, which is generally denoted by α. If the *p*-value is as small or smaller than α, then your null hypothesis is rejected and you call your data or the results are statistically significant at level α. In computer-aided statistical test, you do not need to bother about the critical value and the critical region at all. Conceptually, however, the idea of a critical region is important, especially in view of the difference between a two-tailed test and a one-tailed test. A one-tailed statistical test considers only one side of the sampling distribution, whereas a two-tailed test has to consider both sides that form two

AVOIDING ERRORS IN REASONING AND JUDGMENT

The first point we made at the outset of this chapter was that the ethical life requires that our beliefs and decisions be *justified*. Justifying beliefs, opinions, decisions, laws, and policies, in turn, requires that two conditions be met: (1) that we have *good reasons* for them; and (2) that the beliefs, decisions, etc., *follow from* those reasons. Decisions and judgments "go wrong" when they are made on the basis of any of a number of errors in reasoning. Over the course of the next several segments of our guide to ethical thinking and decision-making, we catalogue several of the more common types of these errors. Before doing so, we need to look briefly at the two above-mentioned conditions for justification.

Conclusions and *Reasons* Are the Basic Units of the Reasoning Process

Though reasoning is a complicated process, on its most basic level it consists of two units of analysis: reasons (sometimes called "*premises*") and *conclusions*.[15]

- A *conclusion* is the "point" of the reasoning process. Conclusions can be *beliefs or opinions* that are upheld or adopted; they can be *laws or policies* that are implemented; they can be *decisions* that are reached or *actions* that are taken. In short, the conclusion is whatever it is that is the point, aim, or purpose of the reasoning process. If you decide, through critical reflection, that "honesty is the best policy" in a given situation, you have *concluded*—through reasoning—that telling the truth is the best moral choice. Ultimately, the process of *reasoning aims at reaching a conclusion*—ideally, one supported by good reasons.
- *Premises* are another way of referring to the "reasons" that justify or lead to a conclusion. Though philosophers use the term "premise," we can just as easily substitute the more common term "reason." If we decide or "conclude" that being honest with a co-worker is the right choice in a particular situation *because* we would want her or him to be honest with us if we were in that same situation, we have offered a reason to support our decision. If we determine that capital punishment is a desirable practice *because* it deters future crime, we have offered a reason in support of our belief or opinion.
- *In the argument, "Abortion is always wrong because taking a human life is always wrong," the conclusion "abortion is always wrong" is supported by the premise or reason "taking a human life is always wrong."*
- *In the argument, "It should be legal to own handguns. I saw a poll in this morning's newspaper that said 83 percent of Americans believe that we should have that right. How can you argue with 83 percent of Americans?" the conclusion "it should be legal to own handguns" relies on the fact (reason) that "83 percent of Americans believe that we should have that right" to support the argument.*

Good Beliefs and Ethical Decisions Require That Two Conditions Be Met

As a *rule*, good beliefs and decisions require that: (1) the *reasons that lead us to have the belief, make the decision, etc., are good, true, or acceptable* and (2) the *conclusion follows from the reasons*. When these two conditions are met, we can say that a belief, opinion, law, policy, decision, etc., is good and justified.[16]

Inference Is the Process of Connecting Reasons to Conclusions

When conclusions are reached on the basis of reasons, we say that we have made an "inference"—we have "inferred" a conclusion from our reason(s). Making decisions, justifying beliefs, and choosing actions all involve the process of inference. Good reasoning, however, requires not only good reasons for the decisions we make and beliefs we hold, but also that the inferences we make that lead us from reason to conclusion be good.

- *Criminologists, for instance, often infer conclusions on the basis of scientific research. If, on the basis of research on serial murder, we find that 80 percent of serial murderers were sexually abused as children, we might infer that childhood sexual abuse has a causal influence on later criminal behavior. In this case, the research data serve as the reason for reaching the conclusion.*

Not All Inferences Are Good Ones

Think of a detective having good evidence, but "misreading" that evidence and being led to the wrong suspect. In this analogy, we can think of the evidence as the "reason" (or pieces of evidence as reasons), while the suspect to whom the detective is led as the "conclusion." Even when we have good reasons, we do not always reach the right conclusion based on those reasons. These types of errors are *errors of inference.*[17]

- *"On average, men are physically stronger than women. Therefore, men make better leaders than women." For this conclusion to be acceptable, we need both good (true, acceptable) reasons and a good inference. The reason offered in this argument is, in fact, true. On average, men are physically stronger than women. The inference, however, is faulty. While inferences can go wrong in a number of different ways, the fault of this inference is that there is no connection between the reason and conclusion. It would be difficult to claim that physical strength has any connection to leadership abilities. The conclusion is poor not because the reason is false, but because the inference made assumes a connection between the reason and conclusion that is absent.*

Not All Reasons Are Good Ones

While problems of inference commonly plague reasoning, equally problematic are errors that involve reaching a conclusion on the basis of poor reasons. Because good reasons are such an important part of ethical decision-making, we will have more to say on this subject in a moment. For now, it is worth noting that just as a detective might have good evidence but arrest the wrong suspect because of a faulty inference, in other cases she or he might arrest the wrong suspect on the basis of faulty or poor evidence. Reaching a good conclusion begins with having good evidence or reasons.

Evaluating Beliefs and Decisions

Because two conditions are required for a belief, decision, etc., to be an instance of good reasoning, the evaluation of our own beliefs and decisions and those of others (including the reasoning underlying laws, policies, etc.) involves two basic strategies. These include the following: (1) assessing the truth or acceptability of the reasons; and/or (2) assessing the quality of the inference that is made. As a good starting point, when assessing beliefs, decisions, and the like:

- *Identify the main* conclusion *(e.g., the belief, decision, law)*
- *Identify the* reasons *being offered in support of the conclusion*
- *Identify any problematic* assumptions *embedded in the reasoning (see below)*
- *Determine whether the reasons might not be* true or otherwise acceptable *(see errors of relevance, evidence, etc., below)*
- *Determine whether the reasons* support the conclusion *(i.e., does the conclusion follow from the reasons)?*[18]

AVOIDING ASSUMPTIONS

In addition to reasons and conclusions, most of the reasoning that we do also involves *assumptions*. We make assumptions when we leave things unsaid or take things for granted. While this may not always be a problem, in some cases the assumptions we make are themselves sources of debate or are otherwise problematic. In most cases, assumptions are *implicit* or not specifically considered in the reasoning process. We may not even be aware that we are making use of assumptions in our reasoning. In other cases, we may be aware that we or others are making assumptions. Either way, we should consider assumptions problematic if we do not have sufficient reasons for accepting them.[19]

- Always be aware of assumptions that we or others may be making. *Assumptions are not always a problem in critical thinking and ethical decision-making. They may be correct, true, acceptable, etc., elements of forming sound beliefs and reaching good decisions or conclusions. In other cases, however, it is the things we take for granted that cause decision-making to go wrong. Always consider whether you or others are making assumptions and, as a general rule, if the assumption might not be true or otherwise acceptable, it is likely a problem that should be addressed or issue that should be taken into consideration.*
- *In the argument, "Abortion is always wrong because taking a human life is always wrong," there is an important assumption. What is assumed or taken-for-granted that may not be acceptable to all people? Hopefully, you identified the assumption as embedded in the premise; namely, this argument assumes that unborn children (i.e., human fetuses) are human beings. It is argued that abortion is wrong because taking human life is wrong. The problem created by the assumption is that we can accept the conclusion if and only if we accept the assumption that unborn children are, in fact, human beings. Of course, this belief is a source of considerable controversy and would need to be supported by a separate argument.*

AVOIDING ERRORS OF RELEVANCE

One of the more common errors in reasoning occurs when we use reasons that are not or should not be considered relevant to the issue or situation. There are a variety of types of errors of relevance. We have chosen to explore only several that seem common in criminal justice: those that rely on authority, popular opinion, expertise, tradition, and emotion as sources of justification. We should note up front that these sources are not necessarily problematic in all ethical thinking and decision-making. In many instances, however, they lead to problems rather than good solutions.

The Use and Abuse of Authority

Authorities are common sources of belief, and authority is a common justification for decisions and judgments. We routinely make appeals to the U.S. Constitution, the Bible or Koran, public opinion polls, books, teachers, or politicians when engaging in ethical arguments or even when making decisions about what to do in our personal and professional lives. Unfortunately, authorities are not always *good* sources and authority is not always a *good* supporting reason for moral judgments. This is not to suggest that authority is without place in ethics; rather, it is to recognize that beliefs held and decisions made on the basis of authority are only as good as the authority itself.[20]

- *Appeals to authority occur when we justify a belief, decision, etc., by appealing to the word of a presumed authority. Appeals to authority typically rely on social institutions (e.g., laws, constitutions), public opinion, social and cultural customs and conventions, religious teachers, and scientific and moral "experts."*
- *When we use authority, we need to carefully assess: (1) the reliability of the source; (2) whether other sources can corroborate the word of the authority (e.g., do other authorities in the field tend to agree); (3) whether the authority is sufficiently trained/educated on the subject matter in question to be regarded as an authority; and (4) whether the authority her-, him-, or itself has good reasons for making the claims that it does.*
- *Be aware of unknown or unnamed authorities. Though we sometimes make such appeals for the sake of simplicity, claims such as "experts agree that . . . ," "research demonstrates that . . . ," or "people in the know say that . . . " may be problematic. Ask yourself, what experts? What research? What people? Apply the same guidelines listed above.*

The Use and Abuse of Tradition

Tradition refers to an established way of doing things. When we make an ***appeal to tradition,*** the reason that we offer in support of a belief or decision appeals to the longevity of the belief, law, practice, and the like.[21] Appeals to tradition are beliefs or decisions based on the fact that something has "always been that way" or "always been done that way." While tradition is not always problematic, it is not a good reason for ethical decisions and moral judgments. In other words, appealing to tradition is not sufficient grounds for ethically good decisions. That women have "always been" regarded as inferior to men, for instance, is not by itself a good reason for continuing to regard and treat women as inferior; because the United States of America was founded as and has always been a democracy is not by itself sufficient reason for claiming that democracy is the best form of government for the United States. If we were to hold tradition to be an adequate justification of policies and practices, we would have to concede that *slavery* was morally acceptable up to the point at which it was abolished.

- *In some cases, there may be good reasons that a tradition exists. Where this is the case, identify and utilize those reasons rather than simply appealing to the tradition itself.*

The Use and Abuse of Majority Belief

Contemporary culture barrages us with statistics everywhere we look—from the front page of the daily paper, to the evening news, political speeches, and scholarly journal articles and books. Problematically, these statistics are often presented in such a way as to appear as authoritative voices. The more we become accustomed to hearing or seeing them, the more we may begin to believe that they are, in fact, authoritative. We may begin to believe that public opinion carries weight of some significance when it comes to current issues and events—that the "majority" must be right. If 73 percent of Americans favor the death penalty, then the death penalty must be morally right or, at least, acceptable. What makes 73 percent of Americans "experts" on capital punishment, war, abortion, or any other contentious issue? We can use some of the same criticism outlined above to judge public opinion: does the public have sufficient knowledge of and education about the subject matter? Does the public itself have good reasons for beliefs?

- *The **democratic fallacy** occurs where we appeal to majority belief to justify a decision or belief. Simply because 88 percent of the population believes X, does not mean that X is good, right, just, etc. Public opinion polls offer us interesting pieces of information about what the public* *thinks and feels, but not a good reason for our own beliefs, decisions, and judgments. Like other sources of authority, the majority can be wrong (remember, the "majority" of people once believed that the earth was flat!).*[22]

The Use and Abuse of Emotion

Many philosophers and nonphilosophers alike have held a deep distrust of emotion. Emotions and feelings have been and are commonly regarded as belonging to that part of our psychological makeup which disposes us to poor judgment, uncritical belief, and harmful behaviors. Emotions are often discussed as irrational forces—collectively, the antithesis of reason—impeding our capacity to think rationally and make sound choices. Because emotions are such powerful forces, they can be powerful influences on our decisions and actions. Many of the beliefs we hold and the choices we make are likely informed in part by emotion. While emotions have many positive functions—even within ethics—they do not always incline us to do the right thing. For every moral action motivated by sympathy, there is likely an equally immoral action motivated by vengeance, hatred, or fear.

- *When approaching ethical issues and decisions, we want to do so in a way that demonstrates what Anne Thomson discusses as* "moral fair-mindedness." *This requires that we: (1) be* self-critical, *judging ourselves by the same standards we judge others; (2) judge and decide without* reference to prejudices and biases, likes and dislikes; *(3) judge and decide* without reference to self-interest *(or those of our race, class, gender, group, or organization); and (4) assess moral issues and make decisions* without reference to our own feelings.[23]
- *As a compromise between eliminating emotions and being driven by emotions, we might consider the ethical need to make assessments as to* whether our feelings are appropriate responses to the situation.
- *Emotions must be governed by the rule of fair-mindedness as well. We must be able not only to assess the appropriateness of our own emotions, but also to make an effort to* understand the emotions of others.

AVOIDING ERRORS OF EVIDENCE

Much of the reasoning we do in the social sciences is *inductive* in nature. **Inductive reasoning** involves making inferences about a population based on known properties of a *sample* of that population. We assume that the properties of the whole population in question will be more or less similar to the properties of the sample about which we know something. Good inductions require a sample that is *similar to the population*. The more similar the sample is to the population as a whole, the more valid and reliable our inferences will be. In addition, if our sample is dissimilar in significant ways to the population, our inferences will be poor ones. Several common errors in reasoning result from our making a poor inference about a population based on a sample that is dissimilar in one or more ways. Though there are others, these include hasty induction, forgetful induction or unrepresentative sample, slothful induction, and exclusion.[24]

Hasty Induction

Hasty inductions are conclusions about a population based on an *insufficient number of cases*. In other words, the size of the sample is too small to make a good inference about the entire population.

- *Research on twenty convicted murderers demonstrates that each of them has an underdeveloped frontal lobe of the brain. On the basis of those twenty cases, we attribute the characteristic of an underdeveloped frontal lobe to all (or most) murderers, claiming that this characteristic is a causal factor in murder. Because there are thousands of convicted murderers around the world and throughout history, we cannot justifiably attribute this characteristic to all (or even most) of them on the basis of twenty cases. Our conclusion was reached on the basis of a hasty induction.*

- *The state of Oregon implements a ban on handguns and, two years later, its crime rate has dropped by 10 percent. We conclude that crime rates can be lowered in all states by implementing bans on handguns. We have committed an error of hasty induction because, even if we could show that Oregon's reduced crime rate was a result of the ban, one state's experience is not sufficient to claim a general rule that would apply to all states.*

Forgetful Induction

While hasty inductions reflect a failure to observe a sufficient number of cases, forgetful inductions fail to observe a *sufficient variety of cases*. This is sometimes referred to as an *unrepresentative sample*. The problem is not that we have observed too few cases, but that the cases we observed are not sufficiently diverse to reflect the diversity of the population.

- *On the basis of interview research with three hundred women who have had abortions, we determine that only a handful of them had good medical reasons for doing so. As it turns out, all three hundred women in our sample were between sixteen and twenty years of age. If we would have interviewed women in other age categories (e.g., under fourteen, over thirty-five), we may have found significantly more cases where good medical reasons existed for the procedure.*
- *Instructors typically have students do course evaluations near the end of the semester. In a particular class, the instructor has exempted all students who have over an 80 percent in the class from taking the final examination. The course evaluations are handed out on the last day of class—a day which is to serve as a review session for the final examination. Problematically, all of the "A" and "B" students in the course—a good number of whom found the course interesting and enjoyable—are not present to do the evaluations. The evaluations ultimately reflect the opinions of those students who struggled with the material or the instructor.*

Slothful Induction

In some cases, we refuse to reach a conclusion (accept a belief, reach a certain decision) even though there is sufficient evidence leading us to that conclusion. We induce "slothfully" when we deny the "correctness" or value of a belief or opinion even when all available evidence tells us that we should accept it.

- *Joey has been convicted of child molestation four times. He has just been released on parole. As Joey's parole officer, he has assured us that "this time is different," and we are inclined to believe that he is rehabilitated. Each time he has been released from prison in the past, he has committed a sex offense within two months. Each of those times, he swore that he was "better" and would not re-offend. While we should not discount the possibility that this time is different, all of the evidence we have should lead us to conclude that Joey will commit yet another offense in the near future.*
- *Dr. Jenks hypothesizes that low serotonin levels cause aggressive behavior in adults, oftentimes leading to violent actions. Over the years, numerous studies have failed to confirm this hypothesis. Many violent persons did not have low serotonin levels, and many people with low serotonin levels did not act aggressively or violently. Nevertheless, Dr. Jenks continues to maintain that a strong relationship exists.*

Exclusion

In some cases, we ignore or exclude important evidence that would have a bearing on the conclusions we reach or the decisions we make. The most problematic instances are those where we refuse to acknowledge evidence because the conclusion to which it leads is undesirable or challenges our accepted and comfortable ways of thinking and doing. Good reasoning requires that we consider *all* available evidence, no matter what implications that evidence may have for the beliefs we hold and decisions we reach.

- *Over the past month, the "Wild Hearts" gang has been linked to thirty-two of thirty-eight crimes committed in the neighborhood. Earlier today, Mrs. Robinson was robbed at gunpoint. Chances are, the "Wild Hearts" had something to do with it. Without any other information, this induction might not be entirely objectionable. However, if we consider that none of the thirty-two crimes linked to the "Wild Hearts" were robberies and none of them involves the use of handguns, our induction becomes poor. With this information, our conclusion would likely be that this crime is not connected to the "Wild Hearts" gang.*
- *One of the more common types of exclusion in social science occurs when we ignore evidence that is contrary to our hypothesis, explanation, etc. Suppose that, in justifying the merit of a theory of crime, we refer to the twelve studies that support the theory, while ignoring or failing to include the fourteen studies that either did not support or effectively refuted the theory. These types of exclusions become especially likely when we become attached to favored ways of seeing and doing.*

AVOIDING OTHER COMMON ERRORS

Errors in reasoning are numerous. Those of evidence and those of relevance represent only two of a variety of categories of faulty thinking. Rather than providing a comprehensive treatment of the remaining categories, we have chosen to single out several additional types of reasoning errors that may be especially useful for thinking about and making decisions within criminal justice.

Two Wrongs Don't Make a Right

This common saying has much validity. Two wrongs always make two wrongs. If, for instance, a suspect assaults a police officer while she or he is in the process of making an arrest, the suspect has committed a wrong. If, in turn, the officer assaults the suspect in retaliation, the officer's actions are no less wrong than the suspect's and certainly do not magically (or morally) make the situation right. Simply because our motive is revenge or retaliation does not mean that actions so motivated will somehow rectify, remedy, or "fix" the initial wrong.

- *Many proponents of restorative justice argue that punishing criminals is an attempt to make two wrongs equal a right. Instead, they argue, if we wish to remedy the initial wrong, we should focus on utilizing restitution, reconciliation, and other strategies designed to restore well-being rather than add harm to harm.*

Stay Focused on the Issue and Relevant Circumstances

There are several common errors in reasoning that involve allowing ourselves to become distracted or attempting to distract others from the real issue at hand or the relevant circumstances as they apply to that issue. At times, we "attack" the source of a claim rather than the ideas offered by that source. Commonly, this attack is of a person's politics, religion, race or gender, groups or organizations to which she or he belongs, her or his character or personal habits and preferences, or the person's situation.

- *If we are politically liberal, we should not dismiss the ideas of a political candidate or commentator because she or he is politically conservative. Alternatively, disregarding a person's argument against capital punishment because she or he is a "bleeding heart liberal" is similarly problematic. In each case, we should seek to refute the ideas themselves, rather than attempting to discredit the ideas by discrediting the person offering them.*
- *If we are interested in whether prisoners should be allowed to train with weights, we should not dismiss the claims made by prisoners simply because they are in prison and have a vested interest in the issue. In such a case, we should consider not the person, but the reasons the person is offering in support of her or his position.*
- *It has recently been discovered that an ethics professor, married with children, has been having an affair with a student and, further, that he lied about the affair when formally questioned. Simply because the professor does not "practice what he preaches," we should not discredit the value of the ideas he taught in his courses.*

Lack of Proof Does Not Disprove and Lack of Disproof Does Not Prove

This statement is self-explanatory. Simply because we have no proof that something is the case, does not mean that it is not the case; similarly, simply because we cannot prove that something is not the case, does not mean that it is. As a general rule, it makes good sense to err on the side of the majority of evidence; however, in so doing we should not exclude alternative possibilities.

Avoid Black-and-White Thinking

Black-and-white thinking relies on *binary* or *either/or logic*—thinking in terms of right/wrong, good/bad, or black/white with no consideration for what lies in between. This type of thinking occurs when we give or are given a limited number of options with respect to a complex issue when, in fact, there are more options available. A recent U.S. president made such a claim with regard to the "war on terror," offering something to the effect of, "either you're with us or you're against us." This type of either/or logic fails to consider that most issues are not "black or white." While commitment is an important part of moral character, we should not forget that good answers and good decisions are sometimes—if not usually—to be found in the gray areas. Always ask whether there are additional alternatives. Can a compromise be reached? Is there room for a creative solution?

- *The defendant is either guilty or innocent*
- *The defendant is either mentally healthy or mentally ill*
- *The defendant was either sane or insane at the time of his offense*

Strive for Consistency in Moral Beliefs and Decisions

Anthony Weston calls this "judging like cases alike." One of the key features of the examined life and of good moral character more generally is consistency in beliefs, decisions, and actions. If a moral belief or decision in a given situation is based on a certain moral value or principle, the same principle should apply to all other similar beliefs and situations. Sometimes we fail to see the similarities between issues or situations; other times, we don't want to see the similarities, as doing so might require us to change our belief or decision with regard to one of them. Valuing loyalty over honesty in one situation, and honesty over loyalty in a different but similar situation may indicate a failure to thoroughly examine one's value priorities. As well, it may simply indicate a failure to see the two situations as similar and, thus, as requiring similar choices. Good ethical thinking and decision-making demands that we be clear about our own values and principles and that we seek to apply them regularly and consistently.[25]

- *The **principle of universalizability** holds that if we judge a practice or behavior to be morally right, we must also judge all morally similar practices to be equally right. If we judge an action to be morally wrong because it causes suffering, then all other actions that cause suffering must be regarded as equally wrong.*
- *To believe, for instance, that abortion is wrong because it is wrong to take a life while simultaneously believing that capital punishment (i.e., taking a life) is desirable or acceptable would likely constitute inconsistency of belief. If you are morally opposed to acts of killing, consistency demands that you oppose all acts of killing (or change your principle).*
- *When inconsistency is an issue, we have only two options: (1) we can determine ways in which what seem to be similar issues or situations are actually different, thus requiring different principles, decisions, etc.; or (2) we can change our minds about one or the other issue or situation. In the above example about capital punishment and abortion, you might determine ways in which abortion is different in morally significant ways from execution. Your guiding principle may not be "it is wrong to take a life," but "it is wrong to take an innocent life." This, in turn, might have implications for whether you support or oppose war, whether you hunt for sport, eat meat, and engage in other practices that involve taking innocent lives. Ask yourself what makes taking life in a time of war morally different from executing criminals; what makes killing animals for food (or sport) different from abortion or execution? To hold different positions on these matters, we must be able to identify exactly how one is different (in a morally relevant way) from the others. If we cannot, then our positions are plagued by inconsistency.*

PUTTING IT ALL TOGETHER: A SUMMARY OF GUIDELINES FOR THE ETHICAL LIFE

- In making decisions about what to believe or what to do, make sure your decisions are justified (i.e., are backed by good reasons).
- Avoid making decisions based on self-interest or the interests of a group to which you belong (e.g., race, gender, religion, political affiliation).
- Avoid becoming trapped in favored ways of seeing the world.
- Recognize that many of your existing beliefs, ideas, and opinions are likely limited and incomplete.
- Seek to develop moral autonomy, developing your own reasons for beliefs and decisions.
- Practice "taking a step back" to see what is in front of you.
- Maintain a healthy, but selectively employed, amount of skepticism.
- Keep an open mind, avoiding dogmatism and defensive posturing.
- Avoid making assumptions.
- Avoid relying on authority as the sole reason for ethical beliefs and decisions.
- Avoid relying on tradition or convention as the sole source of ethical beliefs or reason for decisions.

- Avoid making too much of public opinion.
- Avoid making decisions solely on the basis of emotions, passions, and desires.
- Before making generalizations, make sure you have observed a sufficient number and variety of cases.
- Follow, do not dismiss, good reasons and evidence.
- Do not exclude important sources of information or evidence simply because they do not support preformed ideas.
- Do not add harm or evil to already-existing harm or evil by responding to a wrong with another wrong.
- Stay focused on relevant information.
- Keep in mind that lack of proof does not disprove, and lack of disproof does not prove.
- Avoid black-and-white thinking, thinking dichotomously, and seeing through categories and labels.
- Finally, strive for consistency in moral beliefs and ethical decisions.
- Making an effort to "know thyself" and live an "examined life" will go a long way toward ensuring that you adopt and maintain good moral beliefs and that you make good and consistent ethical decisions.

Endnotes

1. Robert Solomon, *Ethics: A Brief Introduction* (New York: McGraw-Hill, 1984), pp. 101–105; see also, Robert Solomon, *On Ethics and Living Well* (Belmont, CA: Wadsworth, 2005); James Rachels, *The Elements of Moral Philosophy* (New York: McGraw-Hill, 2010).

2. See, e.g., Simon Blackburn, *Being Good: A Short Introduction to Ethics* (Oxford: Oxford University Press, 2001).

3. See, e.g., Emmett Barcalow, *Moral Philosophy: Theories and Issues* (Belmont, CA: Wadsworth, 2006); Anne Thomson, *Critical Reasoning in Ethics* (New York: Routledge, 1999).

4. Thomson, *Critical Reasoning in Ethics*); see also, Louis Groarke, *Moral Reasoning: Rediscovering the Ethical Tradition* (New York: Oxford University Press, 2011).

5. Robert Audi, *The Architecture of Reason: The Structure and Substance of Rationality* (Oxford: Oxford University Press, 2002).

6. Robert Audi, *Practical Reasoning and Ethical Decision*, 2nd ed. (New York: Routledge, 2005).

7. Alec Fisher, *Critical Thinking: An Introduction* (New York: Cambridge University Press, 2001).

8. Zachary Seech, *Open Minds and Everyday Reasoning*, 2nd ed. (Belmont, CA: Wadsworth, 2005).

9. Robert Ennis, *Critical Thinking* (Upper Saddle River, NJ: Prentice Hall, 1996).

10. Gareth Morgan, *Images of Organization*, 2nd ed. (Newbury Park, CA: Sage, 1997).

11. See, e.g., Vincent Ruggiero, *Beyond Feelings: A Guide to Critical Thinking* (New York: McGraw-Hill, 2004).

12. E.g., Morgan, *Images of Organization*.

13. See, e.g., Dennis Q. McInerny, *Being Logical: A Guide to Good Thinking* (New York: Random House, 2004).

14. See generally, Steve Hindes, *Think for Yourself!: An Essay on Cutting Through the Babble, Bias, and Hype* (Golden, CO: Fulcrum, 2005).

15. See generally, Fisher, *Critical Thinking*.

16. McInerny, *Being Logical*.

17. Ibid.

18. See, e.g., Fisher, *Critical Thinking*.

19. Ibid.

20. Ibid.

21. Ibid.

22. McInerny, *Being Logical*.

23. Thomson, *Critical Reasoning in Ethics*.

24. See McInerny, *Being Logical*, for an overview of inductive fallacies.

25. Julian Baggini and Peter Fosl, *The Philosopher's Toolkit: A Compendium of Philosophical Concepts and Methods* (Oxford: Blackwell, 2003).

parts of the critical region. The one-tailed test can only be used when the research hypothesis has a clear direction, which makes the test easier than the two-tailed situation. That is why in chapter six you are advised to specify the direction of your hypothesis whenever possible.

Hypothesis testing can be classified as the test of a parameter (of a single variable) and the test of an association (between different variables). For the former, the mean is most frequently dealt with by researchers. Parameter testing may be applied to the mean of a single population or the comparison of two means. The test quantity is denoted by t (called Student's t) in both cases. The procedure is generally called a t test, though sometimes it is called a Z test when a large sample (N>30) is used. The distribution of t has to do with the degree of freedom (DF) of the sample, which has a value of N-1. In the case of small samples, the impact of the degrees of freedom can be quite considerable. And the critical region is determined not only by the significance level but also the degree of freedom. Since a percentage can be regarded as a special mean, i.e., the mean of a dummy variable, t test can also be used to test the significance of a percentage, or to compare different percentages or rates. In SPSS, the procedure of T-TEST is designed for comparing different means in various situations, including related or paired samples obtained through matching in experimental design. However, you can also use it for testing the significance of a single mean. For example, if you want to test the hypothesis that the mean of the population is m, you can create a constant with a value m (a constant is the special case of a variable, in this case you can name it MEAN). This could be done by using the command of COMPUTE. Then, with the SPSS procedure for paired t test, you can instruct the computer to carry out the single parameter test by issuing the command "T-TEST PAIRS = (variable) MEAN." Here you should note that a single variable test and a relational test is very different.

Hypothesis testing is far more frequently used on the association between two different variables. Similar to descriptive statistics, different test procedures are developed at and applied to different levels. If the two variables are both at the nominal level, the test quantity for testing the significance of their association is X^2. In a contingency table, the calculation of X^2 is based on the difference bet-ween the actual frequency and the expected frequency in each cell. Since X^2 never takes a negative value, the test is always one-tailed. The larger this quantity, the higher the actual significance level. It should be noted that the distribution of X^2 depends on the degree of freedom (DF) of the contingency table, i.e., DF = (r-1)(c-1). Here r is the number of rows and c the number of

12

Applying Ethics: Utilizing Normative Frameworks for Decision-Making

We have dedicated substantial space in this text to examining ethical concepts and frameworks. We were persuaded to do so by our belief that an understanding of these concepts, frameworks, and their accompanying issues are crucial not only to leading an ethical life, but also to having an informed understanding of crime and criminal justice. Whether these ideas are put to use in your personal life, professional life in criminal justice or some other profession, or simply for better understanding the relevance and importance of ethics and morality in crime, law, and justice, hopefully we have succeeded in introducing you to some fundamental problems and issues, and provided you with some basic knowledge with which to entertain these problems and issues.

Particularly with respect to the normative frameworks presented in earlier chapters (consequentialist, deontological, and virtue ethics, respectively), the ideas discussed in this text are meant to be *used*. It does little good to have a firm grasp of ethical perspectives and not be able to *apply* these perspectives to moral issues and ethical dilemmas you may encounter in the process of living your life. At the same time, attempting to live one's life—making choices and decisions with moral impact—without first having some working knowledge of these frameworks and how to use them can be equally problematic. Would we want to undergo major surgery performed by a medical doctor with no understanding of human anatomy and physiology? Would we want our taxes done by an accountant with no working knowledge of tax laws? Would we want convicted criminals to be tried by attorneys and sentenced by judges with no understanding of legal theories, principles, and relevant laws?

Understanding ethical concepts and frameworks is the first step toward adopting good beliefs and making good ethical decisions in all areas of our lives. Knowing how to use or apply those concepts and frameworks is an equally important second step. Though different ethical theories may lead us to different conclusions about ethical issues and to different decisions in the face of ethical dilemmas, understanding them and utilizing the insights they offer is crucial to an ethical life. Notwithstanding the fact that they differ—sometimes significantly, the normative frameworks presented in this text serve as the bases for most analyses of moral issues today. When considering the morality of gun ownership or abortion, or when determining whether honesty is more important than loyalty in a given situation, the tools provided by consequentialist, deontological, and virtue ethical traditions are not only widely employed, but immensely valuable. These tools or considerations can be thought of as "reasons" in ethical decisions. Moral rights, duties, obligations, consequences, and the like can all be utilized as *good reasons* for reaching an ethical conclusion or making an ethical decision.

Having considered these frameworks in considerable detail in previous chapters, we conclude with some consideration for the "how to" of moral decision-making. As an exhaustive consideration is beyond the scope of this chapter and text, what follows are merely suggestions intended to encourage reflection on the practical value or utility of ethical concepts for everyday decision-making in personal and professional contexts. As necessary or desired, we encourage you to revisit the more detailed material on ethical frameworks presented in previous chapters to more thoroughly review the basic ideas and arguments offered from various ethical perspectives.

A BASIC APPROACH

Earlier in the book, we outlined a basic framework (adapted from Tännsjö) for approaching moral issues and situations. This basic framework gives rise to several more specific "steps" that may be of value in contemplating decisions, actions, laws, policies, and the like.

Facts of the Issue or Situation (1 & 2)

+

Moral Criteria (e.g., goods, principles, virtues) (3)
_____

= Practical Conclusion (good decisions, actions) (4)

With this framework in mind, the following questions (adapted from Ruggiero) can serve as guides for thinking about ethical issues and decisions:

1. **Examine the details of the issue or the facts and circumstances of the situation**
2. **Determine what alternatives exist (possible solutions, courses of action)**
3. **Identify relevant and desirable moral criteria (goods, values, principles, duties, obligations, consequences)**
4. **Determine which alternative is consistent with (or furthers, promotes) the criteria identified**

Moral Criteria

Though we have dedicated a section of this chapter to each of the following criteria, the basic moral concerns we will utilize for making ethical decisions can be summarized as follows:

CONSEQUENCES AND GOODS   While the notion of "goods" can apply to all things morally desirable, in this context we mean those goods that are produced by our decisions and actions. *Goods* in this sense include happiness, well-being, and flourishing; relief of pain and suffering; as well as conditions, laws, policies, etc., that serve to promote or protect these goods (e.g., equality, security). Concern with moral goods is a concern with the *consequences* of our decisions and actions.

DUTIES AND PRINCIPLES   While the term "principles" is (like that of "goods") broad, we use it here to refer to morally relevant *duties, rights, and obligations*, including concerns for honesty, fairness, justice, respect for ourselves and others, and other duties and obligations that stem from general moral rules or principles.

VIRTUES As was discussed in Chapter 10, virtues are morally desirable *traits of character*. Here, the term "virtues" is used to refer to dispositions toward honesty, compassion, forgiveness, etc., as well as the avoidance of vicious dispositions such as selfishness, greed, and envy. Actions in accordance with these dispositions tend to be honest, fair, just, etc., and tend to produce good consequences.

When Goods Collide

In some situations, determining what goods are worth pursuing may be difficult. Complex issues such as abortion or gun control often involve multiple, competing goods. Does the good of "life" outweigh the good of "freedom?" Assuming that controlling firearms could reduce crime, does the good of crime reduction outweigh that of freedom or the happiness of those who wish to own and/or carry firearms? In these cases, there is no easy answer. A couple of guidelines may be of assistance:

- Basic Goods Outweigh Secondary Goods. *When goods conflict, the more basic good is typically the more important moral consideration. Determining which goods are more basic is itself difficult. With some critical reflection, however, we could probably develop some general guidelines. As a general rule, for instance, we could probably agree that goods such as life and avoidance of suffering tend to be more basic than that of liberty. My freedom to act in a certain way likely should not have priority over your interest in continuing to live or in avoiding suffering.*
- Intrinsic Goods Outweigh Instrumental Goods. *Another way of thinking about conflicting goods would be to consider which of them are intrinsic and which are instrumental. Intrinsic goods are always more important than and should outweigh instrumental goods. Though what kinds of goods are intrinsic as opposed to merely instrumental is a matter of debate, those such as life, health, happiness, the avoidance of death, pain, and suffering, justice, equality, and other conditions that promote human flourishing are often thought of as "good in themselves."*

When Duties and Obligations Collide

Just as goods can collide with regard to certain issues or in certain situations, duties or obligations can also conflict. Does my duty to keep a promise to a friend override my duty to help another friend who is in need? W. D. Ross (see Chapter 9) suggested that when faced with conflicting duties, we have the following options:

- *Determine which of the competing duties is more important given the facts and circumstances of the situation. In the above scenario, if my promise to friend #1 was to go shopping on Saturday, while my duty to help friend #2 is a matter of life and death, it becomes fairly clear which of the two competing duties is more important. While duties of promise-keeping and aiding others in need may conflict, if we consider what they entail in specific situations it will often become clear which of them overrides the other.*
- *In other situations, however, it may be less clear which duty or obligation is primary. Of these situations, Ross suggests that we identify some higher principle which would serve to resolve conflicts between duties. Thus, if we determine that non-harm is the highest moral principle, this fundamental principle might dictate which of two conflicting duties is more important in specific situations. Of course, higher moral principles should be determined through reason and reflection and may be different for different people.*

When Moral Criteria Collide

Supposing that we regard duties, obligations, rights and principles, consequences, and virtues all as morally significant. What are we to do when issues or circumstances dictate that we cannot promote them all?

EVALUATING CONSEQUENCES

Simply put, considering consequences means considering the *effects* that our decisions and actions have or would likely have on ourselves and others. Consequences have a number of *dimensions*. They can be: (1) predictable or unpredictable; (2) intended or unintended; (3) immediate or long-term; (4) minor or major; (5) physical, emotional, financial; (6) obvious or subtle; and (7) consequential to large numbers of people, or to as few as one. Each of these dimensions carries moral significance.

Applying Utilitarianism

Of the theories we have explored, utilitarianism is that which is concerned primarily with the *consequences of our actions*. More specifically, utilitarianism suggests that in reaching conclusions about moral issues or in making ethical decisions we should consider the *benefits and harms* that it would likely bring, accounting for all people affected by the decision, action, law, policy, etc. The right action, policy, practice, etc., is that which produces the *greatest amount of good for the greatest amount of people*. Ideally, a decision will produce beneficial consequences for everyone it affects. Where this is not possible, priority should be given to the interests of the greater number of people.

APPLYING ACT UTILITARIANISM   Act utilitarianism is the traditional version of utilitarian moral philosophy, where priority is granted to the consequences of individual acts performed by individual agents. Actions are morally right if, considering all available information and evidence, the acting agent *reasonably believes* that it will produce the best consequences for everyone affected.

- *Act utilitarianism requires that we make* predictions *about the likely consequences of alternative courses of action. Because we cannot "know" the future, we must* predict the future.
- *In some cases, we may have specific facts that would allow us to more accurately determine the probable effects of different courses of action. If we are legislators considering abolishing the death penalty in our state and need information about whether homicide rates will increase if we do, we could look to past statistics about changes in homicide rates following abolition of the death penalty in other states. While this in no way guarantees that the effects will be the same in our case, this would constitute good use of available evidence to predict outcomes.*
- *In most cases, we simply need to use our knowledge and experience to make a reasonable judgment.*
- *Act utilitarianism thus requires that we* actively seek out *and* give thoughtful attention to *any and all information that might assist us in predicting the likely consequences of our action (or law, policy, etc.).*

APPLYING RULE UTILITARIANISM   Rule utilitarianism is a modified version of consequentialism that attempts to address problems that arise when otherwise morally undesirable actions might produce good consequences. Rather than focusing on specific acts of individuals in specific situations, it asks that we consider whether the *general practice* (e.g., lying, stealing, cheating) or issue (e.g., abortion, execution) in question has good or desirable *overall consequences*. While abortion, for instance, may in a particular case produce more benefit than harm, as a general practice it may cause more overall harm than good.

- *Rule utilitarianism requires us to consider the overall and long-term consequences of the general practice. In so doing, we need to ask ourselves whether there are general rules that, when followed, produce more benefit than harm.*
- *Good "rules" (those by which we should abide) are those that, if adopted by everyone, would produce the best overall, long-term consequences.*
- *We should ask ourselves not, "what are the consequences of my doing X?" but "what consequences would amount if everyone did X?" If we conclude that doing X would produce the greatest good for the greatest number, then as a general rule it should be practiced.*
- *As with act utilitarianism, consider all available information, all persons and things potentially affected, and all likely consequences.*

EVALUATING DUTIES, RIGHTS, AND OBLIGATIONS

Having moral obligations implies that we have a *duty to do or avoid doing something*. As Ruggiero points out, all of our decisions and actions as human beings occur *in the context of relationships*. In some cases, those relationships are with family or friends; in other cases, with co-workers or clients; in still other cases, with the community or society as a whole. We are mothers, fathers, brothers, sisters, cousins, co-workers, peers, classmates, and members of organizations, communities, cultures, and societies (to name a few). Whether we realize it, we are always already involved in ongoing relationships with countless others. Relationships, in turn, imply duties and obligations to those others. Some obligations result from our having made commitments to specific persons, while others stem from simply sharing a space in the world with others. What duties and obligations can we be said to have?

Applying Kantianism

Kantianism suggests that it is not the consequences of our actions with which we should be concerned, but the *actions themselves*. Actions can be determined to be morally right or wrong irrespective of their potential or real consequences. In short, we should act in accordance with our *moral duties*. These duties derive from the formulations of the *categorical imperative*: (1) our duty to act in accordance with those maxims that we could will to become universal laws; and (2) our duty to act in such a way as to never treat others as a means only. In the first case, if I steal my neighbor's boat so that I can vacation at the lake this weekend, I would be following a rule (maxim) that suggests something to the effect of "one should steal from one's neighbor whenever doing so serves one's own interests." In the second case, if I am nineteen years old and befriend a twenty-two-year-old classmate who I would not otherwise befriend in order to gain access to alcohol, I am using or *exploiting* that person for my own personal gain. Kant would say that I am not respecting the dignity and worth of that person.

- *When contemplating an action, ask yourself whether you would be willing to have that action become a general rule—one which everyone followed when confronted with similar circumstances. What would you want everyone else to do in that situation, and what would everyone else want you to do in that situation?*

- *An implication of Kantian ethics is that we cannot think of ourselves as somehow special or exempt from rules that apply to others. The notion of the "universal law" suggests that we cannot think that a certain action is right for us, while being wrong for others.*
- *We should always respect the dignity and worth of others. Implied is that we should always seek to promote the welfare of others, treating them as human beings rather than as objects or subhuman creatures. Always respect the rights and interests of others, we should refrain from harming them, and, wherever possible, seek to aid them in achieving their own interests.*

Applying Prima Facie Duties

Recall from Chapter 9 that, in expanding on Kantian ethics, W. D. Ross outlined the following list of duties (and corresponding obligations we have to ourselves and others). Along with the general duties Kant outlined as deriving from the categorical imperative, Ross' more specific prima facie duties can serve as guidelines for moral decisions and actions.

- **Honesty.** *We have an obligation to tell the truth and to avoid dishonesty, deception, and fraud.*
- **Promise-keeping.** *We have an obligation to keep promises that we have made to others.*
- **Nonharm (Nonmaleficence).** *We have an obligation not to harm others.*
- **Beneficence (Doing Good).** *We have an obligation generally to "do good" to others, and to aid or assist them where appropriate.*
- **Autonomy.** *We have an obligation to respect the autonomy of others, allowing them to be and do as they choose so long as they are not interfering with the autonomy of others.*
- **Justice.** *We have an obligation to treat others—indeed, all others—as they deserve to be treated (e.g., with respect).*

EVALUATING VIRTUES

In thinking about virtue, we are encouraged to reflect on the types of people we should *be*. Focus is not on our actions or their consequences, but on demonstrating good moral *character* through our decisions and actions. Our task is to embody moral virtues, while avoiding decisions and actions motivated by vice or negative emotions. Importantly, we *become* virtuous people through the regular *practice of virtue*. Thus, if we are motivated by a desire for vengeance, we should overcome that desire and practice forgiveness; if we are motivated by prejudice, practicing tolerance will assist us in overcoming our prejudice and avoiding decisions made and actions taken on that basis. If we focus on "right being" or virtuous character, good decisions and actions will follow naturally. Practicing compassion, for instance, will help us understand the thoughts and feelings of others affected by our decisions and actions and, consequently, increase the likelihood that we will make good decisions and take good actions.

Applying Aristotelian Virtue Ethics

For Aristotle virtue amounts to the *practical use of reason*. In making decisions and undertaking actions, he asks that we utilize our specifically human capacity for reason and rational reflection. As there are no easy solutions to moral issues and dilemmas, we must exercise *judgment*, considering all relevant persons, facts, and circumstances and then "figuring out" what course of action is virtuous and thus best given the specific situation. In other words, being virtuous amounts to exercising *wisdom*. The course of action that is virtuous Aristotle called the "Golden Mean." Practical reason finds those feelings and actions that are midway between deficiency and excess in light of the issue or circumstances. With regard to any issue or in any situation, we can have too much of something or too little of something (e.g., anger, tolerance). The virtuous person is s/he who exercises wisdom in determining the "middle road" between them. In this respect, virtues are *situational*. What is courageous in one situation may be foolhardy in another. How do we know the difference? How do we know what virtue is called for and to what extent? Simply enough, make these determinations by calling upon knowledge and experience. We need to experiment with and engage in life, learning from our successes and mistakes (and those of others) in order to develop our practical wisdom and become virtuous people.

- *To exercise "excellence" is to make decisions and engage in actions such that virtue is expressed in the way that it is done. If we are making an arrest or sentencing a convicted criminal, are we doing so with arrogance and anger or with understanding and respect?*
- *Virtue ethics suggests that we should always try to avoid the influence of negative emotions and, in any given situation, reflect upon their possible influence on our decisions and actions. Are we avoiding the influence of negative emotions? Are we motivated by selfish concerns? Are we engaging in cruelty? Are we deciding or acting out of envy? Greed? Jealousy? Are we being intolerant? Are we deciding or acting out of prejudice or bias?*
- *Likewise, virtue ethics suggests that we should always try to express virtuous character traits in our decisions and actions. Are we demonstrating virtue through our decision or action? Are we being benevolent? Are we making an effort to understand the situation from the perspective of everyone involved? Are we being open-minded? Are we demonstrating courage? Are we being faithful? Sincere? Honest? Loyal? Are we deciding or acting with integrity? Are we demonstrating moderation? Are we demonstrating self-control? Are we respecting ourselves? Are we respecting others? Are we exercising wisdom?*

Applying an Ethic of Care

Though different in some respects, the caring approach to moral decision-making shares many features with the general tradition of virtue. Not least importantly, it emphasizes *ways-of-being* rather than ways-of-doing. It promotes a certain kind of character and the development and utilization of *morally appropriate feelings*, such as understanding, empathy, and compassion, while encouraging us to avoid allowing inappropriate feelings, such as prejudice, hatred, greed, pride, and other vices, to influence our choices. An ethic of care minimizes the significance of impersonal principles and rules such as those found in utilitarian and duty-based frameworks. When faced with an issue or dilemma, we should not be asking what duties or hedonistic calculations apply to a given situation but, rather, *what the caring thing to do would be*. Specifically, caring entails concern for the welfare and suffering of all affected parties, an awareness of underlying relationships between affected parties, and a search for alternative solutions that that take relevant situational factors into consideration.

- *Caring entails seeking to minimize pain and suffering for all parties affected. We must first imaginatively project ourselves into the situation, seeking to understand the perspective of everyone affected and the ways in which they will be affected by different alternatives. In criminal cases, for example, have we considered the ways in which a particular resolution will impact the offender? Victim? Offender's family? Victim's family? Community? Public image of criminal justice?*
- *Relationships between people are paramount. How can we decide in such a way as to create, preserve, or strengthen those relationships? If relationships between people or between people and communities have been damaged, can they be repaired?*

- *The care approach is partly situational. In other words, it asks that we attend to all of the details of the situation, including the ways in which a particular situation may be different (and call for a different decision) than similar situations. Not all like cases can be treated alike, as the people and relationships within those situations necessarily differ. How is this situation unique? How are the people involved unique, including their needs?*
- *The care approach encourages a search for alternative solutions. Is our decision-making constrained by the rigidity of formal guidelines or conventional approaches to decision-making that rely on impartial rules? Is there room for compromise and accommodation? Are there solutions that we haven't considered?*

MAKING DECISIONS

Having reviewed the important features of the ethical frameworks addressed in Chapters 8, 9, and 10, we are in a position to expand upon the basic framework and questions outlined at the beginning of this chapter. The ethical theory employed to evaluate an issue or dilemma will determine what moral criteria are most relevant. What follows are more specific models and series of questions for approaching moral issues and ethical situations from each of the major perspectives outlined above.

Facts of the Issue or Situation (1 and 2)

\+

$$\frac{Moral\ Criteria\ (as\ Emphasized\ by\ Ethical\ Framework)\ (3)}{= Practical\ Conclusion\ (4)}$$

Deciding with Duties

Deciding with duties means first determining what duties, rights, principles, and/or obligations apply to a given issue or situation. Having identified relevant duties (i.e. moral criteria), we are in a position to determine which decision or course of action fulfills those duties or obligations. Our decision-making "steps" and line of questioning might look something like this:

1. **What are the facts of the issue or details of the situation?**
2. **What alternative courses of action exist?**
3. **What duties or obligations apply to the issue or situation?**
   - Which alternative demonstrates respect for human rights?
   - Which alternative demonstrates respect for human dignity?
   - Which alternative could I will to become a "universal law"?
   - What would I want others to do in this situation?
   - What would others want me to do in this situation?
   - Are there relevant duties to be honest? To keep a promise? To refrain from causing harm? To help or assist others? To respect autonomy? To justice and equality?
   - Are there conflicting moral duties or obligations involved? If so, which take priority?
4. **Which decision or course of action is most in keeping with relevant duties, obligations, rights, and principles that have been identified?**

Deciding with Consequences

Deciding with consequences means predicting the likely consequences of different decisions or courses of actions and choosing that which produces the greatest balance of good over bad. From an act-utilitarian perspective, our decision-making "steps" and line of questioning might look something like this:

1. **What are the facts of the issue or details of the situation?**
2. **What alternative courses of action exist?**
3. **What are the likely consequences of each alternative?**
   - Who is likely to be affected by the decision?
   - For all affected, what goods are predicted?
   - For all affected, what harms are predicted?
   - Are there long-term consequences?
   - Might there be indirect or unintended consequences?
4. **Which decision or course of action will likely produce the greatest amount of overall good for the greatest number of people or, alternatively, produce the least amount of overall harm for the greatest number of people?**

Deciding with Virtue

Deciding with virtue means identifying decisions or courses of actions that would be most consistent with admirable or desirable character traits and making an effort to decide or act in a way that expresses those traits. Our decision-making "steps" and line of questioning might look something like this:

1. **What are the facts of the issue or details of the situation?**
2. **What alternative courses of action exist?**
3. **What are the relevant virtues and vices and how do they factor into the issue or dilemma?**
   - Are we being influenced by negative emotions such as greed, envy, intolerance, prejudice, hatred, a desire for revenge?
   - Will a decision or course of action otherwise express vicious character or intentions—cruel, selfish, callous, dishonest, impatient, imprudent, unjust, insincere, rude, servile?
   - Are we expressing traits of character that have a beneficial effect on ourselves and others—benevolent, compassionate, generous, honest, loyal, merciful, nonharmful, respectful, tolerant?
   - Will a decision or course of action be otherwise expressive of virtuous character or intentions—humility, integrity, justice, modesty, open-mindedness, respectful of self and others, trustworthy, wise?
   - What would a morally admirable person do in this situation?
4. **Which decision or course of action will express virtuous character and/or avoid the expression of negative emotions and vicious character?**

Deciding with Care

Though caring is a disposition more than a series of steps, for illustrative purposes we can tentatively offer some suggestions for thinking through moral issues and dilemmas with a care approach. In short, an ethic of care means determining which alternative or solution is most consistent with the philosophy of caring, including its focus on appropriate moral emotions, attention to underlying relationships, situational factors, and the needs of all affected parties. Examples of questions we might ask are as follows:

1. **What are the facts of the issue or details of the situation?**
2. **What alternative courses of action exist?**
3. **What are the elements of a caring disposition and how do they factor into the issue or dilemma?**
   - How is this situation unique? What are the unique needs of all involved (directly and indirectly) in the situation?
   - What solutions exist that include and address the needs of all persons involved?
   - What alternative/s promotes the creation, maintenance, or repair of underlying relationships between people or between people and the community?
   - What alternative/s promotes caring and trust between people or between people and the community?
   - Are we respecting the dignity of all involved?
   - Are we attending to the pain and suffering of all involved, including the greater community, as well as family members and friends of those directly involved?
   - Are there alternatives that we have not considered? Is there room for compromise?
4. **Which decision or course of action best expresses a caring disposition?**

SCENARIOS FOR FURTHER THOUGHT

In this final segment of the chapter, we offer several scenarios intended to encourage the application of ethical frameworks to issues in crime, law, and justice. In the first three, we provide specific questions that might be asked from a given perspective. In the remaining scenarios, we provide only a general context, encouraging you to do your own assessment based on the tools provided throughout this chapter.

1. Suppose that the criminal justice department of a local university consists of two male faculty members and six female faculty members. With a new faculty position open for the upcoming year, the chair of the department would like to hire a male to help offset the dominant female voice of the department. Should the chair's freedom to hire whomever s/he chooses outweigh interests of equal opportunity and nondiscrimination? How might a Kantian ethical framework assist us in approaching this issue?
   - What rights and duties are at issue?
   - Which alternative demonstrates respect for legal and moral rights?
   - What are the relevant obligations to the department? The students? The applicants?
   - Are we treating everyone involved with respect and dignity?
   - If we hire a male, are we exploiting him (using him) as a means only?
   - What course of action could we will that all other chairs in similar situations would take?
   - Can you think of other questions or concerns that might be relevant from a Kantian perspective?
2. Law enforcement agencies often set up sobriety checkpoints on major roadways and highways—especially on weekends, holidays, and other times when people are more likely to be drinking. In theory, checkpoints can get unsafe drivers off of the road, as well as deter would-be drink drivers from getting on the roads. At the same time, some argue that

columns. The value of X^2 needs to be modified when DF = 1, especially when there are cells with less than 5 cases in each of them.

If one variable is nominal and the other is ordinal, we usually treat both as nominal variables to apply the Chi-square test. It is noticeable that X^2 has no direct relations with the measures of association (e.g., Lambda) that we discussed in the descriptive statistics part of this book, although SPSS-X also calculates the approximate significance of Lambda and tau-y based on X^2. X^2 follows a distinctive logic, upon which some other measures of association are developed. These include ϕ (Phi Coefficient of Association), C (Contingency Coefficient of Association), and Cramer's V, which, however, do not possess the PRE (proportionate reduction in error) meaning.

If two variables are both at the ordinal level, we have Goodman and Kruskal's G (Gamma) as a measure of their association. If the two variables are both at the interval level, then we have Pearson's γ. The common logic of test of significance is the same for both cases, that is, to test the hypothesis that the gammas are not zero in the population. For Goodman and Kruskal's G, we can use the Z or t procedure because the sampling distribution of G will approach a normal distribution when sample size is relatively large (actually N≥10 would be fine). For this purpose, G needs to be transformed into a standardized quantity Z so that we can use the Z distribution to make statistical inference. This logic is also the same for Somers' D and Kendall's tau coefficients (tau-a, tau-b, and tau-c).

For Pearson's γ, the popular measure of linear association between two interval variables, a frequently used test quantity is called F ratio. This quantity is considered to have the PRE meaning, though it will not approach a normal distribution. The quantity is important since it is related to a general and very useful technique in statistics, that is, the analysis of variance. The transformation of γ into F takes into account the degrees of freedom, which is determined by the sample size N. In the linear case, the test of the correlation coefficient γ is at once the test of the regression coefficient b since both have the same numerator structure. If the relationship between two interval variables is not linear, you can treat one of them as a nominal variable by appropriately categorizing it.

The relationship between an interval variable and a nominal variable can be tested by grouping the sample cases on the values of the nominal variable and comparing the group means on the interval variable. In the two-group situation, this can be done by using the t procedure mentioned earlier to examine the difference of the group means. To compare the means of more than two groups, however, you need to use a more comprehensive test procedure. This procedure

132

checkpoints are not only inconveniences, but serious infringements on privacy rights. How might act utilitarian aid us in making sense of this issue?

- Who is affected by sobriety checkpoints?
- For all affected, what goods come of checkpoints?
- For all affected, what harms come of them?
- Are there long-term consequences?
- Are there indirect or unintended consequences?
- Do the overall good or beneficial effects outweigh the overall harm caused by sobriety checkpoints?

3. Criminal defense attorneys are sometimes placed in the difficult situation of defending a client whom they know to be guilty of a serious crime. Utilitarian ethics might encourage us to consider the consequences of vigorously defending—to the point of acquittal—a "guilty" defendant. Duty-based ethics might draw attention to the defendant's legal rights and the attorney's relevant duties and obligations to that client. Notwithstanding these concerns, how might virtue ethics inform an attorney's decisions and actions in such a situation?

- What character traits would we want in an "ideal" defense attorney?
- Are attorneys likely to fall victim to negative emotions that would hinder their performance?
- Where do we draw the line between offering a good defense and being dishonest in the courtroom? An attorney's legal duties notwithstanding, is it in some sense dishonest to refrain from revealing information that is pertinent to a case?
- As sincerity is a virtue, how might an attorney overcome tendencies to offer a less-than-sincere defense effort in such cases?
- To what degree are the following virtues desirable in this context: compassion, honesty, loyalty, mercy, nonharm, respect, integrity, and tolerance? How would these traits materialize in the attorney's decisions and actions?
- Would offering a zealous defense in such a situation be at odds with the virtue of self-respect?

4. John Doe attempted to resist arrest for possessing illegal substances and for carrying a concealed weapon without a permit. In an effort to contain/control him, he was seriously beaten by six police officers—ultimately resulting in permanent brain damage. The officers claimed that the use of brutal force, which occurred before Mr. Doe was taken into custody, was necessary. From a utilitarian perspective, on what grounds could we claim that the use of force in this and similar situations is justified? From a Kantian perspective, are there grounds on which we could claim that excessive force was *not* justified?

5. In January of 2009, a four-year-old Ohio boy retrieved a shotgun from the closet of his home, returned to the living room, and proceeded to shoot his eighteen-year-old babysitter (who was not seriously injured in the incident). According to reports, the child was angry that the babysitter had stepped on his foot. Following the incident, local prosecutors had no plans to charge the boy with a crime, but were considering charges against the parents. Utilizing a care approach, how might we resolve this situation in a way that takes into consideration the underlying relationships and the needs of the boy, his family, the babysitter, the babysitter's family, etc.? What relationships have been damaged? How has each person involved been affected by the situation and what does each need from the situation? Would a care approach justify treating the boy as a delinquent? Criminal charges against the boy's parents? A restorative approach?

6. Jury nullification occurs when the jury returns a verdict of "not guilty" despite evidence that the defendant is legally guilty of the crime for which she or he is charged. In effect, the

jury determines that the existing law is immoral or has been wrongfully applied in a particular instance. Jurors may, for instance, refuse to find a defendant guilty of a "mercy killing," despite overwhelming evidence that the killing violated the expressed purpose of the law. Employing utilitarian, Kantian, or virtue ethical perspectives, on what grounds could we claim that the practice of jury nullification in a given case is morally justified? Morally unjustified?

7. In some cases, persons convicted of white-collar or corporate offenses receive lighter sentences relative to those convicted of street crimes. Someone who is convicted of embezzling 1 million dollars may receive a lighter sentence than someone convicted of stealing 200 dollars in a liquor store robbery; a corporation which markets unsafe products, resulting in hundreds of injuries, illnesses, and/or deaths, may be punished less severely than a person who seriously injures or kills one person in a street fight. Utilizing utilitarian, Kantian, and virtue ethical frameworks, are there any grounds on which we can morally justify more lenient sentences for white-collar offenses? Are there any grounds on which we could morally justify *harsher* sentences?

8. Following the arrest and conviction of serial killer David Berkowitz, the state of New York implemented what are often called "Son of Sam" provisions. Recognizing that Berkowitz could have profited substantially from selling the rights to his story, the "Son of Sam" provisions allowed for the confiscation of any royalties that criminals might earn as a result of their crimes. The money, in principle, would then go toward helping the victims and their families. With moral considerations in mind, on what grounds can we justify appropriating monies that criminals (or noncriminals) earn from writing books, selling media rights, selling personal items, or other means?

9. A chemistry professor at a major Southeastern University conducts research on the ways in which drugs interact with the brain. Much of his recent research has focused on illegal substances and involves, in part, creating new compounds that closely resemble current drugs of abuse. His colleagues in academia, however, are not the only ones paying attention to his published research. In fact, makers of designer drugs have been known to use his research to produce new street drugs. A handful of new designer drugs have hit the street as a result of his publications, and several deaths have even been linked to substances produced by amateur chemists based on his research. What moral issues arise from the professor's research? To whom does the professor owe duties? What duties? How might we assess the issue of *free exchange of scientific information* if we were to assume a consequentialist stance on this matter?

10. Dr. Anatine is a licensed psychologist working in private practice. Last month he began treating a new client, Paul. As Paul has grown more comfortable with the therapeutic environment and come to trust Dr. Anatine more, he has revealed increasingly troubling details of his life and lifestyle. In addition to his described affinity for drugs of abuse, Paul is also involved in an emotionally volatile intimate relationship, and occasionally engages in petty criminal activity to support his drug habit. Today, Paul seemed especially agitated. As best as Dr. Anatine could surmise, Paul had had an argument with his girlfriend, Anna, which had turned violent. Though she had not called the police, Anna packed her bags and left "for good"—apparently on her way to stay with her ex-boyfriend, with whom Paul had had more than one unfriendly encounter in the past. Concerning Dr. Anatine are several statements Paul has made that lead him to believe that Paul intends to "hunt her down" and "take care of business." From a previous therapy session, Dr. Anatine knows that Paul owns several firearms, one of which he keeps in his vehicle. What, if anything, should Dr. Anatine do in this situation? What are his

alternatives? What are the relevant duties? Consequences? Rights? If Dr. Anatine were to do nothing and Paul commits an act of violence, to what extent might moral responsibility be placed on Dr. Anatine?

11. Police have received a complaint from community residents about what the residents describe as a homeless man sleeping on a bench in the local park. As far as anyone knows, the man has not harmed anyone and does not appear to pose an immediate threat. There is a local law prohibiting people from sleeping in public, and the fact that a complaint has been received suggests that residents are at least uncomfortable about the situation. Upon speaking with the man, police learn that he is simply very tired, has no permanent residence and no money for a motel room, and no other place to go. He pleads for police to give him just a couple of hours of rest and promises he will then be on his way. How might a utilitarian approach resolve this issue? What moral duties might be relevant? How might an ethic of care approach this matter differently? What alternatives might allow for compromise and accommodation of the needs of everyone?

12. Undercover police work necessarily requires that officers of the law participate in activities that would, under most circumstances, be deemed illegal. For example, police have been noted to transport drugs into prisons, launder drug money, fence stolen goods, and print counterfeit money. These and many other examples involve law enforcement officers' willingly and knowingly engaging in behaviors that are legally prohibited for the sake of gathering evidence against other criminals. Except in cases in which officer behavior goes well beyond what is necessary for their role, they are immune from prosecution. Relying on one or more of the normative theories outlined in the text and above, what moral issues are presented by undercover police work? Do the ends justify the means? Where might we draw the line between moral and immoral?

INDEX

Note: The locators followed by 'b', 'f', and 't' refer to boxes, figures and tables cited in the text.

is exactly the same as the F test discussed above, though the logic for the test quantity is now based on the correlation ratio E^2 (see discussions in the part of descriptive statistics) rather than the squared linear correlation coefficient γ^2. Similar to the calculation of X^2, F will never take a negative value since E or γ is squared in the formula, so the test is always one-tailed. The larger this quantity, the higher the actual significance level. Also similar to X^2, the distribution of F depends on the degrees of freedom of the sample.

If one variable is interval and the other is ordinal, we usually treat the ordinal variable as a nominal variable to apply the F test. F test is more general than t test since it can deal with multi-group comparison as well as two-group comparison. The t procedure is actually a special case of the F procedure. The F procedure is also more powerful because it can conduct the so-called multiple comparison test. To compare any two means in a multi-group situation, the t procedure may not be appropriate since some results may be significant even if there is actually no difference between the means. The multiple comparison test in the F procedure can identify exactly where the difference is between specific groups, not just indicate generally that there is a difference among three or more groups. In SPSS, this procedure is called ONEWAY, representing the very popular technique of one-way analysis of variance. This is because the F procedure actually need not be derived from the correlation ratio E^2. It can be based on the analysis of variance using the same PRE logic. The F quantity is thus the ratio of the between-group sum of squares (BSS, variance that will be reduced) to the within-group sum of squares (WSS, remaining variance).

In today's computerized statistics, you as a consumer of the technology do not need to remember the formulas of various test quantities, much like our predecessors in applied social studies who did not have to understand the derivation of the formulas they had to learn in the past. This is very important since you may not realize that the teaching of statistics nowadays has largely become irrelevant to contemporary research practice. It is fair to say that it has been a failure to many students in behavioral and social fields in view of the courses they have taken and the skills they possess. The ease of producing computer outputs, on the other side, readily leads to the abuse of statistics. The training of quantitative skills in educating the new generation of behavioral and social science researchers, therefore, should emphasize bridging the gap between the operation of computerized statistical programs and the mathematical meaning of traditional statistics courses. The focus is the understanding of the uses, requirements, and the meaning of the results of various statistical procedures and